The Politics of Public Budgeting: Getting and Spending, Borrowing and Balancing

FOURTH EDITION

Irene S. Rubin
Northern Illinois University

CHATHAM HOUSE PUBLISHERS
SEVEN BRIDGES PRESS, LLC
NEW YORK • LONDON

The Politics of Public Budgeting:
Getting and Spending, Borrowing and Balancing

Fourth Edition

Seven Bridges Press, LLC
135 Fifth Avenue
New York, NY 10010

Publisher: Robert J. Gormley
Managing editor: Katharine Miller
Production supervisor: Melissa A. Martin
Cover design: Judith Hudson
Composition: Linda B. Pawelchak/Lori Clinton
Printing and binding: Sheridan Books

Library of Congress Cataloging-in-Publication Data

Rubin, Irene.
    The politics of public budgeting : getting and spending, borrowing and balancing / Irene
S. Rubin.—4th ed.
        p.   cm
    Includes bibliographical references and index.
    ISBN 1-889119-42-3
    1. Local budgets—Political aspects—United States.   2. Budget—Political aspects—
United States.   I. Title.

HJ9147.R83   2000
336.73—dc21

                                                                              99-086159

Manufactured in the United States of America
10   9   8   7   6   5   4   3   2

Contents

Preface to the Fourth Edition

WHEN THE THIRD edition to *The Politics of Public Budgeting* was being prepared, the White House and congressional leaders had just failed, dramatically, to come to agreement on how to balance the federal budget. Without a budget agreement, the federal government had closed down, and much to the amazement of the Republicans, the public was not only aggravated by the shutdown, but blamed the Republicans for obstructing the budget process. In 1996 the atmosphere was thick with mistrust, and it did not look as if any kind of balanced budget agreement could be reached.

By May 1997 the picture had changed. The Republicans had barely maintained their majorities in the 1996 congressional elections. With such slim majorities, they needed to cooperate with Democrats in order to get anything done. The president wanted an agreement. A booming economy provided more revenue than expected, allowing two contentious issues—the proposed reduction in the cost-of-living index and the cap on Medicaid spending—to be taken off the table.

An agreement was reached during the spring and summer of 1997 to balance the budget by 2002 by cutting discretionary programs, including defense, and slowing the growth in Medicare spending. The latter was to produce more than $100 billion in savings over five years. The package included net tax cuts of $85 billion over the five years, ballooning to $250 billion over ten years. In addition, the president got about $32 billion in new money to fund his priority programs, including expanded health care for poor children, welfare benefits for legal immigrants, and more money for Pell education grants. By 1998, well ahead of schedule, the booming economy and the surging stock market had generated enough revenues to balance, or nearly balance, the federal budget (the degree of balance depended on whether surpluses from Social Security were or were not counted). The policy debate then shifted to whether to lift the spending caps a little or to keep them tight and spend the surplus on more tax reduction.

The conflicts surrounding the unexpectedly successful efforts to balance the federal budget illustrate a number of features of public budgeting.

One theme that emerges from the saga of balancing the federal budget is that budget negotiations sometimes deal with major policy issues. Budget observers used terms such as *train wreck* and *budget battles* to describe the ongoing discussions. Every actor who was engaged in the negotiations got something from the final deal. Budgeting was exciting and consequential.

A second theme that emerges from the negotiations to balance the federal budget in 2002 is that unpleasant consequences are sometimes postponed. The negotiations took place in 1997; the deepest cuts in spending were planned for 2001 and 2002. The cost of the tax cuts would balloon after 2002. Budget balance was so attractive a political goal that the decision makers delayed some of the consequences to ease the difficulty of bargaining. If the deeper tax cuts had come earlier, they would have necessitated deeper spending cuts to achieve balance, which might have quashed the deal. By postponing the costs of the tax cuts, the negotiators made the overall package look more balanced than it was, but at the same time made the deal possible. One conclusion from this observation is that accountability—providing an accurate picture of budget decisions and implications—sometimes comes into conflict with acceptability. A second conclusion is that time is a crucial aspect of budgeting decisions. It makes no sense to say a budget is balanced unless one also describes when the budget will be balanced and for how long.

A third idea that comes out of the balanced budget deal of 1997 is that sometimes budgeting events and decisions that look impossible happen anyway. Years of failure may turn out not to be precursors of further failure, but a means of learning what needs to be done and how to do it. Conditions, processes, and negotiators change; new opportunities arise. Nothing is inevitable. The negotiation process is fluid, not predetermined by a fixed structure or any group of actors. The decision making is also open to public opinion. Armed with knowledge, citizens can become budget actors, maybe not determining the outcomes, but influencing the discussion.

Fourth, the budget-balancing negotiations—which initially took place apart from regular budget making—suggest that routine and nonroutine decision making may be segregated. Routine decision making is sometimes punctuated by various kinds of summit agreements that involve a broader range of actors and interests, and that bind future decisions. Routine decision making is highly constrained by such periodic reworkings.

Budgeting can move at a slow and even pace or at breakneck speed. When the budget appears to be most routine, it may be difficult to follow because the real decision making occurred somewhere else at another time; when budgeting is moving at a rapid pace, with many major issues on the table, it may go by in a blur. Without an understanding of the basic pressures and processes, without an understanding of who the players are and the stakes they are fighting for, budgeting can be incomprehensible. Sometimes the actors themselves complain that they do not understand the process and beg for simplification. Citizen observers need some explanation, not only of specific events, but of the underlying patterns. This book describes those underlying patterns.

The Politics of Public Budgeting is not just about the federal government, but about budgeting at all levels of government in the United States. The goal is to describe change over time, to show recent events in the context of institutional constraints, prior agreements, and political jockeying over process and outcomes. In this fourth edition, many of the minicases and tables have been updated, and references to recent budget literature have been included. The emphasis in this edition is on long-term issues, such as accountability and trade-offs, that are highlighted by current events such as the Government Performance and Results Act and the balanced budget agreement. The structure of the chapters is the same as in the previous edition, but there is less intentional repetition and unintentional wordiness. The introductory chapter has been rewritten in places for thematic clarity and contemporary relevance.

Acknowledgments

I WOULD LIKE to thank particularly the people who read and critiqued the manuscript for me in its various stages: Aaron Wildavsky, Allen Schick, Naomi Caiden, Tom Lauth, and Herb Rubin. They have been good and helpful colleagues. Aaron is gone now, but may those of us who remain continue to challenge and encourage one another. I would like to acknowledge particularly the assistance of Professor Schick, whose scholarship and intellectual integrity have been a model for the profession and an inspiration to me.

CHAPTER ONE

The Politics of Public Budgets

PUBLIC BUDGETS DESCRIBE what governments do by listing how governments spend money. A budget links tasks to be performed with the amount of resources necessary to accomplish those tasks, ensuring that money will be available to wage war, provide housing, or maintain streets. Budgets limit expenditures to the revenues available, to ensure balance and prevent overspending. Most of the work in drawing up a budget is technical, estimating how much it will cost to feed a thousand shut-ins with a Meals-on-Wheels program or how much revenue will be produced from a 1 percent tax on retail sales. But public budgets are not merely technical managerial documents; they are also intrinsically and irreducibly political.

- Budgets reflect choices about what government will and will not
  do. They reflect general public consensus about what kinds of services
  governments should provide and what citizens are entitled to as members of society. Should government provide services that the private
  sector could provide, such as water, electricity, transportation, and housing? Do all citizens have a guarantee of health care, regardless of ability
  to pay? Are all insured against hunger? Are they entitled to some kind of
  housing?
- Budgets reflect priorities—between police and flood control, day care
  and defense, the Northeast and the Southwest. The budget process
  mediates between groups and individuals who want different things
  from government and determines who gets what. These decisions may
  influence whether the poor get job training or the police get riot training, both as a response to an increased number of unemployed.
- Budgets reflect the relative proportion of decisions made for local and
  constituency purposes, and for efficiency, effectiveness, and broader
  public goals. Budgets reflect the degree of importance legislators put on

satisfying their constituents and the legislators' willingness to listen to interest-group demands. For example, the Defense Department may decide to spend more money to keep a military base open because the local economy depends on it and to spend less money to improve combat readiness.

- Budgets provide a powerful tool of accountability to citizens who want to know how the government is spending their money and if government has generally followed their preferences. Budgeting links citizen preferences and governmental outcomes.

- Budgets reflect citizens' preferences for different forms of taxation and different levels of taxation, as well as the ability of specific groups of taxpayers to shift tax burdens to others. The budget reflects the degree to which the government redistributes wealth upward or downward through the tax system.

- At the national level, the budget influences the economy, so fiscal policy affects the level of employment—how many people are out of work at any time.

- Budgets reflect the relative power of different individuals and organizations to influence budget outcomes. Budgetary decision making provides a picture of the relative power of budget actors within and between branches of government, as well as the importance of citizens in general and specific interest groups.

In all these ways, public budgeting is political. But budgeting is not typical of other political processes and hence one example among many. It is both an important and a unique arena of politics. It is important because of the specific policy issues reflected in the budget: the scope of government, the distribution of wealth, the openness of government to interest groups, and the accountability of government to the public at large. It is unique because these decisions have to take place in the context of budgeting, with its need for balance, its openness to the environment, and its requirements for timely decisions so that government can carry on without interruption.

Public budgets clearly have political implications, but what does it mean to say that key political decisions are made in the context of budgeting? The answer has several parts. First, what is budgeting? Second, what is public budgeting, as opposed to individual or family budgeting or the budgeting of private organizations? Third, what does *political* mean in the context of public budgeting?

What Is Budgeting?

The essence of budgeting is that it allocates scarce resources and hence implies choice between potential objects of expenditure. Budgeting implies balance, and it requires some kind of decision-making process.

Making Budgetary Choices

All budgeting, whether public or private, individual or organizational, involves choices between possible expenditures. Since no one has unlimited resources, people budget all the time. A child makes a budget (a plan for spending, balancing revenues and expenditures) when she decides to spend money on a marshmallow rabbit rather than a chocolate one, assuming she has money enough for only one rabbit. The air force may choose between two different airplanes to replace current bombers. These examples illustrate the simplest form of budgeting because they involve only one actor, one resource, one time, and two straightforward and comparable choices.

Normally, budgeting does not compare only two reasonably similar items. There may be a nearly unlimited number of choices. Budgeting usually limits the options to consider by grouping together similar things that can be reasonably compared. When I go to the supermarket, I do not compare all the possible things I could buy, not only because I cannot absorb that number of comparisons, but because the comparisons would be meaningless and a waste of time. I do not go to the supermarket and decide to get either a turkey or a bottle of soda pop. I compare main dishes with main dishes, beverages with beverages, desserts with desserts. Then I have a common denominator for comparison. For example, I may look at the main course and ask about the amount of protein for the dollar. I may compare the desserts in terms of the amount of cholesterol or the calories.

There is a tendency, then, to make comparisons within categories where the comparison is meaningful. This is as true for governmental budgeting as it is for shoppers. For example, weapons might be compared with weapons or automobiles with automobiles. They could be compared in terms of speed, reliability, and availability of spare parts, and the one that did the most of what you wanted it to do at the least cost would be the best choice. As long as there is agreement on the goals to be achieved, the choice should be straightforward.

Sometimes, budgeting requires comparison of different, and seemingly incomparable, things. If I do not have enough money to buy a whole balanced meal, I may have to make choices between main dishes and desserts. How do I compare the satisfaction of a sweet tooth to the nourishment of turkey? Or, in the public sector, how do I compare the benefits of providing shelters for the homeless with buying more helicopters for the navy? I may then move to more general comparisons, such as how clearly were the requests made and the benefits spelled out; who got the benefits last time and whose turn is it this time; are there any specific contingencies that make one choice more likely than the other? For example, will we be embarrassed to show our treatment of the homeless in front of a visiting dignitary? Or, are disarmament negotiations coming up in which we need to display strength or make a symbolic gesture of restraint? Comparing dissimilar items may require a list of priorities. It may be possible to do two or more important things if they are sequenced properly.

Budgeting often allocates money, but it can allocate any scarce resource, for example, time. A student may choose between studying for an exam and playing softball and drinking beer afterward. In this example, it is time that is at a premium, not money. Or it could be medical skills that are in short supply, or expensive equipment, or apartment space, or water.

Government programs often involve a choice of resources and sometimes involve combinations of resources, each of which has different characteristics. For example, some federal farm programs involve direct cash payments plus loans at below-market interest rates, and welfare programs often involve dollar payments plus food stamps, which allow recipients to pay less for food. Federal budgets often assign agencies money, personnel, and sometimes borrowing authority, three different kinds of resources.

Balancing and Borrowing

Budgets have to balance. A plan for expenditures that pays no attention to ensuring that revenues cover expenditures is not a budget. That may sound odd in view of historically huge federal deficits, but a budget may technically be balanced by borrowing. Balance means only that outgo is matched or exceeded by income. The borrowing has to be paid off. Borrowing means spending more now and paying more in the future in order to maintain balance. It is a balance over time.

To illustrate the nature of budget balance, consider me as shopper again. Suppose I spend all my weekly shopping money before I buy my dessert. I have the option of treating my dollar limit as if it were more flexible, by adding the dimension of time. I can buy the dessert and everything else in the basket, going over my budget, and then eat less at the end of the month. Or I can pay the bill with a credit card, assuming I will have more money in the future with which to pay off the bill when it comes due. The possibility of borrowing against the future is part of most budget choices.

The following brief example illustrates that time is an important dimension of budgeting, whether one is considering formal borrowing or adopting projects now and committing future revenues to pay for them. In the example, a lobbyist for the university is speaking about funding alternatives likely to be used to pay for a project favored by the Board of Higher Education.

> *Lobbyist:* The Board of Higher Education has an initiative that they would like to put forth during the veto session for $2 million for planning funds for this University Center in Lake County. Whether or not they will be successful in putting that forward will depend on if there is a supplemental budget bill for capital items, and if they can get their issue into that [supplemental] budget, which is tricky. I think that if there is no budget opportunity [through the supplemental], they will try to move forward on the Lake County issue [anyway] . . . they are very committed to it. There are $2 million of planning funds. I would expect that they will fund the planning funds and/or the $10 million construction funds out of next year's fiscal year 2000 higher education capital list. If they do not get the planning money [out of this year's supplementals], then they will probably just fund the planning money out of next year's budget and take the other $8 million out the following year. But they are very, very committed to moving forward on this.[1]

Process

Budgeting cannot proceed without some kind of decision process. The process determines who will have a say and at what point in the decision making, and frames the decisions that have to be made. Budget process typically involves estimates of revenues and limits on expenditures, structures the comparisons among alternatives, and regulates the flow of decisions to see that they are made in proper order and in a timely way.

Back to my shopping example: If I shop for the main course first, and spend more money than I intended on it because I found some fresh fish, there will be less money left for purchasing the dessert. Hence, unless I set a firm limit on the amount of money to spend for each segment of the meal, the order in which I do the purchasing counts. Of course, if I get to the end of my shopping and do not have enough money left for dessert, I can put back some of the items already in the cart and squeeze out enough money for dessert.

Governmental budgeting is also concerned with procedures for managing tradeoffs between large categories of spending. Budgeters may determine the relative importance of each category first, attaching a dollar level in proportion to the assigned importance, or they may allow purchasing in each area to go on independently, later reworking the choices until the balance between the parts is acceptable.

The order of decisions is important in another sense. I can determine how much money I am likely to have first and then set that as an absolute limit on expenditures, or I can determine what I must have, what I wish to have, and what I need to set aside for emergencies and then go out and try to find enough money to cover some or all of those expenditures. Especially in emergencies, such as accidents or other health emergencies, people are likely to obligate the money first and worry about where it will come from later. Governmental budgeting, too, may concentrate first on revenues and later on expenditures, or first on expenditures and later on income. Like individuals or families, during emergencies such as floods or hurricanes or wars, governments will commit the expenditures first and worry about where the money will come from later.

Governmental Budgeting

Public budgeting shares many of the characteristics of budgeting in general but differs from personal and business budgeting in some key ways.

1. Public budgeting is characterized by a variety of budgetary actors who have different priorities and different levels of power over budgetary outcomes. In family and business budgeting there may be only one key actor or a few, and they may have similar views of what they want the budget to achieve.

2. In governmental budgeting, elected officials spend citizens' money, not their own. Generally speaking, individuals and small-business owners spend their own, not someone else's money. Public officials can force citizens to spend their money on expenditures they do not want, but citizens can vote the politicians out of office. Consequently, public officials try not to stray too far from what they think the public wants. Because of the variety of budgetary actors and demands, however, there is no single set of demands to follow. To create enough coherence to guide decisions, budget processes in the public sector involve the negotiation of consent among representatives of competing groups and interests.

3. Because elected officials make spending decisions for citizens, accountability is an important part of public budgeting. The budget document

helps explain to the public how its money was spent. That document is necessarily public, unlike business budgets, and may be the focus of public controversy if citizens do not like what they see or do not fully understand it.

4. Public budgets are planned well in advance of the beginning of the fiscal year and are intended to last a whole year or even two years. Many changes can occur over that period of time, in the economy, in public opinion, in political coalitions, in the weather. Public budgets need to be able to respond to such pressures during the year without major policy changes. If the deals that were necessary to prepare the budget come undone during budget implementation, budget actors will lose their trust in the process. Private-sector budgets are more flexible: they can be remade from week to week or month to month, and policy changes can be adopted at any time. Private-sector budgets are not designed to last unchanged for eighteen months or more. Moreover, private-sector budgets are less open to pressures from the outside, from public opinion or frequent changes in elected officials.

5. Public budgets are incredibly constrained compared to the private sector. There are often rules about the purposes for which revenue can be spent and the time frame in which it can be spent, as well as requirements for balance and limits on borrowing. Capital projects may require public referenda for approval, and taxation growth may be limited to inflation unless citizens approve higher rates in a referendum. Other levels of government may impose spending requirements or limit the permitted forms of taxation. Past agreements may control spending levels or result in tax sharing with other jurisdictions. Courts may play a role in budgeting, telling jurisdictions what they may tax or how their budget process may or may not change. Rather than one bottom line, which is the business model, government agencies may have multiple bottom lines, each of which must balance. Many elements of public budgeting are beyond the control of those who draw up the budget.

The following example, demonstrating that budgeting has a political dimension, should give the reader a feel for governmental budgeting. Any given budget is likely to attract opponents as well as supporters, because no matter how many interests are served by a budget, some claimants will feel they did not get all they wanted or had in a previous budget. Detractors often make public charges against the budget, and budgeters, equally publicly, defend it.

MINICASE: CITY MANAGER REPLIES TO SCATHING BUDGET CRITIQUE

DeKalb, Illinois, has a council-manager form of government with an active, policy-oriented mayor. One mayor, who favored business development and expansion, sometimes at the expense of the existing residents and neighborhoods, was recently defeated by a candidate who advocated balance between new development and existing neighborhoods. Not long after the new mayor and a new manager were in place, the local newspaper ran an editorial excoriating the new manager for his fiscal practices. The editorial was filled with innuendo, exaggeration, and outright mistakes. The new manager responded with a letter to the editor.

The newspaper's criticism of the manager's financial management was a thinly disguised effort to discredit the new administration and its policies of managed growth. The editorial reflected loyalty to the former mayor and longing for the "good old days." It argued that taxes and fees were growing, the city was trying to build too large a fund balance (demonstrating unnecessary taxation), and it was unclear where the increased revenues were going other than into the fund balance. Further, the editorial charged that the former administration had run a tight ship and that the city was in good financial shape when the new mayor took over, but now staff were resigning and were not being replaced, reportedly to save money. The implication was that the new manager and mayor were screwing things up.

The manager, in his reply, pointed out that the previous manager's instructions to the department heads acknowledged that there was too little reserve in the fund balance to provide the necessary margin of safety and that spending cuts would have to be made during the year to improve the situation. The present manager also noted that before he came on board, the city had hired three new policemen in anticipation of a new discount mall that later canceled out. The hiring had been done in the middle of the year, with ballooning costs for the first full year of the new staff. In other words, the manager had inherited a situation that needed to be fixed. The city finances had not been so fine when he began his term.

As for the revenue increases, the property taxes were near long-term averages, but had had to be increased over recent lows because of state mandated costs, over which the city had absolutely no control. The yield from sales taxes had indeed gone up, but the increases were obligated to the Tax Increment Financing district, a district formed a number of years earlier to fund economic development, and to other units of government through existing intergovernmental agreements. The actual amount of sales taxes going into the general fund was decreasing, not increasing, so there was no puzzle about where the increased revenue was going. Finally, the editorial had correctly pointed out that the city had increased fees levied on developers to pay the present and future costs of growth. The administration's goal was for expansion and growth to fund itself, rather than be subsidized by the existing community residents. The manager argued that such policies were common, not only in other cities, but in the neighboring cities with which DeKalb was competing. This fee policy symbolized the policy difference between the current and previous administration.

This story of charges against and defenses of municipal budgeting practices in DeKalb, Illinois, illustrates a number of themes in public budgeting. First, the venue of the debate was the local newspaper. The issues were complex and the newspaper was trying to explain them to the public, but it was not being an impartial observer or educator. The newspaper editor was being given stories that sounded realistic and were supported by some evidence in the budget, but he did not dig deeper. The result was the kind of muffled communication that is common in public budgeting.

Public officials often think they are giving clear signals on the budget and are puzzled by citizen responses. The budget can be harder to explain than elected officials imagine. Public budgeting is complex and rule-bound, while political dialogue is simple, simplifying, and sometimes biased. Accountability does not happen by itself; budgets do not wade into crowds and draw around them circles of admiring readers. Budgets have to be interpreted, and someone has to tell a good story to get readers involved. This is where newspapers come in, but reporters are not necessarily knowledgeable, and newspapers are not necessarily neutral.

Another theme that emerged from the minicase was that the former mayor and manager were still playing political roles, albeit indirect ones. Nearly all new administrations have to run against their predecessors. They come into office and find a mess and try to clean it up. If they get started without a process of reckoning, they are likely to be blamed for the financial mistakes of their predecessors, who, as in this case, may have run down fund balances and put off expenditures until the next administration. The inherited budget may be booby-trapped in a variety of ways, precisely because time is an element in budgeting and expenditures can be put off and revenue moved up.

While prior administrations may still be around to find fault, hoping to return to office, other potential electoral rivals can play a similar role, picking apart the budget, making normal decisions look odd, emphasizing projects that have not been completed or that came in over estimated costs. Taxpayers' groups may also continually pick apart the budget in highly public situations, from their own somewhat narrow point of view. Politics thus infiltrates budgeting whenever the budget goes public. Budgeteers have to be continually alert to the political implications of their actions and the implications of politics for their actions. Keeping governmental finances afloat can be difficult when others are intentionally rocking the boat. There can be great temptation to keep parts of the budget obscure in order to prevent massive criticism from political opponents.

The attack and defense of the DeKalb budget made clear that there is policy in the budget, not just technical decisions about the timing of debt or the level of the property tax rate. The editorial was wrong in some of its charges, but it was right in noting the increase in fees for developers. These fees were not just a way of balancing the budget but reflected a judgment about who should pay for government and who should benefit from public spending. In this case, the former mayor had implemented a policy whereby all residents paid for growth. He claimed that everyone benefited, but it seemed likely that developers and new businesses benefited disproportionately compared to existing residents and businesses. In many cities, growth is highly subsidized, often by citizens who do not benefit directly from growth and who might prefer that additional growth not take place. In DeKalb, the citizens were asked in a political campaign precisely whether they wanted to continue to subsidize growth, and they said no, voting to change mayors to change the existing policy. If elected officials drift too far in their policies from what the citizens wish, they are likely to be turned out of office at the next opportunity.

The manager's letter to the editor made clear that public budgeting is constrained—by other levels of government (state mandates), by prior agreements (the Tax Increment District and intergovernmental agreements), and by competition with surrounding jurisdictions. The manager defended his charging fees for developers not only by noting the condition of the general fund, but also by noting that surrounding towns were doing the same thing, so the community would not lose development by charging a fee.

The overall point of the minicase is that public officials need not only to do the right thing for the community and follow the public will, as best they understand what that is, but also to figure out a way to explain and justify their choices. They are engaged in a dialogue in which there are always other arguments, such as "we have to subsidize business because other governments are doing it" or "if we raise property taxes we will lose businesses." Public officials should not ignore these arguments because there are many in the community who believe them, and their advocates represent legitimate interests. Equally important, engaging in this dialogue is a way of getting the public involved and getting across information about budgetary decisions in a way that people can understand.

In sum, public budgeting is necessarily and legitimately different from personal and business budgeting. These differences help shape the politics of public budgeting.

A Variety of Actors

The first characteristic of public budgeting was the variety of actors involved in the budget and their frequently clashing motivations and goals. On a regular basis, bureau chiefs, executive budget officers, and chief executives are involved in the budget process, as are legislators, both on committees and as a whole group. Interest groups may be involved at intervals, sometimes for relatively long stretches of time, sometimes briefly. Sometimes citizens play a direct or indirect role in the budget process. Courts may play a role in budgets at any level of government at unpredictable intervals. When they do play a role in budgetary decisions, what are these actors trying to achieve?

Bureau Chiefs. Many students of budgeting assume that agency heads always want to expand their agencies, that their demands are almost limitless, and that it is up to other budget actors to curtail and limit their demands. The reasons given for that desire for expansion include prestige, more subordinates, more space, larger desks, more secretaries, and not incidentally, more salary. The argument presumes that agency heads judge their bureaucratic skills in terms of the satisfaction of their budget requests. Successful bureaucrats bring back the budget. Agency expansion is the measure of success.

Recent research has suggested that while some bureaucrats may be motivated by salaries, many feel that one of their major rewards is the opportunity to do good for people—to house the homeless, feed the hungry, find jobs for the unemployed, and send out checks to the disabled.[2] For these bureaucrats, efforts to expand agency budgets are the result of their belief in the programs they work for.

Recent research has also suggested that the bureaucracy has become more professional, which introduces the possibility of another motivation, the desire to do a good job, to do it right, to put in the best machinery that exists or build the biggest, toughest engineering project or the most complicated weapons.

The generalization that bureaucrats always press for budget increases appears to be too strong. Some agencies are much more aggressive in pushing for growth than others. Some are downright moribund. Sometimes agency heads refuse to expand when given the opportunity,[3] suggesting there are some countervailing values to growth. One of these countervailing values is agency autonomy. Administrators may prefer to maintain autonomy rather than increase the budget if it comes down to a choice between the two. A second countervailing value to growth is professionalism, the desire to get the job done, and do it quickly and right. Administrators generally prefer to hire employees who have the ability to get the job done, plus a little, a spare amount of intelligence, motivation, and energy just in case they need to get some extra work done or do it fast in response to a political request.[4] Administrators may refuse to add employees if the proposed employees do not add to the agency's capacity to get things done. A third countervailing value is program loyalty. Expansion may be seen as undesirable if the new mission swamps the existing mission, if it appears contradictory to the existing mission, or if the program requires more money to carry out than is provided, forcing the agency to spend money designated for existing programs on new ones or do a poor job.

A fourth countervailing value is belief in the chain of command. Many, if not all, bureaucrats believe that their role is to carry out the policies of the chief executive and the legislature. If those policies mean cutting back budgets, agency heads cut back the agencies. Agency heads may be appointed precisely because they are willing to make cuts in their agencies.[5]

Bureaucrats, then, do not always try to expand their agencies' budgets. They have other, competing goals, which sometimes dominate. Also, their achievements can be measured by other than expanded budgets. They may go for some specific items in the budget without raising totals, or may try for changes in the wording of legislation. They may strive to get a statutory basis for the agency and security of funding. They may take as a goal providing more efficient and effective service, rather than expanded or more expensive service.

The Executive Budget Office. The traditional role of the budget office has been to scrutinize requests coming up from the agencies, to find waste and eliminate it, and to discourage most requests for new money. The executive budget office has been perceived as the naysayer, the protector of the public purse. Most staff members in the budget office are very conscious of the need to balance the budget, to avoid deficits, and to manage cash flow so that there is money on hand to pay bills. Hence they tend to be skeptical of requests for new money.

In recent years, however, there has been a change in the role of budget office. At the national level under President Ronald Reagan, budgeting became much more top-down, with the director of the Office of Management and Budget (OMB) proposing specific cuts and negotiating them directly with Congress, without much scrutiny of requests coming up from departments or bureaus. OMB became more involved in trying to accomplish the policy goals of the president through the budget.[6] At state levels, too, there has been an evolution of budget staff from more technical to more political and more policy-related goals. When the governor is looking for new spending proposals, these may come from the budget office.

Chief Executive Officers. The role of chief executive officers (the mayor or city manager, the governor, the president) is highly variable, and hence these executives' goals in the budget process cannot be predicted without knowledge of the individuals. Some chief executives have been expansive, proposing new programs; others have been economy minded, cutting back proposals generated by the legislatures. Some have been efficiency oriented, reorganizing staffs and trying to maintain service levels without increases in taxes or expenditures.

Legislators. Legislators have sometimes been described as always trying to increase expenditures.[7] Their motivation is viewed as getting reelected, which depends on their ability to provide constituents services and deliver "pork"—jobs and capital projects—to their districts. Norms of reciprocity magnify the effects of these spending demands because legislators are reluctant to cut others' pork lest their own be cut in return. At the city level, a council member described this norm of reciprocity, "There is an unwritten rule that if something is in a councilman's district, we'll go along and scratch each other's back."[8]

For some legislators, however, getting reelected is not a high priority. They view elected office as a service they perform for the community rather than a career, and while they may be responsive to constituents' needs, they are simply not motivated to start new projects or give public employees a raise in order to get reelected. Also, some legislators feel secure about the possibility of reelection and hence have no urgent need to deliver pork in order to increase their chances of reelection.[9]

Even assuming the motivation to get reelected, holding down taxes may be as important to reelection as spending on programs and projects. The consequence of tax reduction is usually curtailed expenditures. Legislators are bound to try to balance the budget, which puts some constraints on the desire to spend.

The tendency to provide pork is real, but there are counterbalancing factors. Some legislators are more immune to pressures from constituents because they are secure electorally, and legislators can organize themselves in such a way as to insulate themselves somewhat from these pressures. They can, for example, select more electorally secure representatives for key positions on appropriations committees; they can separate committees that deal extensively with interest groups from those that deal with expenditures; they can set up buffer groups to deal with interest groups; they can structure the budget process so that revenue limits precede and guide spending proposals.

Moreover, legislators have interests other than providing pork. Some legislators are deeply concerned about solving social problems, designing and funding defense and foreign aid systems, and monitoring the executive branch. The proportion of federal budget spent on pork-type projects has declined in recent years, despite reforms in Congress that decentralized control and allowed pressure for pork to increase.[10] "Congressmen are not single-minded seekers of local benefits, struggling feverishly to win every last dollar for their districts. However important the quest for local benefits may be, it is always tempered by other competing concerns."[11] The pull for local benefits depends on the program. Some, like water projects, are oriented to local payoffs; others, like entitlement programs for large numbers of people, are not. Programs with local pull account for smaller and smaller proportions of the budget[12] and the trend has accelerated since 1978.[13]

Interest Groups. Interest groups, too, have often been singled out as the driving force behind budget increases. They are said to want more benefits for their members and to be undeterred by concerns for overall budget balance or the negative effects of tax increases. Moreover, their power has been depicted as great. Well-funded interest groups reportedly wine and dine legislators and provide campaign funding for candidates who agree with their positions.

There is some truth to this picture, but it is oversimplified. Interest groups have other policy goals besides budget levels. In fact, most probably deal with the budget only when a crisis occurs, such as a threat to funding levels. Because they can be counted on to come to the defense of a threatened program, they reduce the flexibility of budget decision makers, who find it difficult to cut programs with strong interest-group backing. But many areas of the budget do not have strong interest-group backing. For example, foreign aid programs have few domestic constituencies. Agencies may even have negative constituencies, that is, interest groups that want to reduce their funding and terminate their programs. The American Medical Association sought for years to eliminate the Health Planning Program. Often when there are interest groups, there are many rather than one, and these interest groups may have conflicting styles or conflicting goals, canceling one another out or absorbing energy in battles among themselves. A coalition of interest groups representing broad geographic areas and a variety of constituencies is likely to be more effective at lobbying. Hence coalitions may form, but individual members of the coalition may not go along with measures supported by others, so the range of items lobbied for as a unified group may be narrow. Extensive negotiations and continual efforts are required to get two or more independent groups together for a lobbying effort, and the arrangement can then fall apart. In short, interest groups are often interested in maintaining their autonomy.

Individuals. Individuals seldom have a direct role in the budget process, but they often have an indirect role. They may vote on referenda to limit revenues, forbid some forms of taxation, or require budgetary balance. They voice their opinions also in public opinion polls, and more informally by calling or writing their elected representatives and giving their opinions. Their knowledge of the budget is not usually detailed, but their feelings about the acceptability of taxation are an important part of the constraints of public budgeting. Their preferences for less visible taxes and for taxes earmarked for specific approved expenditures have been an important factor in public budgeting.

The Courts. Another budget actor that plays an intermittent role in determining expenditures is the courts.[14] The courts get involved when other actors, often interest groups, bring a case against the government. Suits that affect the budget may involve service levels or the legality of particular forms of taxation. If a particular tax is judged unconstitutional, the result is usually lost revenues. If there are suits concerning levels of service, governments may be forced to spend more money on that service. There can also be damage suits against governments that affect expenditures. These suits are usually settled without regard to the government agencies' ability to pay. The result may be forced cuts in other areas of the budget, tax increases, or even bankruptcy. When the courts get involved, they may determine budget priorities. They introduce a kind of rigidity into the budget that says do this, or pay this, first.

Typical areas in which courts have gotten involved and mandated expenditures for state and local governments are prison overcrowding (declared cruel and unusual punishment) and deinstitutionalization of mentally ill and mentally handicapped patients. In each case, the rights of the institutionalized population required more services or more space, often involving expenditures of additional funds. From the perspective of the courts, the priority of rights outweighs immediate concerns for budget balances, autonomy of governmental units, and local priorities.

These various actors not only have different and potentially clashing budgetary goals, but they typically have different levels of power. Thus, at times, the budget office may completely dominate the agencies; at times, Congress may differ from the president on budgetary policy and pass its own preferences. The courts may preempt the decision making of the executive and the legislature. Some particular interest groups may always be able to get tax breaks for themselves. The combination of different preferences and different levels of power has to be orchestrated by the budget process in such a way that agreement is reached, and the players stay in the game, continuing to abide by the rules. If some actors feel too powerless over the budget, they may cease to participate or become obstructionist, blocking any agreements or imposing rigid, nonnegotiable solutions. Why participate in negotiations and discussions if the decision will go against you regardless of what you do? If some actors lose on important issues, they may try to influence budget implementation to favor themselves. Or the actors with less budget power may try to change the budget process so that they have a better chance of influencing the outcomes.

Separation of Payer and Decider

One of the major characteristics of public budgeting is that those who pay the bills are not the ones who make the decisions on how the money is to be spent. The possibility exists that elected officials will spend the money differently than taxpayers wish. In some cities in the later 1800s, the problem was solved by having taxpayer groups elect their own representatives, in some cases requiring property ownership and taxpaying history to qualify as a candidate.[15] Nearly all local taxation was based on property taxes at that time. Local government, under the control of these taxpayers, spent money on projects that would benefit them, such as markets, ports, roads, and bridges. When the economy turned sour, and property owners could not afford to pay for these projects, they stopped paying for them.[16] Over the years, however, as more poor folk moved into the cities and voted, with the encouragement of political machines that paid for votes with employment opportunities, the difference between what the wealthy wished to spend tax money on and what elected officials actually spent the money on began to grow. Antitax revolts focused on this gap between taxpayers and "tax eaters," those who consumed public services without paying taxes for them.

During the twentieth century, property ownership broadened as immigrants and blue-collar workers bought their own homes. Also, more recently, taxation at the local level has shifted away from dependence on property taxes and onto sales taxes. The result is that there is not now a class of taxpayers and a class of tax users or consumers of government services. Everyone pays local taxes, including the poor in many cities. The result has been to shift the focus of concern to whether everyone benefits from public taxation or only a few. For those services that benefit only a few, the question arises, why should everyone have to pay for them?

One solution is to charge user fees for services that benefit only or primarily users and not others. Revenue from fees has grown substantially at all levels of government in the past twenty years in response to this pressure against paying for anyone else's services. A second approach has been for those who want narrow benefits to trade support with others who also want narrow benefits. Thus they tolerate some projects that others want in exchange for support on their favored projects. Still, there are expenditures in many budgets that benefit one group or interest that are not balanced by benefits to other groups or interests. Such expenditures can be politically contentious.

Sometimes whether there will be political stress is a matter of perception or presentation, not a characteristic of the actual program. Taxpayers who earn regular incomes often bridle at paying welfare for those who do not work, seeing it as an outlay from which they do not and will not benefit. Viewed differently, however, anyone could end up needing unemployment benefits or even welfare if the economy performs poorly or downsizing throws older workers out in the cold. If taxpayers see themselves as possible future beneficiaries of a safety net, they may be willing to support it; to the extent that they see such expenditures as only for others and believe that they will never need such services, they are more likely to oppose such programs.

The separation between taxpayer and budgetary decision maker highlights the importance of symbolic politics, that is, the way expenditures are presented and viewed. Expenditures that benefit some narrow group may survive if they are represented as being for the collective good. For example, some economic development policies are justified on the basis that everyone benefits from growth. Alternatively, expenditures may be justified in such terms that opposing them appears callow and inhumane or destructive of collective benefits. Thus federal antipollution mandates may pass because it is politically impossible to oppose "clean air"; education mandates for handicapped children may be politically impossible to oppose because who wants to be known for hurting handicapped children or their parents?[17] Sometimes it is difficult to make the argument that everyone benefits from an expenditure aimed at a few, or from a tax break that benefits a narrow group. The argument may not be credible. Then the goal may be to make the expenditure look small instead.

In one illustration, a state university president decided to expand the big-time sports program, in an environment of overall financial scarcity. While some faculty members undoubtedly favored the action, many would have opposed it if they had been asked. The president did not ask their opinions, however; instead, the full costs of the program were disguised to make the budget appear acceptable. Because of progressive underestimates of costs in the sports program, some pundits labeled the sports program the case of the disappearing budget.

To obscure the real costs, the president broke up the costs for the program and scattered them among different portions of the budget. To complicate the picture further, he drew on different pockets of revenue, including student athletic fees, bond revenues, and voluntary donations. When asked, he said money going to the athletic programs was earmarked and could not be spent on other programs, so that professors trying to get more money to teach history or biology would look elsewhere than to sports. The amount of money showing as costs in the athletic program remained constant every year, although the program costs were expanding. Fearing conflict and disapproval, the president hid the costs in the budget.

The more complicated the budget, the more different activities and accounts, the greater the discretion of the administrators. As one university president offered, "Not a day goes by when we do not wish we had a more complex budget." The complexity allows for choice of where to report expenditures, and which revenues to use, to highlight some expenditures and gloss over others.

Because public demands may not be clearly expressed, and because different segments of the public may make different and competing demands, and because public officials themselves may have other priorities, officials may not be able or willing to be bound tightly to public opinion. Nevertheless, if politicians knowingly make decisions that differ from what the public seems to want, there is pressure to present the budget in a way that makes it appear acceptable. That pressure creates a tension between accountability, which requires nearly complete openness, and acceptability, which sometimes involves hiding or distorting information or presenting it in an unclear fashion.

It would be misleading to suggest that the tension between accountability and acceptability always leads to more distortion or more secrecy. Sometimes the balance tends toward more accountability and budgets become clearer and more representative of true costs. The federal budget, for example, has moved toward clearer and more comprehensive portraits of public expenditures in recent years. But the tension is always present.

The Budget Document and Accountability

Because of the separation of payer and decider, the budget document itself becomes an important means of public accountability. How did the public's representatives actually decide to spend taxpayer money? Did they waste it? Did they spend it on defense or police or on social services? The streets are in terrible shape—how much money did they spend on street repair? Citizens do not typically watch the decision making, but they and the press have access to the budget document and can look for the answers. They can hold the government accountable through the budget, to see that what officials promised them was actually delivered.

In recent years there has been pressure to make budgets more readable and more informative. These efforts have included grouping expenditures by program and establishing performance goals and measurements associated with each program. At the national level, the Government Performance and Results Act of 1993 (GPRA) has mandated that all federal agencies provide program plans and performance measures. Agencies are busy trying to comply, with varying degrees of success. The goal of performance budgeting at all levels of government has been to broaden the notion of accountability from a record of where the money was spent to how well the money was spent, and to hold public officials accountable for program outcomes and impacts. It is hoped that such clear reporting will help rekindle public respect for government.

MINICASE: THE GOVERNMENT PERFORMANCE AND RESULTS ACT

The Government Performance and Results Act (GPRA) was to be implemented in stages. Agencies were to come up with overall plans, including goals and program impacts, and then with a series of measures for determining what progress the agency was making, annually and over a period of years, toward the goals. Finally, these plans and measures were to be included as part of the budgetary decision making.

Agencies have had a difficult time coming up with acceptable plans. The political disagreement over what the goals of some agencies should be is intense. Some agencies have found their goals difficult to measure, and success is difficult to attribute to a single agency, because many agencies and societal changes contribute to overall outcomes and impacts. Implementation has been slowed by cutbacks in staffing of precisely those personnel who would have been engaged in creating performance plans. And the budgetary cutbacks built into the 1997 balanced budget agreement require a level of cuts that is no longer necessary because the budget is balanced (more or less), so the level of resources agencies can expect is often unclear. It is difficult to promise a level of service based on uncertain resource levels.

Performance budgeting is often an executive branch activity, changing the budget format in ways that the legislative branch ignores. In the case of GPRA, however, some members of Congress were intensely interested in the reforms, and they were also determined that performance budgeting not shift power away from Congress. Agencies were thus required to consult with their congressional committees before drawing up their agency goals and plans. Key legislators were upset to find in 1997 that the Office of Management and Budget in the Executive Office of the White House expected to review agency plans before they were submitted to Congress for discussion.[18] To the extent that the plans were jointly arrived at by Congress and the agencies, they could be used as a budgetary standard. Agencies could argue that they needed the resources that were in the plan to achieve the goals agreed on; Congress could argue that programs did not deserve the money because they had failed to achieve appropriate portions of their goals within set time limits.

The performance reports were supposed to elevate the level of discussion between Congress and the agency heads about agency budgets. Congress had nearly abandoned the role of examining programs in detail because spending caps had removed a lot of committee discretion. If appropriations subcommittees discovered problems in program implementation, there was not enough flexibility to do much about it. What was given to one agency had to be taken from another. It was easier not to know about problems. But GPRA had the potential for increasing congressional control of programs, making agency heads more responsive to congressional direction, and providing a justification for taking resources from one agency and giving them to another one.

Interestingly, both authorizing committees (in charge of designing and monitoring programs) and appropriations committees (in charge of funding them) have expressed interest in GPRA documents. The authorizing committees have expressed interest in the specific plans for improving services and measuring performance and whether the techniques for achieving the goals hurt or help their constituencies. One subcommittee was concerned, for example, that the administration was trying to reduce the costs of loans by increasing the loan fees beyond the actual program costs. The appropriations subcommittees have been more interested in whether the budget allocations match the goals statements and whether the agencies have clear goals and objectives and performance measures.

Agencies were expected to put their budgets into program formats and integrate those formats with their budget requests. The following testimony from The Office of Personnel Management (OPM) illustrates how one agency framed its budget request in terms of its strategic plan:

> Before considering our request in more detail, it is important to note that, in response to the Government Performance and Results Act, we have included our annual performance plan as an integral part of our budget justification. We have used our strategic goals, and the related series of objectives, as the basis for organizing our performance plan. Some of our objectives relate to overall human resources management concerns; some are limited to specific aspects, such as

staffing or compensation. Some are governmentwide; some are confined to our own agency.

Also, we have included in our budget justification for the first time a crosswalk of annual performance goals and strategic plan goals and objectives, which we have organized by fund and program activity. This presentation clearly links our resource allocations to our strategic plan goals. For example, nearly $60 million and 625 fte's [full time equivalent employees] will be directed to activities designed to achieve our goal of providing policy direction and leadership to recruit and retain the federal workforce required for the 21st century.

As I review with you specific aspects of our request, I will touch on the means we will use to achieve specific goals, as well as our strategies for measuring and validating our achievements.[19]

Increasingly at the federal level, budgets were being prepared and presented to the Office of Management and Budget and to the appropriations committees and oversight agencies in Congress in program and performance format, with at least some measurable goals.[20]

The increased demands for accountability through cost or performance measurement have sometimes been problematic. If particular cost or performance measures make an agency look worse, the agency may want to obscure the results or not use that measure. Also, performance measurement assumes a level of funding that is known with reasonable certainty, a condition increasingly difficult to meet. Moreover, there is no clear linkage between performance measurement and budgeting; that is, it is not clear if a poor performance report warrants additional spending or reduced spending. If the budget is used as a punishment for poor performance, elected officials may send agencies into a downward spiral of deteriorating management quality.

The movement toward improved accountability, better reporting, and more readable budgets suggests more openness after the fact, not during the process. The model suggests that public officials should be free from prior constraints and should be allowed to use their training and best judgment, but should be held accountable for their choices after the fact. Accurate reporting of what they have done and the consequences of those decisions is absolutely necessary for this model to work. But if elected officials have made choices that some members of the public disapprove of, officials may be reluctant to report the details of their decisions, lest they open themselves to attack. Political opponents can use performance data to attack an agency or program or administration, which contributes to a desire not to collect possibly damaging data or not to make it public. If public officials have made mistakes, they may be reluctant to reveal them.

In spite of such difficulties, the level of explanation in public budgets has been rising, not falling. Even so, however, each budget represents some degree of selectivity about what it will present and how. The art of selective revelation is part of public budgeting.

Openness to the Environment

Public budgets are open to the environment, which includes a number of different factors, such as the overall level of resources available (the amount of taxable wealth, the existing tax structure, current economic conditions); the degree of certainty of revenues; and a variety of emergencies such as very heavy snowfall, tornadoes, wars, bridge collapses, droughts, chemical explosions, and water pollution. The environment also includes rigidities resulting from earlier decisions, which may now be embodied in law. For example, rapid inflation in housing prices in California resulted in a citizen referendum to protect against rapidly rising property taxes. The result of the referendum was incorporated in the state constitution, limiting the taxing options of local governments. Constitutional restrictions to maintain a balanced budget or limit expenditures or put a ceiling on borrowing operate in a similar manner. Prior borrowing creates a legal obligation for future budgets, an obligation that may press other possible expenditures out of consideration or require higher levels of taxation. The environment in this sense may frame policy issues and limit alternatives. Public opinion is also part of the budgetary environment, and the perception of change in public opinion will be reflected in changing budgets.

The intergovernmental system is also a key part of the environment for budget actors. The legal sources of revenues, limits on borrowing, strings attached to grants, and mandated costs are but a few of the budgetary implications of the intergovernmental system. The requirement that some grants be spent on particular items or that a recipient match expenditures on grants may result in a pattern of spending different from what the state or local government would have preferred.

Budgeting is open to the environment not only in the sense of changing revenue levels, emergency demands on spending, and the changing intergovernmental system that frames responsibilities and revenue sources, but also in the sense that decision making itself is public. Committee hearings on the budget are public. Revenue and expenditure proposals are public; they are reported in the newspapers and debated in editorials and letters to the editor. The budget as proposed and as adopted is available for public inspection, as are reported comparisons of plans and actual spending. The whole budget process takes place under public scrutiny. Potentially embarrassing mistakes are harder to hide than in the private sector, and this may lead to a kind of caution. Public officials adapt to working in a room with glass walls and no window blinds.

The openness of public budgets to the environment means that budgets have to be adaptable during the year when unexpected events occur. At the national level, supplemental appropriations may help deal with emergencies such as wars, hurricanes, or earthquakes. At the state and local levels, there may be contingency accounts to deal with unexpected events. The goal is to build in enough flexibility to deal with the problems at hand without changing the underlying policies that have emerged from complex, public negotiations between multiple actors with different points of view.

Budget Constraints

Public budgeting is much more constrained than private-sector or family budgeting, because public budgeting is not limited only by the amount of revenue involved. The federal government can mandate state expenditures, preempting state priorities; similarly, states can mandate expenditures for local government. Some state governments tell local governments what format to use for a budget and what information has to be in the budget. States may limit borrowing levels for local governments, or even require that all local borrowing be approved by the state government. The reason for the current emphasis on after-the-fact reporting, rather than prior controls, is that there were so many prior controls that government managers had a difficult time getting anything done. Despite the recent emphasis on after-the-fact reporting, few prior constraints have actually been removed.

One of the constraints in the public sector is the fund structure. Public budgeting is based on funds, separate accounts for separate purposes. Money can be spent only through those accounts and cannot be freely swapped between accounts. Such transfers normally require justification and explicit permission. Each account or fund must balance, that is, revenue must equal or exceed expenditures. The result is not one bottom line, as in a family or business, but multiple bottom lines. Creating some flexibility within these constraints is a continuing trial.

Some constraints have been placed on budgeting by those who oppose higher levels of taxation. They press for tax limits in statutes and constitutions, which may guide decisions for decades. A second source of constraints is prior history of willfulness. Agency administrators sometimes abuse the discretion they have been granted, inviting tighter controls. If the executive branch makes too many transfers between funds or accounts, the legislature may limit the amount of money that can be transferred. A third reason for prior constraints is to facilitate supervision. States cannot easily monitor local budgeting and financial condition if each jurisdiction puts its budget in a different format or includes different information and uses different definitions of balance. Since the states are ultimately responsible for the finances of local governments, they have an interest in keeping them healthy and identifying local governments that may be headed for trouble.

Prior constraints in public budgeting include the fund or account structure and constraints on transfers, tax limits, borrowing limits, requirements for referendums for tax increases or general obligation bond issuance, uniform budget formats, and uniform accounting rules. There may be separate rules for limiting the number of employees and their rank, and additional rules for purchasing and requirements for bidding out contracts or purchases. Reform in recent years has meant reducing some of these prior controls—such as separate limits on total spending and on the number of personnel. But each proposal for reduction in constraints runs into the reason for the constraint in the first place. Changes may reduce the ability of the state to supervise, or the legislature to control policy. Increased discretion may shift power from the legislative to the executive branches, adding a layer of resistance. Or weakening of advanced controls may remove some political or policy tool that is still cherished. Thus in 1993 and 1994 the Clinton administration urged greater discretion for executive branch officials, including discretion over staffing levels. Soon thereafter, the administration and Congress proceeded to pass the Workforce Restructuring Act, reducing federal employment levels by some 270,000 employees. Despite the plea for more agency autonomy, each agency still has an assigned personnel ceiling.

The Meaning of *Politics* in Public Budgeting

Public budgets have a number of special characteristics. These characteristics suggest some of the ways that the budget is political. Political is a word that covers a number of meanings, even when narrowed to the context of budgetary decision making. The purpose of this book is to clarify the meaning of politics in the context of budgeting by sorting out some key meanings and showing how these meanings apply to different parts of budgetary decision making.

The literature suggests at least five major ways of viewing politics in the budget: reformism, incrementalist bargaining, interest-group determinism, process, and policymaking.

- The first is a reform orientation, which argues that politics and budgeting are or should be antithetical, that budgeting should be primarily or exclusively technical, and that comparison between items should be technical and efficiency based. Politics in the sense of the opinions and priorities of elected officials and interest groups is an unwanted intrusion that reduces efficiency and makes decision making less rational. The politics of reform involves a clash of views between professional staff and elected officials over the boundary between technical budget decisions and properly political ones.

- The second perspective is the incrementalist view, which sees budgeting as negotiations among a group of routine actors, bureaucrats, budget officers, chief executives, and legislators, who meet each year and bargain to resolution. To the extent that interest groups are included at all in this view, they are conceived of in the pluralist model. The process is open, anyone can play and win, and the overall outcome is good; conflict is held down because everyone wins something and no one wins too much.

- The third view is that interest groups are dominant actors in the budget process. In its extreme form this argument posits that richer and more powerful interest groups determine the budget. Some interests are represented by interest groups, and others either are not, or are represented by weaker interest groups; the outcome does not approximate democracy. There may be big winners and big losers in this model. Conflict is more extensive than in the incrementalist model. This view of politics in budgeting raises the question whether these interest groups represent narrow or broad coalitions, or possibly even class interest. To what extent do these interest groups represent oil or banking or the homeless, and to what extent do they represent business and labor more broadly?

- The fourth view of politics in the budget is that the budget process itself is the center and focus of budget politics. Those with particular budget goals try to change the budget process to favor their goals. Branches of government struggle with one another over budgetary power through the budget process; the budget process becomes the means of achieving or denying separation and balance between the branches of government. The degree of examination of budget requests, and the degree to which review is technical or political, cursory or detailed, is regulated by the budget process. The ability of interest groups to influence the budget, the role of the public in budget decisions, the openness of budget decision making—all these are part of the politics of process. In this view of politics, the individual actors and their strategies and goals may or may not be important, depending on the role assigned to individual actors in the budget process, and depending on whether the external environment allows any flexibility.

- The fifth view is that the politics of budgeting centers in policy debates, including debates about the role of the budget. Spending levels, taxing policies, and willingness to borrow to sustain spending during recessions are all major policy issues that have to be resolved one way or another during budget deliberations. Budgets may reflect a policy of moderating economic cycles or they may express a policy of allowing the economy to run its course. Each is a policy. Similarly, budgets must allocate funding to particular programs, and in the course of doing so, decide priorities for federal, state, and local governments. This view of politics in the budget emphasizes tradeoffs, especially those that occur between major areas of the budget, such as social services and defense or police. This view also emphasizes the role of the budget office in making policy and the format of the budget in encouraging comparisons between programs.

These five views of politics have been developed over time, and like an ancient document, the messages have been written over one another. Surely they are not all equally true, and certainly they often contradict each other. Parts of each may still be true, and they may be true of different parts of budgetary decision making, or true of budgetary decision making at different times or at different levels of government.

Budgetary Decision Making

This book explores the kind of politics that occurs in budgetary decision making. What is budgetary decision making like? We have already discovered that public budgeting is open to environmental changes and deals with policy conflicts. Policy conflicts can delay particular decisions or prevent them from being made at all; other budget decisions must be independent enough to be made without the missing pieces. They can be corrected later when missing pieces fall into place. Environmental emergencies can reorder priorities and alter targets that have already been determined. As a result, public budgeting must be segmentable and interruptible. The need for segmentation and interruptibility is satisfied by dividing budgeting into separate but linked decision clusters: revenues, process, expenditures, balance, and implementation.

Decision making in each cluster proceeds somewhat separately, but with reference to decisions made or anticipated in other decision streams. Decisions on spending are made with an eye on revenue totals, even though revenue estimates may not yet be firm. Decisions in different streams may be made iteratively, with tentative revenue estimates followed by tentative spending estimates, and followed in turn by updated revenue estimates and a fine-tuning of spending estimates. The order of decision making may be variable from year to year. In one year, there may be no change in the definition of balance, so that prior years' definitions frame this year's deliberations. In another year, the definition of balance may change during the deliberations, requiring adjustments in spending or revenue plans. Sometimes the decision making moves faster in one cluster than in another, and decision makers in the cluster that is ahead may have to guess or anticipate what the decisions will be in other clusters and revise later if necessary.

Each cluster attracts a different characteristic set of actors and generates its own typical pattern of politics. Some clusters have heavy interest-group activity, while others have virtually none; some clusters are marked by intense competition and negotiations and efforts to bind future decisions to restrict open competition; some are marked by deep ideological splits, while others seem not to be ideological at all. Some are marked by dominance of a technical perspective, while others are clearly determined by the priorities of elected officials and the public, and still others represent a blend of the two.

The Revenue Cluster

Revenue decisions include technical estimates of how much income will be available for the following year, assuming no change in the tax structures, and policy decisions about changes in the level or type of taxation. Will taxes be raised or lowered? Will tax breaks be granted, and if so, to whom, for what purpose? Which tax sources will be emphasized, and which deemphasized, with what effect on regions and economic classes, or on age groups? How visible will the tax burden be? Interest groups are intensely involved in the revenue cluster. The revenue cluster emphasizes the scarcity of resources that is an essential element in budgeting and illustrates the tension between accountability and acceptability that is a characteristic of public budgets. Revenues are also extremely sensitive to the environment because changes in the economy influence revenue levels and because the perception of public opinion influences the public officials' willingness to increase taxes.

The Budget Process

The process cluster concerns how to make budget decisions. Who should participate in the budget deliberations? Should the agency heads have power independent of the central budget office? How influential should interest groups be? How much power should the legislature have? How should the work be divided, and when should particular decisions be made? Normally the legislature takes a key role in establishing budget process, although the chief executive may propose desired changes. Interest groups play a minor role, if any role at all. The politics of process may revolve around individuals or groups trying to maximize their power through rearranging the budget process. This jockeying for power rises to importance when the competing parties represent the executive and legislative branches and try to influence the separation and balance between the branches of government. The politics of process may revolve around the policy issues of the level of spending and the ability of government to balance its budget.

The Expenditure Cluster

The expenditure cluster involves some technical estimates of likely expenditures, such as for grants that are dependent on formulas and benefit programs whose costs depend on the level of unemployment. But many expenditure decisions are policy relevant—which programs will be funded at what level, who will benefit from public programs and who will not, where and how cuts will be made, and whose interests will be protected. Agency heads are more involved in these decisions than in taxation or process decisions, and interest groups are also often active. The expenditure portion of the budget emphasizes competition for limited resources and the resulting tradeoffs, choices between specific sets of alternatives. If we want more money spent on streets, does that translate into less money spent on day care? Does more money spent on hurricane relief translate into less money for defense or for housing for the poor?

The Balance Cluster

The balance cluster concerns the basic budgetary question of whether the budget has to be balanced each year with each year's revenues, or whether borrowing is allowed to balance the budget, and if so, how much, for how long, and for what purposes. The politics of balance deals with questions of whether balance should be achieved by increasing revenues, decreasing expenditures, or both, and hence reflects policies about the desirable scope of government. Sometimes the politics of balance emphasizes definitions, as the group in power seeks to make its deficits look smaller by defining them away. The balance cluster also deals with questions of how deficits should be eliminated once they occur and their amounts are pinned down. At the national level, because deficits may be incurred during recessions in an effort to help the economy recover, the ability to run a deficit is linked to policies favoring or opposing the role of the budget in controlling the economy and, in particular, the use of the budget to moderate unemployment. These issues—whether budgets should balance, the proper scope of government and level of taxation, and the role of government in moderating unemployment—are issues that the general public cares about. Citizens may participate in this decision cluster through referendums and opinion polls; broad groups of taxpayers and interest-group coalitions representing broad segments of society may be involved in lobbying on this issue. Political parties may even include their policies toward deficits in their election platforms.

Budget Implementation

Finally, there is a cluster of decisions around budget implementation. How close should actual expenditures be to the ones planned in the budget? How can one justify variation from the budget plan? Can the budget be remade after it is approved, during the budget year? The key issues here revolve around the need to implement decisions exactly as made and the need to make changes during the year because of changes in the environment. The potential conflict is usually resolved by treating implementation as technical rather than policy related. Executive branch staff play the major role in implementation, with much smaller and more occasional roles for the legislature. Interest groups play virtually no role in implementation. The allowance for technical changes does open the door to policy changes during the year, but these are normally carefully monitored and may cause open conflict when they occur.

Microbudgeting and Macrobudgeting

The five clusters of decision making outline the nature of the decisions actually being made, but tell little about how and why the decisions are made. On the one hand there are a number of budget actors, who all have individual motivations, who strategize to get what they want from the budget. The focus on the actors and their strategies is called *microbudgeting.* But the actors do not simply bargain with one another or with whomever they meet in the corridor. The actors are assigned budget roles by the budget process, the issues they examine are often framed by the budget process, and the timing and coordination of their decisions are often regulated by the budget process. The budget actors are not totally free to come to budget agreements in any way they choose. Individual actors are bound by environmental constraints. There are choices they are not free to make because they are against the law, or because the courts decree it, or because previous decision makers have bound their hands. The total amount of revenue available is a kind of constraint, as is popular demand for some programs and popular dislike of others. Budgetary decision making has to account not just for budgetary actors but also for budget processes and the environment. This more top-down and systemic perspective on budgeting is called *macrobudgeting*. Contemporary budgeting gives more emphasis to macrobudgeting than exclusively to microbudgeting.

One way of viewing the determinants of budgetary outcomes is as a causal model, depicted in figure 1.1. In this schema, the environment, budget processes, and individuals' strategies all affect outcomes.

The environment influences budgetary outcomes directly and indirectly, through process and through individual strategies. The environment influences outcomes directly, without going through either budget process or individual strategies, when it imposes emergencies that reorder priorities. Thus a war or a natural disaster preempts normal budgetary decision making.

The environment influences the budget process in several ways. The level of resources available—both the actual level of wealth and the willingness of the citizens to pay their taxes—influences the degree of centralization of budgeting. When resources are especially scarce and there is apparent need to either cut back according to a given set of policies or make each dollar count toward specific economic goals, there is no room for bottom-up demands that result in compromises and a little bit of gain for everyone regardless of need. When resources are abundant, a more decentralized model of process may hold, with less emphasis on comparing policies and less competition between supporters of different policies.

The environment may influence the format of the budget as well as the degree of centralization of decision making. When revenues are growing, there may be more emphasis on planning and on linking the budget to future community goals, to stimulate public demands for new spending. When there is little new money, the idea of planning may seem superfluous. Changing direction, or setting new goals, may seem impossible in the face of declining revenues that make current goals difficult to sustain.

Environment in the sense of the results of prior decisions may also influence process. If there is a huge accumulation of debt and little apparent way to con-

FIGURE 1.1   DECISION MAKING: ENVIRONMENT, PROCESS, AND STRATEGIES

trol it, or if the budget has been growing very rapidly for reasons other than war, there may be attempts to change the budget process in an effort to control spending and debt. In contrast, if the environment suggests the need for additional spending, and the current budget process is delivering very slow growth, the process may be changed to make spending decisions quicker and easier.

The environment influences not only the budget process but also the strategies of the budget actors. Clearly, the level of resources available determines whether actors press for new programs and expansion of existing ones or if they strive to prevent cuts and protect their revenue sources from encroachment by other programs.

The level of certainty of funding influences strategies as well. If whatever an agency was promised may never arrive, agency heads are likely to engage in continuous lobbying for their money. Long-term or future agreements will be perceived as worthless; the possibility of toning down conflict by stretching out budget allocation times will disappear. Attention will focus on what is available now, and going after whatever it is, whether it is what you want or not, because what you really want may never show up and hence is not worth waiting for.

The intergovernmental grant structure is part of the environment that may influence strategies. Because some grant money may seem free, state and local governments may focus their energies on getting grants instead of raising local revenues. Or they may seek to decrease the amount of match required for a grant or increase their authority over how the money can be spent. Intergovernmental grants may make some expenditures relatively cheap, and some cutbacks relatively expensive, and hence frame constraints and choices for state and local budget officials.

The legal environment also influences strategies. For example, if public school teachers want tax raises to fund education and there is a provision in the state constitution forbidding income taxes, the teachers must either campaign for a constitutional revision (a time-consuming and difficult task) or support a tax they know to be more burdensome to the poor. Thus the environment frames choices and influences strategies.

In figure 1.1, the budget process influences strategies directly and, to a lesser extent, outcomes directly. But there is a double-headed arrow on the linkage between budget processes and strategies, suggesting that individuals' strategies also influence budget processes.

Budget processes influence strategies in some fairly obvious ways. If the budget structure allows for lengthy detailed budget hearings, open to the public and interest groups, at which decisions are often made, then various actors are likely to concentrate their efforts on making a good impression at these hearings. If the chief executive prepares the budget, which is subject to only superficial scrutiny and pro forma hearings before being approved by the legislature, anyone who wants to influence the budget—including the legislators themselves—must make their opinions heard earlier in the process, before the final executive proposal is put together. Informal discussion with department heads, or even telephone calls to the budget office, may be the route to influence. If the budget is made two or three times, with only the last one effective, then strategies may be to play out the first time or two with grandstanding—extreme positions to attract media attention—and more detailed and moderate positions later when the final decisions are made. The budget process orders the decisions in such a way that some of them are critical and determine or influence those that come afterward. Budget strategies naturally gravitate to those key decisions no matter where they are located.

When budget outcomes contradict some group's preference, the group may try to change the budget process to help it get the outcomes it prefers. When coalitions of the dissatisfied can agree on particular changes, fairly substantial changes in process may result. A change in process will bring about a change in outcome if the change in process shifts power from one group of individuals who want to accomplish one goal to another group with different goals.

The final link in the figure is between the strategies of budget actors and outcomes. The effect of different strategies on the outcomes is hard to gauge. It seems obvious, however, that strategies that ignore the process or the environment are doomed to failure. Budget actors have to figure out where the flexibility is before they can influence how that flexibility will be used. Strategies that try to bypass superiors or fool legislators generally do not work; strategies that involve careful documentation of need and appear to save money are generally more successful.[21]

Summary and Conclusions

Public budgeting shares the characteristics of all budgeting. It makes choices between possible expenditures, it has to balance, and it has a decision-making process. But public budgeting has a number of additional features peculiar to itself, such as its openness to the environment; the variety of actors involved in budgeting, all of whom come to it with different goals; the separation of taxpayers from budget decision makers; the use of the budget document as a means of public accountability; and the numerous constraints typical of public budgeting.

Public budgeting is both technical and political. Politics takes on some special meanings in the context of budgetary decision making. Budgetary decision making must be flexible, adaptive, and interruptible, which leads to a structure of five semi-independent strands of decision making: revenues, process, expenditures, balance, and implementation. Each such strand generates its own political characteristics.

Budget outcomes are not solely the result of budget actors negotiating with one another in a free-for-all; outcomes depend on the environment, and on the budget process as well as individual strategies. Individual strategies have to be framed in a broader context than simply perceived self-interest.

Budgeting is not well described as an annual process with little change from year to year. Budgetary decision making changes over time: interest group power waxes and wanes, competition in the budget increases and decreases, and the budget process itself varies over time. Changes in process take place in response to individuals, committees, and branches of government jockeying for power; in response to changes in the environment from rich to lean, or vice versa; in response to changes in the power of interest groups; and in response to scandals or excesses of various kinds.

Chapters 2 to 8 describe the patterns of politics associated with each of the decision streams, and the sources and patterns of change over time. The final chapter integrates the decision streams into one model of budgetary decision making and points out the commonalities and differences among the decision streams.

CHAPTER TWO

Revenue Politics

We . . . seem to be able to defy what is supposed to happen. The naysayers all said Social Security was in such trouble, and the Ways and Means Committee pulled it together. It was a doctrine of politics that tax increases could not happen in an election year. We have done it quite often in the last years. . . . There is no doubt we can make tough decisions.

—Representative Barbara Kennelly

PUBLIC BUDGETING INVOLVES a separation of the tax payers and the decision makers who determine tax and spending levels. This separation sets up the possibility of some radical disagreements. Citizens would undoubtedly be happier about paying taxes if they could choose which services they wanted and pay no more for them than they felt the programs were worth. They might be even happier if they could get others to pay the taxes while they received the services. Individual taxpayers usually do not control the mix of services, however, and thus may have to pay for some programs they do not want. Moreover, many citizens are convinced that they are paying for waste and mismanagement. In addition, taxpayers often feel that others are getting away with paying less taxes than they are. They resent being forced to pay more than their share.

Elected officials have the legal power to raise taxes, but they can easily be turned out of office if they raise taxes beyond the limits that citizens formally or informally set. Angry citizens and activated interest groups can, and sometimes do, revolt against taxes. Some politicians respond to this kind of threat by promising not to raise taxes, no matter what.

Never raising taxes is a difficult position to maintain, since expenditures are likely to increase. Even when government does not expand functions, inflation increases the costs of equipment, such as fire trucks and airplanes, and the costs of salaries. Revenue sources that do not grow with inflation, such as water and sewer fees, have to be raised periodically to keep up with the gradually rising costs. When government does add functions, it has to find new sources of taxation or increase existing revenues to cover the increased costs. And when general taxes are eroded by special exceptions or other changes in the laws, some provision has to be made to replace the lost revenues or decrease the size or scope of government. Changes in the environment, such as termination of grant income or a decline in the economy or a natural disaster or war, can create the need for more revenues.

The necessity of increasing revenues and the public's reluctance to be taxed, especially for services they do not want, leads to three major characteristics of revenue politics. The first is that when public officials determine that additional revenues are necessary, they go about getting support very carefully. They may work out a set of strategies, adapt budget processes specifically for taxation purposes, and choose their timing so that overwhelming environmental pressures seem to require tax increases. The second characteristic of revenue politics is that it develops an underside, a mirror image, a politics of protection from taxation and of tax reductions and exceptions. Third, the efforts to raise taxes carefully and to protect individuals, interest groups, and regions from taxation leads to a piecemeal, complicated, inconsistent, and inequitable tax structure that periodically needs overhauling. Revenue politics is characterized by periodic efforts at reform.

Increasing Taxes

Garnering support for increasing revenues is much more difficult than gaining support for spending proposals. Taxation creates a set of opponents and has few supporters. To get taxes passed requires major efforts to create support and defuse opposition.

Following are two examples of efforts to increase taxes. One was only partly and temporarily successful (in Illinois), while the other (in Dayton, Ohio) worked quite well. Both efforts show the tremendous effort that goes into trying to gain support for a tax increase.

The problem in the Illinois case was partly procedural. By initially setting up a blue-ribbon committee to come up with technical solutions, the process stirred up interest-group opposition rather than toning it down. But the more important problem was that there was no irrefutable evidence of need; the governor's past manipulations of the budget created distrust that he just could not overcome. Part of the reason for the success of the Dayton tax increase was the care with which the opposition was defused, by making the increases revokable in the future, by widely airing the need, by guaranteeing the lack of waste to those most suspicious of it, and by linking revenues to specific desired service levels.

MINICASE: INCOME TAX INCREASES IN ILLINOIS

In 1983 the State of Illinois needed more revenues.[1] The state had granted several tax-relief measures, including an expansion of the eligibility for the circuit breaker, a tax-relief measure for the elderly. The state inheritance tax had been repealed in 1982. Both measures lowered revenues. Inflation and recession squeezed state finances, and a long-term decline in heavy industry was eroding the state's economic base.

Cash-flow problems and deficits were revealed immediately after the 1982 election, creating the impression that the governor had hidden the true fiscal condition of the state until after the election was over. This feeling of having been deceived increased the unpopularity of the tax proposal in the state legislature.

The governor set up a blue-ribbon task force to examine the revenue situation. The commission made twenty far-ranging recommendations, including increased revenues, decreased tax breaks, increased fairness, and some economic stimulation. The bipartisan recommendations drew "protests from nearly every special interest group in the state."[2] That was the last that was heard of the seriously thought through bipartisan package.

Governor James Thompson then presented his own proposal for a $1.9 billion tax increase, raising the personal income tax from 2.5 percent to 4 percent and the corporate income tax from 4 percent to 5.6 percent. He also proposed increases in the gasoline tax, license plate fees, and liquor taxes.

The governor's second step was to present his budget proposal for the following year without the tax increases. His so-called doomsday budget included massive cuts in education, local government, public aid, and mental health. It was intended to rouse the beneficiaries of the services facing cuts, to get them to lobby the legislature for the tax increase. The doomsday budget succeeded in rousing these interest groups. The education lobby, the American Federation of Federal, State, and Local Employees, and social service providers all supported various provisions of the tax increase. The Chamber of Commerce, representing an alliance of small business people, predictably opposed the increases, as did the Illinois Association of Manufacturers.

The third step in the governor's strategy was to delay his announcement of how he would allocate the new tax revenues. He wanted to give the impression that many legislators' programs would be funded, without specifically saying yes to one and no to another.

The outcome of the negotiations was partially successful. The legislature granted only a temporary surcharge on the income tax, but the governor was reelected. The financial problems of the state remained and the governor had to go back to the legislature to request increases again in 1987.

MINICASE: A SUCCESSFUL MUNICIPAL TAX INCREASE IN DAYTON, OHIO

In March 1984 voters of Dayton, Ohio, voted overwhelmingly for an increase in the city's income tax.[3] The tax was presented as part of a package, including property tax relief of $50 per person, a tax benefit amounting to more than $1.5 million. Other elements of the approved package included a pledge to reduce municipal employment by more than 100 positions over the next five years, a pledge to maintain services at present levels, a limit on the city's cash reserves, and the establishment of a Chamber of Commerce review committee to study city expenditure patterns. The increase in the income tax was passed with a sunset provision, that is, it was set to terminate in 1990.

City officials engaged in a three-year campaign for acceptance of the increase. The campaign included quarterly reports to council members to build awareness of the problem, reduction of 300 city positions by attrition, and meetings with a group of chief executive officers of businesses in the city to explain the need and ask for support. For the nine months immediately prior to the increase, the mayor and the city manager publicized financial problems, talked to neighborhood groups, and explained the plan to the city unions. The final package was put together by the city council, based on talks with these groups, and then the package was publicized, using "lots of personal contact, targeted selling techniques, and endorsements to explain and sell the package to the voters."[4]

Tax increases need to be planned carefully; consideration must be given to the timing, the choice of budget process, and the selection of the particular elements that will be proposed in a tax increase package.

Monitoring the Environment

The environment affects the timing of tax increases. For example, executives have been more likely to propose increases when the risks were relatively low—

when there was no major opposition party to take advantage of taxpayer discontent or when the overall need for more revenues was very clear, as during a depression or war.[5] When the federal income tax became legal after a constitutional amendment in 1913, most people had to pay no income tax. The law had graduated rates as income rose. The top rate, on incomes over $500,000, was 7 percent.[6] To pay for World War I, the exemption was lowered, so more people with moderate incomes had to pay some tax. Rates were also increased, and the degree of progressivity was increased so that wealthier people paid much higher tax rates. The high rates of progressivity were dropped after the war. But during the Great Depression of the 1930s, revenues fell off because of the shrinking economy and mass unemployment; the need for more revenues resulted in proposals to restore some of the taxes that had been cut. The new proposals shared the burden rather widely.[7] And again during World War II, when the need for additional revenues was acute and unquestionable, the income tax expanded, changing from an elite to a mass tax, vastly increasing its revenue yield.

Choosing a Process

The process of increasing taxes has to be somewhat buffered from interest groups in order to be effective. Individuals and interest groups tend to be both well informed and highly interested in tax proposals; they lobby intensively against increases and for changes that will help them. When information about proposals is open to the public, the public in its various forms tends to turn considered technical proposals into mash. This is what happened with the governor's blue-ribbon panel proposal in Illinois.

But tax-writing legislative committees can buffer themselves against interest groups in a variety of ways. Key elements in the process have to do with openness of the decision making to the public and interest groups, the kind of discipline leaders can exert or rewards they can provide, and the rules under which bills are considered. Open rules allow large numbers of often unrelated amendments, and closed rules prevent amendments after a bill has been passed by committee.

At the national level, the central role in tax decisions of the Ways and Means Committee in the House of Representatives has stimulated much thought on the effect of process on outcomes. For years, the Ways and Means Committee was dominated by its chairman, Wilbur Mills. He carefully worked out compromise legislation that had the full support of his committee; his recommendations were reported to the floor under a closed rule forbidding amendments, and had full committee backing; they were seldom turned down by the House of Representatives.[8] The closed rule prevented House members from sticking a number of tax breaks for special interests onto the tax measure when it came to the floor for a vote, while it enhanced the power of the committee chairman. The closed rule, considerable secrecy in committee deliberations, and the selection of members to the Ways and Means Committee who were from safe districts made the committee less accessible to interest groups. Members of the committee were hand picked, not only because they were from safe districts, but also because they were known to be party loyalists with discipline.[9] The committee operated as a committee of the whole, so the committee chair did not share authority with subcommittee heads. The chair offered support on special-interest tax legislation to get backing on major issues. Once he had forged a coalition of support, it held through the legislative process.

The relative inaccessibility of the deliberations gave the impression of secrecy and of the dominance of an old-boy power structure in tax legislation. The congressional reforms of the 1970s opened up the committee procedures. The chair no longer had the freedom to select members, the committee was expanded in size, and specialized subcommittees were formed. The decision-making process was more open to the public and the press. The ability of committee members to go directly to the press, and their greater independence in getting legislation through, made them less dependent on the chair's support for their special-interest legislation, and hence they were less responsive to his rewards for their loyalty. Members were no longer selected to sit on the Ways and Means Committee because of party loyalty or because they had safe seats. Committee members became more vulnerable to interest groups.

Tax legislation did not markedly improve under this structure; the tendency to give away tax breaks (sometimes called tax expenditures) seems to have increased. "Between 1975 and 1980 the revenue losses for tax expenditures rose faster—14 percent a year—than direct outlays, which increased 11 percent annually during that period. From fiscal 1974 to fiscal 1980, tax expenditures grew by 162 percent while outlays rose by 111 percent. In fiscal 1982 total tax expenditures exceeded $260 billion."[10]

Under the reforms of the 1970s, Ways and Means bills came to the floor under an open rule, meaning that House members could add amendments to a bill when it reached the floor of the House. The Ways and Means bills were more likely to be amended. The Senate sometimes added amendments to House-passed bills, bypassing the Ways and Means Committee completely; these amendments went directly to conference, without any committee consideration. "The process has become so manipulable that in some ways it resembles an open caucus that can be taken over by virtually any group."[11] This environment strengthened interest groups.

After 1980, the structure changed back in the direction of more committee control over the tax process. Representative Dan Rostenkowski took firmer control over Ways and Means Committee members, negotiating support for committee positions and threatening punishment for those not supporting the final agreement. The open rule of the 1970s was replaced by a modified open rule, which allows a few specific and germane amendments, but not an unlimited number for a range of purposes. In addition, more of the committee markups were done in closed sessions, often without a formal vote. Appointments to the committee increasingly included more senior representatives from safer districts. These changes helped to insulate the committee from interest-group pressure and have been credited with helping Ways and Means to design and pass the 1986 tax reform, which reduced the number of tax breaks.[12] After the 1986 tax reform, the rate of increase in tax losses slowed from 14 percent to approximately 6 percent a year (calculated from *The Budget of the United States, 1991*).

The similarities between tax policy and trade policy are instructive. In trade policy, generous giveaways in the form of tariff increases prevailed for a number of years before the Great Depression of the 1930s. The higher a trade barrier, the more protected domestic businesses and industries felt because foreign goods were too expensive, once their producers paid the tariffs, to compete with domestic goods. But the Smoot-Hawley tariff bill, which put tariffs on many items, brought on a world trade war and economic disaster, creating a new consensus for free trade. The consequences of excessive protection were so striking and so negative that the need to change policy was widely accepted. Congress then restructured its trade policy process to bring about the desired outcomes, responsiveness without capitulation to special interests. Congress successfully insulated itself from direct interest-group pressure on bills.[13]

Process by itself cannot control politicians' desires to do favors. If the consensus to provide sound tax policy is there, the structure can be created to allow it to occur. The consensus tends to form when the environment leaves no doubt about the urgency of the need and when the environment suggests that tax increases are low risk, as when there is no effective opposition party. Interest groups do not always determine the outcomes if legislators choose to insulate themselves in the interest of avoiding a clear public policy disaster. But when legislators choose not to create such a structure, they can be overrun by interest groups.

Tax-Raising Strategies

Public officials use a wide variety of strategies to try to get tax increases passed by the legislature and accepted by the voters. Some of these strategies have been suggested in the cases of Illinois and Dayton—for example, the strategy of convincing the public that there is a need for a tax increase and the strategy of proving to citizens that their money will not be wasted.

The chief executive who supports a tax increase can try to trade support on unrelated bills for support on the tax increase. If legislators feel the threat of being thrown out of office, such promises are often inadequate; the tax package has to be structured in such a way as to maximize support. There are basically two ways to do that: (1) tie the tax increase to some highly desired service(s) or capital project(s), which is called earmarking; or (2) raise more revenue than is immediately needed to cover costs and distribute the extra income in such a way as to garner the needed votes.

Earmarking. Earmarking revenues means raising them for a specific purpose so that the money must be spent on that purpose and not on anything else. If the purpose is popular, such as repaving miles of broken residential streets, citizens may be more willing to pay the extra tax for that desired purpose than for general purposes over which they have little control. Earmarking revenues for popular causes can be one way of overcoming popular resistance to tax increases. Those who support a particular program are often eager to have earmarked resources because it means that they do not have to compete with other expenditures in the budget; they can protect their program's funding into the future if they manage to earmark revenues for it. Sometimes powerful lobby groups actually get earmarking into the state constitution to lock in a revenue source for the future.

Earmarking is a major part of revenue politics, with program supporters trying to get revenues earmarked. At the national level, one of the major examples of earmarking is Social Security taxes, which are levied on individuals' paychecks and put into a trust fund that can be spent on nothing else. This arrangement is meant to protect Social Security funding from the demands of other government programs or demands to reduce taxation. There are also special earmarked revenues at the federal level for airport construction, highways, and public transportation. In 1994 $690 billion of federal revenues, or 47 percent of total receipts from the public, were earmarked.[14] Earmarking is also prevalent at the state level. Looking only at taxes and not at all revenues, the National Conference of State Legislatures found a decrease over time from 51 percent earmarked in 1954 to 41 percent in 1963, 23 percent in 1979, 21 percent in 1984, 23 percent in 1988, and 24.4 percent in 1993. While average earmarking at the state level remains much lower than at the national level, recent years have seen a slight rise in earmarking at the state level, primarily for primary and secondary education.[15]

The decrease in the proportion of earmarked state funds from 1954 to 1984 was less a matter of policy choice to reduce earmarking than a side effect of the adoption of broad-based sales and income taxes that occurred in many states between 1950 and 1971. These sales and income taxes were adopted with relatively low levels of earmarking[16] and grew more quickly than earmarked revenue sources.[17] The slight increase in earmarking since 1984 has been a matter of policy choice: ". . . it is clear that legislators now turn somewhat more readily to earmarking taxes than they did in the recent past."[18]

Sometimes taxes are earmarked for the purposes of easing adoption, but then the earmarking is gradually eroded and eventually dropped. One reason this may occur is that earmarking works for popular programs but not for less popular ones. The costs of carrying out routine housekeeping tasks, such as hiring an attorney, become incredibly difficult to pay for if a major portion of revenue is earmarked for the most popular and visible programs. Revenues may not be shifted from earmarked purposes, limiting the flexibility of managers to deal with housekeeping matters, severe needs of small groups, or changing political or technical priorities. Hence there is internal pressure to eliminate and reduce earmarking.

If the earmarking cannot be reduced or eliminated, there may be enormous pressure to take away from the recipient of earmarked revenues any general revenues (nonearmarked revenues) that it may have received, to spend on needy but less popular programs. A recent study indicated that in all seven states studied—New York, New Hampshire, Ohio, Michigan, California, Montana, and Florida—lottery revenues substituted for general revenue that had been going to education.[19] In Florida, after the introduction of the lottery, the proportion of state dollars going to education dropped from 62 to 53 percent.[20] Taxpayers are likely to become angry at such maneuvers. They voted to tax themselves more heavily in order to increase the funding for schools, only to find that the additional earmarked taxes are substituted for the original state funding. When they find themselves in this kind of situation, voters may well refuse to approve future tax increases. A less harmful way of using earmarked funding to pay for less popular programs is to group more and less popular programs together and ask for one earmarked tax increase to pay for both of them. This bundling of more and less popular programs occurred in DeKalb, Illinois, when capital expenditures and social services were linked and an increase in the sales tax was earmarked to pay for them.

Although earmarking can help get a tax passed, it has a number of disadvantages. It prevents comprehensive budgeting. It links specific revenue sources with specific spending programs, but often without any connections between the amount of revenues produced and the amount of revenues needed for the program. Often there is little programmatic connection as well. A portion of the income tax may be spent on local government, as in Illinois, or a portion of income from pari-mutuel betting may be earmarked for mental retardation or indigent patients, as in Arkansas, or taxes on tobacco may be earmarked for education and welfare, as in Alabama.[21] These shortcomings may have helped keep down the level of designating taxes for specific expenditures, despite the temptations of easing public approval of new taxes by earmarking.

Distributing Benefits from a Tax Increase. A second alternative for making revenue increases more palatable is to raise more revenues than needed for the immediate problem and then design a package of expenditures that will gain support for the tax increase. Sometimes, as in the Illinois case, this may be done by keeping the new expenditures secret, allowing many legislators to think that their projects will be included; or the new revenue may be tentatively allocated, pending approval of the tax, to get the new recipients to lobby for the tax increase.

Some revenue-raising proposals have sought to reduce some taxes while increasing others, to gain supporters among those who would benefit from the tax reduction. Thus, in the Dayton case, property taxes were to be reduced for a large number of people as income taxes were increased; a similar arrangement allowed for increases in sales taxes in DeKalb, Illinois, by reducing the property tax. The net amount of revenues is increased, but a large number of people feel they are getting something positive out of the tax increase.

Some other strategies that public officials use when raising taxes include making the increase temporary, spelling out carefully what the increase will be used for, ensuring that any tax increases are gradual and predictable, and taxing those who lack the power or the means to protest.

Temporary Taxes. Specific tactics used to disarm the opposition include making the tax increase temporary. Temporary taxes are distinctly easier to pass than permanent ones, but if the need is not temporary (e.g., a short-term recession continues longer than expected), the problem recurs and the scene plays itself out again.

Accountability. The secrecy with which the Illinois governor handled the finances of the state before his request for tax increases eroded the trust necessary to pass the increases. In this case, accountability was a prerequisite for acceptability. Accountability also frequently plays a role in local school financing elections when citizens' distrust is caused by accumulated deficits and ambiguous statements about how the money will be used. Citizens often want to know what their money is going to be used for, and that it will be well spent, before they willingly part with more of their earnings. Thus openness about government's finances may be part of a successful campaign for tax increases.

Predictability. Successful campaigns to increase taxes are also sensitive to the need for increasing taxes in a gradual, predictable, and unobtrusive manner. Taxes that increase in unpredictable jumps are apt to arouse the most vociferous opposition because people are likely to be unable to pay for them without making major sacrifices. Sudden high increases in property taxes have often preceded tax revolts. Rather than raise one tax by a large and visible amount, politicians may raise a number of smaller taxes by a small amount so that no one group is seriously hurt and citizens feel that the burdens are being widely and equitably shared. In Illinois, the governor proposed moderate increases in an array of taxes rather than larger increases in just one source of funds.

Taxing the Politically Weak. Another way of gaining acceptability for increases in taxation is to place the burden for paying for them on those who have relatively little political power. When business is relatively dominant, it shifts the burden of taxation away from business and on to consumers; when labor is dominant, it shifts the tax burden more on to business and the wealthy. Another version of taxing those too weak to fight back is taxing outsiders. "Outsiders" are those who do not vote and hence cannot throw politicians out of office. Severance taxes on natural resources is one way to pass taxes on to others. For example, states rich in natural resources tax those resources, and the tax is passed on as part of the price to residents in other states who consume the final product. At the local level, sales taxes in shopping centers are popular in part because they tax shoppers from other cities and towns. Hotel and motel taxes are also popular because they tax the out-of-town traveler rather than the resident.

To summarize, public officials plan very carefully for tax increases. They plan the timing, taking advantage of a lack of organized opposition and an environment that seems to require tax increases. They devise and use processes that insulate them somewhat from interest groups. And they strategize to minimize the pain to voters and build coalitions of support. When tax increases are necessary, public officials must be accountable for the way they have been spending money, in terms both of the quality of management (lack of waste) and of following the spending preferences of the public. Their strategies often include conveying to the public the appearance of good management and tying new revenues to particular popular programs. They may back off from these efforts after the tax increase is passed. Hence the need for periodic tax increases is an important linkage between the taxpayers and the spenders, to keep the spenders in line with the desires of the payers.

The Politics of Protection

The politics of raising revenues has a mirror image, that of protecting the population in general or specific groups from taxation or lowering tax levels for individuals or groups. Just as raising taxes necessarily brings a certain amount of blame, the lowering of taxes brings, if not praise, at least a measure of gratitude. Interest groups may hire lobbyists to help deflect needs for more taxation on to others, or even contribute to election campaigns to find candidates who will protect them from tax increases.

The acceptability of taxation is at least in part a function of where the burden falls. Choices revolve around three issues: (1) which taxes to consider; (2) what definition of taxable wealth is used; (3) what pattern of exceptions to grant to broad-based taxes.

The Choice of Revenues to Consider

Part of revenue politics involves pressure to adopt or increase reliance on tax sources that burden others more than oneself. The major forms of revenue currently in use are income and wage taxes, sales taxes of various sorts, tariffs, property taxes, and user fees. Although there are many kinds of each, with somewhat different characteristics, each of these revenue sources works differently and affects the population differently.

Income taxes are taxes paid on different forms of income, including wages and interest on investments, and they are paid by virtually everyone except the very poor. They can be progressive; that is, they may tax the rich more heavily than the poor. Or they can be proportional, taxing everyone the same percentage regardless of income. Income taxes are tied to ability to pay. *Wage taxes* are also tied to ability to pay, but they are a little different, since they are taxes only on wages (earned income), and they tax those who earn their income in the jurisdiction whether they live there or not. Wage taxes are one way of taxing outsiders, commuters to a city who work there but live and vote elsewhere.

Sales taxes are consumer taxes, taxes paid when people or businesses buy something, usually (but not always) a finished product. Sales taxes do not affect wholesale and manufacturing businesses directly, but retailers, who are the ones who collect the tax, may be inconvenienced, and they have to deal with price increases and a possible reduction in demand. Consumers are the most directly affected, but they pay sales taxes in small, almost invisible amounts during the year, so they tend not to mind them too much. Sales taxes are not very tightly linked to ability to pay; they often fall more heavily on the poor than the wealthy because the poor pay a larger proportion of their incomes on taxable items.

Tariffs are fees required for foreign producers to be allowed to market their goods in this country. Tariffs protect domestic industries from foreign competition by raising the price of imported products, but they also raise prices for consumers. Tariffs are ultimately paid by the consumer, without much regard to the ability to pay. Tariffs are levied only by the national government.

Property taxes are those that tax a proportion of the worth or sales value of property people own. This may be personal property (e.g., cars or horses) or real estate (land and houses and buildings). Property taxes on real estate are loosely related to ability to pay because wealthier persons are likely to own more expensive homes, but the relationship is not tight. Older persons on fixed incomes may find property taxes rising because the value of their homes is increasing over time, for example. Or a business may own expensive property and equipment, but not be making much income on it proportional to the value of the property. Owners of commercial property may pass the tax on to their tenants, who may have less income than the owners.

User fees are a revenue source that depends on how much citizens use the service. If you use the local swimming pool, you help pay for it; if you do not use it, you do not pay. Water bills are a form of user fee. User fees have the advantage of allowing those who pay to select only the services they want, and not to use them, and not pay, if the cost is too high. But they have several disadvantages as well. First, they often have little to do with ability to pay. And second, others may benefit although they are not currently using the service, and without their support, the costs of providing some services may be too high for the users to pay. For example, only those currently attending public schools are using the service directly, but every employer of a graduate benefits from the service, and every voter benefits from the education level of other voters. If the whole cost of public schools were placed on those currently taking classes, the costs might easily exceed the students' ability to pay, increasing the number of drop-outs and illiterate unemployables.

Business groups often prefer sales taxes on consumers and oppose income taxes, especially those levied on corporate incomes. Labor groups usually favor income taxes, but as labor's wages have risen, the rank and file have become more reluctant to support high individual income taxes and more supportive of higher corporate income taxes. Many groups support user fees because they seem to be so fair, on the one hand, and so voluntaristic, on the other; if you do not want a service, you do not have to pay for it, and if you use less, you pay less. Those who favor smaller government tend to favor user fees.

The effort to lobby for or against certain forms of taxation becomes particularly visible when a new tax is proposed. For example, when a new tax on imported oil was proposed at the federal level, representatives from the New England states opposed it vigorously because it would raise the cost of gasoline and fuel oil, but the oil-producing states of the South and West supported the tax, because it would help raise the price of domestically produced oil.[22]

Defining Taxable Wealth

The choice of which revenue source to use often revolves around the definition of taxable wealth. In theory, one can levy taxes against any form of wealth. Historically, tax collectors counted windows in houses and taxed people with more windows more heavily. The number of windows was a rough indicator of wealth and one that was less subject to hiding than cash or animals. Choosing the basis for taxation is not merely a technical decision, however; it is also a political decision, and it necessarily hurts some and helps others.

Politicians can protect particular groups of people from taxation by defining their sources of wealth as not taxable. To protect one group, public officials may shift the burden of taxation to some other group or reduce the level of taxation for everyone.

Since particular forms of taxation affect different kinds of wealth, and different regions of the country have been based on different kinds of wealth, the politics of taxation has historically revolved around the choice of taxes that would affect particular regions of the country. Until the late 1930s, ". . . the Northeast favored first tariffs (which protected their industrial goods) and excise, license and land taxes if needed; the South and West resisted all these taxes, whose impact fell disproportionately on them, and favored taxes on income and wealth, of which they had little."[23]

The urban-rural split has also been important in the history of taxation, especially property taxes. Rural areas wanted to make sure the basis of taxation, the measure of wealth, was something they had little of and cities had much of. They worked to define property taxes in terms of both realty (houses, buildings, machinery) and personalty (other forms of wealth, including bonds, mortgages, and other money instruments.) The farmers wanted to define the base of taxation to include the new wealth of the cities, of which the farmers had little; they also sought exemptions of various kinds for their own equipment and herds.[24]

Defining the base of taxation in order to control the burden, especially on the business classes, has a long history within cities. San Francisco during the latter part of the nineteenth century, a city experiencing rapid economic and population growth, illustrates how the tax base may be defined or limited through political choices. Politicians defined the new wealth of the city as not taxable. "In effect, local leaders built a wall between socioeconomic structural development and fiscal policy, refusing to act on the demands created by such development or to accept additional resources provided by such development."[25]

More generally, in the 1800s U.S. cities were growing rapidly, experiencing huge migrations of the poor. The need for revenues to provide infrastructure, especially for streets, water and sewer, and housing, was urgent. The middle and upper classes felt that they were unduly taxed to support the poor and that the burden might be limitless. In response, they tried to buffer the public sector from demands and put their own wealth off limits. By the early 1900s, however, the Progressive movement was strong; part of its thrust was to devise technical solutions to the problems of the cities and to find the resources required to implement them. The Progressives were much more willing to tax the rich to get the capital they needed for public infrastructure.

The effort to define some sources of wealth as nontaxable has continued over the years. In Oakland, California, in the 1960s and early 1970s, an artificially low definition of how much citizens could be taxed kept the scope of services limited and kept City Hall in a perpetual scramble to balance the budget.[26] At the state level, protests by taxpayers in the 1970s reinforced the notion that property taxes are unacceptable to voters. In these instances, the definition of the taxable base was politically negotiated; those who had more political power at the time managed to protect their own wealth. Part of this process involved the systematic discouragement of government response to existing problems. To keep the level of taxation down, the scope of government services had to be kept narrow.

Those who manage to define taxable wealth or acceptable levels of taxation to their own advantage are likely to want to lock in that definition for a long time. One way of doing this is to write tax limits or unacceptable forms of taxation into constitutions and charters. For example, Proposition 13 in California, which limited the property tax, was an amendment to the California constitution. For many years, the U.S. Constitution had a prohibition against an income tax, as did a number of state constitutions.

Writing such constraints into constitutions slows down the rate of change, but constitutions can be amended or rewritten.[27] Introducing a new tax in the face of constitutional restrictions may require larger legislative majorities, public referenda, or even constitutional conventions. The courts are often involved to determine if a new tax is constitutional. Thus the number of actors is often greater, the size of potential veto groups often smaller, and the time lag longer for new tax sources than for increases in traditional sources. Consequently, there is a tendency for historical tax choices to have long-term impact; governmental units tend to stay with whatever taxes they have and marginally increase them as needed; only major economic problems or massive changes in opinion or political strength are likely to provide the background for major changes in the definition of taxable wealth.[28]

Tax Breaks

A tax, once passed, may place the burden of taxation on one group or another, but the location of that burden may change throughout the life of the tax as politicians grant exemptions from the tax. The exemptions are then viewed as political protections for certain groups or economic classes. The nature and politics of tax breaks, sometimes called *tax expenditures*, vary considerably from one

level of government to another, but regardless of the level of government at
which they occur, tax breaks share some common features.

1. They represent dollars that the government is theoretically owed that it
   has decided not to collect. Absent dollars are much more difficult to
   count and account for than dollars one receives in one's hands. Tax
   breaks do not always meaningfully add to one another and hence are
   not always comparable to dollar outlays for expenditures. The amount of
   revenue lost is based on an estimate of the amount of money the taxpayer would owe if the tax break did not exist, but if a particular tax
   preference were eliminated, the government might not receive all the
   money it lost because of the tax break; the money could be spent on
   something else that was tax deductible instead.

2. There is a general tendency for all broad taxes gradually to be eroded
   by exceptions for particular groups. Sometimes when a tax is passed or
   the structure of the tax is changed in a way that hurts some particular
   group, that group tries to get tax breaks so that the new burden on
   them is lessened. Politicians may respond to what they perceive as hardship among a particular group affected by a tax. Those who wish to
   lower their tax burdens may lobby effectively for exceptions for themselves, regardless of hardship. How responsive lawmakers are to these
   pressures depends somewhat on the political strength of the group
   making the demands. At the state level, state officials are often responsive to pressure from the dominant industries in their states. California
   taxes the movie industry lightly, and Wisconsin favors the beer industry.
   North Carolina favors the tobacco industry, and Michigan protects its
   auto industry.[29]

3. During a period of economic stress, there is often a tendency to give
   specific tax breaks to businesses. When the economy began to falter in
   the middle 1970s, pressure increased for government to stimulate investment and capital formation. The national government responded with a
   number of tax breaks, aimed primarily at businesses and upper-income
   taxpayers. The number of tax expenditures greatly increased between
   1975 and 1981, compared to the preceding twenty-nine years.[30] Many
   states have responded to economic problems in similar ways. In the
   middle 1970s, when unemployment hit 8 percent, governors were
   "under tremendous pressure to do something—anything. Most states
   responded with conventional medicine: they cut taxes and offered large
   firms in other states a host of tax and financial incentives to open new

plants across state lines."[31] Cities have responded to weakening economies in similar ways.[32]

4. The money is granted, often with the idea that public policy objectives will be achieved through them, without any supervision or evaluation to see if the policy objective is being achieved. Thus the federal government provides a tax break for investors who loan money to cities so that cities can borrow at lower expense than private-sector companies. The public purpose is to encourage the building of infrastructure, such as streets, buildings, and drainage, that are needed for the economy to function. But there is no supervision to see if the borrowing has indeed gone for such purposes or whether cities are spending money to subsidize private-sector businesses, preparing sites for them, paying for moving costs, or even constructing buildings for private-sector businesses.

Within these overall similarities, there is considerable variation in the nature, use, and politics of tax expenditures at the federal, state, and local levels.

Federal Level. At the national level, the federal income tax has gone through a number of changes since its inception. These changes have been of two basic kinds: (1) the structure of the tax; and (2) the number of exceptions granted.[33] The structure of the tax includes the definition of taxable wealth, policy decisions such as how to treat marriage or children, and the percentage rates applied to families with high, middle, or low incomes. The exceptions are reductions in taxes for those to whom the tax would normally apply. A single individual or a class of people with certain characteristics or certain forms of wealth might get such a reduction, or a company or a particular industry might get a particular tax break.

When the structure of a tax changes, it creates new burdens for different groups of people. As the burden on a group increases, the demand for exceptions for that group is likely to increase. The federal income tax illustrates the relationship between the structure of a tax, the relative burdens it imposes, and the nature of the exceptions granted.

In the early years of the income tax, which was passed in a period of working-class dominance, tax rates burdened the rich particularly. When business dominance was reasserted in the 1920s, the tax structure was modified somewhat, and extensive tax breaks were granted to the wealthy. One example of a tax break for the well-to-do was the lower rate of taxation applied to capital gains compared to wages.

Capital gains taxes offer a separate rate of taxation for income resulting from increases in the value of investments held for a specified period of time, sometimes as short as six months. When the rate of taxation applied to this source of revenue is markedly lower than the rate applied to wages, those who own capital pay lower tax rates than those who earn salaries. This tax break was supposed to provide an incentive for the public to invest money rather than spend it, but it has been available equally during times of capital shortage and abundance.

The capital gains tax was created in 1921. Between 1913 and 1921, there was no differentiation between other income and capital gains. The maximum rate rose from 7 percent to 77 percent between 1913 and 1919, and it was 73 percent between 1919 and 1921. In 1921, the top rate was reduced to 58 percent, in response to the end of World War I and the reduction in revenue needs, and as part of the early period of business dominance. Simultaneously, a separate rate was fixed for long-term capital gains.[34] Initially the special rate for capital gains was set at 12.5 percent, considerably lowering the tax liability of well-to-do investors.

The Tax Reform Act of 1986 eliminated the capital gains tax benefit, but in 1990, when the maximum tax rate for earned income increased, taxes on capital gains were capped at 28 percent, reintroducing a differential, lower rate for income due to growth in the value of investments. The Taxpayers Relief Act of 1997 reduced the capital gains tax rate to 20 percent and 10 percent, depending on the ordinary rate that would otherwise apply, for assets held more than eighteen months. In 1998 the period for which assets had to be held was reduced from eighteen months to a year. Thus there was only a brief period during which capital gains were taxed at the same rate as wages. The U.S. budget for the year 2000 estimated that this tax break would cost about $40.5 billion, the fourth most expensive tax break on the books.[35]

Over the years, there have been many tax exceptions that benefited the rich and businesses, but special tax benefits have not been exclusively for the rich. When the income tax expanded during World War II, many middle- and working-class families were affected for the first time, and attention shifted to assuring that the new burdens were affordable to the aged, ill, and handicapped. For example, medical expenses became deductible. The U.S. budget estimated that that tax break would cost about 3.9 billion dollars in the year 2000.

Most tax expenditures, whether or not aimed specifically at businesses or the well-to-do, benefit the rich disproportionately, because the wealthier you are, the higher the top bracket on your federal income tax, hence the more a tax break is worth to you. Thus if the highest rate you have to pay is 20 percent, a $1 tax break will save you 20 cents; if your highest rate is 30 percent (because you have higher taxable earnings), you would save 30 cents rather than 20 cents from a tax break that excluded $1 of earnings. Tax expenditures have often been criticized for this feature. In 1975, however, a new tax break was created, the Earned Income Tax Credit, which is aimed at lower-income working people and does not benefit wealthier people. That tax break was expanded in 1986, 1990, and 1993. Other new tax breaks have been phrased in such a way that people with more than $60,000 to $70,000 a year in taxable income are not eligible. The goal of these measures is to lighten the tax burden of the working and middle classes and to encourage people to get off welfare, get job skills, and get a job.

While much of the pattern of tax breaks can be explained as reactions to a changing tax structure, in which those suddenly feeling the impact of higher tax burdens successfully pressure for reductions for themselves, some of the tax breaks have been policy responses to currently perceived problems, such as the gasoline shortages of the 1970s. In 1978, as part of its response to the energy crisis, the Carter administration passed a tax-incentive package for individuals and businesses to insulate their homes and save energy. The estimated cost to the Treasury in 1979 was $935 million.[36]

The number and cost of tax breaks accelerated in the 1950s, in part because of the expansion during the 1940s of the number of people who had to pay income taxes. By the 1980s, the rate of growth of tax breaks was described as out of control. "There had been a tenfold increase in the amounts since 1960."[37] The 1981 tax cuts under the Reagan administration contained major tax breaks for businesses, including accelerated depreciation allowances for equipment purchases and reductions in the tax rate on capital gains. Twenty-nine tax preferences were added to the tax code between 1975 and 1981.[38] Most preferences passed at this time were aimed at businesses and upper-income citizens and had the effect of reducing taxes much more for the wealthy than for the poor.

By 1983 tax expenditure estimates were in the range of $295 billion. After 1983 the rate of increase slowed down, and the 1986 Tax Reform Act eliminated a number of tax breaks completely and reduced the value of a number of others. A crude estimate of the impact of the tax reform on tax expenditures is that it reduced tax expenditures by $190 billion, or about 40 percent. About 60 percent of this reduction was the result of lowering the tax rates for citizens with higher incomes, rather than from eliminating or reducing tax breaks. Still some $76 billion of the estimated reduction reflected the elimination or reduction of tax breaks.[39] The Congressional Budget Office estimated the value of eliminated tax expenditures somewhat higher, at $100 billion.[40]

The rate of growth in tax expenditures after 1986 has generally been moderate, motivated in part by the decrease in 1986 in the top bracket of the income tax. When the top bracket is lower, taxpayers have less motivation to look for tax breaks; moreover, the dollar value, in outlay equivalents, of existing tax breaks drops.

Tax expenditures remained lower after the 1986 tax reforms than they had been before, but they began to rise gradually, though differentially, between 1986 and 1996. Corporate tax preferences of the sort that had been granted during the early Reagan administration were cut in 1986, and by 1996 they were still only 30 percent of 1986 levels. By contrast, tax preferences for individuals had regained 79 percent of 1986 levels ten years later.[41] The economy was generally doing well, so the motivation to give tax breaks to stimulate business was relatively low.

The costs of tax expenditures rose in part because the top tax rate increased in 1990 and 1993, making tax breaks worth more to people with large incomes. Tax expenditures also rose because existing tax breaks, without any legislative modifications, became more expensive to the government. Medical costs continued to rise, increasing the costs of medical insurance paid by employers and therefore the value of that deduction. As interest rates fell, many homeowners refinanced their mortgages, starting again with new mortgages and large interest deductions, expanding the cost of that program. A third source of increased expense was legislatively approved expansion of existing programs. Finally, some new programs were added.

The legislative changes included restoration of the lower rate for taxing capital gains, expansion of the Earned Income Tax Credit, and a variety of incentives to increase savings, pay for education, facilitate retirement, and help renew inner cities. President Clinton's 1998 budget emphasized "targeted tax cuts" for middle-class families. The $500-per-child tax credit, higher-education tax breaks, and tax-favored retirement accounts were estimated to cost about $118 billion over five years. For 1999 the administration proposed tax credits for child care (estimated cost $5.6 billion over five years), school construction ($5 billion over five years), low-income housing ($1.6 billion over five years), and energy-efficiency measures such as fuel-efficient cars and rooftop solar systems ($3.6 billion over five years).[42]

From 1988 to 1994, tax expenditures grew about 15.5 percent; from 1993 to 1998, they increased about 42 percent, but then the rate seemed to level out somewhat. Overall—and these estimates are very crude—from 1998 to the year 2000, revenue losses from tax expenditures increased about 8 percent, from about $570 billion to about $617 billion.

The apparent leveling out of tax expenditures was not accidental, but a product of the 1997 balanced budget agreement between the president and Congress. That agreement combined moderate administration proposals with more radical and expensive Republican congressional proposals by backloading the Republicans' proposals. The three important Republican items were a reduction in the capital gains tax, with an additional feature by which the capital gains were indexed to inflation; a higher minimum size for estate taxation; and expanded IRA (Individual Retirement Account) provisions. Fitting all these proposals in was accomplished by slow phase in or delayed beginning of some of the tax breaks; in addition, some of the features, such as indexing, would not begin to have an effect for a number of years. The costs for the Republican tax breaks greatly accelerated in the second five years of the deal, from 2002 to 2007, and then grew even more after that.[43] Moreover, many of these Republican proposals were locked in and could not be revoked later if the budget returned to a deficit position. Not only did these benefits for mainly wealthy people get locked into the budget, but they created the probability that spending would have to be cut further to create enough money to fund the future losses.

The balanced budget agreement illustrates several features about tax expenditures. One is that like many other budget deals, they take advantage of the factor of time. Second, the balanced budget agreement illustrates the ongoing effort to lock in strategic advantages so they cannot be undone by future elected officials who have different priorities. Third, they take advantage of complexity and relative invisibility of tax cuts, since the costs were pushed off so far into the future that they were not visible and therefore seemed free.

The Durability of Tax Expenditures. Each increase in tax expenditures meant less revenue in the future; to keep the budget balanced might mean additional spending cuts. But the reverse also held true. If tax expenditures could be reduced, there would be more money available—translating into smaller programmatic cuts. Hence curtailing the tax expenditure budget was tempting to supporters of federal spending programs. Tax expenditures, however, proved a difficult target for cuts. Over time, the list of tax expenditures had grown to include breaks supported by both Democrats and Republicans. It was difficult to attack the whole list. When a group of reformers on Capitol Hill proposed reducing so-called corporate welfare (a partisan approach), including a series of tax breaks, they did not get enough support to pass the measure. Their next approach was to form a commission, on the pattern of the base-closing commission, that would make tax expenditure reduction decisions impartially and take the political onus off individual members of Congress. That approach failed also.

Tax expenditures proved enduring, despite pressures to balance the budget and the need to offset tax reductions with programmatic cuts or increased taxes. There were several reasons for this impressive record of persistence. One was that tax expenditures for individuals were treated as entitlements. People built these tax breaks into their lives and were unwilling to give them up. Second, the tax breaks covered a wide range of interests and constituencies; nearly every elected official had some constituency to protect. Pork, in terms of grants and projects that could be directed by members of Congress to particular constituencies, had been sharply limited while the country was trying to balance the budget. To the extent that tax breaks substituted for pork, members of Congress were extremely unwilling to give them up. The budget process made it easier to create new or expanded programs through the tax expenditure budget than through direct discretionary expenditures, which were tightly capped. It was easier and more politically acceptable to find an offset to a tax break than it was to raise the caps. A tax expenditure looked simultaneously like a tax cut and a program expansion, and that combination—appearing to give more services for fewer dollars—fit the spirit of the times. Finally, tax breaks did not get the level of scrutiny in Congress that more direct expenditures faced. The estimates of revenue losses were put together with little staff time or analysis, and there was little inclination to examine whether benefits were more efficiently delivered through the tax system or through the direct spending process.

Tax breaks at the federal level are often justified in terms of achieving programmatic goals. They are, in this sense, the equivalent of direct outlays. Thus tax reductions to homeowners for the interest on their mortgage payments are explained in terms of encouraging a stable homeowning class and widespread hope of future homeownership. The good to be achieved also includes stimulation of the economy, since homebuilding requires not only lumber and other raw materials but also products such as washing machines, refrigerators, air conditioners, and heaters, each of which requires raw materials and processing. Such tax breaks benefit the homebuilding industry and realtors, but they are rationalized in terms of a national good.

This attempt to use tax breaks as a policy tool and/or rationalize them in terms of national goals opens tax breaks to a series of tests. Will this tax break help resolve some existing social or economic problem? Would some other form of subsidy achieve more of the goal less expensively than this tax break? When evaluated in these terms, tax breaks often do not look very good.

Lower taxes on capital gains have been justified in terms of encouraging investment and capital formation, but they have been used in periods when capital was generally available as well as when capital was in short supply. This anomaly makes one question whether this tax break was really intended to solve an economic problem or whether it was a redistribution upward, to those earning substantial income from investments.

Even when tax breaks are clearly intended to solve a problem, they may be much more expensive than other forms of subsidy to achieve similar ends. For example, the federal government allows local governments to borrow using tax-free municipal bonds. This lowers the cost of borrowing for cities because investors do not have to pay income tax on the earnings from these municipal bonds. The federal government loses revenues that it would otherwise have earned; wealthy individuals and corporations that invest in municipal bonds get a substantial portion of the benefit; only a limited portion of the money the federal government loses goes to cities to help lower borrowing costs. It would be cheaper for the federal government to give dollars to local governments to build infrastructure than to subsidize construction through tax breaks.

When tax breaks do not meet tests of efficiency and effectiveness, one wonders why they are used instead of more efficient and effective alternatives. One possibility is that the policy goals stated for creating the tax break were just a loose cover for granting favors. Whether a tax break does or does not achieve a stated policy goal may be irrelevant if it is achieving desired political (distributional) goals.

Another reason for using inefficient tax breaks is that they sometimes increase the number of people and institutions that benefit from a program and hence enhance the political support for that program. For example, the tax break on interest from municipal bonds creates a large pool of beneficiaries of a program ostensibly designed to reduce the borrowing costs of local governments. Local governments alone in recent years have not had enough political power to maintain their direct program benefits from the federal government, but the subsidy on bonds has proven difficult to remove because all those who invest in tax-free municipal bonds become a potential lobby to maintain this subsidy to local government. Local governments are aware of this political advantage and have tried to prevent a shift of their subsidy to the direct spending side of the budget, which they see as more vulnerable to cutbacks.

Another possible reason for preferring tax breaks over direct outlays is that they are somewhat less visible to the public. Since 1974 the Congressional Budget Reform Act has required that tax expenditures be listed and at least roughly summarized in the budget, and tax expenditures have to be passed by Congress and the president just like other legislation. The federal government is much more open about tax expenditures than other levels of government are. Nevertheless, it is in the nature of tax breaks to be less visible than program outlays. With welfare payments, it is reasonably easy to estimate the benefit to a mother with five children in a particular state, but it is very difficult, if not impossible, for a journalist or citizen to figure out what the dollar benefit to a business is from combined tax breaks. The public is generally not aware that benefits to the middle class from tax breaks equal or exceed direct spending for the poor in some program areas. Partly because of the lower visibility of tax expenditures to the public, tax expenditure programs can be passed that would not be passed if they were open to the same kind of scrutiny and examination as direct outlays. Paul McDaniel spelled out the policy implications of the tax break for employer-provided health insurance, and then asked if a direct spending program with these features would pass Congress. For example, the tax expenditure covers only those who are employed; the unemployed are not covered. The decision whether employees will participate in the program is left to the discretion of the employer—neither the government nor the employee has any say. There is no limit on the size of the tax expenditure. The federal contribution is proportional to the marginal tax rate of the taxpayer; thus wealthier folks get a bigger subsidy on their health insurance. If a couple earn $80,000 a year, the federal government will pay $31 per $100 of premium; if the couple's taxable income is below $10,000 a year, the federal government will pay none of the couple's premium. It seemed to McDaniel that Congress was unlikely to design a health-care spending program that would have these features.[44]

The Government Performance and Results Act required an evaluation of the efficiency and effectiveness of tax breaks in achieving programmatic goals. But the first level administrative response has been that there is not enough data to establish performance measures, so the data will be gathered for a handful of tax breaks and measures will be set up for them. Progress has been slow, even for this limited number of test cases. Though the idea is clear, that tax expenditures should be chosen as a vehicle for program delivery only when they are more efficient and effective than other delivery methods, this long-desired integration of tax expenditures with other budgetary resources still seems a long way off.

To summarize, because the federal government's budget is so large, tax breaks, even relatively small ones, can have impacts on the economy and on people's behavior, in buying a house or drilling an oil well. Tax breaks can have legitimate policy goals, including improving the equity of the tax burden and stimulating the economy. But this legitimate federal function can easily become confused with more mundane political matters, such as responding to pressure from an interest group that wants to reduce its tax liability. These latter tax expenditures are often rationalized in terms of national goals to be achieved. When programs funded through tax breaks are compared with programs funded with direct outlays, they may be less efficient and less effective, but they may be more politically potent. The rationalizations used to legitimize political giveaways to powerful lobbies can be used by others to leverage further tax breaks.

Nevertheless, federal level tax breaks are not uncontrollable. The amounts involved are clearly listed in the budget. Congressional committees now buffer themselves from interest groups, and requirements to offset every reduction in revenues put pressure on legislators to watch the number and size of tax breaks awarded.

State Level. On the state level, tax expenditures expanded during the 1970s and 1980s. They were primarily used to protect key industries and powerful lobbies, to stimulate the economy, and to alleviate protests against taxes. The protection of key industries has been a function of state tax systems for many years, but the other two sources of tax breaks became more prominent in the 1970s when the economy began to falter. Many governors were desperate to do something when unemployment increased; at the same time, because taxation was increasing more rapidly than people's incomes, tax protest accelerated and many state officials felt that if they did not respond with tax breaks, they would be confronted with rigid, publicly mandated tax limitations.

For example, in Illinois, twenty-eight tax breaks were enacted between 1979 and 1989. Of them, twenty were enacted between 1979 and 1984, just after Proposition 13 in California and the deep recession of the early 1980s. Roughly categorized by purpose, nine of the tax breaks were to encourage economic development; six were efforts to make taxes more equitable or otherwise reduce pressure for tax limits; nine were responses to powerful local industries; and five were responses to other requests or worthy causes.[45]

To encourage economic development and to help head off pressure for tax limits, states have passed a number of tax breaks, in sales, income, and property taxes. Maryland, for example, has constantly eroded the base of its sales and use tax; almost every session of the legislature has added exemptions.[46] As a result, "only approximately 18 percent of consumer income is subject to the sales and use tax."[47]

Maryland also granted breaks from its income tax. To give some idea of the cost of these tax breaks, five discretionary modifications of the tax base for which detailed information was available reduced the state revenues by nearly $1.9 billion in 1987.[48] The largest of the breaks was for exclusion from taxation of income derived from capital gains; that tax break alone cost the state of Maryland $898 million in 1987.[49]

Tax breaks on the property tax have also been widespread. Efforts to head off tax revolts resulted in both homestead exemptions and circuit breakers. By 1992, thirty-six states had adopted circuit breakers, which are provisions to reduce the property taxes of the poor, elderly, or disabled. Most of these provisions were adopted between 1971 and 1977, a time of rapid inflation in housing prices and massive discontent with property taxation. An even higher proportion of states (forty-five out of fifty plus the District of Columbia) adopted homestead exemptions. Of these, nineteen provide benefits to all homeowners who live in their own homes, and most provide additional benefits to the poor, the elderly or disabled, or veterans. The amount of revenue lost by these exemptions was significant, especially in states where eligibility for benefits was broad. Michigan lost $773 million in revenue to circuit breakers in 1990, and five states (including Michigan) lost over $100 million. For homestead exemptions, California lost $3.2 billion in revenues in 1992, Florida lost $1.7 billion in 1991, while Texas school districts lost $1.1 billion in 1990. These are the high-end figures; most states lost considerably less than these amounts. See tables 2.1 and 2.2 for details.

The Advisory Commission on Intergovernmental Relations that reported these statistics was phased out in 1996, and there has been no survey of the states in recent years. Fragmentary data suggests that the cost of these tax breaks continues to rise. Nebraska estimated in 1998 that its 1997 Homestead Exemption losses were $35,095,569 compared to its 1991 figure of $29.3 million.[50] Texas reported the costs of its homestead exemption to school districts in 1999 was $1.365 billion, compared to $1.169 billion in 1990.[51] Washington State reported that its circuit breaker for the elderly cost $80,614,000 in 1998, compared to $50,184,000 in 1992.[52]

TABLE 2.1   STATE CIRCUIT BREAKER PROGRAMS (ESTIMATED COSTS)

STATE (FISCAL YEAR)	AMOUNT (IN THOUSANDS OF DOLLARS)
Arizona (1991)	12,743
Arkansas (1992)	3,950
California (1992)	16,699
Colorado (1992)	14,462
Connecticut (1992)	27,916
District of Columbia (1992)	8,854
Hawaii (1991)	5,819
Idaho (1992)	6,031
Illinois (1990)	104,354
Indiana (1991)	n.a.
Iowa (1990)	10,737
Kansas (1992)	8,700
Maine (1992)	7,494
Maryland (1991)	48,397
Michigan (1990)	773,555
Minnesota (1991)	133,500
Missouri (1992)	17,973
Montana (1990)	4,090
Nevada (1991)	2,636
New Jersey (1990)	n.a.
New Mexico (1991)	3,903
New York (1989)	50,800
North Dakota (1992)	2,381
Ohio (1991)	56,094
Oklahoma (1991)	398
Oregon (1990)	6,365
Pennsylvania (1991)	108,681
Rhode Island (1991)	653
South Dakota (1991)	1,000
Tennessee (1992)	7,026
Utah (1991)	n.a.
Vermont (1992)	22,010
Washington State	n.a.
West Virginia (1991)	n.a.
Wisconsin (1992)	105,505
Wyoming (1992)	n.a.

Source: Advisory Commission on Intergovernmental Relations, *Significant Features of Fiscal Federalism, 1994*, vol. 1 (Washington, D.C.: Government Printing Office, 1994), table 39.

TABLE 2.2 STATES' LOSSES FROM HOMESTEAD EXEMPTIONS

STATE (FISCAL YEAR)	AMOUNT (IN THOUSANDS OF DOLLARS)
Alaska (1991)	9,585
Arizona (1990)	162,744
California (1991–92)	3,290,000
Connecticut (1991)	18,522
District of Columbia (1989)	21,758
Florida (1991)	1,700,000
Illinois (1989)	451,498
Indiana (1991)	274,501
Iowa (1991)	99,613
Kentucky (1989)	9,711
Louisiana (1991)	438,494
Maine (1991)	3,024
Minnesota (1989)	660,000
Mississippi (1990)	110,387
Montana (1990)	1,400
Nebraska (1991)	29,300
New Jersey (1991)	59,583
New Mexico (1986)	8,400
North Carolina (1990–91)	19,072
Oklahoma (1991)	56,639
South Carolina (1991)	37,650
Texas (school districts 1990)	1,169,665
Utah (1990)	1,847
Vermont (1991)	1,000
Washington State (1991)	39,200
West Virginia (1991)	25,829
Wisconsin (1992)	177,600
Wyoming (1992)	0

Source: Compiled from Advisory Commission on Intergovernmental Relations, *Significant Features of Fiscal Federalism, 1991*, vol. 1 (Washington, D.C.: Government Printing Office, 1991), table 42.

Note: Other states have homestead exemptions, but their estimates of revenue losses were unavailable.

States are less able than the federal government to stimulate the economy. Their orientation has been less one of stimulating demand for purchases or increasing the amount of capital available through tax breaks and more one of responding to direct competition with other states. The federal government may feel that it is in competition with other countries, but it has not yet yielded to the easy policy of saying "other countries subsidize this industry, so we have to too." States, however, use this logic extensively and expensively.[53]

This competition increasingly led states to offer the same set of tax breaks as incentives to lure potential industries. For example, in 1974 six states offered tax exemptions to encourage research and development, but by 1992, thirty-one states offered this tax break. In 1974, eighteen states offered an exemption to industries on the corporate income tax, but by 1992, thirty-five states offered this break. The trend is uniform across a variety of tax breaks, with most of the competition and resulting imitation taking place before 1989.[54] As the tax incentives became more similar, in order to compete successfully, states had to outbid each other in the size of the tax breaks. The costs of tax breaks per job created in the automobile industry increased from $11,000 in 1980 (the Nissan plant in Tennessee) to $65,000 per job in 1992 (the BMW plant in South Carolina) to $200,000 in 1993 (Alabama, Mercedes).[55]

Tax incentives for economic development may or may not be phrased as entitlements. Some benefits, such as reduced taxes to companies that expand and hire twenty or more additional employees, are generally available to all and are phrased as entitlements. Other tax breaks are enabled by the state government but are negotiated by state and local governments on a case-by-case basis. Each case is treated as unique, with a specific package of reductions and incentives. Granting benefits to one company does not spill over by logic into granting benefits to other companies. States and local governments can grant more benefits to the first company to get things moving and fewer to companies that come later, after the momentum is established.

Sometimes the design of an individual deal does open up the path for other companies to use the same tax break. For example, in the Alabama-Mercedes case, to benefit Mercedes the state passed a law that would allow any company that was investing over $5 million and creating at least fifty jobs to use the money it would have paid in state income taxes to pay off its debt. Similarly, the law allowed such companies to use the income taxes deducted from employee wages to pay for land, equipment, and plant.[56]

The model of competing with other states in awarding tax breaks may be both expensive and ineffective because if the surrounding states all offer the same incentives, the incentives lose their drawing power. After 1986, states shifted their economic development strategies more toward entrepreneurial efforts, such as loans and loan guarantees and equity or near-equity investments in businesses. This shift occurred at least in part because by then the more traditional incentive approaches, including tax expenditures, had been adopted by most states and failed to distinguish between possible locations for businesses.[57] In the 1990s, there has been some resurgence of interest in tax breaks as a tool because the recession created a sense of greater urgency than long-term high-risk investments could address. Even when tax expenditures did not work well, they allowed political credit taking that longer-term strategies did not, and recessions have increased the perceived urgency of creating jobs or bringing jobs into the state.[58]

MINICASE: LEGISLATURE DENIES ECONOMIC DEVELOPMENT INCENTIVES

In what is either a man bites dog story, of interest for its rarity, or a harbinger of things to come, Washington State refused to provide a tax incentive to lure a new business to the state.[59] In 1998 the governor proposed a big tax break to lure Nucor Corporation to Cowlitz County. The state legislature rebuffed the governor, and the company announced it would go elsewhere. Though the site was not very good for the company's purposes, the company blamed not the site but the lack of an incentive package for its decision.

The incentive package was put together to match or exceed the offer of a neighboring state. Oregon offered about $57 million over twenty years; the cost of Washington State's package was over $100 million dollars over fifteen years. In addition to the high cost, the legislature was discouraged by a study indicating that such expensive tax breaks had minimal effect on attracting businesses in poorer areas of the state. Thus the counties' claims that they were desperate for new jobs fell on deaf ears; this expensive program was unlikely to get them the new jobs they craved. Legislators were also willing to say no in part because existing businesses were actively lobbying against new tax incentive packages because they realized that not only would they not benefit from the tax breaks, but they would bear the burden of increased taxation to pay for the revenue loss.

Tax breaks are not free, and they may become more costly over time. In Washington State, once in place, the tax break incentive program kept on growing until nearly every county had access to some tax break incentives. A tax break passed for one project was often viewed as a precedent for other businesses to take advantage of the same breaks. The fact that the governor argued that this would not happen was an indicator that he thought others felt that it might.

Visible competition and negotiated settlements often create pressure to bring a deal to a successful completion, defined by the company locating or expanding in the state or constructing a building, almost regardless of the cost. The justification is, we have to do this because of the competition (i.e., we will lose the deal if we do not give them what they want), and it is for economic development. While tax breaks for economic development are given one deal at a time, states and local governments avoid a project-by-project cost-benefit analysis by arguing that each project will generate future growth that will not be subsidized or will be subsidized at a lesser rate. The amount and timing of this additional growth is no more than a wild guess, so it is impossible to figure out how much in concessions to give. Any amount conceivably can be justified. Researcher Sam Nunn estimated that it would require anywhere between 750 and 7,300 jobs created by an economic development project to justify a tax abatement of $1 million, if a city had a sales tax. The variation in number of jobs required to break even depended on the assumptions about the income level of the jobs to be created and how much of that income would be spent in the community.[60] The only test of the outcome is whether the company carries out the project; any failure only reinforces the notion that not enough was given away.

The bargaining perspective tends to foster secrecy. Dealings with business, and economic development more generally, are likely to be more secret than other government transactions. The reason given is that business demands secrecy. Presumably, if you want what business has, you do things its way. Nevertheless, by 1992, twenty-one states had reported their tax expenditures. In most cases, the reporting requirement was recently adopted.[61] Many states increased tax breaks in response to tax protests in the 1970s and then confronted the declining revenues of the recession of 1981–82. The recession forced some states to raise revenues and cut spending. In that context, some state officials began to rethink their tax expenditures and report on them.[62]

MINICASE: THE POLITICS OF TAX EXPENDITURES IN MINNESOTA

The history of tax expenditures in Minnesota in the 1980s and 1990s illustrates a number of factors that influence the number and cost of tax breaks. Among those factors is a good information system that lets legislators know the cost of tax breaks they are considering. Minnesota tried to reduce the tax breaks in the income tax in order to provide enough revenue to lower the state income tax, which was high compared to other states. But in the process of reducing the income tax, some of the burden of taxation was shifted to the sales tax. The legislature tried to expand the base of the sales tax to make it more productive, but a poor system of reporting on tax expenditures allowed incremental increases in sales tax expenditures that eroded the sales tax base at the same time the legislature was trying to expand it. What began as targeted reductions to specific industries gradually became deeper and more expensive tax breaks for the same industries and then total exemptions; at the same time, the tax breaks were gradually expanded to other industries, and finally to all new and expanding industries.[63]

When states began issuing their reports on tax expenditures, the results were startling. Of nine states reporting from 1982 to 1984, the ratio of tax expenditures to total revenues varied from a low of 35 percent in California in 1984 to a high of 116 percent in Nebraska in 1982.[64] The average ratio was 69 percent of total revenues. This average may be inflated by some states that include in tax expenditures a variety of "exemptions" that were never a part of the tax base and so do not satisfy a narrower definition of tax expenditure as a deviation from the structure of the tax, exempting what would otherwise, normally, be taxed. A second warning in using these figures is that these states may not be typical of other states because those with higher tax expenditures would be more likely to see them as a problem that needed public documentation and scrutiny.

Even granting that states that have tax expenditure reporting are more extreme in the dollar amounts of tax breaks granted than other states and that some states exaggerate the total losses, the dollar amounts of revenue foregone due to tax breaks is dramatic. California reported tax expenditures of about $17 billion in fiscal year 1999.[65] Massachusetts reported $8.16 billion in tax expenditures for 1997.[66] Texas reported exemptions from sales, franchise, gasoline, and motor vehicle sales at $20.5 billion in fiscal year 1999, compared to general revenue fund totals of $23.5 billion, or about 87 percent.[67]

Revenue losses from tax breaks sometimes grow more quickly than other expenditures. The California tax expenditure report of 1988 noted that the cost of tax breaks had gone up by 8 percent compared to the previous year, while direct outlays grew only 3 percent. The cost increase was due not only to increases in the number of tax breaks, but also to the expansion of the economic base on which the tax expenditures were computed.

Some states have tried to hold down the costs of tax breaks as they realized how expensive they were. Texas reported costs of $12 billion for the sales and franchise tax exemptions in 1991, compared to $15.1 billion in general revenues; by 1999 the figures were $20.5 billion in exemptions, compared to general revenues of $23.5 billion. The increase in tax expenditure losses was 58 percent; the increase in general revenues was 64.2 percent. Even though tax breaks are continuing to grow in cost, they are growing more slowly than general revenues.[68] In Ohio the cost of tax expenditures across funds dropped from $7 billion in 1993 to $5 billion in 1994 and $5.8 billion in 1995. Figures for 1998–2001 suggest further absolute declines, from about $5.4 billion in 1998 to an estimated $4.6 billion in 2001.[69]

Washington State has also tried to reduce the cost of tax breaks, as shown in the minicase above. As shown in table 2.3, the number of tax breaks granted per year has steadily increased from one period to the next, but the average cost per tax break has varied considerably. The tax breaks granted during the Great

Depression of the 1930s are far and away the most costly. The number and cost dropped after World War II, during a general period of prosperity, but increased somewhat during the fiscal stress of the 1970s and 1980s. While the number of tax breaks granted has continued to go up in the most recent period, the average cost of each new break granted has dropped precipitously.

The growing cost of tax breaks made an impact in Maine as well. In 1999 some legislators balked when it became clear that the cost increases in property tax breaks for businesses were preventing badly needed spending on schools and threatening tax breaks that helped poor people pay their rent. One tax expenditure program had become particularly expensive, fully reimbursing about 1,400 eligible businesses for up to twelve years for property taxes paid on equipment and machinery. The program was first funded in 1997, cost $19 million in 1998, and was estimated to cost $31 million in 1999. The next two years were projected to cost $41 million and $51 million.

One proposed solution was to narrow eligibility, by measures such as eliminating from the program out-of-state businesses that were not producing local jobs and were competing with local small businesses. But businesses lobbied for maintaining the tax break, and the governor was reluctant to narrow its scope because doing so would reduce his political support. The governor also argued that a good business climate assumes stability in taxation, that any change so soon after the program was introduced would have a negative impact.[70]

States that do report tax expenditures are able to track the costs of each break from year to year. Legislatures may be made aware of the costs also when governors propose cuts in existing tax breaks to fund new or expanded versions of existing breaks. But many states are still not reporting tax expenditures. The overall costs of tax expenditures over time may not be clearly set down anywhere. The result is that it may be impossible to see trends toward more or less tax expenditures or correlate changes in levels of tax expenditures with increased

TABLE 2.3   STATE OF WASHINGTON, HISTORY OF THE COST OF TAX BREAKS

PERIOD	AVERAGE NUMBER OF BREAKS GRANTED PER YEAR	CURRENT COST OF BREAKS (IN THOUSANDS OF DOLLARS)	AVERAGE COST
1871–1929	.37	$ 1,605,472	$ 72,976
1931–45	4.46	18,056,605	269,501
1947–70	3.39	1,616,713	20,727
1971–85	7.64	2,510,970	23,467
1986–91	10.20	185,488	3,636

Source: Calculated from State of Washington, Department of Revenue, *Tax Exemptions 1992*, Revenue Research Report.

investment, tax yield, or employment. It is also impossible in many states to calculate the distributional impact of tax expenditures.

Local Level. At the local level, tax breaks are normally used to encourage economic development projects. Partly because of the focus on economic development, tax expenditures at the local level are even less visible than at the state level.
They seldom appear in budgets or financial reports,[71] and they are generally
granted on a one-at-a-time basis. The costs of each deal tend to be clear to the
government making the deal, but the tradeoff between costs and benefits may
be obscure. The dealmaking aspect of tax breaks means that benefits are not
known or knowable in advance; builders, contractors, and businesses are encouraged to ask for the moon and see how much they can get. The element of competition that was apparent at the state level is exaggerated at the local level
because the government has so little possibility of influencing the economy and
the bargaining tends to take place when the local community is desperate for
jobs. Companies can promise jobs or threaten to take them away unless they get
most of what they ask for. The bargaining power tends to be one-sided.

There are no aggregate estimates of the amounts of tax expenditures at the
local level, but particular examples that have been studied suggest that individual large projects can be very expensive to both the state and local governments.
The Diamond Star automobile plant in Bloomington and Normal, Illinois, illustrates the size of total incentive packages and the proportion of the packages
that involve tax breaks.[72] The short-term cost of the total incentive package was
$5.384 million for the municipalities concerned; of that amount, $1.2 million
was for sales tax breaks, $206,000 was in local utility reductions, $234,000 was
in reduction in local fees, $78,000 was in reduction in sewer collection fees, and
$486,000 was in reduction in local property tax collections. Over the life of the
project, the two cities would be committing $9.2 million. Of the total package,
reductions in utility charges will cost the two cities $2.4 million and property
tax reduction will cost the two municipalities $5.8 million. Bloomington and
Normal are two small midwestern communities, so these costs are substantial.
One tax abatement granted in 1989 in Fort Worth, Texas, was estimated to result
in an annual loss of revenue of about $6.8 million for fifteen years. The reloca-
tion of Sears' corporate headquarters from downtown Chicago to suburban Hoff-
man Estates cost about $6 million in tax abatements.[73]

Additional evidence of the amounts of local tax expenditures is spotty. In
the early 1980s, New York City was reported to have abated $44 million in
property taxes in a single year; St. Louis, a major user of property tax exemptions, was reported to have exempted nearly $1 billion worth of real estate, about
half the city's tax base.[74] In the mid-1980s in Chicago, a study of a single tax
break estimated that, with ninety-five firms receiving this benefit between

1981and 1985, the cost over the life of the tax break would be $68 million.[75] Losses from this one benefit amounted to $5.7 million in 1985, and the amount of loss was estimated to increase over the next few years as additional firms were granted reductions and old reductions had not yet begun to expire.

By the mid-1990s Ohio local governments granted more than $2 billion in property tax abatements, mostly for economic development programs. The amounts were such that some counties, such as Montgomery County, began to slow down the granting of new abatements. While the rate of growth was lower, the absolute amount was stunning. "Montgomery County granted tax exemptions worth about $1.093 billion in 1995, of which corporate America soaked up about 8 percent, or about $87.7 million." Officials argued that no deal had fallen through because they had not given away enough in tax incentives. While still generous with these tax breaks, county officials attributed their relative caution to desire to protect the school districts, to whom they granted a veto on tax breaks. If the school districts felt that they would be hurt by the deal, they could scotch it. Without such a veto, the county could grant tax breaks that reduced schools' revenue.[76]

Cities and counties are often in a position to give away money that is not theirs. For example, cities have extended their tax-free borrowing status to businesses in order to save them money. These breaks are called Industrial Development Revenue Bonds, and they cost the federal government money.[77] Cities also give away property taxes belonging to school districts. In the Diamond Star case, the school districts negotiated for themselves and chose a shorter maturity for the tax breaks offered than the cities did. In the Montgomery County, Ohio, illustration, the school districts had a veto over the deal. But in many cases, the school districts are not negotiating for themselves; cities may make economic development deals that are good for the cities but reduce the property taxes that school districts would otherwise receive.

There are no reliable data on the extent to which cities reduce the tax revenues of school districts or force school districts to raise taxes to compensate for a frozen tax base. Some states do not even keep data on the impact of tax breaks on school districts. Texas does keep such data, however; it estimated that property tax abatements for economic development, including those for Tax Increment Financing (TIF), would cost school districts $86.5 million in 1999.[78] Indiana does not keep such data, but a recent study gave some indications of the impact of tax increment financing on school districts.

Indiana does not use tax increment financing heavily, so many school districts are not affected at all; moreover, the impact on the general fund is made up by the state, so the school districts are not disadvantaged, although residents of the state more broadly may be. The main impact on the school districts is in those funds in which they are permitted to raise the tax rate to make up for the loss in assessed valuation and in those funds in which they are not allowed to increase the rate and so just have to deal with lower revenues. The state made up $15.4 million in losses to the school districts, and local taxpayers had to pick up another $11.4 million. These figures do not speak to the portion of the funds that school districts lost and were unable to replace. Sixty-seven school districts were affected, but most of them had only a small proportion of their assessed value locked up in TIF. The bulk of the effect fell on a handful of districts. The Indiana case is unusual because relatively few school districts were affected by TIF and because the state made up the majority of the lost dollars. In other states that rely more heavily on TIF, the effects are likely to be greater.[79]

Scattered data on the impact on particular school districts is suggestive of a problem. In Corpus Christi, Texas, in 1990, there were $900,000 in tax losses to school districts reflecting tax breaks for corporations. Wichita, Kansas, school districts lost $1.6 million to tax concessions during fiscal year 1991. In one recent project in Cleveland, the city abated $8 million in property taxes, 60 percent of which would have gone to the school system, which was facing a $34 million deficit for the next fiscal year. An attorney for the school district argued, "Our city council hasn't seen a tax abatement it didn't like."[80] Of the $68 million in lost property taxes from one tax break in Cook County, Illinois, 40 percent will come from the Board of Education.[81]

Thus a peculiarity of local-level tax abatements is that cities and counties can often take the lead in economic development and negotiate with other governments' or districts' revenues, sometimes exacerbating their fiscal stress. The cities are encouraged to offer larger incentives because the money they offer is not their own. As a result, the school districts may look badly managed and may have to come to the public more often for tax increases.

The Politics of Reform

The gradual erosion of the integrity of general taxes is part of a larger process that also includes reform and at least the temporary curtailing of interest groups. Tax expenditures reduce revenues, which means cutting back spending, finding alternative revenue sources, or tolerating chronic deficits. Each of these alternatives has negative political consequences. The more extreme each potential response to the reduction in revenues, the greater the pressure to stop awarding tax breaks or curtail the number of existing tax breaks. Tax expenditures also give the impression of unequal treatment of equals, which upsets taxpayers and encourages them to try to reduce their own tax payments. In the extreme, it may lead to tax protests. When voluntary compliance with tax laws diminishes, the cost of tax collection increases. Thus, despite the political coalitions that support existing tax benefits, there are often counterpressures to reform the tax structure.

The main goal of such reforms is to simplify taxes and reduce special exceptions. The resulting revenue increases may be used to reduce tax rates for everyone, or to reduce the size of the deficit or sustain services and programs. For some, the goal of tax reform has been to see to it that the poor do not pay a disproportionate burden of taxation and that taxes overall are apportioned according to the ability to pay. Since tax breaks are often relatively inefficient ways of accomplishing program goals, curbing tax expenditures may also be seen as an effort to improve efficiency.[82]

Such reforms are difficult but not impossible to achieve. Politically, they have the general weakness that those whose benefits are taken away are likely to be hopping mad, while those whose tax burden is lessened are likely to feel that they deserved it all along. Opponents are likely to be outspoken, and supporters likely to be passive.[83] In addition, the amount of money gained from a large loophole to a relatively small number of people is not enough when spread around to the entire taxpaying audience to win much applause. One way to make tax reform politically attractive is to take away enough tax benefits to moderate substantially the tax burden of large numbers of people.

There was nothing inevitable about the timing of the 1986 federal tax reform, but the conditions were certainly favorable for a tax reform by the mid-1980s. Several decades of accelerated granting of tax expenditures had eroded the revenue base, and the president's 1981 tax reduction had gotten completely out of hand, with Democrats and Republicans competing to add more tax breaks; the result was an increase in the size of the national deficit. Reagan made tax reform an early priority of his second term.

The White House and the Treasury wanted a proposal that would give tax reductions to 80 percent of taxpayers, and set that figure as a guideline. The Senate Finance Committee struggled to reduce the top bracket of the income tax, that is, the maximum rate applied to the wealthiest people, from 50 percent to close to 27 percent. (The final figure was 28 percent.) They wanted to drop the top rate significantly in order to gain enough support in Congress and among the interest groups to pass the reform.

Rather than a mobilized opposition and quiet supporters, the 1986 tax reform had active interest groups on both sides. Business groups were split over the issue. Those in danger of losing benefits lobbied heavily against the reform. Chief executive officers of major corporations, such as IBM, Pepsico, and Reynolds, were active in support of tax reform. Taxpayer groups also created a politically powerful presence. Citizens for Tax Justice, a tiny union-financed group, turned out reports on the amount of taxes paid by major U.S. corporations, many of whom paid nothing at all. The reports received major publicity in the two years preceding the tax reform and helped persuade Congress to remove some of the beneficial tax treatment of these corporations. Citizens for Tax Justice "gave us the fuel for tax reform and for tax increases on the business community," said Representative Robert T. Matsui (D-Calif.), an influential member of the Ways and Means Committee. "I'll bet every member" who favored overhauling the tax code "used CTJ statistics in speeches back home."[84] As an aide to the House Ways and Means Committee chairman remarked, sometimes legislation is based on a few good horror stories, and Citizens for Tax Justice provided those stories.[85]

Despite pressure from proreform interest groups, lobbying to retain tax breaks was fierce;[86] the first time the Senate Finance Committee tried to hammer out its version of reform, it was overwhelmed by resistance to eliminating a variety of preferences. The committee chairman, Robert Packwood (R-Oreg.), may have set the wrong tone initially by supporting Oregon's lumber industry. By the time other senators had protected their constituents, the proposal was no longer revenue neutral—more money was given away in tax decreases than was gained by eliminating or reducing tax breaks.

Senator Packwood went back to the drawing board and started again with a stricter revenue-neutral rule: No benefit could be added without closing a loophole or eliminating a special benefit to pay for it. The committee's recommended package arrived on the Senate floor with an understanding that any amendments would not change the total amount of revenues and would not increase the size of the deficit. This informal rule blocked many interest groups that would have tried to reinstate their benefits on the floor.

One of the particularly interesting aspects of the passage of the reform act was the major role of the conference committee set up to resolve the differences between the House and Senate versions. The many differences between the House and Senate bills created a relatively open conference. The chairs of both the House Ways and Means and the Senate Finance Committee were on the conference committee and conducted most of the negotiations themselves behind closed doors. Other members of Congress reported that such a procedure insulated them from interest groups because they could legitimately say they did not know what was going on.[87]

The final conference committee product did not eliminate all special tax benefits, but it reduced many of them and eliminated others outright. The top individual tax rate was dropped from 50 percent to 28 percent, and 80 percent of individuals and families would be taxed at no more than 15 percent. The top corporate rate was reduced from 46 percent to 34 percent.

In at least one case, the dynamics of income tax reform were similar at the state level. In Wisconsin in 1982, the cost of tax breaks was just about equal to the total taxes collected.[88] A major reform of the income tax occurred by 1985. The reform had the governor's support and was tied to tax reduction. The reduction was partly the result of eliminating deductions and exceptions and partly the result of a favorable revenue projection. The top income bracket was lowered, apparently as an essential part of gaining political support for reform. A high degree of centralization and closed decision rules helped block interest-group demands.[89]

To summarize, broad-based taxes are likely to be gradually eroded by the demands of the interest groups and individuals who feel the burden of the tax. The integrity of the revenue base and the perception that the tax applies equally to all gradually deteriorates. The growing complexity of the tax laws, revenue losses, and inequitable treatment of businesses and individuals in similar financial circumstances generate pressure for reform.

Summary and Conclusions

Public officials need to raise taxes from time to time, but they confront a political minefield when they try to do it. The result is that they raise taxes with great care and try to place the burden of taxation in such a way as to minimize opposition and gain the maximum of support.

The more open the government has been about its finances, and the greater the belief that the resources are really needed and will be spent on items approved by the taxpayers, the greater the acceptability of the tax increase. Tax increases may be precisely the time when the government is held to account.

The actors involved in revenue decisions include the chief executive, the revenue committees of Congress and finance committees of legislatures and councils, interest groups, and the courts. Departments and agency heads are almost completely absent, except when the Treasury Department recommends tax reforms. Citizen commissions, blue-ribbon committees, and task forces of the Chamber of Commerce are also frequent actors, examining the overall need, the current revenue situation, and possible revenue alternatives. An array of interest groups is directly involved at different times. Public employees and service recipients get involved when service cuts are threatened; chambers of commerce and other groups of business representatives get involved when new taxation is being considered. Taxpayers' organizations, unions, and business associations represent broad groups, but there are clearly splits within each broad group. For example, business associations are deeply split about tax reform.

The power that interest groups are able to wield does not depend solely on their finances; small, poor interest groups are sometimes more effective than larger, better financed ones. Small groups, with little financial backing, are sometimes able to manage major impacts through research and symbolic stories that catch the media's and legislators' attention. The ability of interest groups to form and maintain coalitions affects their success, as does the budget process itself. When legislators organize themselves and the budget process in such a way as to insulate themselves from interest groups, interest-group power may be curtailed. This does not happen all the time, but it certainly indicates that interest groups do not always call the shots.

The politics of taxation is characterized by a struggle to shift the burden of taxation away from one's own group, however defined. The pressure may be away from the relatively poor to the relatively rich, or vice versa. Alternatively, the pressure may be to shift taxation from individuals to corporations, or from homeowners to renters or owners of commercial property. Those in one region of the country may try to shift the burden of taxation to other regions. When representatives of any group are in power, they may shift the burden to other groups.

Overall, revenue politics is characterized by a relatively long time span, in which both narrow and broader societal interests compete for position, and by efforts to lock in benefits such as tax breaks and to lock out taxes on particular forms of wealth while backers are powerful enough to do so. Earmarking of revenues is another way of trying to lock in particular favorable patterns.

Taxation often changes by small amounts in a variety of tax sources, but at intervals, there are major changes. New taxes are passed; the burden of taxation is shifted; the definition of taxable wealth is changed; or tax reforms restore the tax base.

CHAPTER THREE

The Politics of Process

If the budget process is to produce anything, it must produce honesty. Only then will the American people learn of and support the difficult choices the Congress and the President must make to restore fiscal discipline.
—SENATOR JOHN EXON

THE BUDGET PROCESS divides up the work of budgetary decision making, assigns particular decisions to particular actors or groups of actors, and coordinates the decision making among them. The budget process sets the rules and determines the parameters of time and money within which the deliberations will take place, and it frames the options and the comparisons that will be considered. It also determines the level of competition between agencies and constituencies for governmental resources.

The budget process can make it more or less difficult to spend public money; it can give one group of actors a veto over the decisions of other actors; it can be inclusive of new groups or reinforce the power of long-standing groups; it can facilitate democratic participation or strengthen authoritarian regimes. The budget process can encourage or discourage careful deliberation and comparison between possible choices of expenditure. Budgetary decision making can be transparent at some times and opaque at others.

The budget process is politically important on a number of levels. It influences the distribution of power between and within the executive and legislative branches of government and between government and the public, viewed both as individuals and as organized interests. It influences budgetary outcomes in broad policy terms, by making it easier or more difficult to balance the budget, make long-term investments, or borrow money. The budget process may tilt toward lower taxes and smaller scope of government or toward higher taxation levels and more publicly provided goods and services. Third, the budget process may influence who benefits from lower taxes or higher spending decisions. For example, the process may have an effect on whether a particular business gets a requested tax break, not only by making tax breaks easier than direct spending, but also by including the business or its representatives in the decision making.

The budget process not only affects the distribution of power and influences policy and spending decisions, it is important in its own right—the process is in a sense an outcome. That is, the budget process is often a key instrument of democratic participation and accountability. The openness of the decision making to public view and to meaningful interest group and citizen participation, the responsiveness of the process to democratically determined priorities, and the quality of reporting in the budget document and in accounting reports all reflect the degree of democratic governance. A top-down model, in which the chief executive determines the budget without consultation about the needs of the agencies, or a model of professional dictation of the budget without citizen participation or direction suggests the nature of governance more broadly. Balancing professionalism on the one hand and executive policymaking on the other is not easy; balancing both of these needs against more direct participation from citizens and interest groups is also complicated; and providing honest and meaningful reporting on decisions being made is a continuing challenge. These are all tasks of the budget process.

Macro and Micro Politics

In light of all these functions of the budget process, the politics of process divides into two broad categories: a politics of macro change and a politics of micro change. In one group, budget actors try to reshape the process to influence broad policy in the direction they espouse. For example, some conservative Republicans want to restructure the budget process to encourage reduced taxation and reduced scope of government services. Some of them consider deeply flawed any budget process that does not bring about this policy outcome. They work together on task forces to forge serious legislative proposals. In the second group, actors jockey for power to influence particular decisions that may have short-run consequences or that may affect only one company or interest group. As they jockey, they may bump against the rules, bend them, break them, or change them.

MINICASE: REPUBLICAN MACRO-LEVEL REFORM PROPOSALS

By June of 1998 it was clear that the federal budget was close to balancing after decades of deficits. Many cheered the contribution of the budget process, revised in 1990, to finally eliminating the deficit. But some in Congress were still frustrated with the budget process. The Speaker of the

House, a Republican, had created a task force to come up with budget reform proposals that would forward the Republican agenda. The Speaker's task force tried to alter the budget process so that it would "enhance our common goals of controlling spending, reducing the debt, and cutting taxes." Task force members argued, "Sensible budget process changes can greatly improve our ability to advance our legislative agenda and to build on the success of the Balanced Budget Act of 1997."

Representative Christopher Cox reported the recommendations of the Speaker's Task Force on Budget Reform to the House Budget Committee's subcommittee on Budget Process Reform.[1] One recommendation was to enforce the spending caps in the budget by requiring a two-thirds vote to exceed them. This requirement would also apply to supplemental appropriations.

A second recommendation was an automatic continuing resolution, at a hard freeze level. Congress uses continuing resolutions when members cannot agree to pass the regular appropriations bills on time; while Congress is working out its disagreements, it usually passes a temporary budget law, to keep the government open. Such legislation is usually classified as "must pass" because without it, the government shuts down. There is great temptation, therefore, to put a variety of riders in the continuing resolution. Representative Cox argued that if the continuing resolutions were automatic rather than discretionary, there would be no threat of closing down the government, and hence no swollen must-pass legislation. What Cox did not say was that such a feature would also encourage conservatives who want lower spending to hold up the budget, with the idea that a hard freeze would then be put in place instead of a new, more expensive budget.

Cox also argued for an end to "baseline budgeting," by which he meant considering budget increases and decreases compared to a baseline that includes inflation. Since the early 1980s, the federal government has used a current services estimate, figuring what it would cost next year to provide this year's level of services. A cut from that level was considered a cut in the budget. Conservatives objected that what was considered a cut could in fact be an increase in dollars. They felt that consideration of inflation pushed up budgeting costs, building in increases by at least the rate of inflation. They also felt, with some justification, that the baselines were not well understood by the public and served to confuse more than to clarify. They argued for elimination of the baseline.

What Cox did not say, however, was that there has to be some baseline; there is no way to budget without one. The issue is what baseline will be used. If politicians are going to talk about cuts or increases, they have to have reference to some kind of base. There are many choices of baseline, including last year's actual budget. What Cox and others wanted was to eliminate the constant services baseline and substitute a different one, which would assume that agencies were cut back each year by the level of inflation, and then advance or retreat from that position. In their model, an agency's budget could in fact be cut, but it would appear to be an increase if the budget increase was less than the inflation rate. The result could be just as confusing to the public, but it would build in a bias toward decreasing spending every year.

The Speaker's tax force wanted the budget process changed so that it would be easier to reduce taxes. It was difficult to reduce taxes when the budget process emphasized balance, because every cut in revenue had to be offset by reductions in spending or other increases in revenue. One proposal was to eliminate the requirement that tax cuts be specifically offset, assuming that revenues were generally sufficient to prevent a deficit. In other words, task force members wanted to eliminate the need for explicit trade-offs when reducing revenues; they wanted to make it less clear what would have to be cut to pay for such tax reductions or who would have to pay for them. Undoubtedly such changes would make it easier to cut taxation.

Perhaps most dramatically, Cox recommended the elimination of all entitlements other than Social Security, making them instead subject to annual appropriations. Entitlements are payments that go to all those eligible, based on criteria such as age, income, or unemployment status. The cost to the federal government of such entitlements goes up and down with the economy and the number of people in need. It would be substantially easier to cut back the entitlement programs if they were annually appropriated rather than permanently authorized and automatically funded.

It is easy to see how these budget process proposals would make it easier to reduce taxes and cut federal government expenditures. They would change the present bias toward growth by building in a bias toward shrinking the federal government—all by changing the rules of budget process.

After figuring out what process reforms would help them achieve their agenda and uncovering the areas of consensus within the Republican ranks for such changes, the next step was to introduce legislation embodying these understandings. The result was a bill, the Comprehensive Budget Process Reform Act of 1999, called the Nussle-Cardin-Goss Budget Process Bill. In some ways, it went beyond the suggestions of the Speaker's task force, but all the proposals were in the same direction as indicated by the task force. The liberal Center for Budget and Policy Priorities called attention to a number of features of this bill and how they would work. In a sign-on letter, the center argued that Congress should reject these proposals.

> Key aspects of H.R. 853 would likely lead to cuts in discretionary spending and impair the appropriations process. In addition, the bill contains troubling changes in the pay-as-you-go rules; it would allow projected non-Social Security surpluses to be used to finance tax cuts or entitlement increases, but if such tax cuts or entitlement increases were enacted and the projected surpluses then failed to materialize, cuts in many important programs—including Medicare, student loans, farm price supports, veterans' adjustment benefits, and the Social Services Block Grant, among others—would be triggered through sequestration [automatic cuts—author]. In a break with past practice, the bill also would allow reductions in the discretionary caps to be used to finance tax cuts. These provisions are deeply disturbing and should not become law.
> Other provisions also are objectionable. For example, the bill's 'lock box' provision would lower the discretionary caps when either the House or Senate approved a floor amendment reducing funding for an item in an appropriations bill, even if the other chamber had soundly rejected the cut and the cut was dropped in conference. Moreover, the caps would be reduced for all years for which caps had been set, even if the item that was cut through a House or Senate floor amendment was a one-year project whose reduction or elimination would produce no savings in subsequent years. At a time when many in Congress and elsewhere agree the existing discretionary spending caps are not sustainable and need to be raised, we find the bill's movement in the opposite direction exceedingly unwise.
> We also are disturbed by provisions of the bill that mandate use of baseline assumptions under which discretionary appropriations would be assumed to be frozen for all years for which caps have not yet been set. Under the bill, the funding level reflected in the rather severe cap set for FY 2002 would be assumed to remain in place through FY 2009, with no adjustment for Inflation. The shrunken baseline would be used to make the surplus appear to be $436

billion larger over the next 10 years than the current CBO baseline shows, paving the way for even-larger tax cuts at the expense of discretionary programs.

Finally, we are concerned that H.R. 853 would weaken the appropriations process. In combination, provisions that would have the budget resolution be signed by the President, prohibit the Appropriations committees from sending appropriations bills to the House floor until work on the budget resolution had been completed, and institute a year-long automatic continuing resolution at the prior year's level if an appropriations bill has not [been] completed by the start of the fiscal year would create a risk of putting the discretionary budget on auto-pilot, with long-term freezes in funding levels. The bias would be toward the status quo, rather than toward setting funding priorities for a given fiscal year and being able to address pressing needs as they arise.

H.R. 853 would both weaken fiscal discipline—by effectively jettisoning the pay-as-you-go rules—and largely abandon a budget process that has helped produce budget surpluses for the first time in many years. It paves the way for sweeping tax cuts at the expense of other important needs. We urge you not to support this bill.

While the first group of actors works for consensus to change the budget process to achieve broad political and partisan goals, a second set of actors is just scrambling for increased budget power, to influence specific short-term or narrowly focused decisions. In the process, they may bend the rules or change them. As an example of violating the budget process rules to influence a specific budget allocation, one group of congresspersons raised the caps on discretionary spending to increase outlays for highways and pork-type projects. These members of Congress did not argue that the caps themselves were wrong. They wanted to influence a specific decision, not the rules that structure the outcomes more broadly. The rules were just in the way.

The chief Democratic counsel for the Senate Budget Committee in Washington, Bill Dauster, gave a partisan speech in 1996, pointing out a number of these rule changes or evasions that the Republicans had devised for short-term advantage. Some of the affected rules were budget process rules and some were rules of procedure in the Senate. It is not only Republicans who do such things when they are in the majority, but in this example, a Democrat was commenting on Republican behavior.

MINICASE: MICRO POLITICS: BENDING THE RULES
TO WIN INDIVIDUAL DECISIONS

Bill Dauster argued that the Republican majority showed a willful disregard for rules and laws when it served their legislative purposes.[2] In one case, in order to approve some unrelated legislation favoring the Federal Express corporation, the Senate Republicans changed a century-old standing rule that limited conference committees to the subject of legislation that was sent to the conference.

Dauster charged that the Senate overturned another century-old rule, this one limiting legislation in appropriations bills. At the national level, there is a difference between bills that provide money and those that design and modify programs. Appropriations bills are supposed to contain money approved for each program; they are not supposed to contain new legislation modifying programs or creating new ones. New or modified legislation can take years to hammer out, negotiating compromises between interests. It can be a slow and contentious process. By contrast, appropriations bills have a must-pass nature—the government will shut down unless there is money appropriated to pay for programs and services. Allowing legislation in appropriations bills empowers a simple majority of the Senate to add unrelated legislative matters to a fast-track budget vehicle that is likely to pass. The reason for such an important change in the rules, according to Dauster, was to adopt an unrelated amendment sponsored by Senator Kay Bailey Hutchison (R-Tex.). What Mrs. Hutchison put in her amendment to an emergency supplemental appropriation was a rescission [withdrawal] of funding for the rest of the year so that no new endangered species could be declared while the authorizing committee was working on revisions in the law that would make it more difficult to declare a species endangered. She thus accomplished quickly and for the short term without a reauthorization bill—through an emergency supplemental budget bill—what she hoped to accomplish with reauthorization legislation later in a broader, more deliberative setting.

Dauster also charged the Republicans with abusing their scorekeeping powers. He argued that on 27 October 1995, during consideration of an amendment by Chairman William Roth (R-Del.) of the Finance Committee, Budget Committee Chairman Pete Domenici (R-N.Mex.) misrepresented off-budget Social Security savings as if they were on-budget savings and thus paved the way for adoption of the Roth amendment without procedural obstacles that would have required sixty votes to waive. Under the Budget

Enforcement Act, Social Security was supposed to be off budget, so counting savings in Social Security was a violation of the Budget Act. One senator brought a point of order noting the violation, but rather than recognize the point of order, Domenici used his discretion as chair of the Budget Committee to make a binding determination of how the cut would be "scored" (counted). It was not that the senator made up a new rule or disapproved of the existing rule, it was just that he chose to ignore the violation of the rule in this case.[3]

Dauster argued that the Republicans expanded the reconciliation process to include nonbudgetary matters and a variety of budgetary issues beyond the basic task of reconciling or cutting back budgets to the level required by the budget resolution. In the 1974 Congressional Budget Reform Act, there was a procedure that required the budget committees to assign totals to the other committees working within the budget, and these committees had to reconcile their own numbers with these figures. The reconciliation process in the Senate was fast-tracked; it allowed only germane amendments; and it limited debate. Most important, it could be passed by a simple majority. Outside the reconciliation process, rules of the Senate had made that body more deliberate than the House and given each member, whether of the minority or the majority, power to obstruct legislation. An individual senator could filibuster a law, delay it by speaking on and on, and it would take a supermajority to cut off the speech. But not so with the reconciliation bills. By putting more ordinary legislation into the reconciliations, the Senate bypassed its own traditions of individualism and debate. Only germane amendments would be considered, and germaneness would be determined by the majority party in committee. In the short run, the Republicans strengthened their ability to pass their preferred legislation in the Senate over Democratic opposition, but in the long run, they altered the deliberative traditions of the Senate and its role in the legislative branch.

Dauster concluded, "This past year, the Republican Senate majority has thus repeatedly arrogated greater power to the majority to use fast-moving legislative trains to move unrelated matters of its choosing. This majority has thus repeatedly torn down the protections that the Senate affords minorities. This majority has shown a disturbing willingness to cast aside long-held precedents and institutions to serve immediate policy ends. That, then, is the unifying theme that runs through the procedural actions that the Republicans took last year and that they seek to take this year. The Republican Senate stands ready to sell its birthright for a mess of pottage. It shows contempt for the institution. It focuses solely on the immediate political gain."

Public Budgeting and the Budget Process

The characteristics of public budgeting help explain the functions and design of the budget process. For example, budget processes are open to the environment. If the economy is weak, there may be pressure to change the rules of the budget process to allow deficits; if public opinion turns to favor budget balance, the budget process may shift to emphasize balance. If public support for government is low, elected officials may change the budget process to give the public more direct control over budget options or to provide more public accountability.

Public budgets involve a variety of claimants who all want different things from the budget and political actors who want to exercise control over budgetary decision making. The budget process regulates who has what degree of control over budget decisions. It also controls the level of competition in the budget by encouraging or discouraging requests and by assigning particular requests to particular pools of money. It may put few requests into a large pool of resources or many requests into a relatively small pool. Some programs may be designated entitlements, or the preferred spending of some group may be earmarked, which is to say spending for that purpose comes first and does not have to compete with other spending priorities. Alternatively, a large group of programs may be shoved into the same limited pool of funds, forcing them to compete with each other in a kind of free-for-all. For example, when the federal government was changing the nature of grants to the state and local governments, it often reduced the total amount of a grant and reduced earmarks at the same time. As a result, a variety of social service providers had to compete with each other for reduced funding. The result was a higher level of conflict in that portion of the budget.

The separation of taxpayer and budget allocator also has important implications for the budget process. The gap between the payers and the decision makers is bridged at least in part by open hearings and planning processes and by reporting requirements that are regulated by the budget process. The budget process can require prior controls, especially detailed controls of inputs, or it can emphasize post controls, based on after the fact reporting, not only of numbers but also of accomplishments. Of course, the budget process can also require a combination of both.

Of all the characteristics of public budgeting, the budget process most clearly represents constraints. One example at the federal level is legislation called (after its legislative sponsors) Gramm-Rudman-Hollings, which reorganized the budget process in 1985. It included new deadlines for decisions, targets for reductions in the deficit over a period of years, and an automatic series of cuts if deficit-reduction targets were not met. This process of deficit reduction framed decisions by requiring across-the-board cuts in particular categories of the budget but exempted many programs from the across-the-board cuts. The Gramm-Rudman-Hollings process thus introduced a number of extremely constraining conditions under which budgeting was to take place. Gramm-Rudman-Hollings was modified in the fall of 1990, but the amended process was still highly constrained.

More generally, budget processes often set limits to expenditures or to revenues at the start of the budget process so that the decision making has to take place within those constraints. Or the process may begin with other kinds of constraints, such as goals for reallocation or productivity savings or constraints on cutting back capital or staff. The specific constraints depend on the conditions and policies then in effect, but they are embodied in the budget process and frame the decision making.

Constraints on decision making may exclude many options from the budget process. The decisions that remain may be very narrow, despite the size of the budget. In one city with a multimillion-dollar budget, the most important decision the budget decision makers were asked to make was between increasing a contingency fund by $20,000 or increasing two part-time secretaries to full-time. The amount of money involved was small and the decision had no major policy implications.

The budget process also reflects constraints imposed by other levels of government. For example, the amount of budgeting autonomy granted to cities by the states varies enormously. Some states mandate uniform budget formats for local governments, while others allow each jurisdiction to work out its own format. States can mandate that the budget be put together by a finance director or budget officer, or allow the city clerk or city attorney to put together an appropriation ordinance (a simple list of anticipated expenditures to help estimate needed property taxes) in lieu of a budget. States can reduce the level of tradeoffs in the budget by allowing the creation of special-purpose governments, by earmarking revenues to local governments, and by mandating expenditures.

Variable Elements of Budget Processes

Budget processes are not fixed. If the actors do not like the outcomes, they can change the process. It is during efforts to change the budget process that the actors' goals are most apparent and the influence of the environment is most clear. Participants' efforts to change the process help make it clear how particular parts of the budget process are intended or expected to work to achieve particular budget outcomes.

Goals

Budget processes can be designed to emphasize and facilitate any of a variety of goals. For example, budget processes can emphasize budget balance, or they can emphasize spending or taxing reductions. They can emphasize productivity or efficiency and effectiveness, or more generally, management improvements. Budget processes can facilitate building public confidence in government. Different budget actors may disagree on what they want the process to accomplish.

A variety of features in budget processes may be used to achieve one or more of these goals. For example, if the emphasis is on building public trust, then the budget process should emphasize openness, solicitation of public opinion, and a variety of means of demonstrating not only that public priorities have been followed, but also that the programs are well managed and effective. Budget documents are likely to be laid out in programs, with performance measures that show what was planned and what was actually accomplished.

If the goal of the budget process is to reduce spending, then the budget process may emphasize constraints such as spending caps and build in incentives for end-of-year savings. Budget rules may create lock boxes or prohibitions on transfers, so that any savings in one area are not used to increase spending somewhere else. Budget actors may change the assumptions on which the future budgets are built, reducing or eliminating baselines that build in inflation costs. There may also be emphasis on various kinds of automatic cuts if various actions are not taken.

Distribution of Budget Power among Actors

Budget processes distribute decision-making power. In normal budgetary decision making, someone makes a budget request, someone reviews that request, and someone has to approve or cut or disallow that spending. But within that overall framework, there is enormous variation, in terms of both what is done and who does it. For example, the budget may begin with extensive policy analysis done by the budget office and policy input from the elected officials. This technical and political input may be given to the departments in the form of guidance and constraints, before departments heads make any budget requests. Alternatively, budget requests may come up from the departments and programs without any top-down guidance about what to include or exclude. In some cases the executive branch dominates the decision making, and in others the legislative branch has an equal or even larger role than the executive branch.

Perhaps the most dramatic difference between budget processes is the degree to which they are dominated by the executive or the legislative branch. In the model of executive dominance, the chief executive is responsible for formulating the budget proposal, which reflects his or her priorities and policy agenda, if any. The chief executive may keep the executive branch agencies completely away from the legislature, other than to present the chief executive's approved version of the proposal. The legislature may rubber-stamp the executive budget, that is, approve it without detailed examination or emendation. Should the legislature make any changes that the chief executive opposes, the chief executive can veto the changes and sometimes even rewrite legislation. In the legislatively dominated budget process, the bureau chiefs write up their requests for spending with the assistance of legislators who want some particular expenditures. The requests are not scrutinized by the chief executive but are handed directly to the legislature for review and approval. The role of the chief executive in the legislative dominance model is slight.

Budget processes normally fall between the extremes of total dominance by the executive and by the legislature. Formally and legally, the legislatures often have the power to initiate spending and approve taxation and proposals for spending, but they may delegate much of that power to the executive. One reason for delegating that authority is the belief that expenditures are out of control and that the legislature cannot discipline itself, especially on capital projects and jobs for constituents. The chief executive is expected to be able to cut out proposals that legislators make to please constituents and impose discipline on the legislature. The belief that legislatures are more vulnerable to interest-group and constituent demands than the chief executive leads to pressure to shift budget power from the legislature to the chief executive.

One way that the executive is supposed to exercise control is to veto any increases the legislature adds to the executive's proposed budget. Strong executive veto powers usually indicate a strong executive and a weak legislature. The political power of the legislature over appropriations is conditioned by the executive's power to veto.

Governors generally have broader veto powers than the president. Constitutionally, the president of the United States has to veto all of a bill or none of it, which permits Congress to package bills to discourage vetoes. Forty-three state governors have line-item vetoes that allow them to strike out any expenditure that appears as a separate line in the budget. Thirty-five governors have the power to veto funding for an entire program or agency. A number of governors have amendatory vetoes, which let them rewrite parts of the law. Only six governors have a veto like the president's, that is, limited to rejecting a bill in its entirety.[4] Thus most state legislatures have less ability to avoid an executive veto by packaging legislation than Congress has at the national level. They also have less ability to exceed the executive's budget proposal.

A second politically significant characteristic of budget processes is their degree of centralization. Centralization refers to two related concepts: (1) the degree to which the budget process is bottom-up or top-down; and (2) the degree to which power is scattered among independent committees, commissions, and elected officials without an effective coordinating device.

Bottom-up procedures begin with the budget requests of bureau chiefs. These requests are scrutinized either by the chief executive and his budget staff or by the legislature, or by both, but the requests form the framework of decision making and set the agenda. There is little or no prioritizing between programs in this model in its extreme form. Each request is judged on its merits, independently of other requests. A loose coordination is achieved by setting revenue or spending limits at the beginning of the process; cost increases are kept within rough limits by giving no agency an increase much higher than the total percentage increase in revenues.

Top-down budgeting at its extreme virtually ignores bureau chiefs. The chief executive may not ask bureau chiefs for their budget requests or may give them detailed instructions on how to formulate their requests. The proposal can be made from whole cloth at the top of the executive branch by taking last year's actual budget and making changes in it in accordance with policy preference, giving more to one and less to another, regardless of what the bureau chiefs would have asked for themselves. A more moderate top-down procedure takes the bureaus' requests and gives more to one and less to another based on policy choices.

In the legislature, too, budget processes can be more top-down or more bottom-up, depending on whether budget and revenue targets are given to spending and revenue committees to work with, or whether the revenue and spending committees do their own work and give the totals to the body as a whole.

Budgeting processes normally combine some top-down elements and some bottom-up elements. Budgeting tends to become more top down when there is a revenue problem or a defined budget crisis that requires reduction in expenditures. Top-down budgeting is associated with spending control and a policy orientation to the budget. That is, if the chief executive has a marked preference for achieving some goal, he or she is more likely to use a top-down process to select some programs and reject others as a means to achieve that goal.

The second dimension of centralization is the extent to which power is scattered among relatively independent actors. For example, the chief executive may have to share power with other elected executive branch officers or with independent commissions. When power is widely shared, the effect may be to immobilize decision making. No one has responsibility or can tell anyone else what to do; approval for any action has to go through a number of different actors. The purpose of a highly fragmented and decentralized budget process may be precisely to limit the amount of spending, and the amount of activist government. More centralization of budget processes is usually more activist and more policy oriented but may be either economy oriented or spending oriented.

A key element in the design of budget processes is the degree to which the public has access to the process, in terms of participation in planning, direct access to useful information and access through the media, and the ability to testify at hearings. To what extent is the public a relevant budget actor?

MINICASE: PARTICIPATORY BUDGETING

Budgeting can be open in the sense of easily visible, or it can be open in the sense of welcoming participation, or both. The more open the budget is to interest groups and the public, and the more democratic the process, the more likely the total of requests will exceed the budget available. Open budget processes tend to push up expenditures unless there is substantial training of the citizens who choose to participate in the process. But if there is training and sufficient staff assistance to local neighborhood groups and grassroots organizations, there may be major gains to be made from decentralizing the budget decision making. Such gains include greater legitimacy of government, greater stability and understanding between groups, and more efficient use of resources.

In the United States, the city of Dayton, Ohio, has decentralized part of the capital budget process to pie-shaped wedges of the city that combine inner-city and outer-city neighborhoods into one budget request.[5] Citizens put themselves forth for election to budget councils and then get substantial training from the city in how to read the budget and how to make budget decisions. City staff receive and examine proposals, but they have to have very good reasons for rejecting community decisions.

Participatory budgeting has also been tried with great success in Porto Alegre, Brazil.[6] The Porto Alegre project begun in 1989 has not only been successful in increasing community participation in budgeting but has also contributed to healthy financial management. "City dwellers have been able to decide about virtually anything related to public resources under the municipal domain—from streets to be paved to reform of the city's main public market, from supporting cultural initiatives in peripheral areas to the publication of a book telling the history of a specific community, from sanitation systems to pay policies regarding municipal civil servants."

Since the beginning of the project hundreds of citizens have been trained to be decision makers and to combine advocacy for a particular clientele with consideration of other requests coming from other neighborhoods and the welfare of the whole city. Staff members present revenue estimates and preliminary budget documents and report on their own performance of the past year. The city is divided into sixteen regions, each of which elects its own representatives who consider the budget options and work on priorities and the final budget format. They then have to negotiate the final options among themselves. City staff provide technical assistance, and priorities are worked out in light of a group of factors based on a description of each region and its particular needs.

The process is "absolutely transparent." The participatory council's meetings are open to the public and the press. Municipal authorities do not vote; they provide technical and legal information. Even a veto by the mayor can be reversed by the citizens' council, forcing new negotiations. The citizens' proposal is sent to the city council to be approved or rejected. It is difficult to reject, however, because it has the stamp of approval of the citizens. The result has been a real shift of power to the public. The outcome has been better, more efficient budgetary decisions, and an influx of capital as a measure of confidence in better financial management.

The most open processes are those that make all decisions in plain public view, before the press, the public, and interest groups. Meetings are held at convenient times for visitors and are announced well in advance. Representatives of various interests are invited to share their views during budget hearings and on advisory boards. The process is closed if the public, the press, and interest groups are not permitted to watch the decision making or allowed to express their views during the budget process. Or their views may be solicited but routinely disregarded. Budget processes are seldom completely open or completely closed.

Open budget processes are more accountable to the public, but they are also more open to interest-group pressure. Closing the budget process is often considered one way to help control increases in expenditures; opening it is usually a way of increasing expenditures. Closing the process is also a way of helping to pass revenue bills, as noted in chapter 2, which means that a more closed process should favor budget balance as a goal.

Format

The key goals of the budget are reflected in the budget format and its relative emphasis on expenditure control, management improvement and cost effectiveness, and policy and planning.[7] The major budget formats are the line-item budget, performance budgets, and program budgets.

A line-item budget lists each department and assigns a sum of money to the department. The money is not granted in a lump sum, to be spent as needed, but is divided into money for specific expenditures—travel, payroll, commodities, and the like. Each kind of expenditure is listed on a separate line; the department then has to spend the money in accordance with the requirements of each line. If the budget is broken into many detailed lines, such as paper supplies, pencils, desks and chairs, typewriters, and stamps, the department head has very little discretion about how the money can be spent. This kind of budget emphasizes financial control. A line-item budget plays down competition because it never compares programs.

A performance budget lists what each administrative unit is trying to accomplish, how much it is planning to do, and with what resources. It reports on how well it did with the resources it had last year. The emphasis is on getting the most service for the dollar.

A program budget divides expenditures by activities so that the costs for juvenile counseling are broken out from traffic patrol, and both of those are separated from crime detection. Sometimes program budgets are formally linked to a planning process where community (or national) goals are stated and expenditures allocated in an effort to reach those goals. The emphasis in this format is on the appropriateness of current spending priorities and the possible need for tradeoffs between programs. Program budgets have the most potential for allowing legislators to review the policy implications of spending decisions.

Zero-based budgeting is a particular kind of program budget. It associates service levels in each program with costs, and then it prioritizes all the options, treating high and low service levels as different program options. All those at the top of the priority list are funded. If there are more items than money, the ones on the bottom of the list are not funded. Zero-based budgeting formally allows for and creates a mechanism for reallocation, since one department may suggest a higher level of service or a new program that is ranked high on the priority list, while another department's programs are ranked low. The new proposal may be funded at the expense of the older. The potential for generating competition and conflict is enormous in this budget format, so that it is seldom used; but a less extreme version, called target budgeting, puts only 5 or 10 percent of the departments' budgets at risk for reallocation. Target budgeting is common.

The information presented in each budget format allows different kinds of analyses to be made. The line-item budget forces attention to changes in accounting categories—why are office supplies more expensive this year than last? These are technical questions of limited focus. When a budget is line item only, it can be very difficult to examine proposed expenditures for sound management practice or the appropriateness of the expenditures.[8] The program budget, especially with its zero-based budget component, forces comparisons between programs on the basis of stated priorities. These priorities are usually statements of policy; for example, when comparing two programs, the one that benefits the poor should have a higher priority than the one that benefits the rich, or programs that emphasize prevention should receive funding before programs that emphasize suppression. Performance budgets lay out not only what programs cost and roughly what they achieve; they lay out the (implied) criteria of productivity for the choices between programs.

Because the different budget formats have different strengths and weaknesses, many actual budgets combine formats.[9] Everyone has to be concerned about financial control, so there is often a line-item budget conforming to administrative units; but sometimes program budgets are added to line-item budgets, and, more rarely, performance budgets are added to the program budget.

In short, there is enormous variation in budget formats. Formats differentially emphasize control, management, or policy preferences. Different formats also influence the kind of review that spending proposals get and structure the level of competition between programs.

Variation between and among Federal, State, and Local Governments

For years, the federal budget process was used by scholars as a model against which other processes could be compared and understood. But during the 1980s, the federal budget was put together in a different way every year. The advent of ad hoc budgeting at the federal level shifted attention to the states and to local governments in the search for a pattern that would convey the idea of a budget process. But a survey of state and local budget processes reveals enormous variation. To come up with an idea of budget process based on this variation requires a description of that variation and the mechanisms that generated it. This chapter illustrates some of the key ways that budget processes differ from one another, while the next chapter describes how and to some extent why federal, state, and local budget processes have changed and discusses some common themes in their evolution.

Variation between Levels of Government

There is so much variation in budget processes between levels of government, and so much variation within levels, that it is difficult to give a concise listing of differences that is at the same time meaningful. What follows is a sketch of some of the major differences in recent years.

One way of describing budget processes is to examine the balance between the executive and the legislature in drawing up and reviewing the budget. Over the past decade, at the federal level there has been more of an equal balance between the branches than at the state or local level. At the state level, the executive tends to be stronger than the legislature, although they are becoming more equal in recent years.[10] At the local level, for all but the smallest cities, the model of executive dominance generally holds. Mayors often hold powerful vetoes, and the councils are often prohibited from increasing the mayor's estimates. Councils have little or no budget staff. They do have to approve the budget in most cities, and in some cities they play a substantial role in reviewing the budget.

One difference between the states and the national level is that the president can veto only whole bills. Congress can seek to avoid a veto by packaging bills in such a way that the president cannot veto them without losing something he wants badly. As differences between the president and Congress became acute during the 1980s, Congress resorted to omnibus legislation, huge packages of legislation combined in a single bill.

One type of omnibus legislation was the continuing resolution. Continuing resolutions are passed when one or more of the thirteen money bills (appropriations bills) are not passed on time. Congress then funds whichever money bills have not passed both houses with one (usually temporary) bill that may cover anywhere from one to thirteen bills, depending on how many have not yet passed. The continuing resolutions thus provide a vehicle for putting together in one bill appropriations that are normally passed separately. The scope is much larger, making it more difficult to veto without harming some absolutely essential spending.

A second occasion for omnibus legislation is the reconciliation bill. Reconciliation is a part of the congressional budget process, in which separate committees take action to comply with the budget resolution; Congress gathers up the committees' changes and passes them as one omnibus piece of legislation. As pointed out by Bill Dauster in the minicase earlier in the chapter, much unrelated legislation has been put in the omnibus reconciliations. Their broad scope makes them more difficult to veto.

At the state level, budgets may be passed in a single measure or in a series of separate bills—practice varies from state to state. But the use of omnibus legislation to avoid vetoes is virtually nonexistent. Only nine states have a mechanism for continuing last year's budget in case this year's budget is late. Omnibus reconciliations are a peculiarity of the federal budget process. State legislatures lack the motivation to package legislation in large clumps; since the governor can generally veto parts of legislation, omnibus legislation provides no protection against a veto.

At the local level, most budgets are passed as a single ordinance, without any unrelated legislation. Agreement on the budget is often worked out in advance,[11] so the council approves the mayor's or manager's budget, and the need for a veto is slight. This is especially true where councils are forbidden to increase the executive's budget recommendations.

Executive staff members carefully monitor council statements throughout the previous year, weigh the spending and tax proposals embodied in such discussions, and incorporate the ones that make sense to them into the budget. By the time the council gets the budget, the ideas they wish to see are usually already incorporated. The executive branch generally lays aside a small amount of money for symbolic additions if council members insist on adding some project the mayor, manager, or budget office intentionally deleted. To the extent that the budget is negotiated with the council, it is generally done in advance, with little open confrontation.

Relations between the mayor and council over the budget can become confrontational if a council member is a potential rival for mayor; even then, the lack of budget staff for the council makes it difficult for council members to pull the budget apart and make their own proposals. The council can become a noisy opposition and, in some cases, can prevent the passage of the budget or force compromises as the price for their support.

In short, there are major differences in the formal powers and patterns of negotiations between the executive and legislative branches at the federal, state, and local levels. At the federal level where the balance is relatively even, executive and legislative members must engage in extensive formal or informal bargaining. The results of these negotiations tend to frame the budget and set limits for departments. While bottom-up budget requests continue to be generated and examined, they may play a small role in determining outcomes because the agreements reached by the executive and legislative branches take priority over the expressed needs of the departments and agencies.[12] The federal government has put a great deal of time and energy into trying to devise budget agreements across branches. The result has been a considerable shift to top-down budgeting.

The situation is quite different at the state level, in part because the governors have more powerful vetoes, and in part because the budget process itself is so different at the state level. There is no reconciliation process at the state (or local) level, and so no occasion for an omnibus reconciliation. Only a handful of states have any form of continuing resolution if the budget appropriations are late.[13] So there is no opportunity for omnibus legislation through continuing resolutions. Moreover, since most governors can reduce or amend legislation or veto parts of it, there is little to be gained from creating omnibus reconciliation at the state level. A governor can veto parts of a big bill as easily as smaller ones.

The federal government is most sensitive to policy issues in the budget, though some states and cities also focus on policy formation and expression through the budget. The policy emphasis at the federal level is partly a function of its large size and the impact of the budget on the economy, so even relatively small changes in taxation or spending have major policy impacts. It is also to some extent a reflection of the more ideological budgeting that has characterized recent years.

The states occupy an in-between position on policymaking. State-level spending has a much smaller impact on the economy, ideological budgeting is less apparent (although it does occur), and the budget process typically does not force the same level of explicit tradeoff between kinds of expenditures.

Cities do not influence the economy much with their expenditures, and they seldom budget ideologically. The portion of the budget that would be affected by ideological budgeting is relatively small in any event. Cities can choose most of the time to obscure tradeoffs in spending completely. When the environment forces a choice between social services and "basic" services (police, fire protection, water, streets, and sanitation), the level of controversy may be suddenly jerked upward. The federal government has to make such controversial decisions almost every year.

Despite the relatively top-down and policy orientation of the federal budget, budgetary power is the most dispersed and fragmented at the national level, partly because the decisions are so important that everyone wants a piece of the action. Before 1974, Congress divided up budget responsibility between legislative committees that designed and authorized programs, revenue committees, and appropriation committees; in 1974, it added budget committees to set spending and revenue targets and coordinate the other committees. The summit agreements between the executive branch and Congress that occurred from time to time during the 1980s and 1990s added an additional level of fragmentation, since they performed some of the key roles of the budget committees, they occurred at unpredictable intervals, and they were negotiated by a shifting set of actors.

By contrast, state and local governments have simpler and less fragmented decision making, in part because the executive branch tends to dominate budgeting. Responsibility for budgeting in the legislature tends to be more concentrated in appropriations and revenue committees, although as at the federal level, sometimes the leadership of each house overrides committee decisions.

The level of coordination between committees is relatively high in state legislatures. In 1988 fourteen states reported a joint tax and expenditure committee in the house, and eighteen reported such a joint committee in the senate. The formation of a single committee is probably the most powerful means of coordination. Another six states referred revenue bills to the appropriations committees, another powerful form of coordination. Seven states reported coordination through joint membership on committees.

While most of the states have somewhat simpler legislative decision-making structures than Congress, some emulate the federal government in complexity. For example, in Colorado, the appropriations committees are staffed by Joint Budget Committee staff, and Joint Budget Committee members sit on their respective appropriations committees; the Joint Budget Committee chair heads his or her appropriations committee. The Joint Budget Committee is the principal deliberating body on the budget. The appropriations committees review new legislation for fiscal impacts. In Florida, the House has five appropriations committees and a revenue committee. The Alabama Senate has four money committees.[14]

At the local level, legislative consideration of the budget may be confined to a single finance committee that is also responsible for revenue and bill approval.

Federal budgeting is fragmented in another sense as well. Some expenditures are approved annually by the Appropriations Committee, but a substantial portion of the federal budget is entitlements, which do not go through the appropriations process. Entitlements are special programs, the spending for which is determined by how many people or governments meet eligibility requirements. They are very difficult to budget for because they are generally open ended. If the economy worsens, the number of unemployed increases, pushing up the costs of some entitlements; if inflation increases, the costs of some entitlements increase; a long and deep recession increases the number of people entitled to some form of welfare. In essence, there are at least two different budget processes, one that applies to entitlements and one that applies to other spending.

States also have entitlements, some in cooperation with the federal government, and they cause problems at the state level as well, because they are unpredictable and mandatory. The state must find the money to pay for them, and spending for entitlements generally increases at precisely the time when the state's own revenues are falling. State governments are also the recipients of federal grants. Such grants are now generally appropriated by the legislature, but they used to form a kind of second budget that was handled differently from normal appropriations.

Local governments generally do not have entitlements and appropriate all or nearly all their budgets every year. Grant revenue may be incorporated into the budget, or it may be budgeted separately. Tax breaks, which operate as entitlements at the federal level and often at the state level as well, are usually handled on a case-by-case basis at the local level, so the costs are known in advance on a yearly basis. There are few open-ended responsibilities. Balancing the budget is thus technically easier at the local level. Expenditures typically do not go up at the same time that revenues go down, as they do for the states and the national government.

Partly as a result of format innovations, a less disparate budget process frequently dominated by a strong executive, and relatively inclusive appropriations, cities often have more explanatory budgets than the states or federal government. The budget is a more important tool for accountability at the local level.

Variation in Budget Processes among States and among Cities

Not only do federal, state, and local governments differ from one another in their budget processes, but states differ from states, and cities differ from cities. Two examples at the state level illustrate the range of possibilities. The budget process in Texas is legislatively dominated. The executive branch is decentralized, with a number of committees and commissions sharing power. Broad coalitions of interest groups dominate key policy issues such as the scope of government and size of the budget. There is little explicit policy focus on programs because the intent of keeping costs down requires deemphasis on comparative needs and a structure that discourages specific interest groups from making program demands. The Wisconsin model is quite different. The budget proposal is prepared by the governor and his budget office, although the legislature also has a major role in the budget. There is considerable centralization in both the executive branch and the legislature, and an explicit program and policy focus. The executive budget office serves also as a policy shop, evaluating and recommending policies; the budget is in program format, allowing for policy tradeoffs in the consideration of the budget.

In Texas, the governor has little budget control, and the legislators have strong linkages directly to the departments.[15] The Budget and Planning Office in the Office of the Governor produces a revenue plan for financing state programs, which provides an expenditure ceiling.[16] The governor has the power to veto items to enforce revenue ceilings, but the plan for expenditures comes from the Legislative Budget Board, which consists of a ten-member joint legislative committee composed of the legislative presiding officers, chairpersons of the appropriations and finance committees, and other members appointed by the legislative leadership. Though the governor is by statute the chief budget officer, the role has not been realized. The Legislative Budget Board creates a working outline. Budget preparation continues in the fiscal committees. The budget is not finished until it is out of conference committee. Then it is voted up or down as a whole by the legislature.

The process is marked by individualistic and personalistic politics in which interest groups "become unchallenged aggregators of political influences."[17] The system produces large amounts of unplanned spending and concentrates power in a small group of people who support one another. The integrity of the original plan is not defended as it goes through legislative committees, so "long range positive policy goals are difficult, if not impossible to make."[18] Administrators of spending agencies work with their boards (note the existence of independent boards, not cabinet-level gubernatorial appointees) and with the legislative leadership "to frame a budget which reflects the low-taxing, low-spending values of the dominant coalition of interest groups."[19] There is little debate over spending "because of the short time, and the lid on government spending and taxing."[20]

The Texas model is extreme in state budgeting. Only a few other states are still as legislatively dominated. Most states have more of an executive budget and more centralization in the executive branch. Wisconsin may come close to the other extreme, where the governor has good policy control over the budget and the Office of the Budget actually helps formulate and sometimes even helps sell the governor's policies in the legislature.[21] The budget office helps prepare a list of upcoming policy issues well before the receipt of the budget requests from the agencies and sorts the agency requests into level of impact on fiscal and policy issues. The state budget office directly negotiates with agency heads on minor and intermediate-level implications of budget proposals, while the governor negotiates directly on the major ones.[22] Select cabinet agency heads may participate in the development of the key policy issues, but noncabinet agency heads have little role. The policy process in the budget is not completely top-down, but is more top-down than bottom-up.

When the budget proposal reaches the legislature, it is reviewed by a fourteen-member standing committee called the Joint Committee on Finance. This committee holds public hearings on the recommendation. The hearings are held on the budgets of each state agency, regardless of size. "In addition to testimony from the Governor's budget staff and administrators of the respective agencies, representatives of particular interest groups and individual private citizens also may testify."[23] A Legislative Fiscal Bureau provides briefings to committee members before the hearings and provides issue papers for committee members to review. The Joint Committee on Finance prepares its proposals as a substitute for the executive proposal, incorporating whatever parts of the governor's recommendations they choose to keep. Then each house votes on the Joint Committee's recommendations.

Although the legislature's consideration is centralized, well staffed, and based on open hearings, the governor still has potent veto power. In Wisconsin, the governor has an item veto, which allows the governor to reject any item in the budget. Governors in Wisconsin have used the item veto extensively, vetoing dollar amounts, appropriations language, and programmatic language. It requires a two-thirds vote of both houses to overturn the governor's veto.

Most states have some form of executive budgeting, but it is common for agencies to submit budget proposals to the legislature either before or at the same time as the governor submits his or her proposal to the legislature.[24] The legislature can choose between the governor's proposals and the agencies' where these proposals differ. This arrangement dilutes executive power over the agencies, providing a ready-made procedure for agency end runs to the legislature.

The major systematic source of variation in municipal budget processes is the form of government. In the town meeting, citizens vote directly on the budget, providing the maximum imaginable level of accountability. This form is necessarily limited to small towns and relatively simple issues. In the commissioner form, which was widely adopted in the early 1900s, the department heads sit as the council and jointly make budget decisions. This form makes no distinction between the executive and legislative branches. It has become rare in recent years, in part because it created problems of accountability.

Most cities today have either a mayor-council form or a council-manager form. In mayor-council forms, the mayor may be chosen by the council and may have little more authority than other council members, or may be chosen by the citizens directly and may have considerably more power than other council members. While small cities may still budget legislatively, with spending recommendations coming from the departments to the council finance committee for review, in medium and large cities, generally the mayor and members of his staff prepare the budget proposal, and the council has limited ability to make changes or even to review the budget. In council-manager cities, the executive-legislative distinction is again blurred, because the city manager, who prepares the budget, is hired and fired by the council. If the manager insists on a budget that departs from council priorities, he or she is fired. Councils tend to play a more active role in budgeting in city-manager cities, at least to the point of making their policy preferences known and ensuring that their interests are represented in the budget. The council-manager form is more common in middle-size cities, while strong (independently elected) mayors are typical of larger cities.

Summary and Conclusions

Budget processes are partly technical, coordinating decision making and keeping the flow of resources to the agencies timely. But they have a political side as well. Because budget power is perceived as such an important component of overall political power, there is considerable jockeying for positions within the budget process and considerable effort to expand the power of some positions at the expense of others. More broadly, many budget actors try to change the budget process to help achieve the goals they value, whether those be growth or decline in the scope and size of government, expansion or contraction of the policy role of the budget, or encouraging or discouraging democratic participation in budgeting.

A decentralized, legislative budgeting process is very open to interest groups and not open to policy concerns. A more top-down, executive-dominated process is more responsive to policy concerns. Budget formats that make comparisons between programs also encourage a policy orientation. The process can to some extent rein in interest groups; and it can exaggerate or tone down competition and encourage and frame budget tradeoffs.

Not surprisingly, budget processes differ at the federal, state, and local levels of government, as well as across states and between cities. The differences depend on the environment and on how particular actors have changed the process to suit their needs and values over time.

CHAPTER FOUR

The Dynamics of Changing Budget Processes

BUDGET PROCESSES ARE highly variable because budget actors keep trying to change them. They are trying to enhance their own power, the power of their committees, and the power of the executive or legislative branch. They are also trying to solve problems immediately confronting them. The belief in the power of the budget process is so strong that actors recommend changes in the budget process to solve a variety of problems.

The belief in the efficacy of changing budget processes may be stronger than the reality. Even when there is a clear linkage between process and outcomes, the same process does not always lead to the same outcome. For example, if budget processes are relatively open to interest groups, that does not mean that expenditures will necessarily be high, because the interest groups may be most interested in keeping expenditures and taxation levels down. This was the case in the Texas example; it is also true in a number of cities. Shifting power from the legislative branch to the executive branch need not reduce spending; at times, the chief executive is likely to be more aggressive in spending, and at other times, the legislature is likely to spend more. Centralizing legislative control over the budget—giving more power to budget committees to set revenue and spending limits—is no guarantee of smaller spending targets. It enhances the possibility of such action, but in no way guarantees it.

Simply shifting power from one location to another has no determinate outcome. Nevertheless, if a particular president is antispending, or is promilitary, shifting power to him is likely to influence outcomes over the period of his administration. If particular committees have been more prospending than others, shifting power to them is likely to increase the levels of spending. For example, in 1885 the House of Representatives reorganized its internal budget process by taking considerable budget power away from the Appropriations Committee and giving it to the legislative committees. The legislative committees were thought to be more program loyal and more interested in program expansion than the Appropriations Committee, so the shift was seen as an attempt to increase expenditures. Expenditures did actually increase more quickly as a result of the change.[1] Later, in 1920, Congress recentralized control in the appropriations committees, in an effort to curtail the growth of expenditures.

Variation in budget processes reflects different adaptations to similar kinds of problems and similar responses adopted at different times. The strengthening of the chief executive officer's power over the budget was a widespread response to the need for increased fiscal and policy control, but it was adopted at different times in different governmental units. Some states adopted very little of the proposed reform, such as Texas, while others adopted most of the executive budget schema.

Overall, budget processes have become more top-down and more centralized, to facilitate financial control and a more explicitly policy-oriented review process. The practice of departments submitting budget requests directly to legislative committees with limited central review gradually yielded to a more executive-dominated budget, where the chief executive was responsible for reviewing the agency and departmental requests. As part of this change, executive budget offices were created, grew in professional staff, and became more politically sensitive and policy oriented. Cabinet government became more prevalent, so that there were fewer elected executive officers and more appointed by the chief executive and responsible to the chief executive.[2]

Over time, legislatures granted more power to chief executives to formulate and execute the budget. The effect was often to enhance the policy-making power of the executive. Depending on the personality of the executive and the degree of difference between the executive and the legislature, the policy-making power was sometimes used for purposes explicitly forbidden by the legislature or was used to bypass legislative approval. Legislators were reluctant to give up their influence over policy and their control over constituency-oriented spending. They responded by strengthening their own ability to perform the functions they assigned to the executive. They increased budget staff, improved their capacity to review budget proposals, and enhanced their capacity to evaluate executive branch performance.

Historically, two features of contemporary budget processes evolved together, the executive budget and increased centralization. On the legislative side, centralization was reflected in consolidating budget power more in a single committee. On the executive side, the increased central control reflected the formation of cabinet government, and especially the development of a budget office under the chief executive. This development aided the capacity of the chief executive to formulate and impose policy choices on the budget.

More recent changes include a rebalancing of the budgetary power between legislative and executive branches and a reshuffling of centralized executive control so that departments have greater control over managerial decisions. At the national level, recent changes in budget process have revolved around how to rebalance the budget; this issue has been of less concern to state and local governments.

Major Changes in the Federal Budget Process

The federal budget process has changed in important ways several times. In 1921 the executive budget process was adopted; in 1974 the Congressional Budget Reform Act was passed, limiting some of the president's budgetary discretion and enhancing Congress's ability to check executive branch revenue projections and economic assumptions; in 1985 Gramm-Rudman-Hollings was passed in an effort to curtail and shrink the deficit. After several iterations, GRH was replaced by the Budget Enforcement Act in 1990 in a further effort to help strengthen the norms of balance. Throughout the 1980s and 1990s the more equal budgetary power of Congress and the president combined with government frequently divided along party lines to result in budget negotiations at the summit between Congress and the president, eventually leading to more centralization of control in OMB and congressional leadership in order to reach and carry out agreements.

The Creation of the Executive Budget at the National Level

At the national level, the 1921 Budget and Accounting Act created the executive budget and the Budget Bureau in the executive branch. This major change in budget processes illustrates both the competition for power over budgeting between branches of government and the role of the environment in fostering increases in expenditures and debt that presented problems that had to be addressed. The existence of a dominant reform movement created a specific agenda for change.

Two major pressures for change were the increase in spending that occurred from 1899 to 1912 and the growth of the reform movement. The level of spending during the last third of the nineteenth century was $200 to $400 million. From 1899 to 1912 the level jumped to $500 to $700 million a year.[3] The full proposal for reform in budgeting at the national level included not just presidential review of agency requests but also a line-item veto for the president and restricted powers of the Congress to change amounts proposed by the president. Clearly, one aim of the reform was to control expenditures.

President William Howard Taft and his secretary of the treasury were very supportive of the executive budget, but Congress did not initially approve of the idea. Part of the reason why Congress did not go along with Taft's plans was that there were budgetary surpluses in 1911 and 1912.[4] The pressure on Congress to give up some of its traditional power in the interest of economy was thus reduced.

President Woodrow Wilson, a Democrat, followed Taft, and Wilson's support of the presidential budget was less intense than Taft's. The Democratic Congress continued to oppose the idea; the Democrats preferred to strengthen Congress and let it do the job of controlling expenditures. World War I intervened, reducing the salience of the issue in the short run but raising the level of expenditures and deficits to such a point that congressional opposition to the presidential budget was reduced. Something needed to be done, and this reform promised lower taxes, lower spending, and elimination of deficits.

In the event, congressional budget reform was carried out in 1920, before the shift to the presidential budget. The House of Representatives consolidated appropriations into a single committee in 1920. Complete integration of revenues and expenditures and comparisons of spending between programs were not fully accomplished, "but the reconsolidation of appropriations power of several committees over the objection of the members of those committees and of the agencies and interest groups involved was still a considerable achievement."[5]

As a result of the congressional reorganization and centralization, some of the pressure for the executive budget was reduced, and the eventual shift of power to the president was not as extreme as originally envisioned by the reformers. The president got the Bureau of the Budget, which was transferred to the Executive Office of the President in 1939, and responsibility for preparing and presenting the budget, but Congress did not give the president a line-item veto and retained for itself its powers of accepting or rejecting or altering the president's proposed budget.

Entitlements and Congressional Fragmentation

Between 1921 and 1974 Congress had tried unsuccessfully several times to centralize its budget process and make it more effective. During the Great Depression, in response to massive unemployment and resulting poverty, a new kind of program was initiated, which gave money to individuals who satisfied criteria established by the programs. Called entitlements, these programs bypassed the appropriations committees and were scrutinized only by the authorizing committees. Hence fragmentation of the budget process accompanied the creation of these new programs. Considerable spending power was shifted to authorizing committees, who often favor additional spending, and control over spending was divided up among a greater number of committees, making coordination more problematic. In addition, during the 1940s there were massive expenditure increases caused by World War II. Congress responded to these problems by trying to integrate the revenue and expenditure process into a legislative budget. The Legislative Reorganization Act was passed in 1946. Had it been implemented, it might have enhanced congressional control over the budget, but Congress never succeeded in using the process and it was later formally abandoned.

Enhanced Congressional Controls

In 1950 Congress tried a more moderate reform, to link all the regular appropriations bills into one omnibus package (except the appropriations for the District of Columbia); this effort failed also, under fire from the appropriations committees. Arguments against the procedure included claims that the size of the budget bill would make it difficult to amend and that the single bill would delay the budget and force Congress to pass continuing resolutions instead. Committee members' complaints about the difficulty of amending the omnibus measure meant that they were unwilling to lose power over particular programs in the budget. The failure of these two efforts at centralization made it seem that any attempts to centralize budget control would be thwarted by members who would refuse to give up power to protect particular programs. These failures discouraged further efforts at reform until the 1970s.

From 1966 to 1973 several environmental changes took place that strained the budget process and gave additional impetus to congressional reform.[6] First were the increased costs of the Vietnam war. Rather than curtail domestic expenditures to help pay for the war and risk exacerbating domestic conflicts, the government ran deficits of increasing size. There was pressure to reduce both the overall level of spending and the size of the deficits. At the same time, there were major policy splits between Congress and the president over the conduct of the war and over domestic spending. President Nixon increasingly withheld billions of dollars of domestic spending that Congress had approved. Mistrusting the president and fearing the of loss of policy control over spending, Congress increased its budgetary role and enhanced its capacity to examine and determine budget policies.

These two pressures—to reduce spending and control deficits and to enhance the congressional role over spending policy—combined into the 1974 Congressional Budget and Impoundment Control Act. Impoundment control prevented the president from unilaterally withholding congressionally approved spending. The budget reform moderately increased the level of centralization and coordination, but equally important, it provided a professional staff of budgeters to help Congress make budget policies.

To the existing authorizing, taxing, and appropriations committees, the 1974 budget reform act added budget committees, whose responsibility was to come up with overall estimates of revenues and spending and targets for spending in broad areas. The other committees were generally supposed to stay within the guidelines established by the budget committees. The new arrangement provided for some coordination between revenue and expenditure committees and some fiscal policy formation, and at the same time did not overly threaten the existing division of power.

Congress's reorganization of the budget process was also intended as a way of taking back some budget initiative from the president. The budget committees could accept presidential policies or, relying on the new Congressional Budget Office, could differ with the president on projections of the economy, the anticipated size of the deficits, and rates of inflation. Congress could make its own fiscal policy.

Though Congress tried to enhance its own power to devise and implement fiscal policy, most of the distribution of power within Congress was left as it was to ensure that threatened appropriations, tax, and authorizing committee members did not squash the whole proposal for change. The compromises reflected in the legislation resulted in budget committees that had little real power or influence. Their ability to act as a brake on spending was thus limited.

Deficit Controls

The influence of the budget committees gradually increased, however, as the size of the deficits continued to grow and began to seem out of control. The provision of *reconciliation*, which had been written into the 1974 law, was first used in 1980, then extensively used in 1981. Reconciliation is a process by which the budget committees can give targets to the other committees that they have to meet, in any way they choose. Reconciliation thus provides a mechanism other than voluntary compliance for enforcing a budget total lower than the desire of a spending committee or forcing a tax proposal higher than a revenue committee might choose.

Despite the new budget process, deficits continued to rise, taking an upturn at the end of the Carter administration and then growing even more rapidly throughout the Reagan administration, reaching historic highs. Some of the problem of deficits had to do with the slow growth of the economy and the effects of rapidly growing social entitlements programs, but deficits also had to do with tax reductions, military buildups, and overestimates of economic growth.

Since so many of the causes of deficits were seen as difficult to control or politically off limits, there was renewed activity to change the budget process. Proponents of discipline applied from the executive branch proposed stronger presidential vetoes; proponents of smaller government proposed taking discretion away from all public officials, of both branches, by passing a constitutional amendment requiring a balanced budget and revenue limitations. Proponents of congressional power suggested further reforms of the legislative budget process. What finally passed was a peculiar compromise that did not change the balance of power much between the Congress and the executive branch but markedly limited the discretion of both branches if they could not meet guidelines on the reduction of the deficit.

The compromise legislation, called Gramm-Rudman-Hollings after its sponsors, was intended to reduce the annual deficit to zero in five years by setting targets that the budget had to reach each year. A failure to achieve the annual targets for deficit reduction triggered an automatic, across-the-board cut (with some exemptions for entitlements). Presumably the across-the-board cuts would be so obnoxious to all parties that they would choose to achieve the deficit-reduction targets on time, so the automatic feature of the cuts would not be invoked. In fact, what actually occurred was that the rules were bent and most of the cuts never occurred. Gramm-Rudman-Hollings was modifed several times before it was finally replaced by the Budget Enforcement Act in 1990.

MINICASE: COMMITTEE RESPONSE TO GRAMM-RUDMAN-HOLLINGS

Representative William Dickinson of Alabama reported in a hearing of the House Armed Services Committee on 5 February 1987 that his subcommittee on Military Construction had the previous year drawn a line in the sand in an effort comply with the limits in Gramm-Rudman-Hollings. "We are going to meet our ceilings," he said, and have no add-ons. "If it wasn't in the budget when it came over here, we will bite the bullet and take the heat and no add-ons." Dickinson called the resulting pressure "uncomfortable," but the line held, in both subcommittee and committee. That the committee even tried to hold the line in an area often known for distributive politics is impressive; that they succeeded at the committee level is even more impressive.

What happened after that, according to Dickinson, was that the Senate Appropriations Committee tried to pressure the authorizing committee to include some of the Appropriations Committee's pet projects. The authorizing committee had already denied their own members any special projects and did not want to go over the ceilings to provide special projects for the Senate Appropriations Committee members. This issue had reportedly come up in prior years as well, but the committee had caved in to pressure. Congressman David Martin added that the committee members were getting a little "suspect" that the Defense Department branches were intentionally leaving out items from the budget request that were legitimate projects in members' districts because Defense officials were confident that Congress would add the projects later.

This story is significant because it reflects not only the real attempts of at least some congressional committees to curb pork-type requests in an effort to comply with Gramm-Rudman-Hollings and the resultant political heat but also the ability to shift the location of the political onus for adding pork projects between the executive and legislative branches without changing the amounts involved. Cutting something out of an executive budget proposal that everyone knows Congress will add back is not a real cut. It makes one branch look good at the other's expense. But the other issue that these committee members were raising was how they could exercise enough power to enforce their line in the sand inside Congress. The complicated committee structure that diffused power among four sets of committees was making it difficult for at least this committee to comply with budget constraints. The committee members were just waiting for a change in the chairmanship of the Senate Appropriations Committee; they were not sure they could develop enough power to do anything else.

Gramm-Rudman-Hollings was not particularly successful. It may have had some marginal effect in reducing the rate of growth of deficits, but deficits continued to grow. Both Congress and the president began "gaming" Gramm-Rudman requirements to reduce the apparent size of the deficit just before the calculation would be made on whether to invoke Gramm-Rudman cuts (called sequesters) to get down to the mandated deficit levels. Gimmicks included overly optimistic estimates of growth in the economy, pushing back spending from one fiscal year to the previous one, and keeping new spending "off budget." Gramm-Rudman's one-year focus encouraged "quick-hit" temporary revenue raisers that would do nothing to help balance the budget in future years.

Many legislators were reluctant to give up Gramm-Rudman because the symbolism was bad—it looked like they were giving up on deficit reduction. Hence they decided to overhaul the legislation, trying to close the loopholes that had appeared and eliminate some of its worst features. In the fall of 1990, after five months of summit negotiations between the administration and Congress, a new plan for deficit reduction was passed.[7]

The budget reforms of 1990 had a number of features. First, the Social Security surplus was taken out of the Gramm-Rudman-Hollings deficit calculations, so the true size of the deficit problem would be clear. Second, instead of trying to control the size of deficits, the new legislation tried to limit discretionary spending, raise taxes, and require "pay-as-you-go" provisions. The agreement set separate spending ceilings for defense, domestic, and foreign discretionary spending, in an effort to keep spending down. The "pay-as-you-go" requirement meant that proposed increases in mandatory expenditures had to be balanced by a compensating increase in revenues or decrease in other entitlements, and proposed reductions in revenues had to be balanced by a decrease in expenditures or an increase in some other revenue source.

The legislation addressed several problems that had arisen during Gramm-Rudman days. Congress had cut the defense budget but had used much of the savings on domestic spending increases; the new process prohibited such transfers. Each area of the budget had to come in at or under ceiling, and savings in one area could not be transferred to other areas. Those constraints made it easier to achieve savings to reduce the deficit.

Another problem of Gramm-Rudman was that the target had to be reached only briefly; there were no sanctions if the deficit estimates increased later in the year. The new law added a feature called "look back," which allowed a check on conformity with the new limits later in the year. If the limits were breached in any of the three caps (defense, domestic, or international), then automatic across-the-board cuts would be invoked in the area that breached the limits. Sequestration, or automatic cuts, would also be invoked if pay-as-you-go provisions of the mandated portion of the budget were violated. If such breaches occurred late in the year, the legislation provided that the amount of the breach be subtracted from the next year's ceiling.

A third problem with Gramm-Rudman was its one-year time span, which encouraged temporary revenue increases that did not solve the problem for future years. The Budget Enforcement Act included a five-year resolution that discouraged that kind of action.

The new budget process was less rigid than the previous one, because it provided for exemptions in emergencies and built in flexibility related to changes in the economy. The rigid fixed-deficit targets were gone, but the mechanisms to help achieve balance were strengthened. The new process was easier to live with, hence more likely to be observed. The process was still laden with constraints, as Gramm-Rudman-Hollings was, and it explicitly regulated and redefined what programs must compete with what programs.[8] Evaluations of the Budget Enforcement Act suggest that it worked better than Gramm-Rudman-Hollings. One scholar observed, "A complete reckoning of what has happened since the rules were devised in 1990 would show that Congress has achieved substantial deficit reduction by increasing revenue and cutting direct spending under existing law while also offsetting any deficit increases resulting from new legislation."[9]

The Budget and Accounting Act of 1921, the Congressional Budget and Impoundment Control Act of 1974, Gramm-Rudman-Hollings in 1985, and the Budget Enforcement Act of 1990 mark the major formal changes in the federal budget process. In addition, there have been some informal changes.

One change has been toward summit bargaining between the president and leaders in Congress. In part because of the increased budgetary power of Congress after 1974 and in part because of a divided government in which the president and the majority in Congress were of different political parties, the authoritative nature of the president's budget proposal deteriorated to an initial bargaining position. During the 1980s the president's proposals were often reported in the press as "dead on arrival," meaning that Congress basically had disregarded the proposal and had come up with its own instead. Congress's willingness to come up with its own detailed budget proposal was reinforced by the election of a Republican majority in Congress in 1994. The result was an increased use of presidential vetoes in 1995 and the protracted set of negotiations between the White House and congressional leadership described in the preface.

Unless Congress can muster a veto-proof majority on budget votes, it still requires the president to sign off on bills. Since neither the president nor Congress has been able to count on the support of the other, an informal system of bargaining has emerged. Throughout the 1980s and 1990s at key points the president and leaders of Congress have met and worked out budget agreements, which have usually then been passed into law.[10] Each of these agreements has covered several years, creating a kind of de facto multiyear budget. Even though annual budgets are still produced, they are drawn up under the constraints of these longer-term negotiated settlements.

Accountability Reforms

There have been many other proposals for budget change, some of which have been partially implemented. The National Performance Review (NPR), an initiative of Vice-President Gore, recommended a number of changes in budget process and implementation in 1993 and 1994, focused on the need to shift from concentrating on controlling inputs and line items to controlling outputs and outcomes. Along those lines, the NPR reports urged more freedom for managers to move money around from one account to another and to use money throughout the year instead of being restricted to quarterly drawdowns. In fact, some greater discretion was granted, but it seems to have produced relatively little impact on management so far.

The emphasis on outputs and outcomes also suited Congress. The result was legislation called GPRA, the Government Performance and Results Act, which required agencies to draw up multiyear plans and measure their progress toward planned goals and the impacts of their programs. This process is well under way. These plans and progress reports are supposed to influence allocations, although it is not clear how much influence they have; it is clear that they have influenced the discussion between the agencies and the Office of Management and Budget and between the agencies and congressional committees.

In short, the history of the budget process at the federal level in the 1970s shows a president taking a disproportionate amount of policymaking power over the budget away from Congress, and Congress reacting by increasing its own policymaking power. By the 1980s the budget process began to deteriorate, for a variety of reasons, including the split between a Republican president and Democratic Congress and large and growing deficits reflecting a budget process poorly matched to a slow-growing economy. The breakdown in the budget process led to a series of ad hoc solutions, punctuated by budget reforms such as Gramm-Rudman-Hollings and the Budget Enforcement Act of 1990. As controlling the deficit became more urgent, consensus began to form on devising a process that would put the incentives in the right places to restore balance and reduce the level of gaming. The Budget Enforcement Act of 1990 was more successful, and it was renewed several times, with slight modifications. Partly due to a booming economy and partly due to the self-constraint of politicians working under the caps and restrictions of the Budget Enforcement Act, the federal budget was balanced in 1998. Only a few years earlier, there had been deficits of hundreds of billions of dollars.

Changes in Budget Process at the State Level

After an initial period of strong legislatures in the 1700s, state legislatures declined in public trust and responsibility. Legislatures tended to be nonrepresentative of voters, and they were often overly large and overly responsive to interest-group and constituency demands. These flaws sometimes led to a series of structural characteristics intended to limit their influence, including short sessions, constitutional constraints on what they could do, and early awards of line-item veto to governors.

To compensate for legislative weakness in yielding to demands, the governor was strengthened in budget dealings with the legislature, but the executive branch, reflecting that same early distrust of state government, remained highly fragmented. Many key state officials were elected rather than appointed by the governor, so they had their own power bases and were not controlled by the governor. A governor and his lieutenant governor might be rivals rather than teammates, and the elected controller might be out to blame the governor for budget problems. In addition, legislatures tended to create many independent commissions. Departments were often headed by commissions that appointed their own heads. Thus the governor's control, even when he gained the power to present the executive budget, was often very limited. The history of the early evolution of the budget process in Illinois illustrates many of these themes.

MINICASE: EARLY BUDGET EVOLUTION IN ILLINOIS

Looking back to the 1800s, the Illinois constitution of 1848 greatly limited the power of the legislature. This was "both because Jacksonian democracy emphasized the executive as the embodiment of the best interests of the people and because excesses of the General Assembly had almost bankrupted the state through the creation of banks and internal improvements."[11] In response to the state's debt, debt was limited under the 1848 constitution to under $50,000.[12] As the power of the legislature was curtailed, the power of the governor was somewhat increased. The governor was given a veto, but only a simple majority was required to overturn.

The 1870 constitution gave a stronger veto power to the governor, requiring a two-thirds majority to overturn. Governor John Palmer was widely respected at the time, which helped him achieve this power, but more specifically, he tried to limit the private and special laws passed by the legislators, many of which were perceived as wasteful. "Palmer had vetoed seventy-two of the twelve hundred private laws passed at the [1869] session. The General Assembly repassed seventeen of these by a simple majority; most could not have been repassed if a two-thirds majority had been required."[13]

Early in the twentieth century, on Governor Edward Dunne's recommendation, the Illinois legislature appointed a Legislative Study Committee on Efficiency and Economy to prepare reform bills.[14] The committee issued over

1,000 pages of reports in 1915.[15] But the legislature did not take action on the proposals during Dunne's administration. Instead, it went in the opposite direction, creating several new boards and commissions.

Governor Frank Lowden, who followed Dunne, believed that industrialization had created new centers of power, such as banks and corporations, but that their growth had thrust on government the unfamiliar role of guardian of the commonweal against mighty and conflicting forces. Power alone could check power. He spoke of the need for more government action, surfacing roads for automobiles, serving the people in state hospitals, and encouraging soil conservation, farmers' cooperatives, and reforestation of wastelands. The governor should have ample discretion and funds to carry out this duty. His proposals provided more centralization, recommending departments headed by single persons rather than committees, and he included the executive budget as a cornerstone of reform. He proposed identical accounting systems for every department, a central purchasing agency, and competitive bidding. He wanted a constitutional convention to modernize the constitution and remove some of its restrictions.

Lowden decided that to maximize support for his more important proposals, he would not include references to the elected officials that kept the executive branch so fragmented; he kept his proposed legal code to departments and officers over which he had jurisdiction. His proposals were passed speedily by the legislature in 1917. They included administrative consolidation into nine departments. The key new position was the director of the Department of Finance. Lowden created cabinet government.

The reforms of 1917 were retained. They were advocated as a model outside Illinois, which contributed to their retention. They brought tax reduction and a virtual end to calls upon the legislature for extra appropriations to cover administrative deficits, both of which worked in favor of keeping the reforms.

Recent changes in budget process at the state level have been somewhat parallel to changes taking place at the national level, in that the extremes of executive budgeting are yielding to more shared power between the executive and legislature. As at the national level, the capacity of state legislatures to review the governor's budget and question the assumptions underlying it has improved.

The difference at the state level is that the states had gone further in awarding the governors budget power, in part because the legislatures were less capable of making policy analyses. Forty-three states have given their governors line-item vetoes (more powerful than the veto power of the president) and nineteen states had an amendatory veto that allowed their governors to reject the language of the appropriations.[16] In the 1960s as a result of Supreme Court mandates of one-man, one-vote, the redrawing of electoral districts, and the election of more representative legislatures, state legislatures began to reform themselves and prepare themselves for a more active policy role, and the budget was a key focus of that increased capacity. Many legislatures increased the length of their sessions, changed from meeting every two years to once a year, and added staff with expertise on fiscal and budgetary matters to advise them.

From 1975 to 1988 (the most recent date for which data are available), the professional staff of legislative fiscal offices nearly doubled, to an average of about fifteen.[17] These staff do many of the same things for the legislature that the Congressional Budget Office does for Congress at the national level. They empower the legislature to question the assumptions in the executive budget and enable it to formulate its own alternatives without jeopardizing budget balance. In 1988 forty-two legislative budget offices (out of sixty-two respondents) listed as a primary task preparing legislative alternatives to executive budget recommendations. Twenty-nine reported as a primary responsibility serving as staff for revenue committees, while thirty-six had major responsibility for analyzing tax legislation and thirty-two had major responsibility for revenue forecasting. About half the sixty-two responding offices described fiscal noting (describing the cost and impacts of legislation as it is being considered) as an important part of their work. Legislative budget staff also reviewed spending proposals coming up from the agencies. In eight states, the legislative finance office actually issues guidance to the executive branch offices for their budget submissions.[18]

In the standard model of executive budgeting, the governor's office gives budget advice to the agencies, then collects proposals from the agencies, cuts them back, and forwards the whole budget proposal to the legislature for its consideration. In that model, the governor's policies form the framework for consideration of the budget. Most of the states have some form of executive budget, but most of them do not actually carry out the budget process in the way prescribed by the model. In reality, many state agencies submit their proposals to the legislature at the same time or before they submit it to the governor's budget office. This submission process enhances the legislature's budget power in comparison to the governor's. On the other hand, it may leave the legislature mired in details of agency operations because the executive budget office has not sifted through the requests before the legislative branch receives them.

In 1983 the legislatures in forty-one states received budget proposals from the executive agencies before the governor's office had put the budget proposal together; by 1988 that number had risen to forty-three, but by 1997 only thirty-two states reported that the legislature received these proposals from executive agencies before the governor prepared his proposal. In 1983 three state legislatures received agency budgets only through the governor; by 1997 eight received the agencies' budget proposals only through the governor.[19] Thus there was more willingness on the part of the state legislatures to work with the governor's proposal, which the legislatures have the capacity to second-guess if they want to. As state legislatures increased their budgeting capacity and expertise, they gradually dropped their agency micro-management.

Legislatures may have been more willing to work with the governors' proposals as those proposals became more readable and informative. In 1997 NASBO, the association of State Budget Officers, listed fourteen states that used performance budgeting as a major budget approach, and it reported that all but two states used some performance measures, whether the results were published or not.[20] But the main reason seems to be that the legislatures were able to exert influence over the executive's budget proposal and therefore did not have to go to the trouble of putting one together all by themselves.

Even when a legislature relied on the governor's budget proposal, it was generally not a rubber stamp, but increasingly put its own imprint on the budget. The Wisconsin legislature was having a much more important effect on policy-laden budget decisions in 1985 than it had a decade earlier.[21] More broadly, the number of states in which participants considered that the legislature was dominant in budgeting or that power was reasonably evenly split between the governor and legislature increased over the 1980s.[22] Part of the reason for the shift back to more balance between executive and legislative budgeting powers was the professionalization of the legislature. Legislators came to budgetary decision making better prepared.

A study of Georgia indicates how state legislatures used their staff to increase their influence. During the 1980s the state legislature began to do its own estimates of the cost of the continuation budget, that is, how much it would cost to provide this year's level of services next year. That figure influenced how much revenue was available to commit. When the legislature estimated the continuation costs lower than the executive, it freed up money for the legislature to use in putting its own priorities into the budget without running deficits.[23]

MINICASE: ILLINOIS STATE BUDGETING:
THE GOVERNOR AND THE LEGISLATURE

The example of Illinois shows a continuing centralization of the executive branch, with the creation of the Bureau of the Budget and the limited reduction in the number of elected executive officers, and with the expanded veto power of the governor. The case also illustrates the legislature's parallel efforts to reform itself and to increase its budgetary powers. Although the executive is still dominant in Illinois, the tendency of the legislature—even in this strong governor state—to increase its policy capacity over the budget is apparent.

On the executive side, the first major change was the creation of the Bureau of the Budget. The Bureau of the Budget grew out of the Illinois Budgetary Commission, created in 1937 by Governor Henry Horner to study revenue problems.[24] He created this committee when his proposed tax increase (3 percent on utility sales) was defeated. Though its initial charter did not include any budgeting functions, it came to review department requests and give informal advice to the governor. The committee included the governor and legislative elites, and hence became a liaison between the governor and the legislature. Its raison d'être was to give the governor advice on spending proposals. When governors chose not to use it, the commission had no legitimate source of power. If the governor accepted its recommendations, legislative-executive cooperation was established.

In the mid-1950s a financial scandal resulted in more responsibility being put on the commission, with a staff and resources assigned to it. By 1969, however, the governor, with the reluctant consent of the legislature, abolished the commission and set up an executive Bureau of the Budget (BOB). The Bureau of the Budget has been strengthened considerably since its founding.

Under Governor Richard Ogilvie (1968–72), the Bureau of the Budget got to make some policy. "Ogilvie's BOB and the often intimidating 'whiz kids' who ran it were usually at the center of, and the source of, major controversies over State expenditures and their policy implications. For the first time, Illinois had an executive budget process and a staff to run it, which could accommodate serious analysis of issues, alternatives, spending levels and finances."[25]

Governor Dan Walker (1972–76) reined in BOB staff, arguing they should "help solve problems and achieve financial accountability but under no circumstances were they to speak for him or to make decisions on matters of program and policy."[26] Walker doubted the usefulness of the planning capacity built into BOB under Ogilvie, and largely dismantled it.[27] Under Governor James Thompson, the BOB continued to play some policy role in its reviews of the departmental budget proposals.

Parallel with these changes, in the mid-1960s the legislature began to reform itself. It created a bipartisan staffing system and standing committees for policy development and oversight and initiated annual and interim sessions. The period of reform culminated in the constitutional convention of 1970 and a new constitution for the state. The 1970 constitution gave the governor a reduction and an amendatory veto, greatly adding to the governor's power to reduce the budget and implement his own budget request. The constitution eliminated only one of the elected executive offices, but made the governor and lieutenant governor partners. The constitution tried to balance the powers of the governor by increasing somewhat the power of the legislature. The auditor of public accounts was replaced by the controller, who provided an alternative to the governor and his budget bureau. And the constitution gave post-audit powers to the legislature.

The legislature remains relatively weak in budget matters, with the governor exercising his veto power with considerable frequency.[28] There is no evidence that the increased powers of the governor have reduced spending or improved the balance in the budget. Recent governors have been concerned with distributive politics, and have often hidden the extent of continuing fiscal problems. The success of the reform in reducing expenditures and increasing efficiency depends on the existence of a legislature that is not overly responsive to interest groups and constituents, and on a reform-minded governor. When both pieces are not in place, giving more power to the governor does not have much visible impact on outcomes. Given the apparent incorrectness of the model that argues that more executive budget power is more financially healthy, there has been an increase in sentiment in recent years to curtail the governor's extremely strong veto. It is not clear when this change will happen, but even in Illinois, which is a very strong executive budget state, there is sentiment for a more balanced role for the legislature.

While the case of Illinois suggests some rebalancing of powers in an extreme case of executive budget powers, the state of Florida offers an example of a state where the legislature has dramatically asserted its legislative budget powers in recent years.

**MINICASE: THE EXECUTIVE AND THE LEGISLATURE
IN FLORIDA'S BUDGETING**

Before the reapportionment of the legislature in 1967, Florida's budgeting was dominated by the governor.[29] The first major change was a relative weakening of the governor's powers when the constitution added six officials who would be elected statewide. These department heads thus had as much political support as the governor, making it difficult for the governor to control the departments. Once the governor had been weakened, the legislature stepped into the vacuum. It began to build up its own staff capability and no longer had to depend on executive staffs for information and research.[30]

The next major change occurred in the early 1980s. One observer suggested that the legislature felt that Governor Robert Graham was usurping its constitutional budget power.[31] Another observer suggested that the governor's budget office "bungled its math."[32] In any case, in 1983 the legislature took the opportunity to change Florida's budget law, mandating the format and content of the budget in considerable detail and requiring the governor's staff and the legislative staff to jointly develop the budget instructions sent to the agencies. Most important, the new law directed the agencies to "submit their independent judgment of their needs to the legislature." The legislature also strengthened its budgetary oversight role, reviewing extensively budget changes initiated by the executive during the year.[33]

Florida's governor is now considered weak in budgeting because, although the governor develops budget recommendations that are released with great fanfare six weeks before the opening of the legislative session, the agencies (his and those outside his purview, such as those controlled by the other six officials elected statewide) and the judicial branch release their budget proposals to the governor and to the legislature at the same time on a shared computer system. The legislature is free to consult with agency personnel and the legislative staff develops its own set of budget recommendations for its appropriations committees. Agency heads, even if appointed by the governor, can do end runs around him, depending upon the individual political power of the agency head. Even powerful people who are below agency-head level can exert more power on their issues if they are backed by an active and interested constituency. Reportedly, one doctor who headed up children's medical services for years could go directly to the legislative leaders for anything he wanted. Agency heads learn that their chief customer is the legislature. The governor's budget recommendations are essentially "Dead on Arrival" when delivered. One long-time observer of budgeting in Florida summarized, "The balance of power in state budgeting in Florida is only slightly less legislatively controlled than in Texas, where a joint legislative council creates the budget."[34]

Changes in Budget Process at the Local Level

The budget process in cities has taken on different characteristics over time, depending on whether budgeting was occurring during a time of economic and governmental expansion or contraction. But there has never been a simple one-to-one relationship between growth or cutback and budget processes.

The financial history of Cleveland, Ohio, illustrates the excesses of many cities in building railroads at public expense in the mid-1800s and the increase in state and local limits on taxing and spending. In the effort to control local spending, governmental structures were decentralized, power was fragmented, and any kind of concerted action or plan became difficult. By 1890, however, Cleveland had created a modern executive budget, centralizing budget power in the hands of the mayor.

MINICASE: CLEVELAND, OHIO

Cleveland was incorporated in 1814 and was granted limited taxing power.[35] Property tax rates were not to exceed 1 percent of the value of property and were to be in proportion to the value of the property. The treasurer collected taxes and paid out expenses on the order of the trustees. In 1833 there was some expansion of taxing powers for public works—there was a limited tax for some areas to protect against lake damage, use of a poll tax for roads, and a pro rata tax for benefits from sidewalks and streets. In the 1836 charter, the mayor and council were granted the right to tax more broadly. Borrowing for railroad projects became excessive, however, and in 1851 the state legislature stepped in and limited taxing and borrowing. Restrictions were tight, and the city had to apply for special grants to cover spending.

In line with the withdrawal of the right to borrow and raise revenues, the city's organization was decentralized between 1852 and 1891 to a series of commissions and boards. A board of improvements was supposed to check ill-considered plans for improvements. In response to the revenue constraints, this board developed a system of special assessments to relieve the stressed general fund. The board consisted of the mayor, a civil engineer, chairman of the council committee on streets, and one street commissioner elected for two years. Its power over public improvements became absolute after 1868.[36]

The municipal code of 1869 carried further the substitution of administrative boards for council committees. Four of eleven boards created were elected; four were approved by the mayor and council and one by the council alone; two were ex officio. The decentralized boards had no interest in the whole. The efficiency and economy of the board system were soon questioned, but it took another fifteen years to bring about change in it.

For the first half of the nineteenth century, the city had no modern budget. There was a specific property tax levy for most of the major departments. The departments, boards, and officers relied on probable income from levies. Before 1873 a large number of funds annually showed deficits, which were funded, and then the process was repeated the following year. The law forbade the practice, but the provision was constantly violated. No department knew what spending would be allowed, since it could go over its levy and have the difference made up later. The auditor borrowed from funds running a surplus to cover those running deficits.[37] The decentralized board system, with its lack of concern for the whole, fueled the problem.

In 1873 the auditor began the first budget when he sent the council a statement of estimated revenues and expenditures with an apportionment to different departments. Requests from the departments were gross and allocations were gross in this early budget form. By 1890 the city passed the requirement for a modern budget in which the council had to pass detailed and specific appropriations for the functions the city had to provide. Within three years, the mayor declared each fund balanced.

The budget pattern adopted in Cleveland in 1890 was distinctly oriented toward fiscal control. The departments were to make estimates to the auditor and the mayor, who were to present statements to the council, along with the previous year's expenses, and the previous five years' expenses. The mayor was to present the annual budget; the council was free to omit items or reduce them, but was not allowed to increase the total. Similarly, the mayor was given the power to alter requests coming from the departments, but was not allowed to increase the totals of those requests. The council's role was to examine and pass the budget, and to set the property tax levy. Its recommendations for taxes had then to be reviewed and approved by a tax board. If the board were to reject proposed tax levies, it would take a three-fourths vote for the council to override. The tax board routinely passed requests in the early 1900s.

Shortly after the budget was modernized, the city succeeded in reforming its extremely decentralized structure. The financial powers of the council were greatly increased. As part of the reform, spending bills, revenue bills, and contracts had to be introduced a week before passage to allow for examination and consideration of the measures. The council's responsibilities included setting salaries for police and fire chiefs, police officers, and firemen. They also set water rates. On the executive side, the reform set up a half dozen departments, each headed by a director, appointed by the mayor with the consent of the council. The mayor, with the department heads of the six departments, formed a board of control, which took over the functions of the old board of improvements and the commissioner of sewers. This form of government was declared unconstitutional in 1902, but it coincided with the period of the introduction of the budget, and the two together probably accounted for the improved financial integrity of the city.

The financial history of Cleveland in the 1800s was not unusual. The 1800s were characterized by initial grants of taxing authority, which were abused; in the rush to control the cities, the states limited their borrowing and taxing powers. Internally, the cities' organization shifted to an extreme decentralization, which was inefficient and lacking in financial control. Limitation of the power of taxation was accompanied by a fiscal demoralization. The early reform period at the end of the 1800s was characterized by reorganization for capacity, with budgeting and financial control as dual focuses.

Municipal budgets originated as a control mechanism after the Civil War, during a period of major spending growth. Early budgets were estimates of how much taxes would be required, based on detailed accounts of receipts and expenditures for preceding years. Officials submitted detailed requests. Typically, the head of the finance department, the controller, the auditor, or the mayor would receive and cut back these requests, or in smaller cities, the departments would forward their requests directly to the council or the budget committee.

To control nonapproved spending during the year some cities adopted annual appropriations, fixing expenditures for the year. Cleveland, Boston,

Denver, Minneapolis, and Omaha all had appropriations budgets, and state law required appropriations in Illinois, Indiana, and New York.[38]

The 1870s and 1880s were years of sharp economic and governmental contraction for most cities. The focus of budgeting became one of keeping government small and inactive. Beginning in 1873 in New York City, a form of budgeting appeared in which budget estimates from the departments went to a board of estimate, variously composed, but generally consisting of the mayor, controller, president of the board of aldermen, and others. It is difficult to get a board of independently elected officials to agree to the same projects, which slows down spending.

The extent to which the boards of estimates were viewed as a way of curtailing tax levies is underscored by a description of how the Board of Estimates actually worked in New York City. In the early days of the board, aldermen would add to the recommended amounts. From 1873 to 1888 they added on average about $500,000 annually. But they were constantly overruled by the Board of Estimates. Over time, the aldermen added less and less. "Responding to consistent pressure for economy in government, particularly from middle-class groups experiencing the brunt of taxation, the Board of Estimates ignored the proposed increases of the council and continued to reduce the level of public expenditures."[39] By 1898 the charter granted the council some formal budget authority, but only to decrease the estimates. If the mayor vetoed any reductions made by the council, a five-sixths majority was required to overturn. There was to be no reconsideration by the Board of Estimates after council action.[40]

During the Progressive era expansion (from about 1895 to about 1920), the focus of budgeting shifted from keeping government small and ineffective to combining activism with efficiency and accountability. The result was a major push for a single executive responsible for the budget. Executive budget reform reflected the Progressive era sense of government as a necessary counterbalance to business and a major provider of services, but at the same time it reflected the perceived need to control government and provide accountability. The single executive reforms reflected as well the notion of government moving on a plan, of change in an agreed-on direction, rather than the random expenditures of a council and a pork-driven budget.

The massive expenditure increases that characterized the early 1900s through the early 1920s stimulated interest in cost accounting and additional techniques for public accountability, and the first tentative steps were taken toward performance measurement. The gradual adoption of the executive budget process in Boston, which culminated in the charter reform of 1909, illustrates the simultaneous increase of the budget power of the mayor, the weakening of the budget power of the council, and the increasing control (centralization) of the mayor over the executive departments. The timing of the major steps to Boston's executive budget reflects Boston's somewhat earlier adoption of Progressive era reforms and increased spending than occurred elsewhere.

The charter of 1854 gave the mayor a veto over all acts of the city council and all acts of either branch that involved the expenditure of money.[41] His veto could be overturned by a two-thirds vote. Despite this important grant of authority, in other ways the charter limited the mayor's powers. The city council "would not limit its executive power" and established "still more firmly government by committee."[42] By 1885, however, a new charter provided for separation of the executive and the legislative and took detailed budget-making authority away from the council and gave it to the mayor. The mayor was given the power to hire and fire department heads and to approve any expenditure over $2000. The mayor's veto power was enhanced to include an item veto.[43] The charter of 1909 extended the role of the mayor from budget implementation and fiscal control to budget proposal. The council's power was limited to reducing or omitting items; they could no longer add new items. The mayor was given an absolute veto power over all acts of the city council—he could veto part of an item, not simply a whole item.[44]

To summarize, the early history of budgeting in cities began with broader grants of taxing powers to deal with rapid growth in the mid-1800s; these taxing powers were often abused, especially with such capital projects as the acquisition of railroads to promote economic development. The recession that began in 1873 ushered in a period of contraction in many cities, which was marked by tax limits and by structural mechanisms to render budgeting difficult, slow, and inefficient. These budget processes indeed kept the costs of government down but did not help cities solve the growing problems of urbanization. As the need for more activist and problem-solving government forged new political coalitions, new forms of budgeting emerged that combined cost controls with the potential for activism; they simultaneously provided accountability, activism, and cost control in the form of the strong mayor who presided over a more centralized bureaucracy and was responsible for the budget.

The themes of activism in problem solving and efficient and accountable government remained strong in succeeding periods when social and economic problems accumulated and became urgent. The council-manager form that began to gain popularity after World War I reflected those themes and added two new ones, the importance of hiring a technical expert (the city manager) to solve problems and the subordination of politics to problem solving.

The issue of accountability became more acute under this form because of its emphasis on eliminating political machines that linked people directly to government. Accountability was to be formally provided by the frequently exercised right of city councils to fire the manager if he (early managers were males, frequently engineers) did not do as they wished. But accountability was also provided by improved budget documents that demonstrated how well public money was being spent.

The major spurts in adoptions of the council-manager form occurred after the two world wars. From 1945 to 1959 the number of council-manager adoptions increased from 637 to almost 1,500.[45] One reason was that the infrastructure of the cities was in a state of neglect and technical problems seemed to require competent staff and an activist approach.

The modern history of budget processes in cities has been parallel in some ways to the state and federal governments, but it has been different in other ways. Cities responded to the same waves of reform that affected the federal and state governments and adopted some of the same reforms. While there was a distinct flavor of efficiency and keeping costs and waste down, there was also a flavor about the city changes that emphasized capacity to respond to problems.

The executive budget reforms went even further in the cities than they went in the states, often limiting the ability of the councils to change the executive's budget recommendations. City councils still do not generally have much budget expertise or a separate professional staff to help them question executive budget proposals or formulate their own. There are still a few cities in which the council prepares the budget, but they are quite rare.

Even so, the direction of change is toward more participation by councils in budgetary decision making. A recent survey of cities over 100,000 population found that 44 percent of city budget or finance officers perceived that the influence of the municipal legislative body in the budgeting and appropriations process had increased in recent years; 8 percent indicated council influence had decreased. The reasons they gave included a more interested and involved and better qualified city council. They also argued that declining federal revenues and fiscal stress were factors.[46]

One reason for increased council participation is an increase in the number of council-manager cities since the end of World War II. More recently, the trend away from completely at-large to at least partly district elections to increase minority and neighborhood representation on city councils may have increased council participation. Neighborhood-based representatives might be more likely to fight for neighborhood capital projects and actively resist cutbacks that affect their territories.[47] Another possible reason for increased council participation is that municipal budgets have become much clearer and easier to follow, even for nontechnically trained elected officials.

The recent history of municipal budget formats begins in the 1950s. Cities began to adopt performance budgeting after the Hoover Commission report in

1949, which advised the federal government to adopt performance budgeting. Los Angeles was one of the early municipal adopters, beginning its performance budgeting in fiscal year 1953.[48] But performance measurement did not suit the needs of the time in the growth period of the 1950s and 1960s.

Performance budgeting focused on efficiency, being good at whatever the public organization does; it is not particularly useful in helping make decisions between competing ends, or deciding what the organization should be doing. It was to meet this need that PPBS (Planning Programming Budgeting Systems) was developed and implemented. During the period of rapid growth of the 1950s, 1960s, and early 1970s, the planning focus of PPB was more attractive, although in some cities, the planning and performance approaches merged.

As with performance measurement, the formal stimulus was from the federal government, which had experimented with PPB first. With the aid of a grant, an experimental program called the 5-5-5 program introduced PPB to five states, five counties, and five cities.[49] The experiment began in 1968. More than five cities became involved with the planning and analysis of PPB, however. In early evaluations, more than fifty local governments reported at least beginning steps on PPB. The George Washington University research team that evaluated early efforts at implementing PPB noted that the prospect that program analysis would be a requirement for receiving federal grants promoted cities' interest. "The cities, with Model City fund applications and approval by the U.S. Department of Housing and Urban Development still ahead, anticipated that a start on PPB would help them gain the federal agency funds."[50] Many of the cities that tried it did so with lukewarm commitment, however, to see how it would work. Some found it too cumbersome or too expensive and dropped it when the recessions of the mid-1970s hit; others tried the system but modified the parts they liked best and dropped the rest.

PPB's emphasis on planning worked best in an environment of growing resources, when choosing programs and defining city goals were immediate policy decisions. But by the middle of the 1970s the financial situation had changed, first with a deep recession and then, in the later 1970s, with the decline in federal aid dollars and taxpayer revolts and then, in the early 1980s, with a second deep recession. In this environment, some cities began to experiment with zero-based budgeting. For example, Oakland, California, drew up a zero-based budget to help it handle anticipated cuts resulting from California's Proposition 13, which was passed in 1978.[51]

Zero-based budgeting was very cumbersome. A number of officials worked out and used modifications of it called target-based budgets. The departments calculate a constant services budget—how much it would cost next year to provide this year's level of service. The budget office, based on its estimates of revenues, then gives each department a target, which may be below the constant-services level. No department's request may exceed the target level. The departments then formulate lists of high-priority items that are unfunded, which include projects or programs that have been squeezed out of their base budgets by low targets as well as some new items. They rank their lists of high-priority unfunded items. Then city officials (which officials actually do this varies from city to city) merge and rerank the departments' priority lists until they can create a citywide list. Whatever money is available from new revenues or from service cuts or giving up low-priority programs is allocated down the priority list until the money gives out.

This system has proven well adapted to pressure to reduce property taxes. The targets are driven by estimates of revenues. Politicians can lower property tax rates and force cuts by reducing targets. This has proven a fairly common use of the system by mayors intent on taking the credit for lowering property taxes. Target-based budgeting also creates some discretion for policy making for political leaders within extremely constrained budgets, since mild cuts plus new revenues can be used to reallocate between departments for high-priority, citywide projects, such as economic development, housing, or crime control. The departments find their chances of getting funding over the targets much improved if they suggest projects high on the mayor's or manager's priority list.

Though the target system also works reasonably well during growth, cities that have adopted it have often done so under the pressure of fiscal problems and with the desire to keep departmental requests to a moderate level. An interesting element of the system is that while it reserves policy decisions to top officials, it forces decisions between projects and expenditures as much as possible back on the departments. It thus offers a new balance between top-down and bottom-up budgeting.

MINICASE: TARGET-BASED BUDGETING IN TAMPA

Tampa uses a form of target-based budgeting. The former budget director, Al Desilet, on whose watch target-based budgeting was begun, explained how it worked and why the city started to use this form of budgeting:

> Each department has a target that is different. We take policy statements and factor them in. And then ask the mayor whether we should have more police or less, more recreation or less. Suppose the mayor says, we need another division in recreation, we factor that in.

Desilet explained that once the departments had been assigned their targets, they had to stay within them, no matter what happened during the year. If oil prices went up, the departments had to absorb the increase by cutting something else. On the other hand, if costs went down, the departments had flexibility to spend the money on high priority items.

Desilet described the origin of the program in terms of his relationship as budget director with the departments:

> I had been there before, but did not like receiving ridiculous budget requests. I spent 10 years receiving budget requests that were 30–40 percent too high. My job was to find what to cut, that is silly, for a budget officer to do that. They did not tell me what needed to be funded. I played the "it's time to cut the budget" game. It was awfully stupid. That is why I did what I did.
>
> It was my opinion a professional in charge of a public service would be capable of doing the best he could, given a level of funding. Only he and his staff could do that. No one else can do that. If the police chief says he needs 30 million, how do you ask him what to cut? He will say, I will take policemen off the streets in the ghetto. That is a stupid answer. He won't tell you the soft, discretionary stuff.

In target-based budgeting, the department heads have to make their own decisions about what to cut, and when confronted with real budget ceilings will cut out the softer stuff themselves. There is no one to play budget games with, just a need to come in under the ceiling while providing a promised level of services. Even unnecessary, politically appointed staff were often squeezed out when the departments found they could not afford them.

Target-based budgeting goes on primarily within the executive branch. The role of the legislative branch is minimal, as suggested by this excerpt from an interview. The council is presented with a package that is difficult to change.

> *Author*: What is the role of the legislature in all this?
> *Desilet*: They have to approve the appropriation. They have a hammer.
> *Author*: But in many cities that does not amount to much power.
> *Desilet*: No, its real. They have power, but once the budget is adopted they have no more say. It's not like the council manager

form, where the city manager develops the budget with the council, it's different. Target setting in other forms of government would not work at all well. If there were a 90 percent target [a 10 percent cut from the constant services baseline], three commissioners would say no. Every proposal would have opposition at the legislative level. But deliver a whole package, you can't tax less and spend more, what do you want to do?

Target-based budgeting assumes a strong executive budget process.

Summary and Conclusions

In an overview of the main lines of evolution of budget processes, four themes appear:

- When there is discontent with budgetary outcomes, either in macro policy or micro political terms, and more direct action does not seem feasible, there may be great pressure to change the budget process. An accumulation of debt that eats away at the flexibility necessary for budgeting, a rise in taxes or a change in tax burdens on particular classes or groups, a sharp rise in spending—any of these may prompt a change in budget process. Whenever the distribution of budget power comes to seem too extreme, it seems to swing back in the direction of more balance.

- The long-term trend toward more executive power and the withering away of legislative budget control may have ended, to be replaced with a period of more balanced power between the two. When the executive's budget power becomes too strong, some kind of balancing mechanism seems to come into play. When President Nixon took too much policy control over the budget away from Congress, Congress responded by taking back some budget control and strengthening its own capacity to make budget decisions. At the state level, when the chief executive has extremely strong veto powers that effectively prevent legislators from introducing expenditures that are higher than or even different from the governor's recommendations, then legislators sometimes seek, formally or informally, a greater role in determining the governor's budget recommendations. Alternatively, the legislatures seek professional staff to balance the executive branch staff, and enable them to examine the budget in some detail and make their own policy and draw up their own proposals when they wish. At the local level, strong executive budget powers have led to adaptations that allow the council to influence the policy in the budget while it is being prepared by the executive.

- Legislators at both state and national levels have been willing to give up power when it seemed that their own discipline was inadequate to control debt or spending. While there is much jockeying to maximize power, there have been restraining forces in which political actors give up power to achieve what they perceive as the common good—in fiscal terms, a stable, balanced budget.

- At least on the executive side of the ledger, the long trend toward greater centralization may finally be abating. Cities in particular have markedly increased their use of target-based budgeting, which helps prevent micromanagement from the budget office and gives back many budgetary decisions to the departments. Vice-President Al Gore's National Performance Review reports included a number of recommendations for changing executive budgeting at the national level. Many of these changes argued for greater budgetary control at lower organizational levels.

CHAPTER FIVE

The Politics of Expenditures: Managing Competition, Accountability, and Acceptability

THE POLITICS OF expenditures is the politics of choice. Some budget actors want one thing, some want something else, and there is not enough money to go around. Many budget claimants may get a little bit of what they want, some may get all or almost all of what they want, while others may get nothing or may actually lose benefits to provide others with what they ask for. The elderly may benefit from increased Medicare payments at the expense of reduced college loans to the young; the Defense Department may grow at the expense of housing programs.

The choices in the budget might be based on policies that imply tradeoffs between areas of the budget. One such policy statement might be that the health of agriculture is essential to the economy, so benefit programs must be targeted specifically at farmers. Another example might be that crime suppression is more important than crime prevention, so police must be funded before social services or education. But the choices in the budget might be framed without obvious policy preferences and tradeoffs between areas. The choices might be between two weapons systems with different technical capabilities, or between two different street-improvement plans. The choice might depend only on which claimant has enough support or can negotiate enough support to succeed. The environment might favor some claims over others, exaggerating some needs and toning down others. Jobs programs have more appeal during a long and deep recession; drainage programs have more appeal after a period of serious flooding.

When revenue increases or budget cutbacks are allocated across the board—that is, the same percentage increase or decrease is given to all existing programs—there may not seem to be much choice in the budget. No one program expands faster than others, no program is cut back disproportionately to preserve others. There may be little change from year to year. Nevertheless, budgets make choices between expenditures even when priorities seem to remain the same from year to year. Each year (or each budget cycle) there is a choice of spending revenue increases the same way money was spent in the past, or doing something different with it. There is also a choice of reallocating funds among existing programs or from old to new programs. The decision to keep this year's expenditures the same as last year's is also a choice.

Tradeoffs

Because public budgeting involves a wide variety of actors with different spending goals, the necessity of choice in the budget leads to competition between actors, between programs, and between beneficiaries. Sometimes this competition results in highly visible tradeoffs.

MINICASE: TRADEOFFS IN THE BUDGET UNDER THE FEDERAL BUDGET ENFORCEMENT ACT

Budgets are inherently conflictual; there is always more demand for public spending than there is money. Some requests are cut while others are funded. When revenues are increasing, it is difficult for citizens to see what request is being cut to fund what other priorities. But since the 1990 Budget Enforcement Act instituted spending caps, tradeoffs have become more visible. It is now possible to see what trades for what.

Each appropriations subcommittee has a spending cap; if a subcommittee wishes to give one agency in its jurisdiction more money, it must take the money from elsewhere in its jurisdiction to stay under the caps. How a program fares depends not only on national priorities, but also on what other programs compete with it on the same subcommittee.

One of the appropriations subcommittees has jurisdiction over the Department of Housing and Urban Development (HUD), the Veterans Administration, and assorted independent agencies such as the Federal Emergency Management Agency (FEMA). These agencies compete with one another not because they are similar or working toward the same goals, but because they are in the jurisdiction of the same subcommittee.

Similarly, Commerce, Justice, and State are all in the jurisdiction of a single subcommittee, so Department of Commerce programs such as the

TABLE 5.1   OUTLAYS BY AGENCY, 1980–1997 (IN MILLIONS OF DOLLARS)

| | AGENCY | | |
YEAR	Commerce	State	Justice
1980	3,129	1,940	2,538
1981	2,296	1,902	2,641
1982	2,054	2,186	2,695
1983	1,925	2,273	2,617
1984	1,895	2,404	2,849
1985	2,140	2,645	3,586
1986	2,083	2,865	3,768
1987	2,127	2,788	4,333
1988	2,279	3,421	5,426
1989	2,571	3,722	6,232
1990	3,734	3,979	6,507
1991	2,585	4,252	8,244
1992	2,567	5,007	9,802
1993	2,798	5,384	10,170
1994	2,915	5,718	10,005
1995	3,702	5,344	10,708
1996	3,702	4,951	11,954
1997	3,783	5,237	14,310

Source: Historical Tables of the U.S. Budget, 1998.

Census Bureau and the National Weather Service have to compete with programs of the Department of State and the Department of Justice (which
houses the FBI and the Drug Enforcement Agency). If one of these departments or programs is highly popular and/or seems to require an increase,
the others have to take a hit or grow more slowly. Table 5.1 illustrates the
relative budgets of the three departments from 1980 to 1997. Starting with
budgets of about the same size, Commerce grew 20.9 percent; the Department of State, 169 percent; and the Department of Justice, 463 percent.
These figures are a little misleading, however, because they start Commerce
off from a very high level established by the extra funding for the 1980
census, making its rate of growth seem slower than it was. Changing the
base year to 1983, after the Commerce Department had come down off the
census level (and experienced cuts in addition), the growth figures are Commerce, 101 percent; State, 130 percent; and Justice, 446 percent.

Administrators in programs located in the Department of Commerce
reported that they felt they were competing only with those on their subcommittee. For example, Wilbur Hawkins of the Economic Development Adminis-

tration (EDA) in the Commerce Department argued that "Commerce, Justice and State are tied together. EDA in Commerce, competes with programs in CJS [Commerce, Justice and State]. Irrelevant to Interior or other committees."

Not only do departments compete with other departments and programs on the same subcommittee, they are increasingly forced to make tradeoffs within their own departments. If one program absolutely requires an increase, such as the Census Bureau when it is approaching the decennial census, that increase means cuts in other programs in the same department. The Commerce Department was told to find the money in other programs to pay for the census count:

> Your budget request for 1998 totals $4.223 billion, which would be an increase of $466 million or 12 percent above the amount that Congress provided for the current year. Let me start by saying that this is going to be another year of tough budget constraints. We understand that you're in a ramp-up mode for the census.
>
> The difficulty for the Subcommittee is that we're likely to be faced with overall budget constraints. So, in order to fund increases in one place, we may have no option but to find reductions in other places.
>
> We're going to look very hard at all programs to squeeze out any additional funding that may be needed. And certainly your ideas are going to be the driving force in that job of setting priorities.[1]

Just as regular appropriations come under the caps, so does (nonemergency) supplemental spending during the year. Any proposed nonemergency supplemental had to be offset with a reduction in spending somewhere else. Tradeoffs were even more visible and problematic in supplemental than in regular appropriations. The norms indicated that offsets should be drawn primarily from the same subcommittees that had increased spending, in order to stay under their own caps, but the possibility remained that one committee could raid another by proposing an offset from another subcommittee. The range of possible tradeoffs thus expanded during the process of funding supplementals.

Funding supplementals was often accomplished by gathering up unspent funds, even if they were only temporarily unspent. Thus unspent funds became highly precious sources of revenue, leading to uneven trades whereby some agencies gave more heavily than others because they were more likely to have reserves or to be able to create unspent funds through scoring changes. As Congress became more assiduous in searching out and using carryover funds of various sorts, some agencies became more cautious about leaving those funds uncommitted. The National Oceanic and Atmospheric Administration (NOAA) at one point committed funds for a major purchase well in advance of need, thereby preventing Congress from using the funds, much to the aggravation of its subcommittee.

One of the major trades was from low-income housing to FEMA. One congressperson estimated, "In the past 2 years, including this [supplemental] legislation before us today, we have cut almost $12 billion from other VA-HUD programs—principally low-income housing—to pay for FEMA disaster relief." The need to come up with money from low-income housing for FEMA resulted in part from prior years' efforts to take money from FEMA for presidential initiatives. Funding for FEMA varies from year to year, and it can be difficult to predict not only when a disaster will strike, but how long before all the bills come in for that disaster. Thus in one year costs may be lower than budgeted for, and in another year higher. Budgeting for FEMA in advance helped reduce its impact on the deficit, but created an unevenness in spending that had to be covered somehow.

Taking the money from HUD Section 8 to fund FEMA was problematic because HUD was going to need that money to pay for renewing contracts. The "savings" from reducing the size of reserves should have gone to HUD to help pay for the program itself. Some members of Congress, disturbed by the implications of the tradeoffs, tried to set up a fund in which HUD savings would be put aside in anticipation of increased housing contract renewals.

For 1998, however, Congress did not abide by its own policy. The unobligated reserves for Section 8 were set aside to fund the contract renewals, but when it came time for supplemental appropriations, the temptation to spend those balances on something else proved too great. Representative Lucille Roybal-Allard (D-Calif.) objected to the tradeoff. She called attention to the fact that the defense allocation was not paying for the military part of the supplemental; housing for the poor was paying for the war in Bosnia:

> It is unconscionable that badly needed funding to support our troops in Bosnia and Iraq, and disaster relief for states like California, which have sustained upwards of $500 million in damages this winter, are unnecessarily being pitted against important programs which benefit the American people.

> Despite the fact that more than 80 percent of the funds in this bill are for the Department of Defense, the Republican majority has not offset these costs by making one cut in defense spending. Instead, they have chosen to play partisan political games by making cuts in programs they know the administration and Democrats cannot support.
>
> For example, Republicans have chosen to make cuts in education, the AmeriCorps Service Program, which gives disadvantaged youth a chance, and the Section 8 Program, which provides critically needed housing for our Nation's families, the elderly, and the disabled.[2]
>
> All budgets contain tradeoffs. The budget process and its constraints determine how clear these tradeoffs will be. They also frame the comparisons, so some particular programs compete with each other.

How is this competition handled in the politics of expenditures? One model prevalent in the 1960s and 1970s envisioned the politics of expenditures as bargaining between individuals, each with personal goals, to influence budget outcomes. This competition was constrained by shared understandings that developed over time, and by decision rules, often formulas, that created fairness in the distribution of resources. The result was that no one asked for too much and that new revenues were allocated in small amounts, pretty much in the same way that previous revenues had been allocated. Competition was minimized by mutual consent. This model may have been accurate at some times and in some places, but it has to be modified considerably to describe most of contemporary public spending.

One of the reasons that this model (called *incrementalism*) is inapplicable to contemporary budgeting is that norms of moderation in making budget requests and norms of fairness of allocating increases in revenues can only operate to limit claims on the budget and constrain allocations if every budget actor knows what every other actor gets from the budget process. An agency head is not likely to be constrained in asking for more if he or she feels that other agencies may have received more in the previous year. In recent years, especially at the national level, the variety of resources spent and the relative invisibility of some of those resources make it nearly impossible to compare budget outcomes; moreover, multiyear projects, cutbacks during the year, and supplemental appropriations may introduce changes during the year, making keeping up with others' funding levels very time-consuming if not impossible.

A second problem with the incremental model of moderation is that norms of fairness and moderation apply only to actors in the government who have to deal with one another year after year; they do not apply to interest-group representatives whose goal is to get as much as possible from the budget and have no interest whatsoever in what anyone else receives.

To the extent that internal actors cannot compare the increments they received to make sure they were fairly allocated, and to the extent that external actors such as interest groups are involved in making budgetary demands, competition may be intense and may not be regulated by shared understandings and decision rules. The result is more variability in budget proposals, more range of choice, and more competition between expenditures.

The model of restrained bargaining among actors is flawed in other ways as well. It underestimates the importance of the budget process in regulating competition; it underplays the fact that various budget actors have different capacities to mobilize support, which means that the playing field is not even to start with; and it underemphasizes the role of the environment in setting constraints on revenue totals, and on preferences for particular programs. Budgeting takes place in a political environment in which spending has to match public preferences at least roughly. Citizens may rebel against certain programs they do not want to fund or demand the continuation of existing programs. These preferences may become constraints that budget actors have to work around. Allocation of expenditures is not just a matter of bargaining between a limited set of internal actors.

The constraints of the environment and the budget process make the success of individuals' budget strategies conditional. A particular strategy might be successful at one time and fail at another time, or be successful in one budget process and fail in another. For example, an agency that tries to bypass the budget scrutiny of the executive budget office and make its presentation directly to the legislature might be successful in a legislatively dominated budget process and fail dismally in a centralized executive budget process. Even the best-conceived plans for program expansion will fail if the environment dictates cutbacks because of sharp revenue declines. The politics of expenditures is not an open competition of all against all, with the best strategists winning; it is bargaining among unequals, within a changing environment that shifts the goals and the level of discretion; it is also bargaining within a process that structures the level of competition and gives some interests a better chance than others.

The four characteristics of public budgeting outlined in chapter 1 help explain the politics of expenditures. These characteristics are: multiple actors with different goals; a budget process filled with constraints about what can and cannot be done; decision making that is open and vulnerable to the environment; and a separation between those who make spending decisions and those who pay taxes.

Multiple Actors Compete for Spending Preferences

All budget processes involve choice, but the number of actors involved in public spending decisions, their variety, and the variety of their spending preferences all contribute to a structurally high level of competition. The chief executive is likely to have a policy or a series of programs that he or she would like to support or terminate; legislators may support some of those programs but not others; agency heads are likely to support the narrower goals of their own programs, each agency head representing some potential demand on the budget. Interest groups typically request spending that favors that interest group, introducing a wide variety of possible requests. In a city, the animal protection league, the historical preservation society, the public housing board, the downtown business association, the library, the spouse-abuse center, the student association of the university, and supporters of the airport might all make spending proposals in a given year.

Groups can make narrow or broad demands. On the narrow end are demands such as providing shelter for the homeless or requesting sewer repairs in a given neighborhood. On the broad end, political parties or coalitions of interest groups of the political right or left may demand particular patterns of spending. Many Republicans, for example, favor increases in defense spending and oppose spending on regulatory agencies and many social services; many Democrats favor more social spending and less spending on defense. Party activists may try to implement these spending preferences through the political party organization.

Competition is keen because there are more demands than revenues, but it can be made keener when the competing interests are in some sense oppositional, so that the gains of one group may be seen as losses for another. Spending on agriculture and interstate highways is seen as spending for rural areas; spending for urban renewal or mass transit is viewed as spending for cities. These are viewed as oppositional. Spending for the elderly, such as on Social Security or Medicare, is viewed as oppositional to spending on the young, as in programs for educational loans. Spending for the downtown area is often seen as antagonistic to spending for the neighborhoods. And spending for defense is seen as antagonistic to spending on social services.

How this competition is reflected in budgetary decision making depends a lot on the budget process and the budget format. If comparisons are framed between antagonistic programs, the amount of competition may be severe enough to slow down or even disrupt decision making. For example, when DeKalb, Illinois, had to deal with the loss of revenue sharing, decisions about what to cut were framed as basic services (police, fire, streets) versus social services (transportation for the elderly, counseling for abused spouses, and day care).

The resulting controversy was emotional and held up approval of the rest of the budget pending the solution to this problem. Similarly, in 1995, at the national level, budgetary decisions were phrased in terms of health care for the elderly and poor versus tax breaks for the well-to-do. These and other emotionally laden comparisons derailed the budget process, actually closing down portions of the federal government twice because appropriation bills were delayed and the controversy prevented the passage of continuing resolutions.

If the comparisons are framed so that antagonistic programs are not in direct competition with one another, the level of conflict may be dampened. Thus, if there are multiple appropriation bills, one for defense and one for housing, and targets have been set for spending for each one based on the existing allocation plus inflation, housing programs compete with housing programs, and defense programs compete with defense programs, but individual housing programs do not compete with individual defense programs. Budgeters do not ask, Do you want to house the homeless or buy the navy a new helicopter?

No matter how decisions are grouped, there is likely to be competition within the categories for particular pots of money. For example, suppose a budget is divided into capital and operating expenses. (Capital items are goods purchased and/or built by governmental agencies that have a life expectancy of more than two or three years. Operating expenses recur regularly, such as salary, lighting bills, and postage.) If $500,000 is set aside for capital improvements, then all proposed capital improvements must compete with one another for that $500,000. Competition is likely to be acute within the capital budget. If $120,000 is set aside for all social services, then the social services have to compete with one another for the $120,000. When the budget process determines how much money will be set aside for what groupings of expenditures, it regulates who will compete with whom, and for how much money.

One way of dealing with intense competition is to try to raise the priority of one's spending proposal, and one way of increasing the priority of projects or programs is to represent them as solutions to crises or emergencies. The emergency need not be imminent, only easily imaginable. Thus a fire department can make arguments for new equipment in terms of its capacity to save lives in a fire; the Defense Department can argue for new weapons systems because the Russians have more firepower, and what would happen if they attacked us. The possibility of such events may have to be exaggerated to make a powerful case. Supporters of the defense budget, for example, often gave different and sometimes exaggerated estimates of Soviet troop and armament strength in order to justify military buildups in the United States. The information was not blatantly false so much as misleading—saying we had fewer divisions of men under arms than the Soviets, for example, although the size of our divisions was much larger.[3] The tactic of selectively presenting a threatening portrait of the environment in order to justify budget increases can be called "The Russians Are Coming."

At the local level, at a recent budget presentation, a fire department official presented a film of a fire in a residence, with the blaze going from room to room; the film showed the temperatures in each room, the smoke and toxic fumes and the damage done, second by second. One had to conclude that the house could be one's own, and that the quicker the fire department's response time, the safer one's own house and family. The department requested an extra ambulance that year, complete with emergency equipment, and got it, although the justification was garbled and technically weak. The agency could probably have gotten anything it requested after showing that film.

The threat of disastrous consequences if expenditures are not made is particularly common in defense. For example, in 1986, President Reagan argued for a real (above inflation) increase in Defense Department spending because failure to provide increases would risk a return to the problems of the 1970s, "a hollow army, ships that can't sail, and aircraft that can't fly." It would encourage adventurism on the part of the Soviets, and it would weaken the administration's ability to negotiate a satisfactory arms reduction agreement.[4]

The "just imagine what would happen if this purchase were not made" argument has widespread applicability. It requires an imagination and a word picture, or a film or photographs, or even props. A budget presentation at a state university library included a seat back, to illustrate that furniture purchased with the construction of the library was falling apart. The staff member went on to paint a verbal portrait of a crowded library where there were tables but no seats and the students had to sit on the floor. In another example, a director of water and sewer at City Hall argued that he had to have certain new equipment because if he did not, the city sewers would back up into peoples' homes, and council members would get angry complaints from citizens. His brief argument was very vivid and suggestive, both as to events and the probable political consequences.

Another way of reordering priorities is to imply that the current prioritization is too political or too ignorant and that technical scientific analysis indicates that whatever one is after is absolutely necessary and highly desirable. One instance of this argument occurred several years ago in a city that was considering its capital budget, when staff insisted on building a water tower rather than digging a well as was required by a grant the city had received. The staff recommendation tripled the estimated expense. The project was in an undeveloped portion of the city, and the project's intent was to create a visible sign of the available infrastructure to help lure in new business. A well that provided water alone could not provide the same symbol.

When a citizen advisory board member asked why a water tower was necessary when a new well would satisfy the conditions of the grant, the city manager angrily replied that the decision was a technical one and would be made by staff; it was beyond the citizen's competence.[5] The staff later came up with a technical reason for a water tower, to save costs in electricity. The argument then turned on whether there would be a rate increase, and how much it would be; city staff invited a representative of the power company to speak at the budget session, to convince the advisory board that the move to water towers would be cost effective. The project was approved, and the technical argument was the clincher.

The argument that the current allocation scheme is too political was used successfully, with some modification, by universities looking for federal earmarks from Congress (allocations for specific projects). Such projects were identified by opponents as "pork" (benefits that a high-ranking congressperson is able to bring to his or her district). In support of these earmarked, or pork, projects, many university presidents and their supporters in Congress argued that the main method of allocating grants for basic science through peer review was biased, because it was based on an old boy system (a network of people who knew each other and worked together, perhaps went to school together, and all accepted the same orthodoxy) that provided grants only to a handful of elite universities. Other schools, with ideas potentially out of the mainstream, could not get access to federal money. Science as a whole would benefit, these presidents argued, if nonelite schools were funded through earmarked funding specifically reserved for them.[6]

An argument for increasing the priority of routine maintenance or construction of undramatic capital projects is that "it will cost more later." Maintenance projects may be routinely delayed because other needs seem more urgent. To push up the priority of routine tasks, proponents sometimes argue that the costs are inevitable and that doing the projects now will be cheaper than waiting, so the only logical choice is to do them now. Public works directors routinely argue that if roof repairs on public buildings are delayed, rain will cause structural damage and the eventual costs will be many times greater than if the work is done soon. If street maintenance and repair is delayed, the streets will fall apart and have to be rebuilt at much greater costs. Another version of this argument is that whatever project is being proposed is most cost effective—that is, a dollar spent here will have (by implication) a more positive effect than a dollar spent elsewhere.[7] At the federal level, spending for children's programs is justified as an investment. For example, the Children's Defense Fund argued that research proved that such programs as prenatal care and immunization save more money than they cost.[8]

Yet another way of dealing with high levels of competition is to argue that the project will not cost much anyway. One can just slip it into a list of projects and not worry about the priorities because it will not cost much. Sometimes the programs really are not very expensive, but sometimes they are, and the budget strategy is to make them look less expensive than they are. One way to make programs or projects look cheap is to use "free" money, or money whose costs are not obvious. At the local level, grant money from the state or federal government often appears free. From the perspective of the federal government, loan programs often appear cheap or even free because they are usually paid back by the borrower.[9]

Many other techniques have been employed at all levels of government to make programs look inexpensive. Sometimes these techniques revolve around substituting leases for purchases, which shifts expenditures from highly visible capital budgets to much less visible operating budgets. Sometimes governments make costs of programs less visible by using tax breaks instead of outlays; in this manner, revenues are never collected or due, and hence they may never appear in the budget as an outlay, though the money is spent as surely as if the revenue were collected and then disbursed. Recent trends in tax expenditure reporting at the state level have made this strategy less effective in reducing the visibility of these expenditures, but there is very little tax expenditure reporting at the local level.

A whole set of techniques revolves around making project or program costs look less expensive by ignoring or underestimating later years' costs, or pushing current costs off into the future. One way of doing that is to budget a project's first-year costs starting in the middle of the year, so that the costs of a whole year do not show up until a year later. A second approach is to push costs off until after the end of the budget reporting period; if there is a five-year budget, the costs for the program might begin to balloon in year six. For example, the 1997 balanced-budget agreement in Washington granted huge tax reductions whose costs swelled after 2002, while the agreement only went as far as 2002 in recording the costs. The result was to make the tax reduction look more affordable than it was.

Another way of making programs look inexpensive is by allowing them to charge fees or otherwise recover their costs. Because the program seems to pay for itself, there may be no expenditure recorded in the budget. This practice may be quite common at the local level in economic development activities, where a city invests in extending water and services to an undeveloped parcel with the idea that it will recapture these outlays in the future when the land is developed and sold. The time lag between the initial outlays and the recapture may be many years, during which time the city has collected taxes and spent public money with no budgetary record. To a reader of the budget, it may be unclear how much was spent and how much is owed; moreover, the land may never be developed. The federal government has used fee income to offset spending, sometimes making spending appear lower than it is.[10]

In an effort to push their programs up on funding priority lists, program advocates sometimes try to define their program outputs as so valuable and so politically untouchable that no tampering with allocations is possible. For example, the goal of paramedic service is lifesaving. Politicians are politically unwilling to estimate the dollar value of a life saved. Hence they may not be willing to calculate the cost of paramedic service or may not hold the program to the same standards of cost effectiveness as other programs. It is politically difficult to deny requests to the paramedic service when the implied consequence of not spending the money is loss of life.

At the national level, the Export-Import Bank and the closely related Overseas Private Investment Corporation have successfully used the strategy of linking the program to goals with unlimited value. Both agencies provide loan assistance and insurance to make it easier for US companies to sell their products abroad. Opponents of both agencies have argued that they represent corporate welfare, providing government-subsidized benefits to large and successful companies. Program supporters argue that there is a war, a trade war, and without such tools as OPIC and the Ex-Im bank, other countries that do have such tools will win out. Moreover, they argue that such agencies create jobs and improve trade. They also argue that OPIC covers its own expenses and makes a profit, which opponents deny. The success of these agencies in getting reauthorized in the face of such stiff and principled opposition depends at least in part on their ability to link their activities to successful trade, whether in fact that trade would have happened without them or not. The goal is so valuable that it has been difficult to question the agencies designed to achieve it.[11]

A variant of this strategy is to create programs with symbolic outputs. To the extent that the outputs are symbolic, their worth cannot be priced; hence the programs seem to justify spending any amount of money. Putting a man on the moon was such a program. Its costs were not estimated or even estimatable at the time the program was announced. The outcome was symbolic. We were going to do it, no matter how much it cost. A positive climate for business is another of those symbolic goals that seem to justify a wide range of expenditures. How much is it worth? How much will it deliver in terms of economic expansion? No one knows, but a good climate is perceived as of value in itself.

For agencies that want to grow, but whose goals are not sufficiently valued to escape cost/benefit calculus, a frequently used strategy is to try to hook on to more highly valued goals. Thus a local airport serving private airplanes is running at a loss; it is providing a service valued by some but paid for by all. The ratio of costs to benefits will be a political and budgetary red flag unless the airport can be tied to a more valued (preferably an unlimitedly valued) goal, in this case economic development. Even if the case is weak for linking private airplanes and economic development, if the agency and its backers gain general acceptance for the argument, the airport's funding too can be treated as not requiring cost/benefit analysis. Similarly, at the state level, university funding had been fairly low on the priority ranking of state programs, but received a boost when higher education officials managed to redefine higher education as the nucleus of economic development. But not every agency or program can take advantage of the strategy of overvalued ends. For most programs, even with valued outputs, it still matters how much they cost. When costs get out of line, the result is embarrassment and a search for alternative programs that provide as good a service at less cost.

One of the key strategies that supporters of farm subsidies used over the years was to link their programs to the symbolic worth of protecting the family farm. But it gradually became clear that a substantial proportion of the funding was going to large, wealthy corporate owners, not to struggling family farmers. In the face of continuing pressure to reduce the deficit and continuing pressure to deregulate and increase the use of market forces, farm programs lost considerable support after the passage of Gramm-Rudman-Hollings. Funding for farm programs had been cut by roughly 60 percent between 1986 and 1995, from $26 billion to $9 billion, and it looked as if the reductions were going to continue over the next few years. The linkage to a valued goal has to be credible in order to work.

Another strategy to help gain backing for a proposal is to put forward proposals for spending that seem in line with stated policy objectives of the chief executive. Thus, at the federal level, some of the agencies whose programs were disapproved by President Reagan in 1981 tried to design new programs that were more in line with the president's goals. Sometimes the policy guidance may not be as clear as it was in 1981, leaving agencies to hunt for hints about what might be approved or desired.

To summarize, the variety of claimants on the budget and the variety of expenditures they ask for creates a situation of choice and competition between objects of expenditure and between programs. The budget process frames the comparisons between expenditures and can damp down or increase the level of competition. For those programs and projects that must compete, especially for those that perceive themselves low on a priority list, budget actors may devise a variety of strategies to help them compete successfully.

Budget Constraints Can Reduce Competition

Because competition can be fierce in parts of the budget, the participants sometimes strategize more about how to reduce competition than about how to compete effectively. They seek to put constraints on budgeting that give their own programs automatic funding and/or make their programs untouchable. They seek to take their own programs out of the rough and tumble of policy-related tradeoffs.

Earmarking

Just as revenues can be earmarked for a specific program or project, so can expenditures be earmarked, with similar effect. A spending earmark means that within existing revenue sources, a legislative or constitutional mandate requires a particular level or amount of spending for a specified purpose. Earmarking is the opposite of lump-sum budgeting, in which a total amount of money is granted, with agency administrators maintaining discretion on how the money will be spent. Supporters of a program often seek earmarks when they fail to succeed in normal competition, as illustrated by the minicase on the San Francisco Children's Amendment.

MINICASE: CHILDREN'S AMENDMENT IN SAN FRANCISCO

Between 1987 and 1991 in San Francisco, spending for children's programs had declined 20 percent. Continuing budgetary shortfalls threatened to reduce the amount of funding each year. Advocates for children found they had to fight for funding each year, with limited success. While they would have liked to earmark new revenues for children, the antitax sentiment was so strong that supporters decided to try to earmark existing revenues instead and set a minimum level of funding for children's programs.

Supporters put a proposition on the ballot to amend the San Francisco charter and then actively campaigned for the proposal. Using the argument that spending money on children would save money for other programs later and applying generously the symbolism of the importance of children, supporters won a major victory at the polls. They had managed to restructure the budget to reduce the level of competition for their program.[12]

One of the main reasons for earmarking is the failure to compete successfully in a free-for-all, despite the importance of a program to some constituents or interest groups. The group or program may not have a large constituency, or it may not have the resources to compete successfully, but it has powerful symbolic appeal or strong legislative support by key members. Earmarking may thus be a totally legitimate way to reduce competition.

Nevertheless, earmarking has been highly controversial. Public managers often resent earmarking, because it limits their discretion, and hence their ability to manage. From the viewpoint of legislators, administrators may abuse their discretion by ignoring the obvious preferences of members of the legislature.

Small programs that a few members care intensely about may be starved of resources by agency heads trying to protect broader programs.

Sometimes earmarks are merely authoritative restatements of priorities that are legitimately determined by legislative committees. At other times, earmarks are just pork, distributive benefits to particular companies or industries or organizations in the home district of the legislator. Distributions of pork often result in lower-priority spending being pushed up to the top of the list; they may result in funding projects that would not survive on their merits. But even pure pork may have positive functions. As a reward for support on particular bills, pork provides a way of building coalitions for important legislation, such as the Civil Rights Act at the national level. Pork projects, generally small in size, provide resources to committee and subcommittee chairs to help build coalitions and maintain discipline. Small amounts of pork can be the lubrication that makes the political system work, but pork looks and sometimes is wasteful, and it can generate substantial controversy. A small coalition of congresspersons has taken a public stance against earmarking, defining it all as unnecessary pork.

MINICASE: SCIENCE FUNDING AND EARMARKING

Funding for basic research in science illustrates the kind of controversy that earmarks can create.[13] The federal government subsidizes basic scientific research in the United States primarily through a system of competitive grants to universities and their professors. Though the amount of these grants has grown over the years, the number of universities and the number of researchers has grown much more quickly, so fewer grants are available for each applicant. The competition between researchers and universities has become more intense as efforts to balance the federal budget have put tight caps on discretionary spending.

Grant applications for major funding agencies are reviewed by "peers," other academics who are engaged in doing similar work. Not surprisingly, these peer reviewers support applications whose authors make the same assumptions they do; they also tend to support those in a handful of major universities with famous faculty and well-supported laboratories. Part of the grant includes funding for facilities, so those universities that get the grants often have better-funded facilities. Under this model, the richer, more successful universities get richer and more successful, while universities just under the top ones often struggle unsuccessfully for grants.

In frustration, some of the second-tier university presidents presented facility improvement projects directly to supportive members of Congress, or indirectly through consulting firms that would look for congressional support, in the hope of gaining earmarks. Associations of universities that contained both first-tier and second-tier universities were stymied, because their members seemed to have conflicting interests. The only thing all the members could agree on was to lobby for a new grant with additional funding for improved facilities. If the total amount of the pie could be increased, the competition would be minimized. But Congress never passed legislation increasing the amount of money for research facilities. Competition for limited grants continued unabated.

Despite the opposition of the first-tier universities who benefited most from the competitive grant process and did not want to see grant funds bled off, second-tier university presidents and their consulting firms were generally successful in winning earmarks. In response, first-tier university presidents began to double-dip, getting the competitive grants and also requesting earmarks. The results were a reduction in the amount of money available through the competitive grant formula and an increasing proportion of money allocated by appropriation committee and subcommittee chairs to universities in their districts.

Mandates

Mandates are a little like earmarks, but instead of being requested by an organization, a mandate is often imposed on an organization. A mandated project or program is not in competition with any other project or program; it must be provided and paid for, regardless of other priorities. Mandates can come from accrediting associations, from banks or other lenders, or from federal or state legislatures. They are requirements that a particular good or service be provided at a given, required level or cost. Alternatively, mandates may require minimum salaries or benefits to be paid to particular groups of employees. Mandates may be funded or unfunded. Earmarking is an agreement among friends: one requests money for a project, the other provides it. Mandating requires that a service be performed by someone else, it is an authoritative requirement; and it may not be requested or desired at all.

One form of mandating is the professional accreditation model. The model occurs in universities, where accounting associations, journalism societies, bar associations, planning associations, and public administration associations set standards for academic programs. In many cases, the accreditors set restrictions on transferring money out of the program (as in law schools) and set staffing as well as academic standards. These standards become mandatory minimum levels for funding because if the program (or the whole school) loses its accreditation its ability to attract students seriously diminishes. The accreditation model also applies to some other public-sector agencies. For example, cities are rated on their capacity to handle major fires, and fire departments use these ratings as arguments for what they must have in the way of staffing and equipment.

While the accreditation process may be presented as an outside force, subject to no internal control, agency heads and interest groups can help form professional societies and urge them to set up standards in order to reduce the competition they face in the budget. Professional societies can play the role of accreditor or help to set standards that are set into law.

Mandates may also come from the federal government to the state and local governments and from the state governments to their local governments. The federal government can pass a law requiring states to implement laws on clean air or water or require state and local governments to provide equal transit services for the handicapped. Carrying out such laws can cost state and local governments hundreds of millions of dollars. State governments often make laws with spending implications for local governments, which the local governments have to carry out. Thus if the state passes a law requiring municipalities to dispose of toxic wastes in a certain way, the cities must comply; if the state also passes the money along, fine, if not, the cities must pick up the burden themselves. State governments can require a certain level of salary for police or a particular increase in pension contributions; they can mandate collective bargaining, too, which may have major implications for spending.

Spending mandates from the states are constraints on budgeting that reduce competition. Internal actors can try to use this process to reduce the competition they face. For example, public employee unions can form a statewide coalition and lobby the capital for mandated increases in salaries. This creates a kind of end run around the entire local political and administrative system. When the costs are mandated, there is no competition with other requests for spending.

Entitlements

Offering a program as an entitlement as opposed to a normal appropriation also reduces competition. An entitlement is a particular kind of program that offers public money to individuals, companies, or governmental units that fit particular requirements. All those who are eligible and apply for benefits receive them.

The costs of entitlements are uncertain from year to year, since those costs depend on the number of eligibles who apply for benefits. Entitlements make a prior claim on the budget; they must be funded first. Other expenditures may have to be cut to pay for entitlements. Otherwise, entitlements would cause deficits. At the state level, for example, the costs of health care entitlements keeps growing. Because many states treat tax increases as politically unacceptable, the increase in entitlements often forces cuts in other more discretionary programs, such as highway maintenance or higher-education spending. Similar tradeoffs have been required at the national level.

Under the Budget Enforcement Act of 1990, there are walls between mandatory and discretionary spending. Mandatory spending includes entitlements and other expenses, such as interest on the federal debt that are more or less automatic. According to the budget rules, the costs of existing mandatory programs can go up because of increased numbers of eligible applicants or inflation, without requiring reductions in discretionary spending. But if the increases are not offset in some way, increases in entitlement spending will increase the deficit. Efforts to reduce and eliminate the deficit put pressure on Congress to cut the discretionary side of the budget to offset increases in costs of entitlements. Appropriations committee members, who deal with the discretionary portion of the budget, freely expressed this relationship.

> House Appropriations Committee—Newly confirmed chairman Ted Stevens announced on Jan. 8 that discretionary spending for 1998 will likely remain the same as that for 1997, if entitlement spending continues to rise. On a similar note, Nebraska Sen. Bob Kerrey, who sits on the Agriculture Committee as well as Appropriations, told reporters that a $1.6 billion cut in the FY98 budget for the Agriculture Department may be needed to help offset a 1.5 percent growth in federally-funded entitlement programs.[14]

Some entitlements are so rooted in the values of what government should do for citizens that they are treated as rights.[15] For example, people may have a right to basic protection or a roof over their head or a right not to starve or freeze to death in a society that can afford to feed and warm them. Basic health care may also be considered a right. Once an entitlement is treated as a right, it is virtually nonnegotiable in a budget. Entitlements, when they are treated as rights, represent an extreme form of the strategy of locking in benefits.

Part of the politics of entitlements relates to the changing social definition over time, sometimes over centuries, as to what constitutes a right-based demand on the budget. Some entitlements can be relatively weak for many years and gradually grow stronger, as public consensus grows that the benefit is a right. The actual beneficiaries may not be organized or may have little political power, such as the unemployed or the homeless. Their plight must catch the public imagination, and the public must define their situation as worthy of collective aid. Right-based programs may be terminated or reduced if popular belief in their necessity wanes, or if the need for the program is reduced.

For program advocates, trying to design programs as entitlements is a strategy to reduce competition. They may also try to change the social definition of the right underlying an entitlement, by bringing dramatic instances of socially caused suffering to the attention of the public and of politicians. Documenting need is an important part of this strategy, and the ability to rouse public sympathy may be crucial.

Public Enterprises

Public enterprises are governmental services that are run like businesses, in the sense that they sell the goods or services they produce on a fee-for-service basis. Public enterprises may be owned or operated by government agencies. They are intended to pay for themselves through the sale of what they do or make. To the extent that they succeed, they involve no direct expenditures and hence appear free. They are segregated from the rest of the budget, and the revenues they generate are supposed to go exclusively for the expenses they incur. They typically have great policy independence because of their own revenue base.

There are public enterprises at all levels of government. At the national level, the Tennessee Valley Authority (TVA), which provided electric power, is one example of a public enterprise; the postal service is operated as a public enterprise, as is Amtrak, the passenger rail company. States have historically run a number of enterprises, but currently the state university systems are probably the most widespread enterprises at the state level. At the local level, common public enterprises include water and sewer services, and parking. In Illinois, about 20 percent of local budgets are derived from such enterprises. This is a substantial share of government activity.

Public enterprises may be either on-budget or off-budget. If on-budget, they are listed in the budget along with regular services. Tradeoffs between on-budget enterprises and other traditional services should be limited, but may occur to some extent through interfund transfers. If the enterprise is off-budget, however, the degree of tradeoff with other services may be minimal.

A wide variety of techniques may be used to reintegrate the enterprises into the budget. In some cases, the general fund may subsidize the enterprise, say by providing free services, such as snow plowing or water. Or the general-purpose government may issue general obligations bonds for the enterprise, which would otherwise have to offer revenue bonds, which carry a higher rate of interest. In other cases, the enterprise may be making money that the general government covets, either for cash-flow purposes, or to keep taxation down. The enterprise may make payments in lieu of taxes to the city (called PILOTs, these payments take the place of taxes from a private corporation). Enterprises, especially when off-budget, can become repositories of patronage hiring, thus paying for a kind of general political overhead that other departments and programs cannot afford.

Special-purpose Governments

Special-purpose governments are created at the local level to provide a single ser-vice or perform a single major function. In Illinois, there are special-purpose governments to provide library services, sanitary sewers, mosquito abatement, drainage, education, parks, special recreation, and airports. Special-purpose gov-ernments may charge fees, but they can usually also collect taxes and issue debt, much like any other local government. The difference is that other local gov-ernments provide a variety of services, while special-purpose governments pro-vide only one. By creating a special-purpose government, supporters are reducing to zero the competition with other governmental functions.

Some states have a huge number of these special-purpose local governments. The variation between metropolitan areas in the number of special-purpose gov-ernments led one researcher to investigate whether provision by special-purpose government led to a higher level of spending than would have occurred in a multipurpose government. She found that pulling out a single function and pro-viding it with its own taxing powers made that function more successful in get-ting and spending resources.[16] Thus, though creating a special-purpose government can be time-consuming and difficult, it is often a successful fund-ing strategy for supporters of services that are not doing as well in the highly competitive environment of general-purpose local governments. From the point of view of public policy, however, special-purpose governments prevent the kind of prioritization and tradeoffs that are part of democratic governance.

Trust Funds

Trust funds are budget entities that separate out specific revenues and expendi-tures for a particular purpose. Money deposited in a trust fund is supposed to be spent only for those purposes specified in the creation of the trust fund. Among the best-known trust funds are Social Security and the Highway Trust Fund. Social Security provides income to elderly people after retirement to ensure that there are not a lot of elderly poor people who cannot pay for food or shelter. Social Security is supported by a payroll tax collected explicitly for Social Security. The Highway Trust Fund, which builds and repairs the interstate highway system, is supported by a gas tax that is earmarked to support highways. Because trust funds have their own revenue sources, program supporters may seek this kind of budget entity to reduce competition with any other spending programs.

Trust funds are different from enterprises in that they are not businesses, making a product and selling it for a fee. Trust funds normally rely on taxation rather than fees for service. In neither Social Security nor the Highway Trust Fund does the trust fund sell a service directly to users or beneficiaries, as would, say, a toll road.

MINICASE: IS SOCIAL SECURITY GOING BUST?

Social Security is an example at the federal level of a trust fund set up to ensure that money for the program is not spent on anything else. The recent history of Social Security has been tumultuous and suggests the difficulty of keeping trust funds truly apart from the rest of the budget and the long-term success of program supporters in maintaining the integrity of the fund. Many people think that Social Security will not be there for them when they retire, but the reality is more promising.

Over the years, Social Security has had very little surplus. Unlike most pension funds, which try to build and invest a reserve against the time when larger numbers of people will retire, Social Security has been payout funded, that is, money paid in by those currently working has been spent on those currently retired. Payout funding has some serious problems. If the economy weakens and current workers earn less or many become unemployed, revenues going into the system fall. If more people than expected apply for disability benefits, expenditures rise, independent of income to the trust fund. Other demographic changes can also affect Social Security. If there are many more retirees than younger people working and contributing to the system, the younger people may have to pay more into the system to sustain the larger number of older people. The costs of the system go up as longevity goes up. People are living longer, which is wonderful, but they draw Social Security over a longer period of time, which is expensive.

According to Gwendolyn King, commissioner of the Social Security System, in 1983 the system was near collapse. "Social Security Trust Fund reserves were nearly exhausted."[17] Senator Dave Durenburger reminded Senate Finance Committee members that in 1983 "things were so bad the government had to borrow from the Medicare Hospital Insurance Trust Fund."[18]

A Social Security Commission was established to work out a rescue plan and ensure the integrity of Social Security into the twenty-first century when it would have to deal with larger numbers of retirees and relatively smaller numbers of workers who were paying into the fund. As a result of the commission recommendations and the support of the president and the Speaker of the House, the problem was resolved, and Social Security taxes were increased.

The increased Social Security taxes contributed to rapidly growing surpluses. That should have been a good thing, but it turned out to be a difficulty of unanticipated proportions. Senator Daniel Patrick Moynihan accused Social Security of thievery; Senator John Heinz elevated the charge to embezzlement.[19] Other senators charged that the government was taking Social Security money and spending it on other things. These charges were intentionally flamboyant; they suggested that the sanctity of the trust fund had been violated, which was an exaggeration, but not completely without foundation.

What was happening was that the government was borrowing from the Social Security Trust Fund surplus to fund the deficit. That made some supporters of the trust fund nervous about how the government was going to repay the borrowing, and if the trust fund was going to be cheated in some way. The Social Security Trust Fund was required by law to invest its surplus in U.S. Treasury securities, so there was less of a conspiracy involved than the rhetoric implied.

Some of the problems were addressed during the 1990 Omnibus Reconciliation. Social Security was taken off budget for purposes of calculating the budget deficit, effective right away, not in 1993. It was to be excluded completely from the requirements of Gramm-Rudman-Hollings. Once Social Security was on its own, some senators feared that Congress might spend the reserves if there were not additional protections preventing such action.[20] Hence, the Omnibus Reconciliation contained a "firewall" protection for Social Security. It was to be considered out of order in the House or Senate to propose changes in Social Security that would seriously deplete the surplus. In addition, some effort was made to make the tax burden lighter on poorer people, by increasing the Earned Income Tax Credit.

Social Security's financial problems are real, but not irresolvable. They have often been exaggerated for political purpose. The trustees of the Social

Security System issue a regular report on how long they estimate they will be able to pay full benefits. As of 1999 they estimated that they could pay full benefits through 2034 and 67 percent of benefits through 2075, without any changes in the system. Elected officials have been discussing and actively debating a number of proposals to ensure full benefits after 2034. Part of the debate is about how the surplus in the Social Security Trust Fund, which has been invested (loaned to the government), will be repaid; part of the discussion is about whether any part of Social Security should be privatized.

People have argued that Social Security isn't really a trust fund, and that the money it has collected isn't really there, just a pile of IOUs in place of the surplus being collected for later payout. But Social Security has been treated like a trust fund, and it is required by law to invest its balance in federal notes. The federal government has been paying off its debts for many many years; there is no reason to think that it will default on its Social Security obligations.

Taking Spending Off Budget

In general, taking something out of the budget makes it less visible. At the federal level, this strategy has led to the seeming surrealistic tactic of taking a program off budget. Congress took the Export-Import Bank off budget in 1971 and restored it to on-budget status in 1976; Section 202 Housing for the Elderly and Handicapped was taken off budget in 1974 and restored to budget status in 1978; the Strategic Petroleum Reserve program was declared off-budget in 1981. The reason these programs were taken off budget was to protect them from cuts. More recently, Social Security was taken off budget.[21]

Supporters try to take a program off budget when they think they will be more successful in spending money that way. The Highway Trust Fund presents a clear example of a recent effort to take a program off budget with the goal of increasing expenditures.

MINICASE: TAKING THE HIGHWAY TRUST FUND OFF BUDGET

The Highway Trust Fund revenues were derived from gasoline taxes. Supporters of the federal highway program felt that all the money collected from gas taxes should be spent on highway projects within a few years of collection. When, in 1990, an additional gas tax was passed to balance the budget rather than to pay for highways, program supporters were incensed. Several years later, they managed to get these new taxes added to the Highway Trust Fund. Program supporters in and out of Congress itched to spend the increased money in the trust fund, but the trust fund expenditures were included under the spending caps for transportation. The increased revenues could not be spent without breaking the caps, so the trust fund balance swelled. Authorization committees were generally for an increase in spending, while the budget and appropriations committees were for continued constraint.

To solve the problem and get out from under the caps, program supporters proposed to take the trust fund off budget, which incensed old budget hands like Representative Charles Stenholm (D-Tex.), who explained his opposition to the plan at some length:

> This bill would reduce controls on federal spending, the exact opposite of what we should be doing as we work toward a balanced budget. Next week the Budget Committee, on which I am privileged to serve, is scheduled to begin the process of putting together the budget resolution for fiscal year 1997. This process will require many tough choices as priorities are set among worthy programs . . . essentially all programs will be together in the same boat, competing for priority status. . . . This bill is an effort to circumvent this process for one segment of the budget. The debate today is really about whether the transportation trust funds should be exempted from the priority-setting process that tests every other program. A vote for this bill says that spending on transportation programs automatically should receive a higher priority than every other program of the federal government.
>
> We have heard good arguments today about the value of investing in our national infrastructure. I agree with much of what was said but I disagree with the venue. This debate should be heard in the midst of arguments about the value of every other program, not standing alone without programmatic competition for numerous hours on the House Floor.
>
> We're talking about much more than the simple bookkeeping activity of moving the trust funds onto a different side of the ledger. The real impact of the bill is in removing trust funds from the statutory budget enforcement mechanisms and, to a lesser extent, the congressional budget process.[22]

Stenholm argued that instead of exempting a major spending program from the caps, the caps should be raised for all programs as the budget came into balance and created a surplus. In the event, highway spending was increased, without taking the Highway Trust Fund off budget. A firewall was set up around the highway fund (earmarking), so other programs could not get it. The increased highway spending was offset, as required by the budget process. Oddly, however, the offset included a reduction in veterans' benefits for smoking-related illnesses. The effect of the firewall and required spending on highways was similar for supporters of highway spending to what they would have had if the trust fund had been pulled off budget, but without the same level of threat to the whole budget process. Stenholm and others were concerned that if programs began to opt out of the budget process, the caps would become meaningless and there would be no pressure to maintain the discipline required to balance the budget.

Budget Processes

A budget process can tone down competition. One way of doing that is through formula allocations. Formulas include simple across-the-board increases or decreases, where the same percentage increase is given to each department or program, and more elaborate distribution schemes that include measures of need, such as size, case loads, enrollment, or age of housing stock. Many grants from federal and state governments are based on formulas; recipients do not have to apply for them, and once the formula has been established, there is no competition between recipients. They get their money automatically. There may be intense competition between potential recipients as the formula is being designed, because some will lose and others will gain from the actual formula used, but once the formula is in place, competition is eliminated.

A second way of using the budget process to tone down competition is to limit the portion of the budget that departments and programs can compete for. If most of the budget is treated as fixed and only a small portion as potentially variable, the scope of competition is limited. Incremental budgeting, which is said to concentrate mainly on the difference between last year's actual budget and this year's proposed, is one way of limiting the scope of competition. Or, in the more extreme case, this year's budget is basically the same as last year's, and most new money is allocated in proportion to last year's allocation; only a tiny bit may be held out to respond to changing priorities or emergency demands. Target-based budgeting allows a bit more competition but still limits its scope. The budget office may assign each department only a large percentage of its last year's budget, but not the whole amount; the difference is set aside in a pool that all the departments have to compete for.

Another way of using the budget process to tone down competition is to provide a list in priority order of the programs that will be cut in case revenues are less than projected. In this situation, some programs are more at risk, but some are relatively less at risk; for the latter, the level of competition is markedly reduced. Some state governments use this kind of process. In a more extreme model, some programs are exempted completely from cuts. For example, Gramm-Rudman-Hollings, which revised the federal budget process, specified that if deficit reduction targets were not met, there would be across-the-board cuts in defense and domestic spending, but some programs would be completely exempt. The minicase of the Children's Amendment in San Francisco illustrated a related strategy of establishing a floor of funding below which a program cannot be cut.

In sum, strategies to reduce competition are widespread and varied. However, if programs are competing successfully, program advocates generally do not try to reduce or eliminate the competition. Second, those who do try to reduce competition cannot select from a vast array of possibilities; not all strategies will be possible for them. For example, to make a program an enterprise fund requires the ability to charge fees for service, fees large enough to cover or almost cover expenditures. To make a program an entitlement, especially a right-based entitlement, implies a public perception of the need for and worthiness of the program. Third, these techniques have varying degrees of reversibility. Even trust funds, which are almost inviolate, may end up sharing their funding with unrelated expenditures. There is a counterpressure to break down the rigidity and increase the amount of competition, and hence flexibility and responsiveness, in the budget.

The Environment Can Affect Spending Priorities

Spending strategies are framed by the environment. A change in the environment can overwhelm all strategies, temporarily reducing the scope of activity of individual actors. Or it can create a situation in which policy mandates are clear and urgent.

The environment can change in a variety of ways. There can be tornadoes or floods, natural disasters of many sorts; there can be wars, cold or hot, and arms races; there can be elections and changes of policy resulting from the change in the composition of the elected officials; and there can be a change in popular opinion, elevating some benefit programs to rights and demoting others from rights to formula funded grants. These changes may occur once in a while or gradually over a long period of time. In addition, the environment continually affects the politics of spending because it influences the level of resources and rate of growth of revenues, and because it influences the certainty that revenues will appear.

One major change in the environment that affects budget strategies is the difference between relative abundance and continuing growth, on the one hand, and ragged stability or revenue decline, on the other. During growth, budget actors may argue for minimum staffing levels and high levels of specialization; during decline, they may work to undo minimum staffing levels and hire for flexibility. During decline, general skills, overlapping capacity, and redundancy may be more important. You can add new people or equipment during growth; during decline, the existing staff and equipment have to do more different kinds of jobs.

Even more important, the model of incremental growth, with a line-item budget, allocation of revenue increases by fair shares, and general suppression of conflict, is premised on moderate, gradual, but continuous growth. If growth is more rapid or if there is no growth, this pattern is likely to be disrupted. Rapid growth in revenues may lead to a burst of planning and search for new missions and programs; there may be an outreach to new potential interest groups or service beneficiaries; new needs may be documented and new programs designed. Outsiders might be involved in the budget process and in weighing alternative new programs. None of these things is likely to occur when the margin for growth is small and divided up proportionately among existing actors.

A change in the environment from rich to lean may mean the elimination of the increase in revenues from last year to this that is the focus of the internal actors' bargaining in the incremental model of politics. The set of strategies associated with this model may become less relevant during decline. Budget processes are likely to become more centralized, making the competition between individual actors subordinate to the achievement of collective goals. If there is a need to cut back departments and programs, then each department's budget may be at some risk, vastly increasing the scope of competition. Agency heads are more likely to use defensive strategies, such as linking current programs to politically valued ends, distorting program goals to make them look like they are within an approved policy set, and trying to reduce competition and lock in current spending levels.

Even governments that are reasonably well off financially may not be able to count on their revenues—the environment may be unstable, or revenue sources unpredictable. At all levels of government, there may be reductions in the level of budget during the year if revenues were overestimated or if the economy declines unpredictably during the year. Uncertainty can be introduced for state and local governments by changes in tax laws at other levels of government. Taxpayer revolts may change the amount of revenue that can be collected, or redefine taxable wealth. As national economies are increasingly open to the world economy, changes in the price of oil or droughts in the former Soviet Union can have an impact on spending programs. If the price of fuel suddenly increases, then operating costs go up; if other countries purchase unforeseeably large amounts of grain, the cost of agricultural subsidies may suddenly go down.

When revenues become uncertain, spending behavior may change. Planning assumes long-term stability; with continual disruption and reallocation from project to project, planning makes little sense. The idea of being patient and giving up current programs or capital projects to someone else with the assurance that you will succeed in the future, vanishes. Being on top of the current list is all that counts. This pattern makes it difficult to save money for a large project or allocate one large project in one area one year and another large project somewhere else another year. Instead, the emphasis is likely to be on a number of smaller projects each year, even if none of them can solve real problems because they are too small. Also, one is not likely to break a larger project or program into parts, assuming that one part can be achieved this year, and another next year; the later parts may never arrive, and the project may remain incomplete and useless.

Uncertain revenues also affect spending by encouraging higher-level executives to hold back on the budget, allocating a little at a time so that there is uncommitted money to eliminate from the budget if cuts come suddenly. Requests for spending may pile up, awaiting release during the year, generating a continuing competition between agencies to get portions of their budgets released.

In short, changes in the environment provide an overriding consideration. They may directly impose policy mandates that cancel out other kinds of politics; thus a war, or warlike peace, may impose defense spending. Or they may simply make policy directions clearer, as in a major shift in the political party in power or a major shift in public opinion. Such a shift may be the result of urban uprisings in the ghetto, which supported increases in police spending, or the result of changes in the balance of trade, which may generate a variety of policies. Changes in the environment may alter the budget process and thereby alter appropriate budget strategies. Changes in revenue levels are likely to affect the politics of spending as well.

The Separation between Payer and Spender Requires Public Approval of Spending Choices

The separation between those who pay taxes and those who make the decisions about how those taxes should be spent introduces the concepts of accountability and acceptability. *Accountability* means transparency to the taxpayers about what budget decisions have been made; *acceptability* means that whatever decisions are made should not stir up too much public opposition. In some circumstances, accountability and acceptability go together; in others they are clashing opposites.

For example, if elected officials' spending decisions agree with the opinions of the majority of citizens, as when a service clearly benefits everyone, currently or in the future, then accountability and acceptability go together; the decision is acceptable and can be openly arrived at and be highly visible. But if spending decisions favor only one small group and the majority of citizens would not approve the expenditures if given the choice, then accountability and acceptability may be opposites—to gain acceptability may mean obscuring or making less clear what the decisions were or how much they cost.

Spending decisions at some level have to gain public support, or at least acquiescence. That may mean providing services that nearly everyone wants, and no others; or it may mean trying to deliver programs to smaller or more targeted groups and either convincing the whole public to go along or offering other programs to the people who do not directly benefit from particular programs. When neither of these options seems to work, then supporters may represent the costs as low or free, and hence not important, or obscure the costs in a variety of ways so that they do not rouse too much opposition.

Providing Services Nearly Everyone Wants

Direct service delivery means using public employees or using tax money to hire someone to accomplish a public goal, such as providing road and street repair or snow plowing. Governmental services normally benefit many citizens at some point in their lives. Fires can occur in any neighborhood and can spread from one house to another, so almost everyone can perceive that he or she receives benefits from the fire department. Most people use public streets and are sensitive to their level of repair. Everyone benefits from an effective national defense and from inspection of meats for cleanliness. Because services generally benefit wide sections of the population, they are not particularly controversial, and expenditures for them need not be obscured. The services portion of the budget is the most open one. The costs are the clearest and most meaningful, the numbers typically are the most accurate, and the departments are the most accountable for what they are doing.

When they are threatened with cuts, budget actors often defend direct services by describing the negative consequences of reduction in services. For example, a director of public works may argue that it will take more time to clear the roads of snow if the council cuts staffing levels. It is clear that the public wants this service to work well and speedily and that the council will get citizen complaints if this service is cut back. But agency heads have to pick services that are really popular, or decision makers are likely to say, "OK, go ahead and cut." In its extreme form, this strategy is called the Washington Monument ploy because, at one time, in response to threatened cuts, the National Park Service offered to cut staffing of the very popular national monument in Washington, D.C., forcing a closing of the monument or reduction in the hours it was available to visitors. Congress, knowing the public outcry that would have resulted, restored the cut.

Even with popular services, the Washington Monument ploy does not always work. It depends on a fairly decentralized budget process in which the departments and agencies have considerable power. In a more centralized process, the executive budget office will catch such ploys and simply force the agency to make cuts elsewhere. The particular service that is so popular will not get cut, but the agency's other, less popular programs remain vulnerable.

Given the nature of direct services, such as their general popularity and the relative openness with which they are treated because of their popularity, it is interesting to note that services are more often provided by state and local governments than by the federal government. The federal government provides defense services directly, and some regulatory services, such as inspections of meatpacking plants for cleanliness and places of work for employee safety. State governments often provide mental health services, some police and highway services, and higher education. Local governments typically provide police, fire, street repair, public schools, and water and sewer services.

Services like police and fire are characterized by broad distribution of benefits across groups and little geographic specificity. They tend to generate little public conflict and little specific interest-group support. When the services are targeted to particular groups or neighborhoods, or are allocated unevenly, more citizen and neighborhood group involvement may result. Thus, if a recreation department closes services in a particular neighborhood, or a branch library reduces its hours, or a fire station in a particular neighborhood is closed, then those benefiting specifically from those services may organize and protest. If street repair is neglected in some neighborhoods and carried out routinely in others, neighborhood activism may develop.

The general sense of approval that clings to direct service delivery also applies to some entitlement programs. After a long and painful depression in which many people lose their jobs and suffer downward mobility, there is likely to be a general awareness that unemployment and need can happen to good people, hardworking people, as well as the shiftless. Citizens can see welfare and food programs as available to all, and feel some security that the programs are there for them if they are needed. But after years of continuous high employment and increasing incomes, they may come to feel that they are succeeding because they deserve to succeed, that the economy has little to do with it, and that others are failing because of personal or moral flaws. They no longer see welfare as a safety net for everyone, but a dole or gift from the many hardworking to the few and lazy. The safety net may lose its general public support.

Expenditures That Do Not Help Everyone

Not every program or service gives benefit to every taxpayer in even measure. Leaf pickup may benefit disproportionately the wealthy, who have large wooded lots on tree-lined streets; municipal airports may benefit the owners of private aircraft; various federal programs benefit middle-class students or underprivileged youngsters or owners of private boats. How do these programs get the approval they need?

Geographic Dispersion. One way is to spread out the benefits so that even a narrowly conceived program acquires a number of different beneficiaries. A program for repairing naval ships may be divided into ten parts, when location in a single city might make more sense; a program for helping cities recover from economic problems may be expanded to affect a larger number of cities in more states. The support base is expanded to get more geographically diversified backing for the program.

Positive Spillovers. Another approach is to convince people that there are positive spillovers, that is, people in general benefit from a program even if they do not use the service directly and never intend to. Public subsidies to mass transit are often justified in terms of positive spillovers. It is not just the transit riders who benefit from mass transit. The users of automobiles also benefit because if all riders on mass transit took their cars, there would be traffic jams of immense proportions, and the costs of road repairs would be much higher, a cost paid in part by automobile users through their gasoline taxes. Downtown businesses and mall owners also benefit from mass transit because buses and trains bring in customers during the day and increase the pool of available employees, increasing the quality and reducing the price for workers. Mass transit is more fuel efficient, slowing down the need for imported oil and the depletion of nonrenewable resources and keeping gas prices down for everyone. In addition, some elderly or handicapped people can become economically self-sufficient through the use of mass transit, reducing the public cost of supporting them.

Programs can be sold in terms of advertising their actual positive spillover effects or by exaggerating potential spillover effects. An example of an exaggerated positive spillover effect is the claim that local airports should be subsidized by general taxpayers because they aid economic development. The argument is that small airports, which directly serve only wealthy owners of private planes, contribute to economic development because businesses will not locate in the city unless it has an airport. Every taxpayer presumably benefits from economic development because there will be more taxpayers sharing the burden, and so taxes for each resident will presumably drop. The impact of the airport on economic development may never be measured or questioned. The supposed impact on economic development becomes a rationale for public support of a program with a narrow group of beneficiaries.

Balancing Benefits to a Variety of Groups. If a program benefits a particular group, and there are not clear positive spillovers to help rationalize public expenditures, then several other strategies may be employed. One is to see that everyone gets a little something from different programs. Thus there may be rent subsidies for the poor and low-cost loans for education to the middle class and a coast guard fleet to maintain the safety of pleasure boaters among the wealthy. There may be water subsidies to farmers in the Southwest and dairy subsidies to farmers in Wisconsin and New England. The interstate highway system that served primarily rural areas may be balanced by the public transit program that serves primarily urban areas.

In order to make this model work, not only must the key interests each get something but the benefits should be roughly even to each group or else those receiving less are likely to protest. For example, a recent program to provide long-term home health care for the elderly was defeated in the House, at least in part because the elderly had just been given an expensive new program to protect them from the costs of catastrophic illness. Critics of the proposed home health care measure argued that the elderly were being greedy, that they had just had a turn, and now other needy groups should get their turn.[23] Opposition to the home health care bill was framed in terms of intergenerational splits: The elderly were getting more benefits, while the young were actually losing theirs. Lobbyists for the elderly tried to redefine the situation and create the perception that care for the elderly helped the entire family (positive spillovers to everyone), not just the elderly. They argued that if family funds went to take care of the elderly, families would have less money to send young people to college.[24]

In the case of the elderly, less money for them does not automatically translate into more money for the young and middle classes; there is not an explicit agreement among supporters of these programs to balance the spending. Since the elderly have been so politically powerful, they have been able to get much of what they want without forming any coalitions. But among some competing interests, such informal agreements to balance expenditures may emerge.

One example involves urban and rural interests concerned with subsidies for agriculture. Agricultural subsidies have been both expensive and in some cases quite visible. The agriculture program was created during the depression of the 1930s when 25 percent of the population or more was on the farms and poor. Subsidies to agriculture were not considered payments to a small, undeserving minority; farmers were a substantial part of the population, and the extent of their need was widely known and accepted. Since then fewer and fewer people own farms; farming has become more productive; there are more big industrialized farms, and fewer poor family farmers. The logic of paying huge subsidies to so few large businesses has come under attack. The agriculture lobbies have had to work for continued legislative support.

The politics of farm support has a geographic bias, since rural states are more likely to benefit directly, and more urban states are likely to pay the bill in terms of higher food costs as well as higher tax bills. To offset this potential urban opposition to agricultural subsidies, advocates of agricultural subsidies have supported programs like food stamps, school lunch programs, and mass transit, which aid the poor and big cities.

When farm subsidies were being reconsidered by the budget committees in Congress in 1990, advocates of continued subsidies testified at the hearings. Charles Rose, chairman of the Agriculture Subcommittee on Tobacco and Peanuts, argued not very subtly that he expected loyalty from representatives of large northern cities who had received his votes before.

> Mr. Downey had a good time poking fun at wool and mohair and laughing about that and about the honey bee program. I would like for you and him to know that a lot of people I represent do not think subsidies for New York City and the Long Island Railroad and mass transportation up north are very funny, either, but we continue to vote for them and we continue to support them. . . .
>
> I remember when Eddie Koch [later mayor of New York City] was here and he led the whole Congress against the farm bill. I believe he even beat major farm legislation . . . and then he turned right around and said everybody has to sign on in the bailout of New York City. I wrote Eddie Koch a letter, and I said I believe that must be what you call "chutzpah," Mr. Koch. I think that you need to know that the problems of this country extend beyond the Hudson River and the Long Island Railway. Do not ask us who represent the farms of America to come to your aid when you take cheap shots at us in the farm bill.[25]

Dan Glickman, representative from Kansas and chair of the subcommittee on wheat, soybeans, and feed grains of the Agriculture Committee, made a similar argument that sounded just short of a threat. "I have supported food stamps, urban programs . . . as have most of us. . . . I would hate to see a lot of programs jeopardized because of an attempt to drive a train through agriculture programs. That could happen. I am serious about that."[26]

In fact, as these farm state representatives suggested would happen, the tight linkage between farm supports and food to the poor appeared to have broken down by 1995. The Senate's version of the budget resolution for 1996 cut heavily into spending for school lunches, Women, Infants, and Children (WIC) food support, and food stamps. These programs represented the support for urban poor that farm state legislators had used to build their coalitions of support for farm spending.

Agriculture has not represented a single interest but a range of interests, from apple growers to dairy farmers, to sugar and peanut farmers. The interests of the different agricultural lobbies have sometimes been antagonistic, which has weakened their lobbying power. To compensate for these differing demands, representatives from farm states and agricultural supporters in Congress have tended to trade off support for different agricultural products, the same way they do on pet capital projects. As long as the amount of money to be allocated was allowed to increase, this arrangement stood, but the threatened reductions during the Reagan administration broke this coalition apart and increased competition between the lobby groups. "In 1981 budget pressures created such bitter conflicts among commodity groups involved in omnibus farm legislation that Congress came close to killing target prices—a major crop price support—and the federal tobacco and peanut programs. The legislation finally passed the House by a scant two-vote margin, with a significant number of farm state members voting against it."[27]

Making Program Costs Look Cheap. Pairing antagonistic interests is one way to broaden support for programs aimed at narrow groups. Such pairing is not always possible, however. Another technique for funding narrow interests is to make the costs small or even free. As long as the public does not feel that it is funding the costs, their objections to programs they do not benefit from should be limited. Three ways to make programs look cheap or free are grants, loans, and insurance programs.

Grants are transfers of money from one level of government to another or from a governmental unit to an outside agency to accomplish some particular program goal. The national government often awards grants to the states and sometimes directly to local governments as incentives for compliance with national policies. States may pass on federal grants to their local governments, and add some further aid.

Grants may seem free to the state and local governments that receive them. To the extent that money comes from another level of government to accomplish some purpose, the provision of that desired good or service by local governments may be noncontroversial. If the local government has to put up some of its own money in order to get the grant, however, applying for or accepting the grant may be much more controversial.

DeKalb, Illinois, provides services to the elderly and poor. As long as these services were provided from federal revenue sharing, and not from local taxes, there was little opposition to the program. When there was a question of paying for the social services with local taxation, a brouhaha ensued, and comparisons were made between basic services, economic development, and social services. Once the programs were paid for from local money, they had to compete with other programs, especially programs targeted to larger groups or the whole community. The support for the social services survived the transition, but at a lower level of funding. The reduced costs lowered the level of controversy.

Grants sometimes require a local match of money. One level of government offers a grant to another level of government, with the requirement that the recipient also put up some money. Every 75 cents of federal money may require 25 cents of local match. The local match may be in dollars or in labor or even from other grants. When the local match can be taken out of nontax revenues, it may seem like magic, and the project may seem free or nearly free. Such projects are likely to go to the top of the priority list, even if the beneficiaries are a narrow group. If the city has to put in some of its own money, or an increasing portion of its own revenues over a period of time, more thought may go into the priority of the project. Still, a project with a state or federal match is cheaper to undertake than one without any grant support, and hence there may be a bias in its favor even if everyone does not clearly benefit.

Government loan programs often charge less than market rates for interest. Below-market rates for interest on loans is often the least visible form of subsidy. The difference between the government rate and the market rate is the rate of the subsidy. Typically, no one has bothered to calculate what it would have cost a businessman to borrow without the government loan; hence the degree of subsidy was often not recorded or known. Since the government should get its money back plus interest to keep the loan pool going and cover defaults, it has been difficult to perceive these subsidies as expenditures.

Sometimes the costs of a loan program exceed what has been set aside to cover costs, and the capital for loans is depleted. Sometimes the loans are forgiven, or perhaps it was never intended that they be repaid. In one agricultural program, farmers deposited their grains in special storage facilities and then could borrow from the government (usually at subsidized rates) up to the agreed value of the crop. If the farmer could not get that price for his crop, he did not have to pay back the loan; the government got the crop instead, which was not worth the loan amount. While loans may appear "free," they may actually cost a substantial amount of money.

Loan guarantees are a form of insurance. When loans are considered too risky by commercial bankers, but the demand for loans seems to reflect larger social problems, the government may guarantee the loan, that is, agree to cover the debt if the borrower is unable to pay it back. From the bank's perspective, the loans are almost risk free. If the loan is guaranteed, the borrower can pay less interest, since interest is to some extent proportional to risk. Such loan guarantees are a form of subsidy to the borrower, who pays less than market price for interest, and to the lenders, who gain interest with virtually no risk.

The cost to government agencies of loan guarantees is typically low, since costs occur only if the borrower fails to pay back the loan. For most of its life, the guarantee is an obligation, but not an expenditure. It is difficult to estimate outlays for guarantees in advance, but if and when they come due, they must be paid. Such obligations are called contingent liabilities. Since the government only gets involved when there is high risk, the costs are not totally negligible.

Many loan guarantee programs involve particular narrow groups. Some are for college students, some are for private businesses developing alternative fuels, some are for farmers, and some are for housing. Major loan guarantees have been issued to specific businesses that were in financial trouble, such as Lockheed and Chrysler, and to industries, such as steel. Despite the targeted nature of the guarantees, with the exception of the Chrysler guarantees, these programs generated little public opposition, since they seem virtually free. In recent years, however, the high costs of defaults in the Higher Education Loan Guarantee program made that program politically vulnerable. When the costs become more apparent, opposition to the program increases.

In addition to grants, loans, and loan guarantees, government provides some forms of insurance. Because insurance is based on the collection of premiums from those who buy the insurance, it should cost taxpayers little money. The government offers insurance at times when there seems to be a national need or when private insurers find the risk too great. The federal government often charges much less than the actual risk might warrant. The federal government offers insurance to farmers, in case weather conditions wipe out a crop. The program goal is to prevent farmers from going out of business and hence to ensure a continuing supply of food without extremes of price fluctuations. The national government also provides flood insurance that commercial dealers do not handle. Another insurance program that is both national and state is the unemployment insurance program.

Insurance programs became visible and controversial when the federal government discovered that it had to pay out large sums on insured accounts for failed savings and loans. Other programs that look low in cost, such as loans and loan guarantees, may also turn out to be expensive. When the costs become apparent and burdensome, the political dynamics change.

MINICASE: FEDERAL CREDIT REFORM

At the federal level, loans, loan guarantees, and insurance grew enormously from 1970 to 1989, at least in part because they seemed cheap or free. Total credit and insurance outstanding was $861 billion in 1970; that figure had increased to $5.7 trillion by 1989 (see table 5.2). This amount represents total exposure; only a small portion of the amount is likely to be translated into actual governmental outlays. Nevertheless, recent experience with rising rates of default on student loans, massive expenditures for failed savings and loans, and scary experiences with government-sponsored enterprises such as the Federal Housing Administration convinced many officials that the contingent liabilities were real and needed to be controlled. In 1982, loan defaults and writeoffs were $3.7 billion; by 1989, the figure had increased to $14.4 billion. These numbers, although sobering, were dwarfed by the savings-and-loan crisis. According to the 1991 budget, insurance losses in 1989 were $67.2 billion, 96 percent of which was for 400 insolvent savings and loans. In 1982, insurance losses had been only $4.6 billion. The Congressional Budget Office, writing in early 1991, estimated that outlays for insurance losses for 1989–96 would total $155 billion, more than three times the amount estimated in 1989 legislation.[28] Continual upward revisions of costs contributed to the impression that matters were out of control.

TABLE 5.2   **FEDERAL CREDIT AND INSURANCE OUTSTANDING**
            (IN BILLIONS OF DOLLARS)

PROGRAM	1970	1975	1980	1985	1989	PERCENTAGE INCREASE 1970–89
Direct loans	$51	$74	$164	$257	$207	306
Guarantees	125	189	299	410	588	370
GSE loans[a]	24	49	151	370	763	3,096
Deposit insurance	445	837	1,465	2,227	2,927	558
Other insurance	216	187	831	1,021	1,286	495
Total	$861	$1,337	$2,909	$4,285	$5,771	570

Source: Budget of the United States Government, FY 1991, 229.
   a. Government Sponsored Enterprises.

These numbers created widespread pressure in Washington for credit reform. Congressman Charles Schumer summarized the case for credit reform:

> Too many of our credit programs have spun out of control. Our perverse budgetary accounting procedures have led us to dish out credit as if it were cost free. As a result of this painless overindulgence, we have placed ourselves at the brink of financial disaster. If we don't apply the brakes now, we will speed off a trillion dollar cliff.[29]

Schumer explained that the cash-flow accounting of the federal budget obscured the true costs of lending and insurance programs. Loan guarantees and insurance involved no immediate cash outlays, and because guarantee fees and insurance premiums are recorded as income, new loan guarantees and expanded deposit insurance coverage appeared to reduce the deficit in the short run. When direct loans slowed down, loan guarantees actually increased after the passage of Gramm-Rudman-Hollings. Schumer argued that there should be some reported costs at the time the loan and guarantee programs are approved so that Congress would be more aware of what it was doing and make better decisions.

The hearings on credit reform reveal the concerns and intent of the backers of the reform. Congressman Bill Gradison argued that failure to control the credit programs resulted in spending that absorbed limited funds for other activities and reduced capacity to expand social service expenditures. And Congressman Schumer argued that the separate ceiling on credit should be eliminated, and credit included in one massive ceiling, so that tradeoffs between grants, loans, guarantees, and direct expenditures could be made.[30] Without their agreeing explicitly to it, their priorities had been reordered by massive obligatory spending, and what might be a loan or insurance program of lesser importance was driving out what might be more important expenditures made through grants, entitlements, or direct services. Part of the goal of credit reform was to enable Congress to recover its capacity to define priorities.

In the fall of 1990, Congress included credit reform in the Omnibus Reconciliation. One feature of the reform is that the cost to the government of the loan or guarantee over its life is to be estimated, appropriated, and included in the spending ceilings required by the Budget Enforcement Act of 1990. The older notion of a separate spending ceiling for credit was dropped. These changes make the real costs of loans and guarantees clear at the time of approval and treat loans and guarantees like any other expenditures, allowing for both comparability and tradeoffs. The reform was limited in its scope. It omitted several key programs and did not address the issue of insurance, but it effectively eliminated the perverse incentives that resulted from Gramm-Rudman-Hollings and the cash accounting system.

HAS CREDIT REFORM BEEN EFFECTIVE?

Credit reform was to be implemented beginning in 1991. To evaluate how effective it has been requires the answers to several questions. First, how well have the federal agencies that provide credit complied with the law?

Second, how well has the law succeeded in enabling Congress to make tradeoffs and choices between direct loans and loan guarantees? Third, what have been the incentives built into the new scoring system? Has scoring under credit reform led to a new kind of gaming and overestimates of future savings or underestimates of costs? Has credit reform led to a more realistic evaluation of costs of guaranteed and direct loans?

How well have agencies complied with credit reform? Initially, not well, not because they were unwilling to comply but because they had inadequate historical data on which to estimate what their loss rates were likely to be over the life of loans and inadequate staff and skills to redo the books for prior years' loans in order to get more adequate figures.[31] It will take time to redo the accounting systems of those agencies with large loan portfolios to get accurate numbers. As of 1995, four years after the beginning of the credit reform requirements, major lenders, including the FHA, the Export-Import Bank, and Veterans' Affairs credit programs, still had not complied with the requirements of credit reform.[32]

Despite some compliance problems, comparability between credit and noncredit programs has increased, and legislators have actually made some tradeoffs between the credit budget and the noncredit budget. Tradeoffs are required under the Budget Enforcement Act's spending caps; if one program is to be increased, another has to be cut to pay for it. Congress increased the enforcement provisions of the Student Guaranteed Loans to reduce the number of loan defaults, decreasing the long-term costs to the government. Congress then used the estimated savings from this loan guarantee program to extend unemployment benefits for people who had been out of work a long time. The action generated some controversy, since how much money would be saved through the new procedures for collecting loan repayments was not known with certainty.[33] Nevertheless, a real tradeoff did occur as intended by the supporters of credit reform.

Part of the intent of the legislation was to be able to compare credit and noncredit programs, but the legislation also made it more feasible to compare credit programs. President Clinton supported a program, passed by Congress, in which a federal agency would offer student loans to supplement the bank-administered student loan guarantee program. The direct service was estimated under credit reform to be cheaper. The new Republican-dominated Congress elected in 1994 opposed any expansion of direct federal services and argued that under credit reform administrative costs were excluded from the subsidy costs, making direct federal delivery look more cost effective than it was. Their goal was to return this program to the banks, for whom the program was profitable. The result was an imbroglio over how to count administrative costs and how to evaluate which program delivery mechanism was really more cost effective. While the issue may have been motivated by an attempt to increase the profits of bankers, the argument took place in the context of figuring out how to compare costs of two different service delivery vehicles.[34] That this debate took place in this way should probably be scored as a plus for credit reform.

As for the incentives built into credit reform and how Congress is responding to them with reasonable data in hand on the real costs of loans and loan guarantees, Congress and the administration have worked to bring down the subsidy costs of loans. One incident is suggestive. In 1993 Congress proposed and the president signed a reduction in the subsidy cost of loans guaranteed in the Small Business Administration. This reduction was achieved by reducing the proportion of large loans that the federal government guaranteed from 85 percent to 75 percent. "In the summer of 1993, legislation from our committee was enacted and signed by President Clinton, reducing the subsidy cost of 7(a) loans from 5.4 percent to 2.2 percent and more than doubling the 7(a) program level with the same amount of appropriated dollars."[35] In 1995, legislation was passed to reduce further SBA subsidy costs. As the chairman of the Small Business Committee described the proposal, which further reduced the guaranteed portion of loans and increased the loan guarantee fee, in 1996 only $133 million needs to be approved to support $10.5 billion in loans, a reduction of 39 percent with a 35 percent increase in loan volume.[36]

Under credit reform, by reducing the proportion of each loan that the government guaranteed, Congress would have to appropriate less money to cover likely losses. Congress took some of the freed-up money for new loan guarantees. Banks were probably going to make the loans anyhow, whether 85 percent or 75 percent of the loan was guaranteed. As long as loan guarantees were considered free, as in pre-credit-reform days, such a tradeoff between percentage of each loan guaranteed and total dollar amount of all loans guaranteed would not have been made. There would have been no motivation to do so.

The numbers in terms of dollars and subsidies since the credit reform was implemented suggest that Congress and the administration have worked hard to keep the subsidy rates down, and have generally been successful in doing so (see table 5.3). Figures for the ratio of subsidy dollars to total loans and loan guarantees issued suggest that more dollars are going out at less cost per dollar to the federal government. Note also that loan guarantees, which were generally cheaper in subsidy costs than direct loans, grew more rapidly than direct loans (71 percent growth in guaranteed loans compared to 22 percent growth in direct loans). Moreover, the ratio of direct loans outstanding to guarantees outstanding was about .4 in 1989, but on an annual basis was much lower from 1995-2000. In the year 2000, based on projections, the ratio was only .16. These figures suggest that Congress and the administration responded to real costs of the two programs by increasing direct loans more slowly than guaranteed loans. Decision makers responded to the changed incentives built into the scoring system. Under Gramm-Rudman-Hollings, loans looked cheaper because loan initiation fees appeared to lower the cost of the direct loans in that year to below zero. Under credit reform, the long term costs, not just the first year costs showed up. Direct loans no longer appeared free. They were thus issued more carefully, at the same time that great effort was made to bring down the subsidy costs.

TABLE 5.3   DOLLAR SUBSIDIES PER DOLLAR OF LOAN AND LOAN GUARANTEE, 1995–2000 (IN BILLIONS OF DOLLARS)

	1995	1996	1997	1998	1999[a]	2000[a]
Direct loans						
Obligations	30.9	23.4	33.6	28.8	38.5	37.9
Subsidy BA[b]	2.6	1.8	2.4	6.5	1.1	−0.2
Ratio	.084	.076	.071	.22	.028	−.005
Loan Guarantees						
Commitments	138.5	175.4	172.3	218.4	216.5	237.6
Subsidy BA[b]	4.6	4.0	3.6	2.6	4.3	3.2
Ratio	.033	.022	.020	.011	.019	.013

Source: Data from *Budget of the United States, FY 2000*. Ratios calculated by author.
   a. Estimated.
   b. BA = budget authority.

Obscuring Costs. While there are a variety of ways of getting public support for spending programs that do not benefit large groups of taxpayers, sometimes, perhaps only occasionally, decision makers go ahead and spend money on something that the taxpayers would probably disapprove of if they knew about it or understood its impact. At the least, the expenditures would rouse controversy. On these occasions, the costs of programs may be intentionally distorted downward or even hidden. The intention of budget actors to obscure costs is difficult to prove, but the level of invisibility is clearer. Unpopular costs may be hidden in the budget; subsidies may be virtually invisible; expenditures may be made with relatively hard to trace money; and costs may be systematically underestimated.

For example, if a particular project is likely to arouse controversy, or even has been forbidden by the legislature or by higher levels of government, administrators may shift the costs of the program into other programs or simply not break out costs in a way that shows how the money was spent. The Illinois Board of Higher Education forbade all but one of the state's universities from doing research at public expense. To appear to comply with the state board, administrators at one of the universities not approved for research buried the costs of doing research. The library budget was presented, but the costs to the library of serving faculty and students doing research was not broken out; the cost of faculty salaries was reported, but the extra expense of hiring a research (as opposed to a teaching) faculty was not described. Travel lines were reported, but the amount of travel related to research (as opposed to teaching or administration) was not summarized.

Some forms of subsidy are difficult to see and estimate. For example, some public enterprises sell their services at differential rates, charging some groups less and others more. The cost of the subsidy to those paying less may be completely invisible. Sometimes price reductions to large users are justified as based on economies of scale, that is, it is cheaper per unit to produce and deliver large amounts to a single address. But the size of the economies of scale may never be calculated or documented, so any amount of reduction may be justified in this way. One would have to know the real costs of producing and delivering the service in order to compute the level of subsidy, an impossible task without the enterprise's cooperation. In these cases, where a service is provided at less than the cost to produce it, an expensive and almost invisible subsidy is being provided to narrow groups of beneficiaries.

Most public enterprises do not break even and are subsidized by general taxation. Sometimes these subsidies are clearly labeled in the budget, but sometimes they are not. The postal service, for example, is subsidized by tax dollars, to keep rates low. Postal subsidies to newspapers and news magazines are direct and widely known, but postal service personnel costs have been subsidized in a less visible way. The postal service has paid two-thirds of the pension and health benefits of employees, while the U.S. Treasury has paid the rest. The subsidy in 1984 was $.8 billion, and was projected to increase to $4.4 billion by 1989.[37] By the end of 1987, however, the level of subsidy was reduced.

The subsidies may be intentionally secret if the level of subsidy is politically controversial. Subsidies at the local level may involve unrepaid (possibly unrecorded) interfund transfers or transfers in kind. A city government may provide an enterprise with free space or subsidized rent; the true market value and hence the amount of the subsidy is not calculated. "Free" snow plowing of the municipal airport or "free" engineering services are additional examples. People who want to increase the political acceptability of an airport enterprise by making it look cheap (if it pays for itself, how can anyone object?) may try to hide subsidies or minimize their amounts.

When subsidies to public enterprises are not hidden, they may be highly controversial. Not all subsidized enterprises benefit the poor or handicapped; some benefit farmers (with subsidized electricity) or rural residents (with subsidized train services)[38] or other particular target groups. What makes subsidies so controversial is that ultimately all taxpayers, most of whom do not benefit from the service, are paying to reduce the cost of selected services for others. In the case of airports, it is often the owners of private airplanes whose costs are being subsidized, a group that is certainly not poor.

**MINICASE: BETWEEN A (LITTLE) ROCK AND A HARD PLACE:
SITING AND FUNDING A PRESIDENTIAL LIBRARY**

Locating a presidential library in a city may be viewed as a form of economic development, but the immediate beneficiaries are not likely to be seen as poor or otherwise needy of public subsidy.[39] In addition, those who oppose the president whose library it is may oppose public spending on such a project. What to do if you are determined to build a project with public subsidy, cannot keep the costs secret because you have to ask for the money, but you think the public if asked, might reject the project because of the narrowness of the group of beneficiaries?

Long before the vote to impeach President Clinton came in the House of Representatives, many citizens in the capital city of Arkansas were skeptical about honoring him with a presidential library there. On the other hand, there were many others—including city officials—who projected that the economic benefits of such a siting would be beneficial to the city and its residents no matter how citizens felt about the president. City officials envisioned a revitalized downtown surrounding the potential site and hired a Philadelphia consulting firm, which estimated that the library investment would provide a return of $10.7 million per year for the city. But siting the library in this location required some creative financing that will have fiscal impacts on the city for many years to come, and the project provides an excellent example of what happens when elected and appointed officials do not consult the public before spending public money.

The land that Little Rock officials wanted for the project came at a price of $13.5 million—a sum that was (understandably) not readily available but had to be raised before the site could be announced. The initial proposal to pay for acquisition and clearing of the land involved an increase in the hotel and restaurant tax that required no public vote. But the public protest was so resounding that this approach was eventually dropped and alternative funding mechanisms considered. The decision was then made to issue $16.5 million in park revenue bonds to pay for the land and the cost of the bond issue. In March 1998 the city board approved the issuance of the bonds, in spite of the fact that citizen groups called for the measure to be put to a vote in a special election. Citizen groups failed to get the needed signatures in time to put the referendum on the ballot in April 1998, however, and the bonds were issued and the land purchased in May of that year.

The city then pledged fees from parks and golf courses to pay back the bonds, taking dollars from the general fund that would have to be replaced later. In response to these actions, one community activist blamed the postal service and downtown retailers for defeating the proposal for a voter referendum on the bonds, resulting in the filing of a court case. The complaint was later amended to add that the city was illegally using park fees to buy the land. While some citizens were still focused on the inappropriateness of honoring an impeached president, others made the more compelling argument that infrastructure needs in the city were more crucial and that a revenue bond issue to repair streets and drainage received much slower action. Still other citizens expressed concern that city parks and the zoo also needed improvements and that the park and golf fees should have been used to pay for these needs instead of being diverted to pay off the bonds for the presidential library.

The mayor proposed a solution to this dilemma in January 1999, announcing a plan to offer something for everyone by fixing up all sections of Little Rock through the passage of a one-cent sales tax. The proposed tax consisted of a .75-cent temporary tax to pay for $150 million in capital improvements and infrastructure needs over the next five years, and a .25-cent ongoing tax or $9.3 million a year to go for city operating expenses. But many citizens were by then aware that the sales tax was really needed for the first payment on the park bonds issued for the presidential library site. The mayor continued to hold public meetings around the city to promote his plan for the tax, tailoring his presentations for various interest groups. But he was constantly plagued by questions regarding the use of the money to pay for the library, causing it to be dubbed in the press the "Clinton Lie-berry." A group of Little Rock residents even vowed to raise $25,000 to help defeat the tax, and terms like *arrogant* and *irresponsible* were used to describe City of

Little Rock officials, who, the press also reported, hoped that most voters would be "asleep" while the package passed.

Although foes of the tax spent only $3,288 to fight it and the city spent $31,264 to promote it (a ratio of 1:10), and voter turnout was lower than expected, the tax package failed by a margin of 2 to 1. Many citizens viewed this result as proof that even those residents who saw the advantages of building the library were upset by the way the site was funded. But the problem remained that the city was in sad financial state because the payments on the park bonds had to continue, and there was no "Plan B" for financing these payments. Meanwhile other reports were circulating about bad financial practices in the city, including the illegal investment of funds over the past several years and early reports of a projected deficit of $4.1 million in the FY 2000 operating budget. As a result, the City Board of Directors passed a resolution to put the budget at the top of its priority list, cutting a whole city department, initiating layoffs and a hiring freeze, and reducing expected pay raises by half for all city employees. Because of these cost-cutting measures, the City Manager then projected instead a surplus of $1.5 million in FY 2000 and asked elected officials to consider funding some of the projects listed in the mayor's January proposal without referring to the dilemma over the bond payments.

When the court case regarding the issuance of the bonds was heard in June 1999, the judge ruled that Little Rock had not spent the money illegally or used it improperly to buy the land for the library. But the antitax advocate who filed the original suit vowed to appeal, meaning the issue would not go away anytime soon—as either a fiscal problem or a political one. The budgeting lesson in Little Rock is clear: whether elected or appointed, officials must consult the people before spending public money, even if they believe the expense is ultimately in the best interest of the public. When officials do not take the opinions of taxpayers into consideration, they may find themselves between a rock and a hard place, with land for a presidential library that many citizens are still not sure they want, and the obligation of bond payments that must be made from public funds.

Subsidies that are public and visible can become highly controversial. As a result, some subsidies, such as a reduction in competition that allows businesses to charge higher prices, are particularly difficult to see and count. Farmers may receive such indirect subsidies to keep competition low.[40] The actual mechanism of delivering the subsidies has varied enormously over the years. One approach has been to limit the amount of land planted to certain crops, to reduce the total yield and thereby improve prices. Another regulatory approach has been to limit foreign imports of some crops so that U.S. farmers will not have to compete with less expensive crops from abroad. U.S. consumers pay for these market interventions when they pay routinely higher prices for their food. Taxpayers directly bear the costs of paying farmers for not planting certain crops; they indirectly pay for the subsidy in higher food prices at the supermarket.

Another example of a subsidy that is difficult to estimate is called a land writedown. Its intent is to be an economic development tool, to help attract new businesses to an area and hence generate local jobs. The city or other jurisdiction acquires land, possibly through its legal right of eminent domain, which allows it to purchase land against the owners' will for a public purpose, presumably at a fair market price. Since a private developer would have to deal with holdouts—those who refuse to sell, and those who pretend to refuse to sell to bid up the price—the government's action in putting together a large plot of land for development is a benefit to the private sector. The land may then be sold to the developer for considerably less than the parcel would now go for on the market. The difference between the worth of the land and the cost of the sale to the developer is called a writedown. The amount of the writedown may never be calculated, because it depends on estimates of the current value of the land for its intended use. How much money state and local governments spend on such incentives is difficult, if not impossible, to ascertain.

Land writedowns are an example of using almost invisible money to make what might be controversial an expenditure for a single company. The expenditure is rationalized in terms of positive spillovers, that is, the resulting economic development. But the amount of future development and the distribution of benefits from that development are highly uncertain. The company may not hire many local residents; or it may take the subsidies, make profits for a few years, and then leave the city and the state. Current costs should be weighed against potential future gains. If the costs of the development are high and visible, and there are many competing projects, some of which may have more certain return, such subsidies may generate much discussion and possibly opposition. Businesses already located in the city are likely to wonder why the city spends so much on a company that has yet returned nothing to the city, while they pay their taxes, generate jobs, and get nothing back from the city. Homeowners may question why they pay taxes that go for single companies to lower their costs when there are a variety of needs in the city, such as street, water system, and sewer improvements.

Using invisible or nearly invisible money can head off controversy. Another example is the use of pensions to increase the total compensation package for public employees. Little public information is distributed about how pension funds are run. While perhaps not intentionally hidden, they tend to be secret on a secret-open continuum. Their relatively secret nature combined with the fact that they generally involve future rather than current expenses make them ideal salary incentives in governments where salary increases to local employees would be looked at askance by taxpayers. For example, mayors can give raises to employees through pension funds while seeming in public to be holding the line on salaries, being tough with employee demands and easy on the taxpayers' pocketbooks. Labor is kept content, presumably avoiding embarrassing strikes. The cost of this strategy is ballooning future obligations. Although later officials will be stuck with the tab, current politicians will be long gone by the time the consequences are felt.

Perhaps the epitome of intentional secrecy in budgeting is the Defense Department's "black budget," the portion of defense spending that has been classified and is not subject to public discussion or debate. It includes most of the Central Intelligence Agency and all of the National Security Agency and the National Reconnaissance Office. It pays for secret wars and secret police, at the discretion of the president. While there are undoubtedly some legitimate national secrets in the black budget, during the 1980s it expanded to include controversial weapons systems, and by extension, the policies that drive their invention and intended deployment. None of these policies may be discussed, and some of the projects cannot even be named in public. By 1989, the black budget peaked at about $36 billion a year. The declassification of the Stealth bomber and MIL-STAR, a complex computerized communication and coordination project to run a nuclear war, brought the black budget down to $34 billion by 1991.[41]

From 1981, at the very beginning of the Reagan administration, to 1985, the Pentagon budget doubled, but the secret portion for weapons increased eightfold.[42] During that period, there was no outside scrutiny of secret spending, not by the General Accounting Office and not by the Pentagon's own auditors.

After the GAO was allowed in, it discovered that the air force and navy refused to tell "their civilian overseers about new black programs they . . . created."[43] The military had created hundreds of unauthorized programs during the 1980s. The lack of oversight suggested not only that civilians had lost control of the military but also that the quality of management might be worse in the secret portion of the defense budget than it was in the overt part. Secrecy made it possible to hide mistakes and made economizing unnecessary.

Congress began to try to take control of the black budget in 1986. Procurement horror stories in the regular Defense Department budget roused Congress and made many wonder about the waste that might be occurring out of sight. Congressman John Dingell, who chaired the Subcommittee on Oversight and Investigations of the House Committee on Energy and Commerce, spearheaded the effort; also important was Les Aspin, who took over the House Armed Services Committee and was the first chair in many years who was willing to question what the generals asked for. Dingell asked the secretary of defense for a list of air force black programs over $10 million; the secretary ignored the request. Then Les Aspin and the ranking minority member of the House Armed Services Committee, writing for the committee, argued with the secretary that too many defense programs were being put into the black budget and that the budget numbers for the Stealth bomber and the advanced Cruise missile should be released. The secretary did not release the figures. In the face of this intransigiency, Congress passed a law the following year, requiring the Defense Department to reveal the information. The information was not revealed until 1989, by which time much of the weapons research had been completed.[44] In 1992 the secret satellite program was made visible; its budget was about $6 billion.[45] Though technically still part of the secret budget, the satellite program has been opened to financial oversight. That oversight further erodes the sanctity of the black budget. By 1995, newspapers were estimating the size of the black budget at about $28 billion.[46] In 1997 the CIA reported, as the result of a freedom of information lawsuit, that the black budget totaled $26.6 billion.

MINICASE: THE IMPACT OF BEING IN A SECRET BUDGET

The spy satellite program, in the National Reconnaissance Office, was made public in 1992 after operating for more than thirty years as a supersecret agency. While it was secret, the satellite program got into the habit of ignoring the bottom line. In some cases, spending estimates for the expensive satellites were too low by about half, but Congress approved the overruns "because the technology was essential for monitoring the Soviets."[47] With the collapse of the Soviet Union, the agency's rationale disappeared, and with it, its cloak of secrecy. Pressure to make the agency public was intertwined with the need to make budget cuts. The agency's mission was scrutinized and its budget deeply cut.

After the agency went public, the level of scrutiny of its budget increased, calling attention to a series of peculiar financial maneuvers. The agency had developed a certain laxness about budgetary responsiveness and accountability. In 1993 the agency had signed a multi-billion dollar contract for ocean surveillance satellites, in direct contradiction to congressional instructions. Then the agency built a $347 million building for itself, without telling Congress that it was doing so, drawing from accounts that were not labeled for construction. In 1995 financial overseers discovered that the agency had built up a contingency fund of $1.5 billion, a substantial proportion of its total budget, ignoring congressional directives to reduce the size of the fund. Reportedly the contingency fund began because the agency did not want to compromise its secrecy by asking Congress for supplemental appropriations to keep production lines going. The fund was allowed to grow from year to year, however. Congress cut back the discretionary fund in 1995 when it discovered the size to which the fund had grown.[48]

Congress has not yet developed general controls over the black budget, but after a period of expansion in the 1980s, the size of the secret budget has begun to come down. The collapse of the Soviet Union has taken away a major excuse for secrecy at the same time that efforts to control the deficit have made it imperative to control agency spending and eliminate waste. Especially when agencies flout congressional will, they may lose their secret status and some of their discretion. The Department of Defense may actually find this loss of secrecy advantageous because it both allows and requires the department to gain public and congressional support for weapons and surveillance programs earlier in their development instead of presenting such programs as done deals later on. At the least, greater openness allows the Defense Department to demonstrate managerial improvements and reduced waste in procurement; at best, greater openness suggests that the Defense Department, and especially its spy agencies, is controllable by elected officials.

Summary and Conclusions

In the public sector, because of the wide variety of budget actors and the variety of their preferences, the amount of competition underlying the budget is necessarily high. The chief executive and his or her staff, the department heads, and legislators and their staffs all play a role in formulating or approving proposals for expenditures. A variety of interest groups may lobby for particular expenditures, and the public at large may have marked preferences about what government should and should not spend money on. The level of competition may be exaggerated or reduced by changes in the environment and in the budget process. The budget process frames choices and hence determines what expenditure proposals compete with one another.

When programs or departments are forced to compete with one another for resources, they develop a variety of strategies to improve the priority of their spending goals. In the capital budget, project supporters may argue that the technical requirements for some project absolutely require this expense immediately; or they may argue that delay will only cost more. In the operating budget program supporters may argue the political consequences of failure to provide a popular service, or they may try to link their programs to widely accepted policy goals.

Competition in some parts of the budget and under some budget processes may be so keen that the actors, rather than try to compete successfully, switch to strategies to reduce the level of conflict. They do this in a variety of ways. In the capital budget, competition can be defused through the use of a long-term plan; projects not funded this year can be kept alive and possibly funded later. There are winners, but no absolute losers. In the service portion of the budget, competition may be defused by norms forbidding sudden termination or deep cutbacks in one program to build another. Change occurs in small amounts at the margins, limiting the scope of competition. In trust funds and enterprises, competition is defused by taking revenues and expenditures out of the general fund, isolating them from potential tradeoffs. For some program expenditures, competition is defused by setting them up as entitlements, distributing funds by formula, or by imposing particular expenditures by mandates. One cannot understand these adaptations and the direction of change without appreciating the intensity of competition that underlies them.

The direction of change over the past fifty years has been to lock up more and more of the budget, to take out programs and projects from the competitive parts of the budget. There has been an increase in the use of trust funds and, even more dramatically at the national level, in the use of entitlements. At the local level, services that charged fees have been increasingly segregated from the municipal budget, and in some states have been set up as special, single-purpose governmental units. Contractors may push for long-term sole-source contracts, to lock in particular spending for capital projects; coalitions of interest groups, legislators, and bureaucrats may, when the environment favors them, push to lock their programs into the budget for as long a period as they can manage.

The result of the changing composition of the budget is that budgets may now look more interest-group dominated, and it may be difficult to perceive competition over the short term. But trying to lock in expenditures at the peak of one's power is part of budgetary politics; if anything, it underscores the waxing and waning of interest-group influence and the responsiveness of expenditures to outside contingencies. Coalitions of support for a particular program may peak at some point, and at that point supporters try to lock in their programs through a trust fund structure or an entitlement. The coalition may not be able to stay together after that, or the environmental conditions that made their program seem desirable may disappear. If they were successful in locking in their program or project, their programs will survive future changes in environmental conditions.

The process of locking up expenditure decisions and reducing budgetary competition is not permanent and one-directional. There are major pressures in the opposite direction, to reduce or weaken entitlements, to borrow from public enterprises or use their revenues for other purposes, to use trust funds for other purposes or use general funds to pay for programs funded by trust funds. But the time frame for unlocking expenditures may be relatively long. Politicians find it extremely difficult to terminate entitlements that are popular with a broad segment of the public. If, over a long period of time, that support erodes, politicians may be able to change programs from entitlements to block grants, making them easier to cut. It took many years and a massive reduction in the number of family farms before cuts in the agriculture support programs became acceptable. Efforts to break into trust funds may take years, but have sometimes been successful, as in the Highway Trust Fund.

Handling competition is one key theme in the politics of expenditures; the second one is managing accountability and acceptability to the taxpaying public. The budget choices do not depend only on what the budget actors want and can get from one another; they are constrained by the preferences of the public that pays the taxes. Accountability and acceptability are handled differently depending on how popular particular expenditures are, and what techniques are used to gain support for less popular programs.

The delivery of services that benefit citizens broadly is generally publicly acceptable, and the costs are open and clear. In situations in which the benefits are targeted at a narrower group, and costs can be pinpointed, program supporters may offer their support to other groups to help them get their programs, in order to widen the support base. Thus supporters of agricultural subsidies to rural areas supported school lunch programs for the urban poor. Coalitions of support may be engineered between various interests. Spending under these conditions may occasionally be controversial, but the strategy generally works. In areas of spending where individual groups or geographic areas benefit without any apparent trades of support, the costs may be deeply submerged or made invisible. Controversial issues may be kept off the policy agenda.

The politics of expenditures is not dominated by the motives and strategies of a limited set of actors. Instead, varying groups of actors, with strategies framed by the budget process and the environment, strive to achieve their goals. Elected officials who make budgetary decisions are ultimately accountable to the public; the need to gain public acceptance of spending decisions influences the openness of spending, the geographic distribution of beneficiaries of spending, and the formation of coalitions among rivals for spending. The result is simultaneously highly competitive and highly constrained, open to the environment, and accountable, more or less, to the public.

CHAPTER SIX

The Politics of Balancing the Budget

> *. . . We still need to constrain the deficit. We still need ways to impose budgetary discipline. . . . Yet . . . Gramm-Rudman has accomplished neither reduction nor restraint. . . . the time has come for something more effective.*
>
> —SENATOR JIM SASSER

THE MOST IMPORTANT constraint on budgeting is the requirement for balance: Revenues must equal or exceed expenditures. Balancing is a key part of budgetary decision making, but it is not always successful. Budgets may look balanced but not be really balanced. Even if budgets are truly balanced at the beginning of the budget year, they may become unbalanced during the year. This may occur by accident, if revenue projections were not good enough or if some expenditures were unintentionally underestimated. But governments sometimes run deficits intentionally. There may be an emergency—a war, a diplomatic initiative, or a natural disaster—that requires spending whether budgeted or not. Or government can run deficits to moderate negative trends in the economy (at the national level) or to maintain spending for unemployment benefits and welfare during a recession. Government can also run deficits because the budget actors are unwilling to make difficult choices.

When deficits are caused by emergencies or by declines in the economy, the borrowing required to cover the deficits is temporary and is not usually particularly harmful. Budgets have to be flexible and responsive to the environment, and some borrowing may be necessary to that end. But sometimes deficits occur because revenues are growing more slowly than expenditures and decision makers are unwilling to make the politically difficult choices of cutting expenditures and increasing revenues. This kind of imbalance may be chronic rather than temporary and is more serious than deficits that occur briefly during economic downturns.

The most serious deficits occur when decision makers ignore the constraints of balance or treat them as more flexible than they are. They may choose to cut taxes without cutting back spending proportionately; or they may increase the rate of spending beyond the rate of growth in revenues, causing potential deficits down the road, especially if the increases in spending are in entitlements or other hard-to-cut areas of spending. This kind of deficit spending is attributed to a lack of discipline or a lack of will; the proposed solution is often more rigid constraints, embodied in constitutional amendments, new statutes, or new budget processes.

While decisions that have to be made to avoid deficits may be politically unpopular, the solution of ignoring hard decisions and running deficits is not popular either. Both the public and the financial community oppose deficits. Since the 1940s, opinion polls have shown that the public favors balanced budgets by approximately 2 to 1. The Harris survey in 1982 found that Americans agreed by more than a 2 to 1 margin that a constitutional amendment to balance the federal budget would be "an effective way to keep federal spending under control."[1] Financial markets that loan governments money also insist on balanced budgets.

Because deficits are embarrassing, when governments run chronic deficits, those responsible for them tend to deny them or minimize their size and importance. The quality of the budget numbers suffers under these circumstances, and it can be extremely difficult to figure out the real size of the deficits. Once the numbers are obscured, pressures to reduce the deficit are also diminished, making it more difficult to gather the necessary political support to return to balanced budgets.

By the time budget actors decide to eliminate deficits, those deficits may be very large and proportionately difficult to cut back. Whose programs should be cut back, and by how much? Where can cuts legally be made? How can resistance from interest groups be minimized? Whose taxes should be raised, and by how much? Can expenditures be shifted to other levels of government to reduce the size of the deficit? How can the appropriate actions be taken while maintaining accountability and acceptability to the public? How can politicians make such unpopular choices and still maintain their support base?

The politics of budget balance revolves less around the routine decisions made in most budgets to make them balance than it does around how and why budgets get unbalanced, and how to rebalance them when they get out of balance. This kind of budgetary politics can be explored by returning to the characteristics of public budgeting: It is marked by constraints, it involves multiple actors with different budgetary goals, it is open to the environment, and it has to resolve the separation of taxpayer and budget decision maker through techniques of accountability and acceptability.

Balance as a Constraint

Governments define what balance means, making the constraints looser or tighter depending on the circumstances. They may include or exclude savings from prior years when they calculate balance. The requirement for balance may cover all funds or only some of them. The balance constraint is eased if surpluses from one fund can be used to defray shortages in another fund. Some governments allow the budget to be balanced with borrowed money, drastically loosening the balance constraint.

Another way that the constraint of balance can be loosened or tightened is to adjust when the budget must be balanced. For example, in some states, such as California, New York, and New Hampshire, the governor is required only to present a balanced budget to the legislature; after that, anything can happen. In Alaska, the legislature has only to pass a balanced budget, but there are no features describing what happens after the budget is passed. In some states, any deficit that occurs after the budget is passed must be eliminated within that fiscal year; in others, it may be carried over into the next fiscal year or biennium.[2]

Most of the time, balance is determined year by year, but sometimes balance occurs over several years. If all outstanding obligations were to be deducted from this year's revenue, the budget might not be balanced, but if those same obligations were matched against several years' anticipated revenues, that same budget might be balanced. The Federal Highway Trust Fund illustrates this somewhat looser definition of balance.

MINICASE: BALANCE AND THE HIGHWAY TRUST FUND

The Highway Trust Fund is an account, based primarily on user fees, that is set aside for the purpose of building and repairing the nation's highways. The trust fund operates through contract authority, rather than more normal budget authority: when projects are finished, the states bill the federal government for reimbursement, which comes out of the Highway Trust Fund. As a result, a simple definition of balance (and surplus) is not possible for the Highway Trust Fund. That is, if the trust fund defined itself as balanced because its revenues this year were greater than its outlays this year, the result would be highly misleading. Revenues have to be greater than obligations, not just outlays, because the states are toting up bills that have not been submitted yet. By next year, there will be more money in the trust fund to pay off the bills that are being incurred now but will not be presented until next year or the year after. So how can anyone tell if the trust fund is really balanced at any one time? How can Congress or the president ensure that the states do nòt exceed revenues in their spending? And if there is a surplus, how does anyone know how much it is?

When money is committed by the states, it shows up in the trust fund as obligated but not yet spent. So the total remains high, although much of the money is already committed and cannot be spent on anything else. The result of not subtracting this committed money from the trust fund total is to make the balance in the fund look higher than it really is, which can be an advantage if the goal is to make the federal budget as a whole look balanced by counting the "surplus" in the Highway Trust Fund as part of the consolidated balance of the federal government. But the result is misleading.

> In FY 1994, for example, the highway account showed future commitments of $42.6 billion. If these commitments had been charged against the balance in the highway account at that time, it actually would have shown a deficit. To guarantee the ability to make good on these commitments, Congress, through the Byrd amendment to the Federal-Aid Highway Act of 1956, as amended, restricted the growth of these commitments to a level not to exceed the current year's unexpended balance plus projected income for the following two fiscal years.[3]

> The result does provide some protection against overspending, but it does not yield an exact figure for budgetary balance or an exact estimate of surplus. To calculate a surplus in this situation, one has to subtract the actual obligations from the present and future revenues. The number is spongy, in part because until bills are actually presented for projects approved or underway, the exact amount is not known. Also, the calculation depends on estimates of revenues for the present and the next two years.

The size of the margin required for balance also varies. In some states, revenues are expected to exceed or equal expenditures in order to have balance; other states require that revenues exceed expenditures by a specified margin. This excess becomes part of a balance that can be used to apply against revenue shortfalls when they occur.

When governments run deficits, public officials have a tendency to increase the number and severity of constraints as a way to restore balance. The additional constraints can vary from a moderate change in the budget process that makes the linkage between revenue and expenditure decisions tighter and more authoritative, to a change in statutes making the requirements for balance more inclusive and more difficult to get around, to a change in the constitution, narrowly specifying the conditions under which deficits may be run, or generally forbidding deficits.

Multiple Actors, Ideologies, and Deficits

Who gets involved in the politics of balance, and how do these actors come down on a variety of policy issues involved in budget balancing?

The public plays an indirect role, putting pressure on elected officials to balance the budget. Citizens seem to feel that their personal budgets have to balance and hence governmental budgets should also balance.

Interest groups may contribute to deficits by making it difficult to raise taxes or cut programs. When cuts are being proposed, interest groups may be vociferous in protecting programs that benefit them. But interest groups that represent narrow constituencies do not generally have distinct policies toward deficits (as opposed to policies toward maintaining the programs that benefit them) or play much of a policy role in the politics of deficits.

Because many of the policy issues surrounding balance of the budget affect broad social classes, broad coalitions of interest groups that come close to representing social classes may play a more active policy role. A coalition of labor unions may oppose a coalition of business groups. Politicians sometimes use the requirement for balance as a vehicle for arguing about the appropriate size of government and level of taxation. These are issues that affect the rich and the poor differently, and thus class-based coalitions often take sides in debates on budgetary balance.

Officials at different levels of government also become actors in the politics of deficits because of the possibility of one level of government balancing its budget at the expense of other levels of government. There are at least four major policy issues in the politics of balance that these actors take sides on.

The Appropriate Size of Government

Budgets may be balanced by allowing revenues to increase, by freezing revenues at current levels and cutting expenditures to match, or by reducing revenues and cutting expenditures deeply to create a new level of balance. Allowing revenues to increase to reduce deficits is a fiscally conservative but socially more liberal position, without major implications for current program spending. Achieving budget balance by deeply cutting programs is a more politically conservative position. Some conservatives press for cuts in taxes, to force cuts in expenditures, using the requirement of balance as a vehicle to reduce the scope of government.

The Role of the Budget in the Economy

Should the budget be a tool of control over the economy to dampen economic swings, to control inflation and unemployment levels? Political liberals have accepted the need for deficits during recessions because the need to increase unemployment benefits and welfare spending occurs at the same time that government receipts decline as a result of falling incomes. Some conservatives oppose deficit spending as a technique to help stimulate the economy when it is weak, possibly because such spending has had a bias toward the poor and the unemployed. They prefer that the budget not be responsive to economic cycles at all, and argue that expenditures should be cut back when revenues fall during recessions. Other political conservatives will tolerate deficits during recessions if the deficit is caused by tax reductions to businesses and the wealthy. This policy is supposed to increase the supply of capital and thus stimulate the economy. Not only conservatives and liberals line up on this issue, but also aggregates of interest groups that represent business and labor.

The Role of Each Level of Government

Where should the burden for providing services and benefits be placed? If balancing the budget becomes a valued goal at the federal level, there may be a strong temptation to balance it at the expense of other levels of government, cutting back grants and passing on program responsibilities. The states may do the same with local governments. Local governments may try to give service responsibility back to the state government or to townships, counties, or special districts, or the private sector. In theory, each level of government has an interest in passing on expenditures to other levels of government and preventing expenditures from being passed to themselves.

The Choice of Outcomes

Which functions should continue to be performed? Whose benefits and programs should be maintained or cut? The politics of balance may lightly veil a bitter politics of outcomes with protection or termination of particular programs or benefits as the goal. Interest groups, service recipients, and agency heads may take sides on this issue to protect their programs.

These four issues summarize what many of the actors in this portion of the budgetary decision-making process are trying to achieve. Liberals are trying to maintain the scope of government, while conservatives are trying to shrink it; working people and their representatives want the budget to be used to keep the level of employment high, while business people and their representatives prefer that the budget be used to keep taxes low; each level of government wants to balance its budget, possibly by shifting the burdens of programs and projects elsewhere, so that the tough decisions of what to cut or how to increase taxes do not have to be made; and interest groups, legislators, beneficiaries of programs, and agency heads are trying to protect their programs from cuts that are made to balance the budget.

The Environment, Unpredictability, and Deficits

Deficits occur in part because budgets are open to the environment, which can challenge the budget in a variety of ways. The courts may declare that mental patients cannot be committed to a mental hospital without treatment or that overcrowding of prisons is cruel and unusual punishment, so governments have to increase treatments in mental hospitals and build more prisons and hire more guards. State or federal governments may mandate expenditures, requiring local governments to list all their toxic materials or provide higher pensions for the police. Or natural events can provoke increases in expenditures, for example, hurricanes, floods, blizzards, or exceptionally cold weather. Violence, such as riots, crime waves, or political demonstrations, can require extra staff hours, increased communication equipment, improved training or better public relations, more jobs, new programs, and additional housing. War, with its overriding urgency, can increase expenditures without reference to current revenues.

Unexpected losses of revenues can result from courts declaring some tax unconstitutional, which may require the restoration of the revenues to the taxpayers. Or sudden declines in tax revenues can result from changes in state laws that affect local governments. There may be a sudden change in the type of bonds that cities may legally issue, or some forms of borrowing may become unexpectedly expensive or hard to get when a government is planning to borrow for a large project. A sudden downturn in the economy can shrink revenues below expectations. At the local level, a business may close unexpectedly, or move to another state, causing a decline in property taxes and leaving employees without jobs and without income, reducing sales tax revenues.

The intergovernmental revenue system introduces considerable uncertainty for state and local governments. Some grants are competitive, and so the potential recipients do not know in advance if they will receive the money. Sometimes intergovernmental aid is phrased as an entitlement so that all those cities, for example, who have over 6 percent of their population unemployed for longer than a certain number of months are eligible for particular kinds of aid. Those paying for the program cannot estimate its cost; those who might receive the aid do not have any way of knowing in advance whether they will be eligible. They may find out in the middle of a fiscal year that they will get the aid.

When state governments give aid to local governments in the form of entitlements, the problem is exaggerated because the state governments themselves have to balance their budgets. To meet unexpected increases in costs, they have to set aside contingency funds. Some states at times incur obligations to their local governments that they in turn do not have the money to fund. Local governments that planned on revenues from the state and included them in their budgets have to guess how much they will receive of what they were entitled to.

Another, related problem with intergovernmental revenues is that when the donor-level government is in financial trouble, it may hang on to the money it is supposed to give to the recipient for weeks or even months, so it can earn interest on the money to solve its own financial problems. Or it can simply delay payments into the next fiscal year, forcing those who needed the money and planned to use it at the normal time to borrow in anticipation of receiving the money later.

Some expenditures are demand driven rather than revenue driven. That means that the cost depends on the demand; the supply of the service is not determined by how much money is budgeted. For example, fire departments are to some extent demand driven; they respond to calls, and the calls are not limited to or even related to the supply. One response to such a situation from the budgetary perspective is to create an overcapacity and budget for it so that no matter what the demand, it is budgeted for. But that is a very expensive solution. Ambulance calls are demand driven; social service agencies that deal with battered spouses or abused children are demand driven. You cannot turn someone away in the middle of a crisis in which they are in physical danger, yet costs are proportional to the number of clients. Environmental changes may push such costs up beyond plans or expectations. For example, the increasing use of crack, an addictive form of cocaine, seems to increase the number of abandoned children and the incidence of spouse abuse, but it is hard to predict when it will hit a particular community or with what force. A poor economy in other parts of the world may set the jobless migrating, and an influx of non-English-speaking immigrants may tax the capacity of the Immigration and Naturalization Service and all the social agencies that deal with poor immigrants.

The problem of demand-driven costs is particularly acute at the federal level because so much of federal spending is now composed of entitlements, many of which are open ended. That means that if there is an increase in the number of people eligible for a given benefit, the money must be found to pay them, regardless of what is happening on the revenue side. Entitlements decouple revenue and expenditure decisions, and hence contribute to deficits.

Long and severe recessions contribute most directly to budgetary imbalance because they simultaneously increase expenditures for unemployment relief and welfare and reduce revenues because so many people are out of work or earning less. It is politically very difficult to raise taxes when many people are unemployed, and perhaps equally difficult to reduce the benefits of people who are desperate for them because they have been thrown out of work. Moreover, reducing public spending in order to balance the budget may have the effect of worsening the recession because people have even less money to spend to keep the economy going.

The environment may also contribute to deficits when the economy of a whole region is gradually declining and the amount of taxable wealth is stable or declining. The costs of delivering programs and projects may continue to increase, since costs are often not proportionate to the size of the population but to the number of lane miles, or the number of square miles of area. There may be a long-term disequilibrium between the cost of government and the availability of revenues. Either governments must continue to raise tax rates, taking a higher and higher share of people's income, against which the public will eventually rebel, or continue to cut back the level of programs and projects, potentially exaggerating the decline. In the face of such continuing negative choices, officials may from time to time run deficits. Such deficits are not inevitable and not acceptable to the public or the financial community, but they are perhaps understandable.

In short, many deficits, perhaps most of them, stem from changes in the environment. These changes may require more flexibility than the budget can deliver. Despite the best of intentions, deficits happen. Forbidding deficits, which is one response to them, seems futile in the face of the openness of the budget to the environment. The budget can be made less open to the environment, and it can be made more flexible, so that it can adapt without deficits. But the most common response seems to be to run the deficits, and then worry about how to eliminate them in a timely and fair manner.

Increasing Stress between Payer and Decider

The potential difficulties created by the separation of payer and decider may become acute when governments run deficits. The public wants balance, but it simultaneously wants to maintain services and programs that it likes, and does not want to increase its tax burden. Decision makers are faced with what appears to be a series of impossible choices from the perspective of political acceptability. Citizens may argue to tax someone else, and cut someone else's programs, but for the decision maker, there may not be many legal options that satisfy those conditions. The result in these cases may be a reduction in accountability.

On the simplest level, in cities, cuts may be taken where they are least visible, in order to prevent citizens' complaints. Such cuts break the visible link between taxes paid and services produced; it appears as if cuts can be made without reducing services. The costs of such a strategy, besides the long-term decline in trust of the taxpayers, include the increased costs of delayed maintenance, of capital projects deferred, and the inability to downsize in a logical way.

The unpopularity of deficits when combined with the unpleasant options to reduce them may lead to a tendency to hide or minimize them, and to pretend they are not there. The budget in this case loses much of its capacity to act as an instrument of accountability, transparently telling the citizens how their money is being spent. Balance may be redefined, the system of accounting may be changed to a cash basis to hide deficits, long-term capital borrowing may be used to cover operating deficits, expenditures may be pushed off into the next year, funds may be borrowed between accounts inappropriately and possibly without record (presumably with intent to repay). Revenues may be overestimated or expenditures underestimated to make the budget, as passed, look more balanced than it is. The longer this hiding goes on, the more convoluted and uninformative the budget becomes. The worse the situation looks, the more unwilling those responsible for it may be to have the situation revealed.

How, then, can the deficit situation ever be fixed? What kinds of pressures are there to reveal the problem and restore balance? Actually there are a number of such pressures. For example, if there has been a lot of internal borrowing, those agency heads whose budget is being borrowed may become desperate enough to complain, especially if they are not being left with enough money to run their programs and they are being publicly criticized for poor management. Second, the problems of internal borrowing may become so tangled that auditors can no longer certify the honesty and integrity of the financial records, a sure warning sign of trouble that may begin unraveling the situation and bringing it to public attention. Third, if the problem goes on long enough, there is likely to be an election, and if there is competition, the rival for chief executive is likely to be more than willing to discover his or her opponent's financial misdoings. If and when new politicians are elected they have the incentive to reveal as much as they can attribute to their predecessor, and make a highly publicized effort to clean it up, casting the blame on the previous incumbent. Fourth, the amounts involved may become so large that they are impossible to keep quiet. If these amounts grow large enough, they necessitate public borrowing, which means turning to a public market for funds. Banks and other investors normally require evidence of sound financial practice. The more desperate a government is to borrow, the more it needs to restore its fiscal integrity to be able to do so. The cost of borrowing may become so substantial that it interferes with the ability of the government to carry on its routine activities, adding to the pressure to restore balance.

Once the need is recognized, the difficult task of restoring balance remains. When many programs are entitlements and difficult to cut back or trim, and other programs have intense interest-group support, it may be difficult to know where and how to cut expenses while maintaining acceptability to the public. These problems have been particularly intense at the federal level, where the size of the deficit became astronomical before serious efforts were taken to reduce it.

The four characteristics of public budgeting—constraints, variety of actors and goals, openness to the environment, and the separation of payer and decider—provide some common themes for the politics of deficits at different levels of government. Nevertheless, some important differences between federal, state, and local budgeting give different emphasis and different interpretation of deficit reduction efforts at different levels of government.

One difference between levels of government is that state and local governments are required to balance their budgets; the federal government is not. When changes in the environment push up the costs of entitlement programs at the federal level, the increased costs show up as increased deficits; at the state level, the costs have to come out of a contingency fund or reduced spending for other budgeted expenses. Alternatively, the state may try to delay payments or push more of the burden for the entitlements on to local governments. At state and local levels, budgetary surpluses are sometimes built up to guard against deficits. Another aspect of the state and local requirement for balance is that efforts to hide deficits may be more intense.

A second difference between the levels of government is that the role of deficit spending in regulating the economy is most salient at the federal level of government. State governments are only marginally involved in efforts to control the economy, and local governments are generally too minor a part of the economy to control it no matter how they spend their money.

A third difference has to do with overall size. At the federal level, the tremendous size of budget deficits and their chronic nature created a noisy and stubborn problem with potentially major impacts on the national economy. Deficits are more rare and more tractable at state and local levels. The state requirements for balance make rebalancing the budget during the year a frequent activity, so that it is more difficult for large deficits to accumulate from year to year.

The Politics of Deficits: The Federal Level

Deficits were a fact of life at the federal level for many years, but they became particularly large in the late 1980s and early 1990s (see table 7.1, p. 226, for the size of deficits by year). Deficit spending has historically been of three types: borrowing for wars, borrowing to deal with economic recessions, and borrowing to cover a long-term imbalance between revenues and spending.

From the beginning of the republic to the 1930s, deficits were associated primarily with wars, and debts were paid off after the wars were over. During the Great Depression of the 1930s, politicians responded to falling revenues and the urgent need for aid for the poor by allowing deficit spending. The depression forged a new role for the federal government, to help minimize swings in the economy and the attendant social and economic distress. After the depression, an economic theory (Keynesianism) emerged, arguing that deficits for this purpose were not necessarily harmful to the economy, that spending during recession actually helped stimulate the economy. Deficits incurred to offset recessions and stimulate the economy are supposed to be temporary. Since the middle of the 1970s, deficits have occurred regardless of the state of the economy.

Politicians who promised to eliminate deficits have often failed to do so, creating the impression that deficits were out of control. Whatever acceptance there was of moderate-size and occasional deficits began to evaporate when the deficits became huge. In 1974 the federal government had a deficit of $6.1 billion, which was .4 of 1 percent of the gross national product (GNP). By 1992 the deficit had reached a peak of $290 billion, or $340 billion if the Social Security surplus was subtracted.[4]

David Stockman, in a candid speech in spring 1985 just before his resignation as director of OMB, summarized the reasons for these deficits. He argued that the first cause of the deficits had to do with demobilization after the Vietnam war. Instead of reducing expenditures, the newly freed-up money was absorbed in increased income-support programs. Outlays for defense were reduced, allowing the massive inventories created by the war to be drawn down. But lower defense spending could not continue; the hostage situation in Iran highlighted U.S. military weakness, contributing to a consensus for increases in military spending, beginning with President Jimmy Carter in the late 1970s and continuing well into the Reagan administration. The rate of inflation increased, contributing to higher interest rates. The result was a major increase in interest payments on the federal debt. The Reagan administration's policy of tax reductions added one more major factor to the increased deficits. When these tax reductions were combined with the recession of 1981–82, the deficits soared.[5]

Stockman pointed out that the Reagan administration strategy of cutting back discretionary programs (while maintaining support for defense, Social Security, and tax cuts) could not possibly reduce the deficits because there was not enough money in these discretionary programs. "We argue with Congress over $80 or $90 billion of nondefense appropriation, but those that are truly discretionary amount to only a few billion dollars a year—not enough to fix a $200 billion problem."[6] Taxes had to be raised, or entitlement programs reduced, and defense curtailed. Thus deficit reduction was framed in terms of major policy priorities. There was no easy way or even relatively easy way to cut the deficits.

Citizens favored balanced budgets and increasingly supported efforts to control or limit the level of taxation. This sentiment spawned a number of revenue and expenditure limitation movements in states across the country. Many of them were not successful, but some, such as Proposition 13 in California and Proposition 2^1/$_2$ in Massachusetts, were very successful, and convinced politicians across the country that public desire to limit growth of public revenues was real and deeply felt. Moreover, taxpayer groups were organized and began to press the state legislatures to vote for federal balanced budget amendments. Under pressure from national taxpayer associations, many states did pass calls for a constitutional convention to add a balanced budget amendment to the constitution.

President Reagan was interested in reducing the scope of government activities and wanted to reduce taxes. He advocated a balanced budget in his election speeches, but there is considerable evidence that his administration was not terribly interested in reducing deficits, in comparison to achieving other policy goals.

> The Reagan administration, while it does not like deficit spending, has opted for this course of action because deficits facilitate the achievement of some of its other policy objectives. Deficits have enabled it (1) to preserve the 1981 tax cuts; (2) to blame Congress for fiscal irresponsibility; (3) to pressure for cutbacks in domestic programs; and—at least in its first years—to finance additional defense spending.[7]

At least one of President Reagan's entourage admitted that the tax cuts of 1981 would increase deficits. He confided: "Reagan's main goal is not to balance the budget—it is to reduce the role of government . . . if we don't cut taxes and generate big deficits, spending will never come down . . . with huge deficits, their choices are tougher, . . . they'll have to cut spending."[8]

Having been pressed by its own policy goals to accept a growing deficit, the Reagan administration attempted to minimize its size and importance, purposely underestimating the size of the deficit by overestimating revenues. Those giving financial advice to the president knew that he was underestimating the deficit.

David Stockman, director of OMB in the Reagan administration, was reported in the *New York Times* as stating, "The economics of Mr. Reagan's successful drive to cut taxes and restrain government spending in his first year in office . . . was predicated upon an economic forecast for 1981 that its authors, Mr. Stockman and the president's chief economist then, Murray Weidenbaum, knew to be false but a politically expedient device."[9]

According to Stockman, the administration used accounting gimmicks to make the deficit look smaller. In 1981, he reported, a series of spending reductions and revenue measures was inadequate to close the gap opened by tax cuts. "Bookkeeping began its wondrous works. We invented the magic asterisk: If we couldn't find the savings in time—and we couldn't—we would issue an I.O.U. We would call it 'future savings to be identified.' "[10]

The administration also minimized the importance of deficits. In hearings before the Ways and Means Committee in 1983, after Chairman Dan Rostenkowski described the size of the deficits in the $200 billion range, he asked Secretary of the Treasury Donald Regan if he still opposed new taxes. Regan responded that he did: "We think that to have tax increases over the next two years would be folly, because it is not needed at this point. The deficits can be handled."[11]

President Reagan pressed for spending cuts in Congress, with considerable success in the first year of his administration. As his ability to dictate cuts to Congress waned, he threw more of his support to the movement for a constitutional amendment that would combine a balanced budget with spending limitations. Such an amendment would accomplish more of the president's goal of cutting back the size of government than the balanced budget amendment alone.

Constitutional approaches to eliminating the deficit vied for years with more flexible legislative approaches. Every time a legislative approach failed, it gave impetus to the movement for a constitutional amendment; every time the constitutional amendment came up for a vote and appeared likely to win, it gave increased impetus for finding a legislative formula that would work.

Proposed Constitutional Amendments

The U.S. Constitution can be amended in two ways: Congress can adopt an amendment by a two-thirds vote in each house and then put the matter before the states to ratify by a three-fourths majority, or two-thirds of the states can vote for a constitutional convention, at which an amendment would presumably be discussed. Then three-fourths of the states need to ratify the proposed amendment. Partly because of the legal ambiguities in the second route (it is not clear that the constitutional convention could be limited to consideration of the balanced budget amendment), there was mounting pressure in Congress to head off the states and present a carefully considered congressional proposal.

As early as 1939, states began petitioning Congress to propose an amendment limiting federal taxing power. The movement continued on and off until 1963, when thirty-four states had passed it, but some of the resolutions were fifteen to twenty years old. Twelve states had withdrawn their applications, so the convention was never called.[12] More recent budget-balancing calls began in 1975 and received impetus from the success of Proposition 13 in California. The National Taxpayers Union and the American Farm Bureau Federation were active in starting this movement.[13] By 1985, thirty-two of the required thirty-four states had passed a resolution calling for a constitutional convention.

As the pressure mounted in the states for a constitutional amendment, Congress began considering its own proposals. The Senate passed a proposed constitutional amendment in August 1982; the House of Representatives voted down the measure in October 1982. A budget-balancing amendment was voted on in the Senate in March 1986, where it narrowly failed because a competing form of limitation had been passed several months earlier, draining away some of the support for the constitutional amendment.

Proposals for a balanced budget amendment to the Constitution gained much support in 1992, 1994, and 1995 but did not pass both houses by the required two-thirds majority. In 1990 Congress had passed the Budget Enforcement Act, closing many of the loopholes in prior legislative efforts to balance the budget, but the deficit got worse in 1991 and 1992. Legislators kept telling each other that a balanced budget amendment was the only remaining possibility, that nothing else could possibly work.

Robert Reischauer, who was then director of the Congressional Budget Office, explained in the fall of 1993 why Congress felt so disempowered with respect to its ability to control the deficit: "That agreement [the 1990 budget accord] was billed as the largest deficit reduction in American history, yet it was followed by back to back record deficits in Fiscal Year 1991 and 1992."[14] Reischauer explained the anomaly as resulting in part from a misunderstanding about when the deficit reduction would show up in the deficit numbers, and in part from a slower than expected recovery from the recession. In addition, a lot of technical factors went in the wrong direction, including better-than-average farm weather, large crops, and below-average prices, requiring high federal payments to farmers. By the end of 1993, the deficit was finally headed downward, reflecting the 1990 spending caps and more technical factors going the right, rather than the wrong, way.

The version of the amendment that came up before the House in 1992 included a requirement of a two-thirds majority to increase the debt limit, in addition to the requirement of a two-thirds majority to suspend the requirement that outlays not exceed estimated receipts. An alternate proposal that would have limited revenue increases to the rate of increase in national income died in committee. The proposal that was voted on (H.J. Resolution 290, the Stenholm proposal) was inclusive in terms of covering all revenues and expenditures, including Social Security, and did not deal with the possibility of shifting the burden of spending to the states. This particular version of the proposal reportedly earned the opposition of the Chamber of Commerce, because it suggested to them that taxes might increase to balance the budget; organized labor and the American Association of Retired Persons also lobbied against the measure, fearing that cutbacks in Social Security and Medicare would be the result.[15] The measure was defeated in the House.

Although the deficit situation did improve as the economy recovered from recession and the effects of the 1990 spending caps were felt, the prospect of large deficits resuming later in the decade, as a result of entitlement spending, remained in the foreground. When the elections of fall 1994 created a Republican majority in both the House and the Senate, an ideological passion for change swept over the House in particular. New energy was expended to get a balanced budget amendment passed.

The question on whom the burden would fall if a constitutional amendment was passed was partly resolved with the passage of a limitation on unfunded mandates in 1995. Although this legislation does not protect states from cutbacks in grants, it should help prevent the federal government from setting standards and requirements that states have to implement at great cost. With new and enthusiastic Republican majorities, and the problem of state opposition out of the way, it seemed more likely than ever that the constitutional amendment would pass Congress and go on to the states for ratification. The measure did pass the House of Representatives, but failed in the Senate by one vote. The closeness of the vote suggested that legislators were trying to maximize their popularity by taking a public stance in favor of a balanced budget amendment as long as the measure did not actually pass. In fact, legislators charged each other with taking symbolic stances.

Each time that the balanced budget amendment came up, fairly standard arguments were made for and against it. The arguments on the positive side included the following:

1. Deficit spending is detrimental to the economy, it increases inflation, and it crowds out other uses of capital.

2. The need for flexible economic policy is overstated. Keynesian politics doesn't work, and monetary policies (controlling the economy by regulating the amount of money in circulation and influencing interest rates) are sufficient to influence economic cycles.

3. Growth of government should be checked.

4. Congress, if left alone, will not act or cannot take effective action.

The arguments against a constitutional amendment requiring a balanced budget included the following:

1. There is little relationship between either deficits or the size of government and inflation, and a balanced budget/revenue limitation is likely to have major negative economic impacts.

2. Constitutional budget constraints will impede the government's ability to respond to economic and other crises.

3. A constitutional requirement for a supermajority to allow an unbalanced budget will have the effect of magnifying the power of a small minority of congressmen who could demand a high (and unrelated) price for their votes.

4. A constitutional amendment is unenforceable.

5. Spending cuts are likely to fall on social services and aid to state and local governments.

6. A constitutional amendment will shift budget-making power to the courts (because of enforcement issues).

7. This is not a proper subject for a constitutional amendment.

8. The same result can be achieved through legislation.

Ultimately, the rigidity of a constitutional amendment, the support for different versions of its wording that allowed or did not allow much revenue growth, and the loss of budget power in Congress that would result from such an amendment shifted support to a legislative solution. Unfortunately, it was not clear what an effective legislative solution would look like. It took several iterations and a number of years to work out a legislative solution.

Statutory Approaches to Budget Balancing

Some of the proposals for legislative solutions were more oriented toward revenue constraints and constraints on the growth of government; others were more exclusively directed toward balancing the budget and eliminating the deficit. The proposals to limit spending growth varied not only in technical mechanism but also in scope. Some included loans, some included tax expenditures, and some both of these; others pointedly excluded loans and tax expenditures. Some of the limitations were much more severe in the level of cuts required than others.

One of the proposals seriously considered by the House was Congressman Robert Giaimo's proposal (H.R. 6021) to limit spending to a percentage of the GNP. In Giaimo's proposal, the limit could be breached by a simple majority of both houses if economic circumstances warranted. This proposal allowed for much easier adaptation to economic cycles than constitutional amendments that required a two-thirds majority to allow a deficit in an economic downturn. Giaimo's proposal included tax expenditures and loan guarantees to prevent increased spending in these areas to bypass controls on program spending. Congresswoman Marjorie Holt introduced a bill that included loans in the controls on spending but ignored the issue of tax expenditures; and Congressman James Jones introduced a spending limit as percentage of GNP without spending limits on either tax expenditures or loan guarantees. The issue of whose programs would be cut back—those of business and the wealthy or cities and the poor—was debated under the guise of how inclusive spending limits should be.

Business groups testifying on congressional proposals to limit spending and balance the budget uniformly approved the general idea, but opposed Giaimo's proposal to curb tax expenditures. For example, the National Association of Manufacturers (NAM) offered its support for spending limitations and a balanced budget, but specifically excluded tax expenditures from controls.

> Balancing the budget is essential to reduce and then eliminate inflation. This policy goal should be implemented by forcing down spending levels rather than allowing tax levels to rise . . . NAM strongly endorses the approach in H.R. 5371 to limit fiscal 1981 spending to 21 percent of the estimated GNP and subsequent years to 20 percent. We oppose including "tax expenditures" in a higher percentage.[16]

NAM piously argued that Congress should have the strength to sacrifice some legislative sacred cows while arguing to maintain its own tax breaks.

Congressman Richard Bolling opposed any new formal procedures to limit expenditures or balance the budget, but he was more sympathetic to Giaimo's proposal, which included tax expenditures in the limitation, than to those of Holt or Jones which excluded tax expenditures from controls. Bolling was sarcastic about the Business Roundtable (a lobbying group of chief executive officers of big businesses), which was calling for congressmen to curb their requests for special projects while businessmen were trying to protect their tax breaks.

> I think the best case that can be made for a gimmick like this [a spend-
> ing limitation that includes tax expenditures] is that the business commu-
> nity comes in through the Business Roundtable and tells us what an
> outrage it would be to include tax expenditures, but of course, these [tax
> expenditures] are different in kind [from other expenditures], and I
> honor their view. It's about as unselfish as the view of those of us who are
> for our own water projects.[17]

The issue of legislative approaches to budgetary balance and spending limitations
was also discussed on the grounds of whether such ceilings were necessary or
workable. Congressman Richard Gephardt, for example, argued that new limits
were not necessary because strengthening the existing budget process would
achieve the same goals, with the greatest degree of flexibility. Strengthening the
existing process maintained congressional budgeting power, instead of giving it
away or constraining it, but it also gave more power to the budget committees
in Congress, as opposed to the appropriations, authorizing, and tax committees.

The debate as to whether a ceiling was necessary was phrased by some congressmen and interest groups in terms of the need for discipline and the need to
provide an excuse to constituents when congressmen said no to requests. The
opponents of ceilings argued that constraints were artificial and could not substitute for will. Congressman Bolling argued, for example, that fiscal decisions
were "a whole lot more a matter of will than procedure."[18] Jamie Whitten, chairman of the Appropriations Committee, agreed with Congressman Bolling.

> Let us not kid ourselves that some artificial gimmick will ever substitute
> for the real will of Congress. Congress by its very nature is unlikely to
> lock itself into a room without keeping a key. And when the confinement
> begins to pain us, we tend to be all too willing to use the key.[19]

Whitten, as chair of the House Appropriations Committee, stood to lose a lot
of power if Congress hamstrung itself with limits or gave the budget committees more enforcement power. Thus, while his description of congressional behavior is undoubtedly true, his argument against additional controls on spending
probably also reflected his desire to maintain his power.

The proposals made by Giaimo, Jones, and Holt were aimed primarily at
limitations on spending, and though their proposals aimed at balanced budgets,
they did not guarantee them. Some other proposals discussed in the House were
focused more on the balance aspect, assuming that revenue raising has its own
natural political limits. James Wright, majority leader in the House in 1980, and
Phil Gramm, both of Texas, offered a proposal to require a three-month review,

after the budget year began, to project deficits for the remainder of the year. "If the deficit were to represent 5 percent of the controllable expenditures for the remainder of the fiscal year, then the president would be instructed to reduce every such item by that same 5 percentage points."[20] Gramm explained that to avoid such cuts Congress would pass balanced budgets.

In the Wright-Gramm proposal, the budget could be unbalanced if both houses voted to approve a deficit resulting from unforeseen circumstances or overriding concerns. The bill was thus fairly flexible in terms of adaptation to the economy, requiring no supermajority, but it did require positive congressional action to unbalance the budget. Gramm noted in the hearings that although Wright's and his proposal addressed budgetary balance, they were willing to consider adding Jones's proposal to limit spending as a percentage of GNP and Giaimo's proposal to limit tax expenditures and loans.

Among the proposals to balance the budget and limit revenues or expenditures were a number of suggestions for strengthening the existing congressional budget act. One recommendation was to use the existing reconciliation procedures. This process allowed Congress to make cuts in any spending that was over the targets formulated by the budget committees. This proposal was the first major one to be adopted. Reconciliation was used a little in 1980 and in a major way in 1981, and the result was major budget reductions. Because Congress also passed the president's tax reduction package, however, little progress was made in closing the deficit gap.

The use of the reconciliation process gives somewhat more power to the budget committees because it allows them to set targets for the appropriation and authorizing committees and gives the budget committees a procedure for gaining compliance. If the targets set are lower than their own preference, the appropriations and authorizing committees can pare down their requests in whatever way they see fit. Reconciliation thus shifts power away from the appropriations and authorization committees, but not drastically so. In 1981, however, President Reagan and OMB director David Stockman were not content with the House reconciliation. OMB drew up an alternative version and had two representatives, Phil Gramm and Delbert Latta, introduce the administration's version as an amendment; and the Gramm-Latta amendment passed the House. The OMB version became the Omnibus Reconciliation Act of 1981. The work of the appropriations and authorization committees in attempting to comply with the reconciliation instructions was bypassed, creating considerable resentment against using the process again.

In December 1985 the Balanced Budget and Emergency Deficit Control Act of 1985, popularly called Gramm-Rudman-Hollings, was passed. Gramm-Rudman-Hollings was oriented toward deficit reduction and budget balance rather than expenditure or revenue limitations. It allowed some rise in revenues to balance the budget, rather than rigid limitations on revenues. It protected entitlement programs such as Social Security. It reduced the shock of cutting back the deficit by phasing in balanced budgets over a five-year period. The law stipulated that Congress could vote to allow deficits in excess of targets in case of economic recession. The requirements for balance were to lapse during a war.

The goal of Gramm-Rudman-Hollings was to achieve budgetary balance by 1991 by reducing the size of the deficit by specified amounts each year from 1986 to 1991. If the deficit in any year was larger than the target for that year, an automatic provision would take over, cutting programs across the board after certain special rules had been considered. The cuts were to be divided evenly between defense and nondefense expenditures. The threat of cutting all programs, on the one hand, was supposed to be more fair, and on the other hand, was supposed to be so distasteful that it would force Congress to eliminate the excess deficit before the automatic cuts could take effect. In the event, Congress exempted many programs from the across-the board-cuts, so that if such cuts, called sequesters, were necessary, they would fall disproportionately on a relatively small number of programs.

In an effort to get down the size of the deficit so that sequesters would not be necessary and the programs covered by Gramm-Rudman-Hollings would not be decimated, both the president and Congress began to "game the system," by such means as selling off assets, building trust fund balances by freezing trust fund spending in the Highway Trust Fund and the Airport Trust Fund, and increasing revenue estimates. Spending was pushed over into the succeeding year to make the current year look more balanced that it was. When a portion of Gramm-Rudman-Hollings was declared unconstitutional, a new version was passed, with easier deficit targets.

Gramm-Rudman-Hollings was not successful, in either its original or its revised form. It encouraged stopgap measures and overestimates of economic growth, and created incentives to take existing programs off budget and create new off-budget enterprises. Senator Herbert Kohl observed, "Since we enacted Gramm-Rudman, we have created five off-budget government sponsored enterprises. Only one was created in the previous thirteen years."[21]

Senator Nancy Kassebaum summed up a lot of accumulated congressional frustration with the budget process in 1989 when she decried the use of such emergency devices as continuing resolutions as a substitute for the budget. She claimed that Congress had routinely failed to make timely fiscal decisions. "In doing so," she argued, "we lose the power to allot money among programs of greater or less merit. We lose the chance to weigh revenue options thoughtfully. In fact, we lose the ability to do anything other than affirm the aggregate spending, taxing—and borrowing—decisions of earlier years. That is not policy making."[22]

Pressure increased to reform the budget process as deficits grew beyond the ability of Gramm-Rudman sequesters to cure without doing unacceptable damage. The Budget Enforcement Act was passed in the fall of 1990. Like Gramm-Rudman, the Budget Enforcement Act of 1990 picked from and blended a large number of different proposals. As a result, it was a complex measure. But its essential feature was that it strengthened the constraints for balance, rather than tried to reduce the size of the deficit.

One portion of the measure focused on limiting spending on domestic "controllables," those programs that regularly go through the congressional appropriations process. Another portion of the reform focused on entitlements and other mandatory spending. The goal for entitlements was less on keeping spending down than on maintaining balance; pay-as-you-go (often called PAY-GO) provisions required compensating increases in revenues or decreases in other noncontrollables to pay for any increases in entitlements. Similarly, revenue reductions were to be controlled by strict requirements that they be offset with either increases in revenue or spending reductions. The linkage between revenues and expenditures was intentionally tightened in two key areas, entitlements and tax expenditures.

Part of the thrust of the reforms was to make the real costs of spending apparent when decisions were being made in order to restructure the incentives more toward balance. For example, credit reforms included in the budget reforms of 1990 make the costs of loans and loan guarantees more visible at the time when the programs are being approved. Before the reform, approval was separated by many years from the actual costs, which were routinely underestimated.

The removal of the Social Security surplus from the calculation of the deficit also had the effect of making the costs of current spending and revenue decisions more apparent at the time the decisions were being made. When Social Security balances were included in the deficit calculation, the deficit looked like it was decreasing even when it was growing, which encouraged a lack of fiscal discipline. With Social Security surpluses subtracted out, each action that increased the deficit would have an immediate, visible, and negative consequence.

The budget reforms of 1990 were especially significant because they show the budget process starting to adapt to a slower-growing economy. The reform discouraged increases in expenditures and reductions in revenues and strengthened the expectations for balance. It helped make costs clearer and raises revenues. Its scope was broad in the sense of including regular appropriations, entitlements, loans, and loan guarantees, and it was more inclusive of time, requiring enforcement at several points during a year and over several years. Instead of a rigid series of goals intended to last only until the problem goes away, the new process was much more flexible, leaving room for choices among programs, for adaptation to the economy, and for emergencies. The Budget Enforcement Act did not set a specific date for the elimination of deficits; it linked revenues and expenditures more tightly and restructured the incentives to make it easier to achieve balance over the long haul.

The Budget Enforcement Act of 1990 was much more successful than Gramm-Rudman-Hollings. Its more flexible approach to deficit reduction and its explicit closing of the loopholes in prior legislation have markedly reduced the manipulations that marked the Gramm-Rudman-Hollings period. After 1992, for a combination of reasons including the budget caps in the Budget Enforcement Act, the deficit actually began to fall. From its peak of $290 billion in 1992, the deficit dropped, until the budget was more or less balanced in FY 1998.

Although the basic approach underlying the Budget Enforcement Act remained intact, it was modified and extended several times. Finally, in 1997 Congress and the president agreed on a proposal to balance the budget by 2002, with specific spending cuts outlined for each year, and tax reductions that extended beyond the end of the agreement. A booming economy brought balance to the budget well before expectations, setting up a great deal of speculation about whether the caps would be maintained, cutting agencies and programs deeply closer to 2002 in order to fund more tax cuts, or whether the caps would be partially lifted or modified in some way to spread out the projected surpluses more widely.

Deficits in the States

When they are facing deficits, the states, like the federal government, have to decide whether and how much to raise revenues or cut expenditures, with similar implications for the scope of government. Just as at the federal level, there are problems of defining what constitutes a deficit and problems of measuring the size and importance of deficits. Just as the federal government has to decide how much of a financial burden it can shift to the states or the private sector, states have to decide how much expense to absorb from or pass on to local governments, and how much of a service burden they can unload on local governments. Nevertheless, the requirement, variously interpreted, of annual balance at the state level normally prevents the buildup of large, long-term deficits, and makes rebalancing the budget both more routine and somewhat easier.

Although there is considerable variation between states in who has power to make reductions in spending to restore balance after the beginning of the fiscal year, the responsibility is generally given to the governor. In 1998 twelve states reported that the governor had unlimited authority to cut the budget during the fiscal year if necessary. Ten states reported that the governor could make cuts during the year but that they could be only across-the-board cuts. Twelve states reported that the governor must consult with the legislature before making midyear cuts. In 1988 only seven state legislatures had required the governor to consult over midyear changes, indicating that the legislatures were taking a some-what more active role in budget implementation issues.[23]

The issue of which interests will be protected and which will be cut back has been less salient at the state level because deficits, when they have occurred, have usually been caused by recessions and hence been relatively short term. Because the deficits are considered temporary, states can adopt temporary mea-sures to handle them, including temporary taxes or surtaxes. They can tighten belts and make across-the-board cuts. They can often avoid making difficult choices between programs or types of programs.

For example, Michigan has responded to recent recessions with budget cuts rather than tax increases, but these cuts have tended to be across the board. "It is clear that there is a tendency to accommodate budget reductions by cutting across the board, and that further reductions would lead (at least initially) to cutbacks in all services, and not in any particular targeted programs."[24] The tendency to cut across the board or make cuts according to preset priorities takes some of the bitterness out of allocational battles concerning the elimination of sizable deficits.

When financial problems occur that cannot be categorized as moderate in severity and short term (e.g., when the bottom fell out of the oil market), they are likely to provoke much argumentation about priorities as well as tradeoffs between additional taxation and additional cuts.

MINICASE: CONNECTICUT CUTS BACK TO BALANCE THE BUDGET

Connecticut was particularly hard hit during the recession of the early 1990s, and when the recession was combined with the effects of growth in entitlement spending, the result was a deficit of a billion dollars in an $8 billion budget.[25] The enormous size of the deficit combined with continuing growth in entitlements that outstripped revenue growth meant that ordinary across-the-board cuts and delaying action were not viable options. The unusual depth of the recession also suggested that the economy might not snap back in a short period of time. Fears about long-term economic growth helped shape the response to deficits.

Over a two-year period, the governor increased taxes (in a highly unpopular move) and then cut $1.1 billion in services to slow down the rate of increase in spending. Governor Lowell Weicker argued that the budget had to be not only cut but restructured because annual uncontrollable increases were outstripping revenue increases. His restructuring included tightening eligibility standards for welfare and reducing the increasing costs of long-term health care, reducing employee benefits, downsizing the state workforce, and changing the relationship between the state and local governments. Forced to cut back on a variety of support programs to local governments, the state tried to compensate somewhat for the damage it was causing by reducing the burden of state mandates on local governments.

The reductions in state aid included lowering the funds for public schools, eliminating or reducing various kinds of property tax relief, cutting back on general assistance (a form of welfare) funding, and reducing benefits for the teachers' retirement fund. Among the more burdensome mandates the state proposed to reduce were those that required all heart disease and hypertension among police and firefighters to be considered work related, and the state recommended a modified set of binding arbitration rules for municipalities.

Although the governor argued that the cuts would be spread evenly across the public, responses to the recession and to the deficits included major new and expanded tax breaks for business to facilitate economic recovery. The cost of these tax breaks was expected to increase from approximately $100 million in 1992 to over $350 million in 1995.[26]

Although states sometimes face long-term fiscal stress, most of their experience with deficits results from handling downturns in the economy that simultaneously reduce revenues and increase social services expenditures such as welfare and unemployment payments. Because deficits incurred for this purpose tend to be temporary, and because deficits are almost always illegal at the state level, states have frequently engaged in temporizing, stalling cuts and hiding deficits until the economy improves.

Obscuring the Deficit

States wrestling with balanced budget requirements frequently try to obscure or minimize the size of the deficits they are running. For example, Representative David Obey of Wisconsin reported, "I come from a state with a balanced budget requirement. In the six years that I served in the legislature, Wisconsin's indebtedness doubled, because they engaged in all kinds of phoney-baloney devices, off-budget accounting, dummy building corporations, all the rest, that simply defined out of the budget all kinds of spending that was really governmental. And they are still doing it today."[27]

Another gimmick to make a budget look balanced is to accelerate tax collections, which produces a one-time windfall for the state. For example, if a state changes from a quarterly to a monthly collection schedule, it can collect fifteen months' revenues in twelve months. On a quarterly basis, it could collect taxes the first of the year, for the preceding three months; the second payment would be at month 3 for the preceding three months; the third payment would be at month 6 for the preceding three months; and the final payment for the year would be at month 9 for the preceding three months. But if the state goes to monthly collections at that point, it can collect the taxes for months 10, 11, and 12 that they would normally have to wait for until the next fiscal year.[28]

A similar gimmick is to delay some expenditures so that they occur in the next fiscal year. That increases the next year's expenditures, but the hope is that by then the recession will have ended and increased revenues will cover the extra expenditures. A way to push expenditures into the following year is to change the basis of accounting from modified accrual to cash. Under cash accounting, expenditures that are incurred this year, but not paid until next year, are officially counted as next year's expenditures. Under accrual accounting, they would be counted as part of *this* year's expenditures. By switching the basis of accounting, some items that would have been counted as expenditures this year get carried over into next year.

In Illinois, the governor changed the accounting system from modified accrual to cash in 1978. He made the budget look more balanced in that year because the cash accounting system pushed off some expenditures into the next year's budget.[29] In addition, the cash budget changed the definition of a deficit. A cash budget measures deficits by looking at the available cash balance at the end of the year rather than matching revenues and expenditures during the year. The result is an easily manipulable deficit.

The available cash balance is eminently suited for manipulation: Any cash on hand goes into the available balance, even if its source is a loan. The available balance is also affected by speedups in revenue collections or delays in paying vendors or by manipulating the timing of drawdowns of federal funds. "When an administration commits itself to a specific end of year available balance, it can manipulate the revenue processing system to bring about an available balance consistent with its prediction."[30] Perhaps most important, the cash balance is always positive and hence makes it look as if the state is always running a surplus, whether or not it is in deficit.

Other common gimmicks include borrowing between funds to make the general fund look more balanced than it is, and using one-time revenues to make the budget look more balanced than it is. For example, California, in order to address an incipient deficit in FY 1981–82, began its deficit-reduction plan mainly with one-time revenues. These included financing capital outlays previously funded from the general fund with one-time use of tidelands oil revenues; anticipation of increased federal funding for Supplemental Security Income/State Supplemental Income; and temporary elimination of the state bailout for local governments required to replace revenues lost by Proposition 13. One-time revenue increases totaled nearly $514 million; one-time expenditure reductions totaled $208 million.[31]

Taking expenditures off budget, manipulating the cash balance by borrowing or moving expenditures forward or revenues backward, closing the gap with one-time revenues, and internal borrowing are all techniques to reduce the amount of cuts or tax increases that might otherwise be necessary. They are part of a politics of avoidance and delay to help avert hard political choices, the kind that make enemies. These techniques are not necessarily bad; it makes sense to avoid deep cuts and expensive restructuring to eliminate a deficit that will disappear on its own within a year or two as the economy recovers. If state laws allowed more time to recover from a deficit resulting from a downturn in the economy, less effort would be taken to hide such deficits.

Creating Buffers

While some states temporize to get past the worst of a recession without deep cuts in service levels, the routines of handling deficits require action during the year, when the deficits are discovered. It is often the governor's responsibility to make those cuts, which are perceived as a political liability. The governor may try to avoid them by creating buffer funds through underestimating revenue.

The politics of balance is intimately related to the politics of revenue estimation. In Illinois, for example, the governor and the state Office of Management and Budget have a tendency to underestimate revenues, to build in a buffer in case some revenues do not show up. Such a buffer prevents deficits, and hence the politically awkward cuts the governor would otherwise have to make in the middle of the year. The legislature has pressed for higher estimations of revenues, knowing that if a deficit occurs during the year, the governor, not the legislature, will have to cut back expenditures.[32] The higher estimates of revenues allow legislators to make a more generous budget and satisfy more claims.

In Michigan, a different dynamic has emerged. Michigan had for many years met recessions with tax increases, but in the late 1970s began to respond to recessions with expenditure reductions. The prior history of growth of expenditures was reversed in the early 1980s. The governor proposed budgets with high estimates of revenue for 1980, 1981, and 1982. The legislature passed the budget pretty much as proposed, but then, in each of the three years, the economy did not grow as expected, "forcing" the governor (with the approval of the legislative appropriations committees) to cut expenditures, reduce state employment, and cut programs.[33] The projected deficits provide apparently irresistible pressure to make cuts while reducing the level of blame. Presumably if the governor had just recommended the cuts initially, he would have run into more opposition. One observer remarked, "Fiscal crises have been an important agent through which the majority of state political officials have chosen to shield their aim of reducing the scope and level of government programs in the state."[34]

In the Michigan case, the politics of balance became linked to the politics of government size. Cutting back on expenditures became the option of choice for dealing with deficits—so much so that the deficits may have been created for the purpose of forcing cuts and gaining political legitimacy for doing so. Of course, the state need not have depended on a cutback strategy; it could instead have chosen to raise revenues. But, since the mid-1970s, there has been increasing pressure in the states to limit revenues and expenditures. By 1996 twenty-seven states had some form of tax or expenditure limit; of these, sixteen were written into state constitutions.[35]

Many states found that they had to cut expenditures and/or raise taxes during the recession of 1991 despite the fact that the recession was neither terribly deep nor terribly long. The states just did not have enough money set aside to tide them over without drastic action to balance the budget. But that drastic action is politically unpleasant. Rather than raise taxes during a recession, which may exaggerate the economic downturn and will almost certainly raise a public outcry because taxes will take a bigger bite out of people's shrinking income, or cut expenditures, which are needed more acutely during recessions, some states in recent years have tried to create special funds to carry them through a recession. The idea is to put more money in during periods of economic growth and take more money out when the economy is in a slump, without running deficits. Such funds are called *rainy-day funds.*

As of the end of 1983, nineteen states had rainy-day funds, most of which had been set up in the early 1980s. ACIR, using a looser definition, estimated that thirty-five states had some kind of stabilization fund in 1988.[36] By 1992 ACIR reported that forty-four states had some kind of fiscal stabilization fund.[37] The Center for Budget and Policy Priorities reported that 45 out of the 48 states they looked at had some kind of rainy-day fund in 1999.[38] Some of these funds were tiny or even had a zero balance, however, so their impact during a recession would be minimal, especially if the recession lasted for more than a year.

It is not easy for a state to maintain a high level of annual balance without stimulating demands to either reduce the level of taxation or spend down the surplus. The very large balance held by the State of California before Proposition 13—$4 billion—is said to have contributed to the passage of Proposition 13. If the state was running that large a surplus, then it must have been collecting too much tax money. The farther away politicians get from the last recession and its painful cuts, the greater the temptation to spend down the year-end balance.

Separate rainy-day accounts with automatic provisions for buildup and spenddown may lessen this temptation somewhat. Rainy-day funds, as differentiated from an annual positive balance, set aside money for a specific purpose under state statutes. They are somewhat easier to defend than unearmarked year-end balances that look as if the state collected more revenues than it needed. The formula for funding the rainy-day account is decided first; then the money is set aside each year, generally in a special fund, and is drawn down when economic conditions cause a decline in revenues.[39]

Passing the Buck to Local Governments

For states without effective rainy-day funds, there may be great temptation to balance the budget without cutting expenditures or raising revenues. Since local governments are the subordinates of the states, and have to take orders from state governments, the states can decide to pass the burden of paying for programs and projects to their local governments. Richard Lamm, governor of Colorado, described the politics of passing the buck:

> The Gramm-Rudman bill is the result of Washington's inability to deal rationally with its mounting deficit. My hope is that this bill will be a catalyst for more careful analysis of Federal programs. My fear is that it will be an excuse for fiscal federalism at the point of a budgetary bayonet. I would be more critical of the Federal Government but for the fact that Colorado state government plays the same tricks on its cities and counties. Every election year, legislators brag that Colorado ranks forty-eighth nationally in the level of state taxes based on personal income. What they don't tell the public is, local governments are having to shoulder the tax burdens that the state passes along.[40]

When Michigan passed a constitutional amendment in 1977 to limit expenditures, it wrote into its constitution that the state had to maintain the current proportion of expenditures on local governments. The state was forbidden to economize by disproportionately cutting intergovernmental transfers to local governments.

In California, after Proposition 13, the state government provided aid to local governments to make up the losses in revenues. To protect its own finances, however, it passed a law providing that if the state's fiscal condition deteriorated, the aid to local governments would be reduced.

These three examples—Colorado, Michigan, and California—illustrate the three possibilities of passing the burden on to local governments, protecting local governments from increased burdens, and absorbing some of the burden and passing on the rest. To get some idea of which pattern is dominant, one can look at the laws states have passed requiring them to absorb costs resulting from mandates they impose on local governments and at the proportion of state and local spending that the states have picked up over time.

By 1988 fifteen states had passed laws and constitutional amendments requiring state reimbursement for imposed costs. Those laws and amendments overestimate local ability to resist state imposition of costs since half the laws are statutory, and they may be overlooked in practice.[41]

More direct evidence is provided by looking at the state proportion of state and local expenditures (excluding federal aid) over time. If the state proportion is going up or is constant, then the state is not passing on any burden to the local governments. The proportion of state and local expenditures picked up by the state governments increased continuously from 44 percent in 1942 to 58 percent in 1982, but in 1983 and 1984 it began to decline, to 57 percent in 1983 and 56 percent in 1984. By 1991–92 the state share had dropped to 43 percent. In welfare, the state share increased to a peak of 89 percent in 1982 and then declined to 82 percent in 1984, rising to 83 percent in 1986. The state share of welfare costs has remained steady at between 81.5 and 83 percent since then. Between 1992 and 1996 (the most recent data posted by the census) states have on average slightly increased their shares of health, welfare, and corrections costs, but have not increased their overall share of state and local expenditures.[42]

The timing of the downturn in state share of state and local expenditures is suggestive. States were hit with a deep and long recession in 1982 and 1983, and in 1983 the state share began to decline. Fiscal stress in the states became worse in the early 1990s, raising the question again of the extent to which the states would balance their own budgets on the backs of the local governments. These fiscal problems included a recession in 1990–91, explosive growth in Medicaid expenditures, increased enrollments in public schools, and tougher sentencing laws and higher numbers of people imprisoned. General end-of-year balances and rainy-day funds that had averaged 8 or 9 percent of general fund expenditures in the late 1970s and early 1980s dropped as low as 1.1 percent in 1991 and had only risen to about 2.6 percent by 1994.[43]

Since the mid- to late 1980s, the states seemed either more willing to shift the burden to local governments or had less flexibility to do anything but cut higher education and aid to local governments. More of the tax burden is being borne at the local level. "In every year since 1985, local taxes have risen faster than state taxes."[44] Aid to local government generally lost out in comparison to other state spending priorities. From 1990 to 1992, aid to local governments became a smaller percentage of state spending in forty states.[45] California shifted some of the property tax from local governments to the school districts, and then cut the state payments to the schools. It only partially compensated the local governments for this loss. Thus the state reduced its own payments while increasing the financial stress of the local governments.[46] In Minnesota, state aid to local governments dropped from 26 to 18 percent of general fund spending between 1990 and 1995.[47] As fiscal stress intensified at the state level, local governments took a disproportionate hit.

The figures given here on declining state shares of state and local spending do not address changes in individual states, but they do suggest that on average, states have not picked up an increased share of state and local spending; instead, they seem to be balancing their own budgets and keeping their tax burdens down by passing along the burdens to the local governments. Continuing reforms in education finance may change this picture in the future.

The Politics of Balance in Cities

Cities, like states, are required to balance their budgets. But, unlike the federal government, local governments have virtually no role in influencing cycles of the economy with their budgets. Generally, their budgets are too small and their economies too open for local governments to be able to have an impact on the economy. The result is that cities do not have to worry about whether they should run deficits. They try to maintain year-end balances to tide them over when recession hits, but they are often unable to predict downturns in the economy and have to reduce expenditures during the year to balance the budget.

At the local level, as at the state level, considerable effort may be spent to hide or minimize the size of deficits, especially those that are not the result of immediate environmental exigencies. Many of the same tactics used at the state level are employed, including "borrowing" between funds (sometimes invisibly and without intent to repay), changing the basis of accounting so that some expenditures are counted in the next year's budget, delaying paying bills and "borrowing" from pension funds by not putting in the required amount of employer contribution. Cities may also hide deficits by borrowing outside the city for operating expenditures, pretending they are borrowing for capital. Cities sometimes shift expenditures from a fund that is poorer into other funds that are richer.

Depending on the definition of deficit used, cities can make the budget look balanced by drawing down reserves, which is usually technically legal but obscures the fact that the city is running an operating deficit. Or the budget can be balanced with one-time revenues, resulting from the sale of property or grants or other one-time income. Overestimating revenues also makes the budget look more balanced than it is.

When deficits occur unintentionally during the year, the normal response is to gather unspent money and defer spending it until the crisis is over or the council has had a chance to act on priorities. The result may be heavier cuts in some areas than in others; the intent is not to choose program areas but to find money that is as yet unspent. Capital projects are often delayed because the money is not yet spent or irrevocably committed.

When a deficit is imminent in the following year's budget, or when a deficit is carried over from one year to the next, then the manager or mayor makes recommendations for how the deficit gap is to be closed, and the council must approve or disapprove the recommendations. In this situation, program priorities must be decided, revenue increase and expenditure decrease weighed, and scope of services reevaluated. Formally, the council has the power to make these decisions, but in fact the distribution of power between the mayor, manager, or administrator on the one hand and the council, on the other, is highly variable.

The council may give the chief executive officer general policy for the upcoming budget, such as balance the budget without tax increases this year or figure in a 1-percent increase in local sales taxes. The manager or administrator may make recommendations for the figure to use for inflation and give estimates of yield for revenue sources. Council members may accept or reject these estimates, or give alternate estimates. The council may give general guidelines about what services may be cut, and which ones sustained, or it may get involved in the details of line-by-line, program-by-program cuts. Whatever balance of power exists in one year may change the next as council members lose interest or the manager or mayor restructures the budget process and asks for a different kind of input or asks for input at a different stage of the process.

The issue of scope of services is unlikely to arise in response to a midyear revenue decline, but it can arise as local governments wrestle with what appears to be an impending imbalance in the next year's operating budget. For example, in the 1970s when cities were dealing with recessions, economic base erosion, and the effects of the leveling out and decline of federal revenues, if the cities were responsible for a range of functions they often tried to shift some of those functions to other levels of government. Services such as courts, city universities, and museums were either shifted to other levels of government or to the private sector. Some cities gave their planning functions to the county. In some states, cities were able to shift some or all of their share of welfare to the state, and some of the cost of police.[48] More recently, one city wrestling with slow growth in property tax revenues and termination of revenue sharing tried to give a city sewer to the sanitary district, the city bus system to the local state university, the dog pound and animal-control function to the county, and the airport and economic development office to regional authorities.

The option of solving local financial problems by shifting burdens of service delivery elsewhere and begging more revenues from state and national governments may have been cut off by the 1980s. The shift in burden may actually go the other way, toward the cities. If states can build and maintain their rainy-day funds, they may be able to buffer themselves from the worst of the financial pressures and hence not place additional burdens on local governments during recessions. But the states still have to deal with diminished federal aid. How far the federal government will cut back on aid to states and local governments is not clear, but it seems likely that the financial pressure on state and local governments will continue. The ability of the states to absorb the fiscal problems of the local governments has diminished in recent years.

The issue of scope arises not only in terms of shifting the level of government at which some services are performed but also in the question of what services will be cut back or eliminated. During the 1970s, when the public seemed determined to hold the line on revenues, cities perceived they had little choice but to cut back services. They chose to do this, insofar as they could, in ways that would not overly affect the public. They cut back in invisible ways, such as delaying maintenance and deferring capital projects. When deep service cuts appeared necessary, their choice was to find some other unit of government to perform the task.

The following example of a city running deficits illustrates several themes about how city budgets get unbalanced, the tendency to obscure deficits when they occur, and the kinds of pressure necessary to force a city to rebalance its budget. The case also illustrates how difficult it can be to cut spending when every expenditure seems to have a political protector or be exempt from cuts. A change in structure was required, with an increase in constraints, in order to force a linkage between revenues and expenditures and create enough central authority to cut back spending proposals. The example occurred in the 1970s, when the option of increasing federal aid was still open. The same story told in the 1980s might have a different ending.

MINICASE: THE POLITICS OF DEFICITS: AN URBAN EXAMPLE

The city of Southside (a fictional name given to protect the anonymity of those involved) ran deficits that were hidden in the budget from 1972 to 1976.[49] During the later part of this period, there was no recession to blame. The initial causes of the deficit include hiring at the same time a young and inexperienced city manager and an inexperienced budget officer. But the city's problems went well beyond hiring a few inexperienced people. It was suffering from a long-term economic base erosion as heavy industry in the region declined and left behind many unemployed and a reduced demand for housing. The result was frozen or slow growing revenues from both sales and property taxes. Department heads and elected officials seemed unwilling or unable to cut back expenditures proportionately. Elected officials at one point actually reduced property tax rates despite increasing costs. The young city manager did not have enough power to force the elected officials and department heads to cut expenditures, so he tried to reduce labor costs instead, aggravating the city's employee unions and actually increasing labor costs.

The young manager initially hid the deficits, then tried to publicize them as a tool to force the council to make the requisite cuts. He used his budget message to warn council members about emerging deficits, but council members later argued that they did not understand that the budget had to balance fund by fund; they said they were looking at the bottom line, in effect, a cash balance. Cash balances are nearly always positive at the end of the year, and are misleading indicators of deficits. The council in effect chose a loose definition of balance.

The deficits were kept secret in part by inappropriate, secret internal borrowing, especially from the cash flow of the water fund. The director of the water department worried that he could no longer do his job properly. He pleaded his case at a budget hearing in an emotional tone. When auditors came to examine the financial records of the city, they refused to audit the water fund, because the records were not complete—the first public acknowledgment of serious financial trouble.

The second key event in forcing the deficits into the public view occurred as the council and manager struggled to deal with the long-term decline of the economic base of the city. They helped promote a new regional shopping center on the edge of the city. To carry out their end of the bargain required annexations, property acquisitions, and capital outlay for water, roads, traffic signals, and a new police substation. The city had to borrow, issuing a bond. The bond issue meant that Moody's, one of the major bond evaluators, would have to examine and certify the city's creditworthiness, or potential bond buyers would not risk their money. The evaluation of the city's creditworthiness was a disaster; the staff had to struggle to retain any rating at all. The problem was now public, and the city had to take action to avoid complete humiliation, as well as to maintain the marketability of its bonds.

The manager tried to cut back expenditures of the departments but was hampered by the independence of the department heads. The police and fire chiefs were hired and fired by a police and fire board, appointed by the mayor, and so were not directly responsible to the city manager and felt free to ignore his budget advice. The fire department was spending more than its budgeted allocation; police department expenditures had grown rapidly in response to urban riots a number of years earlier, and the manager seemed unable to cut them back. He requested cuts from the department heads, which they refused to make. The manager also tried to cut out council members' pet capital projects, but found that he did not have the power to do that either. In frustration, the manager tried to cut some of the union agreements and restructure the unions so that they would be easier to deal with, but ended up with some very expensive arbitration settlements that further unbalanced his budget. The manager was fired, and replaced with a more senior manager.

The new manager froze departmental budgets and increased revenue by increasing federal aid, an option still open in the late 1970s. Perhaps more important, he changed the budget process. He had control over the street department head who was responsible to him, and fired him. The manager forbade department heads to communicate directly to the council without going through him, to prevent end runs in which department heads got protection for expenditures from the council before they put them in the budget request. The new manager insisted on the right to hire the police and fire chiefs, and was successful, so they reported to him. The fire department was broken out of the general fund and set up with its own earmarked taxes, so the temptation to overspend by borrowing from other departments was reduced. These changes vastly increased the manager's ability to control budget requests and spending of the departments. The departments and the council were burdened with more constraints, but the manager had more authority to enforce balance.

The case study of Southside indicates that despite balanced budget requirements, cities sometimes do run deficits, but because of the balance constraint, the size of the deficits may be obscured. When that happens, the size of the deficit can grow to a substantial portion of all spending and make remedies politically difficult. Because many of the actors shared a belief that the property tax could not be increased because the public would not tolerate it, the expenditure decrease option was explored. But the political coalitions that supported expenditures were stronger than the young manager, and he failed to make significant cuts. When the manager was finally fired, and the city resolved to handle its deficit problems, they chose budget process reform as a key to the solution. Give the manager more power to make cuts and balance the budget; centralize the executive budget process. The deficits seemed to result as much from failure of structure as from economic circumstances, so a reform of structure seemed a logical response.

Summary and Conclusions

Budget balancing is a lot more than a technical activity that readjusts spending and revenue decisions. It is structurally linked to issues about the scope of government because balance depends on decisions to raise taxes and maintain scope, or cut spending and reduce scope. Balance is also linked to spending priorities because when cutbacks in expenditures are used, some programs will be protected and others cut back disproportionately, or all programs will be cut across the board. Balance is linked to federalism because the scope of responsibilities and the relationship between revenue capacity and spending responsibilities can easily be changed as one level of government seeks to balance its budget at the expense of others. Finally, the politics of balance is linked to the politics of process, as governments shift budget-making power in an attempt to increase discipline, control expenditures, and systematically and authoritatively link revenues and expenditures.

Many of the issues involved in budget balance are not immediate distributional questions, but questions of the structure and size of government, questions on the level of taxation, and sometimes even questions on the form of government. These questions bring out ideological differences between people, between Democrats and Republicans, liberals and conservatives, farmers and city people, business and labor. Even the public at large may be involved, in terms of preferences for taxation levels or insistence on the constraint of balance.

Those who want to limit the size of government have striven to link spending caps with balanced budget requirements and have sought to reduce flexibility to a minimum, striving to place simply worded amendments in the constitution. Business groups have sought to limit the size of government while maintaining their own tax breaks by excluding tax expenditures from controls. Those who want government to continue to provide existing programs or even expand them have sought to maintain balance without constraints on revenues.

More specialized interest groups and department heads may become involved in the politics of balance if particular programs are threatened by cuts; they increase the constraints on cutting the budget, making the political choices more difficult, and hence encourage options that do not rely on deep budget cuts. One consequence of the political difficulty of making cuts is delay, minimizing the size and importance of the problem, hoping it will go away. When governments resort to delay, at state and local levels where they are normally required by law to provide balance, the result has been the use of gimmicks that make the budget appear balanced.

The politics of balance is closely linked to the politics of budget implementation. A budget can become unbalanced during the year because of environmental changes. Also, some of the gimmicks used to make the budget look balanced cause problems during the budget year. Budgeters may overestimate revenues and underestimate expenditures so that the budget as submitted looks balanced, but it will become unbalanced during the year. At the state and local levels, the budget may have to be changed during the year to rebalance it. At any level of government, departments may request supplemental appropriations if their initial estimates of expenditures were too low. Requirements for balance also encourage interfund transfers during the year, to make the budget look more balanced than it is. The importance of changes that occur during the budget year is discussed in the next chapter.

CHAPTER SEVEN

Budget Execution: The Politics of Adaptation

Budget execution is the fun part of budgeting, and the most important part. You get to see how good your estimates were, and whether it all works. You can't just put a budget on the shelf and expect it to work.
—Neil Neilson, City Manager

A BUDGET IS passed at the end of a long period of analysis, debate, disagreement, and compromise. As a result, it often seems to be the outcome and end point of the budgetary process. But budgeting does not stop completely once the budget becomes law. Because of a changing economy, poor predictions of revenues and expenditures, continuing political battles, changed leadership, and the altered salience of public problems, the budget may change after it is passed. Accommodating to changes due to unavoidable circumstances while assuring that the policy agreements underlying the budget are observed is the task of budget implementation.

The implementation stage often involves formulas for disbursements and rules about how much money can be shifted from one item or program to another after the budget has been passed. The emphasis in budget execution is on carrying out the budget exactly as it was enacted, which makes budget execution seem highly technical, the proper sphere of administrators and accountants, devoid of political content. In reality, budget execution is also political because it regulates the degree of public accountability in the budget, because it involves battles for policy control between the executive and the legislature, and because even the most technical of issues, such as the elimination of waste, fraud, and abuse, may become part of political campaigns.

The people who draw up a budget have to make predictions about revenues and expenditures, predictions based on guesses about the future performance of the economy, the rate of inflation, and even the weather. When the economy improves, revenues increase, and outlays for programs such as unemployment compensation and welfare go down. When the economy slows down, revenues drop off, and expenditures for unemployment compensation and welfare go up. Inflation affects the price of goods and services purchased during the year, as well as the payout for pensions that rise with the cost of living. Weather conditions affect the cost of heating bills, street repairs, and cleanups after hurricanes, tornadoes, or floods. If the guesses underlying the budget are wrong, the budget may be adjusted in midyear to reflect the real revenues and expenditures. If the budget is required to balance before the end of the fiscal year, environmental changes may force budget changes.

A budget may change during the year because the budget process was not complete before the beginning of the fiscal year. The budget year may begin under one set of figures but continue under a different set after the decision making is completed. Budget actors may tentatively resolve an issue, expressing the result in the budget, but later back off from the agreement, bringing about a new set of negotiations. Sometimes actors distort information in order to get an agreement that will pass, but end up with an unworkable budget and have to modify it later.

A budget may represent the best thinking and compromises of actors involved during budget preparation, in reaction to situations that were pressing at the time, but the salience of problems and the composition of the actors may change by the time the budget is executed, requiring changes in the budget itself. When leadership changes, which often occurs during a budget year, the new insiders may be eager to implement their policies and hence may make changes in the existing budget.

For all these reasons—a changing economy, continuing political battles, a changed leadership, and the altered salience of public problems—the budget implemented may not be the same as the budget passed. A certain amount of flexibility and change during the budget year may be both necessary and desirable. But changing the budget during the fiscal year raises potential problems.

Granting the executive branch wide discretion to implement the budget and make such changes as may be necessary may give agency heads or chief executives a disproportionate amount of decision-making power not allowed during the regular budget process. If agency heads or the chief executive use that discretionary power to reverse the intent of the legislature, the result may be a major battle between the executive and legislative branches. And changes in the budget during the year, if they are extensive or clearly policy related, may create a shadowy second budget process, outside public scrutiny, threatening the ability of the budget as originally passed to represent government decisions to the public.

The need for flexibility in the budget, to adapt to changing conditions, conflicts with the need to implement the budget as it was passed. Public account-ability requires that the budget passed in full public view, with public and inter-est-group participation, be the budget implemented.

How is this dilemma resolved? First, budgets are generally implemented as passed. The requirement to do so is taken seriously, so that consideration of important policy issues that arise during the year is often delayed until the next full budget process. Second, flexibility is allowed and discretion is granted by the legislatures to the executive branch to make necessary minor or technical changes during the year. These technical adjustments may be carefully monitored (con-strained) to ensure that more important policy decisions are not slipped in among the more routine adaptations without due consideration and participation.

Policy-laden budget decisions may be allowed during the year under particu-lar conditions. When a new president is elected, he may be given fairly broad dis-cretion in reshaping the existing budget to fit his policies. Or Congress may design and implement new programs for relief of farmers in the middle of a drought or to help the unemployed during a deep recession. These decisions are made in the normal way, by the usual committees; what is unusual about them is that they feed into the budget in the middle of the year, and they may be made in haste. In these cases, the changes have high visibility and widespread public acceptability. Conse-quently, they do not threaten public acceptability or accountability.

Despite the care with which budgets are normally implemented, deviations from the budget that are not routine and minor sometimes occur. These devia-tions may be of two kinds. The first is a violation of fiscal control, resulting in overspending or waste, fraud, or abuse. The second is a violation of policy con-trol, in which some budget actor makes policy changes in the budget without going through the whole formal, public business of lawmaking. If the conse-quences are serious enough, or irritating enough, or embarrassing enough, the chief executive or the legislature may increase control over budget implementa-tion. The legislature may increase its control over the executive, the chief exec-utive may increase his or her control over the agencies. The result may be an increase in the number and severity of constraints over budget implementation.

Adapting to Economic Changes

Budgets can be affected by declining economies either through decreases in rev-enues or increases in program expenditures triggered by increased unemploy-ment and poverty. At the federal level, the pattern has been to increase supplemental expenditures when the economy declines in order to cover increased program costs. The result is to add to the size of the deficit during the year. The data in table 7.1 (p. 226) show that the level of supplemental appropriations increased during the recessions in the mid 1970s, in 1982 and 1983, and again in 1991.

The Congressional Budget Office estimated that for 1970 to 1980 about 28 percent of supplemental appropriations was for expenditures that were underestimated as a result of changing economic conditions.[1] Of supplemental money spent in the mid-1970s because of recession, a substantial proportion was caused by new programs enacted during the year, such as the extension of unemployment benefits in 1975 and the enactment of antirecession fiscal assistance to cities in 1976. A similar story could be told of the 1980s, when supplemental appropriations jumped up during the deep recession of 1982–83. Not only were costs increased for unemployment benefits—the total cost of unemployment compensation was reported at $32 billion in 1983[2]—but a new jobs program was enacted (P.L. 98-8). The cost of the Emergency Jobs Appropriations Supplemental Appropriation was over $16 billion, or about two-thirds of the entire supplemental appropriations for the year. The extension of benefits through new legislation is by no means automatic; it is a political choice made possible by changing economic and hence changing political conditions. During a deep recession, political pressure for relief creates increased political salience for new legislation.

At the state and local levels, because deficits are formally forbidden, supplementals are rarely used to adapt to negative changes in the economy. Midyear adaptations to economic declines are more likely to include budget cuts, tax increases, and reductions in reserve accounts. Because these adaptations are so much more politically painful than supplemental appropriations, more effort is taken to prevent or delay such midyear action. The tough political decisions are likely to be postponed at least until the next budget cycle when they can be considered at length as part of the normal budget preparation process. If the recession is brief, the economy may have recovered by the next budget cycle, preventing the necessity for tax increases or deep service cuts.

The adaptation of states to recessions implies that if politicians delay, they will not have to make serious budgetary changes. But for some states, a downturn in the economy may be of long duration rather than temporary. For example, states affected by long-term economic declines in farming and energy prices found themselves faced with midyear reductions in expenditures in 1986. Mississippi reduced its budget midyear by 4.67 percent; Oklahoma, by 4.5 percent; Arkansas by 4.3 percent.[3] Texas led the way, with midyear budget cuts totaling 13 percent of the budget. Texas is dependent for about one-third of its state revenues on taxation of gas and oil production. The drop in oil prices that occurred in 1986 created a severe midyear decline in revenues, and a shortfall of $1.3 billion. The initial state response was to delay, to belt tighten, and to borrow cash from other funds to put into the general fund, until the issue could be addressed as part of a full budget discussion.[4] It takes a long time to build a consensus for new policies in response to a long-term decline. Texas was still wrestling with these revenue problems in 1991, with an estimated budget gap of $4.6 billion in a two-year budget of $53 billion.[5]

At the state level, the cost of delaying a response to economic decline is often short-term budget manipulation and a reduction in the usefulness of the budget as an instrument of accountability.[6] The long-run effect, however, is to ensure that policy decisions reflected in the budget are made in the open, during the regular budget process by the authorized and appropriate budget actors. The slow building of consensus for radical changes in spending or revenue structure encourages public participation. The public nature of the decisions guarantees substantial public accountability.

The response of cities to apparently temporary downturns in the economy is similar to that of the states, that is, there is a general belt tightening during the year and a delay of consideration of major changes in taxation or program levels until the following budget cycle. Two ministudies of council-manager cities illustrate the responses to temporary revenue shortfalls. The first case, Rock Island, Illinois, illustrates the belt-tightening phenomenon and the delay of policy decisions until the following year. The city avoided major cuts at the expense of running deficits briefly. The second case, DeKalb, Illinois, illustrates a response in which deficits were avoided by making fairly severe cuts, but the cuts were taken in such a way as to avoid major policy choices. The DeKalb case also shows the efforts cities take to avoid policy decisions in revising the budget during the year, even when revenues are unexpectedly large, as opposed to when they are unexpectedly small.

MINICASE: ROCK ISLAND, ILLINOIS

Rock Island is a council-manager city that was seriously affected by the deep recession of the early 1980s. The city manager described it: "We had about a $300,000 deficit that one year [1983]. The personal property replacement tax failed [this is a payment from the state] and sales and income tax revenues declined." The city addressed these problems the following year; but during 1983, the city did not make hasty policy changes in the budget; the major response was belt tightening. The result was that the city ran a deficit in 1983.

The manager described the process of belt tightening that goes on when a revenue shortfall is detected during the year. "You get the department heads together, and tell them you need help. Where can you give me money? They know I'm fair. They will help. Someone may say to me, 'We can delay our purchases of new radios until next year.' Sometimes you freeze capital improvements, but there are some projects you can't stop. Then you try to coast it out for the rest of the year."

The actions taken often assumed either the economy would improve or the council would increase taxes and make appropriate cuts for the following year. But the manager had to be prepared for the possibility that the council would not raise taxes. To prevent deeper cuts and reduce the size of the deficit, he tried to build up the size of the year-end balance, despite the deficits. The year-end balance is carried over to the following year. In order to build up the balance, "The departments will underspend. You need 'cash carry forward.' If the council won't increase taxes, you try to make savings this year [for next year]. If you overstated the cost of something [this year], don't spend the difference."

The Rock Island case illustrates several points. First, during the year in which revenues dropped, there was no major rebudgeting, that is, no deep targeted cuts that changed program priorities. The budget was carried out pretty much as passed, despite the looming deficits. Responses included new procedures to respond more quickly to falling revenues, deferral of capital expenditures, job freezes, and delays in refilling positions. The departments cooperated with the cuts, the content of which was not centrally dictated. The city staff worked on creating a buffer/contingency fund for deficit reduction, carrying a small amount of one year's money into the next year.

Getting the departments to go along with the deferrals required the political credit of the manager. His modest statement about their reason for cooperating was that "they know I'm fair." In other cities, such trust may not be there. If the departments are not cooperative, it can be very difficult to make cuts during the year. The degree of authority of the mayor or manager is an important part of these informal "voluntary" cuts.

MINICASE: DEKALB, ILLINOIS

The DeKalb case illustrates the budgetary adaptation both to a revenue shortfall and to a revenue windfall, and shows exactly where the money was cut during the shortfall.

In 1980–81, DeKalb experienced a revenue shortfall in the general fund. They had planned to receive $5,637,472 in revenues, and to use some of the year-end balance from 1980 for 1981 expenses. Actual revenues were only $5,420,793, and the year-end balance never materialized. To avoid deficits in 1981, the city had to cut $635,936 (about 10.4 percent of the budget) in midyear. Then it had to find what funds it could to build a year-end balance to carry over into the following year. (No balance at all is considered very risky. Cities and states normally keep year-end balances of about 5 percent of the budget.) The city managed to cut expenditures by $654,332, avoiding a deficit, but was not able to contribute much to the fund balance.

What expenditures were reduced in the middle of the year? An amount totaling $282,005 came from Public Works (overtime, repairs to traffic signals, sidewalk repair, snow and ice control, vehicle maintenance, and labor for storm sewers); $255,000 came from general fund support, including $175,000 budgeted for storm sewers and $80,000 for contingency. About $50,000 came from the legislative section, from underspending by the Economic Development Commission. About $40,000 came from police (travel, training, and office equipment); $30,000 came from fire (training, vehicle maintenance, training overtime, and personal services); $18,000 came from code enforcement. Slight increases from other departments reduced the savings from $680,000 to $654,332.

These cuts were in no sense across the board. The bulk of the cuts came from public works. Some of it came from delayable projects, such as storm sewers and sidewalk repairs. Some of it came from small earmarked contingency funds, such as for snow removal and traffic-signal accidents. The next largest amount was from general fund support, which was primarily for the capital portion of the sewer project, and from a small contingency fund. Other departmental savings were minor—from travel, training, vehicle maintenance, and office equipment. In short, the process of cutting and postponing picks up money wherever it is available—from large capital projects with low immediate need and from contingency funds.

Interestingly, in 1983–84, as the city was pulling out of the recession, it found that it had underestimated revenue. Did it then allocate the surplus during the year? No. Instead, it replenished the year-end balance.

Budgeting has to be adaptive not only to economic declines, but also to economic recovery and growth. When the economy first begins to improve after a recession or a slowdown in growth, revenues often come in higher than budgeted. The typical response is to use the extra revenues to build back reserves depleted during the recession, without changing expenditures. But what happens if revenue growth continues after fund balances are replenished and revenues are continuously underestimated? What happens to the surplus of uncommitted revenues that appears during the year?

A case study of the state of Georgia for the period 1977 to 1986 is suggestive about how such uncommitted revenues may be used. Under conditions of continuing economic growth and systematic underestimation of revenue, Georgia made midyear appropriations a standard feature of the budget.[7] While the average increase over the general appropriation was only 2.9 percent, in some years 5 percent or more over the general appropriation was allocated midyear.

The money was allocated differently from the general appropriation. "Legislators view the midyear budget amendment as an opportunity to fund local projects that do not compete very well with statewide projects when the General Appropriation Act is initially approved . . . there is generally much more pork in the midyear amendment."[8] Some agencies are able to do much better in the midyear allocation than in the normal annual budget, but not because priorities are redetermined or changed in the middle of the year. Fiscal conservativeness leads "legislative leaders and the governor to prefer capital construction projects which will not have recurring obligations in years when the surplus may not be available."[9] Similarly, they prefer projects that have a potential of producing revenue.[10] The result is that departments having appropriate projects get more of the midyear revenues, which are treated (properly) as one-time revenues.

Georgia's budget behavior may or may not be typical of other states, but it suggests an underlying principle. When increases in revenues are seen as resulting from unpredictable growth in the economy, the money is appropriately treated as one-time revenues to be spent primarily on one-time expenditures. Just as cuts during a recession come disproportionately from departments with major projects that can be delayed, some departments will do better during economy-induced windfalls because they have the right kind of projects to absorb temporary money. Over the long term, and as part of routine budget decision making, politicians may alter the emphasis on one program or another,[11] but during the year, there was little reprioritizing. While there were midyear changes in response to change in the economy, the budgeting process was not repeated on a smaller scale during the year, either by bureaucrats or by elected officials.

Budgetary Changes for Noneconomic Reasons

There are many other reasons for changing the budget in midyear besides adapting to the ups and downs of the economy. Programs may become obsolete, making expenditures unnecessary; a new president may come into office eager to make a policy impact on his predecessor's budget; agencies may not accept decisions made during the budget approval stage and may request changes; contingencies such as weather conditions or changing political situations may require increases in state or foreign aid or in emergency services. Some of the changes that occur in the budget are for technical and relatively nonpolitical reasons, but some are more policy related. This section describes the kinds of budgetary changes and explores the relative policy content of each kind of change. Changes include supplemental appropriations, rescissions and deferrals, reprogrammings, building and depleting contingency and reserve funds, and interfund transfers. In all instances, the proportion of the budget involved in these adjustments is small; the proportion of these changes that is policy related is also small.

Supplementals and Rescissions

Supplemental appropriations are formal additions to the budget after the initial budget has been passed. *Rescissions* occur when the law authorizing an expenditure is nullified; permission to spend that money for that purpose is withdrawn. Both supplementals and rescissions are ways of reshaping the budget during the budget year. They are often used to help respond to events that cannot be anticipated during the regular budget cycle. While they can be used separately, supplementals and rescissions often occur together. In theory, unspent money is identified, permission to spend it is rescinded, and the new need is funded instead.

While both supplementals and rescissions are often employed for technical reasons, they can also be used for political and policy purposes during the year. For example, they are often used to allow a new president to reshape the budget of the current year when he begins his term of office. Supplementals can be used to fund programs that were cut during the year or to fund politically popular pork projects. Rescissions can be used to drain funds from programs that are less popular after they have been funded during the regular budget process. Supplementals can take on added political significance when the president tries to fund his high-priority programs in the supplementals while Congress, dominated by the opposite party, tries to block action or cut those items. Because supplementals often contain must-pass legislation to fund emergencies, holding them up for political purposes becomes a high-risk, high-visibility strategy. Both the level and content of rescissions and supplementals have to be monitored to assure that they are being used primarily for unforeseen events and not for undoing the agreements underlying the budget that was passed. Supplementals, in particular, have the potential for unbalancing the budget with all manner of distributive or pork projects.

At the national level, supplementals and rescissions have become more highly political because of increased efforts to balance the budget. Some legislators who thought that rescissions might provide a way to balance the budget were willing to give the president enhanced powers to rescind spending, changing the balance of power between the legislative and executive branches. The president used the authority only in a limited way. Even so, members of Congress whose projects were cut by the president were predictably infuriated, requiring some of the cuts to be reversed. The president's relationship with Congress suffered, ensuring that such presidential rescissions would be a limited tool at best. After only a short time in effect, enhanced rescission authority was declared unconstitutional.

A second source of controversy surrounding supplementals and rescissions occurred because under the Budget Enforcement Act of 1990, nonemergency supplementals had to be paid for by rescissions, forcing Congress and the president to make explicit tradeoffs. Legislators who proposed supplementals had to say what would be cut to fund their proposed projects, stirring up opponents.

As the federal government tried to balance the budget, it became much more concerned about supplemental appropriations that might swell the deficit. Supplemental appropriations were small as a proportion of the total budget authority, but larger as a proportion of the deficit. Table 7.1 shows the relationship of supplementals net of rescissions through 1995 as a percentage of total budget authority and as a percentage of the deficit. After 1990 and the passage of the Budget Enforcement Act, supplementals were broken into two categories, emergency and nonemergency supplementals. Beginning in 1991, nonemergency supplemental budget authority was supposed to be completely offset by rescissions; emergency supplementals did not need to be offset. In most years since 1990, Congress has fully offset nonemergency supplemental spending, and in some years since 1994, Congress has also offset some of the emergency supplemental spending.[12] Table 7.2 lists emergency spending, in supplementals and in regular appropriations from 1991 to November 1999, in millions of dollars of budget authority, and as a percentage of the deficit. While this emergency spending could have added to the deficit, some of it was offset by rescissions. The percentage of the deficit column thus exaggerates somewhat the effect of the emergency spending on deficits. Table 7.3 gives the size of the rescissions each year from 1976 to 1997 and rescissions as a percentage of total budget authority.

TABLE 7.1   SUPPLEMENTAL APPROPRIATIONS, NET OF RESCISSIONS, 1970–95

YEAR	SUPPLEMENTAL BUDGET AUTHORITY (IN MILLIONS OF DOLLARS)	PERCENTAGE OF TOTAL BUDGET AUTHORITY	DEFICIT (IN BILLIONS OF DOLLARS)	PERCENTAGE OF DEFICIT
1970	5,994	2.8	2.8	na
1971	9,871	4.2	−23.0	42.6
1972	11,599	4.7	−23.4	49.1
1973	11,371	4.1	−14.9	75.8
1974	14,796	4.7	−6.1	240.9
1975	27,588	6.7	−53.2	51.6
1976	24,636	5.9	−73.7	33.3
1977	36,724	7.8	−53.7	68.3
1978	16,054	3.1	−59.2	27.0
1979	13,858	2.5	−40.7	33.9
1980	19,461	2.9	−73.8	26.2
1981	6,923	.9	−79.0	8.7
1982	21,020	2.6	−128.0	16.4
1983	21,123	2.4	−207.8	10.1
1984	16,222	1.7	−185.4	8.7
1985	14,804	1.4	−212.3	6.9
1986	2,249	.2	−221.2	1.0
1987	9,370	.9	−149.8	6.2
1988	1,302	.1	−155.2	.83
1989	5,615	.5	−152.5	3.6
1990	2,253	.16	−221.2	1.0
1991	45,771	3.30	−269.4	16.9
1992	16,107	1.09	−290.4	5.5
1993	7,345	.49	−255.0	2.8
1994	8,229	.53	−203.1	4.0
1995	−889[a]	na	−163.9	na

Sources: Supplementals net of rescissions, 1970–89 from Congressional Budget Office, *Supplemental Appropriations in the 1980s,* x. For 1990–95, unpublished data were provided by the CBO through 17 May 1995. Total budget authority and size of the deficit were drawn from the Historical Tables of the U.S. Budget. Calculations by the author.

a. This figure represents only two of the three major supplementals in that year. The third, which occurred after 17 May, included about $7.4 billion in supplementals and about $15.5 billion in rescissions, for a net supplemental total of about −$8 billion. When added to the negative $889 million from the first two supplementals, the total for 1995 comes out a whopping negative $8.8 billion.

The generally successful effort to control the impact of supplementals on the federal deficit had two prongs. On the one hand, the government sought to reduce the size of supplementals by budgeting in advance for unpredictable expenditures, such as for crop failures and storm damage. On the other hand, as many supplementals as possible were offset with cuts in other spending. Some of these cuts were programmatic, but others were in various kinds of contingency accounts. The very savings accounts intended to buffer against future emergencies were then used to offset supplementals, setting up a system of borrowing from future years.

TABLE 7.2   EMERGENCY SPENDING, IN SUPPLEMENTALS AND REGULAR
APPROPRIATIONS, FISCAL YEARS 1991–99

YEAR	EMERGENCY BUDGET AUTHORITY (IN BILLIONS OF DOLLARS)	DEFICIT/SURPLUS (IN BILLIONS OF DOLLARS)	PERCENTAGE OF DEFICIT
1991	45.846	−269.4	17.0
1992	16.168	−290.4	5.5
1993	6.029	−255.0	2.3
1994	13.860	−203.1	6.8
1995	7.935	−163.9	4.8
1996	5.051	−107.4	4.7
1997	9.536	−21.9	43.5
1998	5.898	69.2	na
1999[a]	21.574	(est.) 79.3	na

Source: Congressional Budget Office, *Emergency Spending under the Budget Enforcement Act,*
December 1998, Appendices A1 and A2.
   a. Data current as of November 1998, only two months of FY 1999.

TABLE 7.3   FEDERAL GOVERNMENT RESCISSIONS, FISCAL YEARS 1976–97

YEAR	BUDGET AUTHORITY RESCINDED	PERCENTAGE OF TOTAL BUDGET
1976	$ 148,331,000	.035
1977	986,412,943	.208
1978	585,819,000	.114
1979	771,109,000	.135
1980	4,015,902,546	.590
1981	14,617,426,150	1.900
1982	4,413,918,000	.540
1983	310,605,000	.034
1984	2,224,064,000	.23
1985	5,632,320,000	.524
1986	5,552,620,000	.517
1987	12,395,390,675	1.120
1988	3,888,663,000	.327
1989	327,966,000	.025
1990	2,304,986,000	.168
1991	1,706,886,000	.123
1992	24,594,499,054	1.670
1993	2,411,586,643	.163
1994	3,667,894,830	.239
1995	19,713,768,252	1.280
1996	5,938,252,131	.375
1997	7,666,364,000	.466

Source: General Accounting Office, *Summary of Proposed and Enacted Rescissions,*
Fiscal Years 1974–1997 (Washington, D.C.: Government Printing Office, 10 June
1998), for the dollar amounts of rescissions. Amounts for the total budget authority
are from the *Budget of the United States, FY 2000,* Historical Tables.

Budgeting for Unpredictable Events

Given the real increase in emergencies due to hurricanes, wars, and earthquakes, keeping the level of supplementals down was increasingly difficult. One goal became, in so far as possible, to anticipate the level of spending for emergencies and budget for them in advance, rather than allowing them to swell the supplementals and hence the deficits. Several major programs that had been funded by supplementals were shifted into the regular budget and anticipated from year to year, including agricultural crop emergencies and recovery assistance after floods, hurricanes, and earthquakes. Fire-fighting programs of the U.S. Forest Service and the Department of the Interior are also based on advance funding.[13] In addition, efforts were made to make populated areas more emergency-proof so that hurricanes or floods would cost less when they hit.

In 1994, partly in response to budget pressures, the administration and Congress passed P.L. 103-354 (the Federal Crop Insurance Reform and Department of Agriculture Reorganization Act of 1994) to reform crop insurance for agricultural disasters. Though funded by insurance, the program had never paid for itself because too few participants paid insurance premiums, so the risk could not be spread across a large enough pool. The gap between premiums and indemnities was paid through ad hoc bills treated as emergencies under Gramm-Rudman-Hollings and the Budget Enforcement Act; these costs typically ran about $1.5 billion per year. P.L. 103-354 amended Gramm-Rudman-Hollings to allow regular appropriations for agricultural disasters. The money to pay for the program still had to come from somewhere, however. If the insurance program could be expanded sufficiently, even with the federal government paying the premiums, the risk could be spread broadly enough to help the program pay for itself because the loss ratio would be reduced.

> A major program reform was enacted in 1994 to address a growing problem caused by the repeated provision of Federal ad hoc agricultural disaster payments. Participation in the crop insurance program had been kept low by the availability of post-event disaster aid to farmers from the Federal Government. Because disaster payments were no-cost grants, farmers had little incentive to purchase Federal crop insurance. The 1994 reform repealed agricultural disaster payment authorities and substituted a "catastrophic" insurance policy that indemnifies farmers at a rate roughly equal to the previous disaster payments. The catastrophic policy is free to farmers except for an administrative fee. Private companies sell and adjust the catastrophic portion of the crop insurance program, and also provide higher levels of coverage (which are also federally subsidized.) The reform was implemented in crop year 1995, and [as of FY 1998—author] no ad hoc

crop disaster assistance bill has been enacted since 1994. In 1995, 82 percent of eligible acres participated in the program—140 percent over 1994. However, the 1996 Farm Bill eliminated the requirement that farmers participating in USDA's commodity programs carry crop insurance, and participation dropped in 1997 to an estimated 61 percent of eligible acres.[14]

By shifting from ad hoc payments for agricultural losses to a larger insurance program in which the government paid the premiums for commercially provided insurance, the newly redesigned program shifted from emergency spending in supplementals to predictable premiums budgeted in advance. The program change in 1994 expanded the number of insured, helping to finance the program by spreading the risk more widely. After the 1996 changes, however, the number of those covered dropped, and in 1998, when farm income dropped precipitously, neither the insurance program nor the revamped commodity programs were sufficient to compensate. A big ad hoc emergency payment was included in the 1999 Omnibus Appropriation (P.L. 105-277). Though this situation seemed a throwback to the pre-1994 days, a certain percentage of the emergency payment was set aside to subsidize insurance payments for higher coverage, and those who were not covered by insurance but received the emergency payments were required to purchase insurance over the next two years. Thus the legislative effort still focused on trying to expand the insurance program and minimize the need for future ad hoc emergency payments.

The second major effort to reduce the amount of emergency supplementals occurred with the Federal Emergency Management Agency (FEMA). In the 1992 Desert Shield/Desert Storm supplemental, a requirement was added that $320 million be budgeted each year for disasters and that additional amounts be considered emergency spending, which would not necessarily have to be offset. The $320 million figure was picked because it was close to the prior ten-year average for annual outlays for this purpose, so the effort was to budget for the best prediction of the level of expenditures, based on prior history. Unfortunately, the number and severity of natural disasters increased substantially over the next few years, continuing to leave a large portion of the outlays in emergency spending. FEMA's response was to change its emphasis to reducing the damage, hence the costs, from natural disasters.

The FEMA director explained,

Our costs have gone up for three main reasons. First, we have the busiest period of disaster events in recent memory. Second, an unprecedented number of large-scale natural disasters have occurred. And third, the types of events that have occurred have cost us a lot more.

For the 10-year period prior to 1989, total obligations from the Disaster Relief Fund were $4 billion; since 1989 we have spent $21 billion.

The 1992 Desert Shield/Desert Storm supplemental bill says that all amounts appropriated for Stafford Act disaster assistance over $320 million or the President's budget request, whichever is lower, will be emergency requirements. When that bill was passed, $320 million was our 10-year average obligational level. And I remember that in the 10 years before that, we did not have much disaster activity.

FEMA's current 5-year average is $2.5 billion, less Northridge earthquake. For the 1997 budget, FEMA first adopted a new basis for estimating what we need for Disaster Relief Fund, the 5-year average less Northridge. We expected that our annual requirement for Disaster Relief would equal this level. This has been pretty much on target since then.

Because of the language in the Desert Storm supplemental, the President's budgets have usually requested something in the $320 million range. We've gotten additional funding as emergency supplemental appropriations usually in response to a large disaster event. And over the past 10 years, FEMA has spent over $21 billion to help people and communities repair and rebuild after natural disasters.

. . . The administration has made an effort to address rising costs in recent budget submissions, but what we have to do and what we have to change is the way we deal with disasters or we're going to be doomed to pay for this over and over again in our poor planning, lost lives, and lost property. We must put an end to the damage, repair, damage, repair cycle that we have been in. The most effective way to break this cycle is to reduce the cost of damages of the disaster by preventing them through mitigation and prevention. Money spent now on mitigation, either pre- or post-disaster, will save us money later.[15]

FEMA manages flood insurance through the National Flood Insurance Program (NFIP), which has focused on prevention of inappropriate rebuilding in flood plains and on restructuring its fees. For the 1999 budget (prepared in 1998) OMB noted that revenue from premiums was up, and that incentives were in place for communities to enforce their flood plain ordinances, to prevent building or rebuilding where flooding could be expected, and to require owners to build to code to help prevent expensive flood damage.

Flood insurance premium revenue grew by approximately 45 percent from 1994 to 1997, exceeding the goal of 20 percent set three years ago. The NFIP's "Cover America" initiative, which is a major marketing and advertising campaign, should continue to increase awareness of flood insurance and educate people about the risks of floods. FEMA is using three strategies to increase the number of flood insurance policies in force: lender compliance, program simplification, and expanded marketing.

The NFIP's Community Rating System (CRS) now allows policyholders in over 900 communities to receive discounts of at least 5 percent on their premiums by undertaking activities which will reduce flood losses, facilitate accurate insurance rating, and promote public awareness of flood insurance and flood risk.

In 1997 the NFIP expanded mitigation insurance as authorized by the National Flood Insurance Reform Act of 1994. Mandatory Increased Cost of Construction (ICC) coverage, which took effect May 1, 1997, allows repetitively flooded or substantially damaged structures to be rebuilt in accordance with existing flood plain management requirements. This will reduce the amount and cost of future flood damage and allow those structures to be actuarially rated.

In 1998 and 1999 FEMA will continue efforts to reduce future flood damage by educating Federal regulators about mandatory flood insurance requirements for federally backed home and business loans on property located in flood hazard areas; simplifying policy language; using mitigation insurance to allow flood victims to rebuild to code, thereby reducing future flood damage costs; and using flood insurance premium adjustments to encourage community and State mitigation activities beyond those required by the NFIP.[16]

Efforts to reduce emergency spending that could swell the deficits had some effect, but even in programs in which a portion of the emergency costs were anticipated and budgeted for, emergency appropriations were not eliminated. Since this spending could not be eliminated, minimizing its impact on the deficit meant that it had to be offset in some way. The main tool available for curtailing the impacts of supplemental legislation was a rescission—something else had to be cut to fund the new unplanned or unfunded expenditure. Political attention then shifted to the issue of what would be cut to fund what expenditures.

Deferrals

Under the 1974 Congressional Budget Reform Act, the president had to propose deferrals to Congress, and if Congress did not disapprove, the spending was deferred. Some or all of the money for a particular project or program could be delayed for some specified period of time. Deferrals are common at all levels of government, but they were perhaps most formalized at the federal level. The amounts of money deferred at the federal level were substantially greater than the amounts involved in rescissions from 1975 to 1979 (see table 7.4). Rescissions were more permanent than deferrals and required positive approval from both houses of Congress; deferrals were easier to get because they involved only a temporary delay in spending, and unless Congress actively disapproved, spending was deferred.

Deferrals are generally classed as routine and technical or as policy related. In policy-related deferrals, the president disapproves of some spending that Congress approves and recommends that the spending be delayed. Congress normally accedes to the president's requests on routine deferrals, which averaged about $8 billion a year from 1981 to 1988. But Congress gets very touchy when the president refuses to spend money that has been legally appropriated and that represents Congress's preferences. In 1981 and 1982, Congress allowed almost all the president's requested policy deferrals; he was a very popular new president with an apparent mandate to reshape the budget quickly, and Congress went along with his initiatives. From 1983 to 1988, Congress got more balky about approving the president's proposals to defer spending for policy purposes. Although Congress had approved $6.1 billion of policy deferrals in 1981 and 1982, it approved only $7.7 billion in policy deferrals for the next six years.[17]

The timing of the change was probably related in part to the two difficult years of 1981 and 1982, during which Congress had acceded to many cuts it might have preferred to have opposed, but felt that the political risks of opposing the president were too formidable. During those years, the president not only invoked the reconciliation procedures of the 1974 budget reform act but also bypassed those procedures by substituting his own amendment for the work of the congressional committees. Reportedly, the president used a lot of pressure tactics to get support on these measures and amassed considerable resentment for his seeming lack of respect for congressional ways. When the Supreme Court

TABLE 7.4   FEDERAL DEFERRALS, 1975–79

YEAR	AMOUNT DEFERRED (IN THOUSANDS)	AMOUNT DISAPPROVED (IN THOUSANDS)
1975	$24,574,236	$9,318,217
1976	9,209,780	393,081
1977	6,831,194	25,600
1978	4,910,114	69,531
1979	4,393,328	13,852

Source: Adapted from Allen Schick, *Congress and Money* (Washington, D.C.: Urban Institute Press, 1980), 404.

nullified Congress's ability to veto presidential requests for deferrals in 1983 (*Immigration and Naturalization Service* v. *Chadha*),[18] it must have seemed one more powerful blow to congressional power. In fact, however, the congressional veto of deferrals was declared unconstitutional because it required only one house to take action and therefore did not have the force of law.

Congress responded to the elimination of its veto powers over deferrals by putting its rejection of deferrals into supplemental appropriations, and passing them as they would other laws. In 1986, when Reagan deferred some $10 billion that he did not want spent, "Congress's response was to insert a provision in that year's supplemental appropriation bill nullifying most of the policy deferrals."[19] In 1987 the Senate report on the supplementals rejected the president's request for deferrals, arguing that the president was using them for policy purposes, not programmatic technicalities. The report questioned the president's legal ability to defer the funds.[20] Indeed, in 1987 the U.S. Court of Appeals for the District of Columbia barred any kind of policy-based deferral.[21] On 1 April 1987 the controller general advised Congress that twenty-five policy deferrals submitted by the president after the decision by the court of appeals were illegal. The administration decided not to appeal the decision to the Supreme Court. Consequently, it is currently illegal to defer spending for policy purposes, although spending may still be deferred for technical reasons.

At state and local levels deferrals have never been clearly policy related. Projects are deferred when there is no cash to pay for them. Because governors often have line-item vetoes, and sometimes have amendatory vetoes, it is not necessary for them to withhold spending on projects when the legislature increases their budget requests.

Reprogramming

Reprogramming means taking some or all of the money that has been budgeted to one program or project and transferring it to another in the same account or fund during the fiscal year. Reprogramming may make good managerial sense if the money cannot be appropriately spent as budgeted and other urgent needs for the money occur during the year. A labor strike may result in budgeted salary remaining unused, or a change in accounting for pensions may free up some funds that were budgeted for that purpose. At the federal level, a change in program structure may reduce the amount of money necessary to keep in reserve in case of emergency. Or expenditures may have been inadvertently overestimated, because they are difficult to predict, such as money set aside for plowing snow at the local level in the northern part of the country. Such funds can and should be released for other purposes that arise during the year within the same fund or appropriation account.

Reprogramming can help an agency adapt to unexpected contingencies without requiring a supplemental appropriation. Some agencies, however, may intentionally underspend in order to create a pool of funds that can be spent elsewhere on items that have not been approved. Extensive reprogramming can alter the approved budget and change the legislative priorities reflected in the appropriations. To prevent such changes, the legislature may set guidelines for reprogramming, limiting the total amount that can be shifted, reducing the size of the units within which flexible choices can be exercised (say, from accounts to subaccounts), requiring advance notice and explanation of reprogramming, or requiring extensive quarterly reporting after the reprogramming has taken place.

Reprogramming does take place at the state and local level and sometimes becomes controversial, but it has been a more visible issue at the national level. Congress has tried to maintain agency ability to adapt to changing situations while preventing agencies from using reprogramming to thwart its will. It does so by issuing guidelines to control rather than prevent reprogramming. Guidelines often include wording such as, "Reprogramming may be used for unforeseen events but only if delay until the next budget cycle would result in excessive costs or damage." Proscriptions often include any projects for which Congress has already denied funding, and reprogramming into areas where Congress has just cut the budget is usually forbidden. These guidelines normally appear in committee report language, rather than in actual legislation, to convey the intent of committee members without binding the agency through law. Committees often ask the agencies to report in advance reprogrammings above a given dollar amount, which gives the committee members a chance to object if the reprogramming has policy implications or is otherwise questionable.

Overall, Congress's experience in controlling reprogramming has been successful. The number of requests for reprogramming has been moderate over the years and there have been few major controversies. Nevertheless, especially in those agencies where there has been a history of tension between committees and the departments or agencies over reprogrammings, Congress has remained vigilant. Moreover, efforts to balance the budget and reduce spending, especially in the discretionary portion of the budget, have restimulated interest in reprogramming. Legislators needed to grant agencies more discretion to move money around that was not being fully used, to soften the cuts, but they worried that their legislative priorities might be cut if reprogramming authority was broadened.

In 1994, when congressional appropriations committees were wrestling with cuts, several subcommittees reiterated or changed language in the reprogramming guidelines. The Interior Subcommittee of the Senate Appropriations Committee included such revisions in Senate Report 103-294. The language simultaneously increased the minimums necessary to trigger a formal reprogramming action, thus increasing agency discretion, and tightened other areas of discretion. The minimum trigger for reporting a reprogramming to congressional committees was raised from $250,000 or 10 percent to $500,000 or 10 percent, with exceptions for the Forest Service, the Bureau of Indian Affairs, and the Bureau of Land Management. In the Bureau of Land Management and some Forest Service programs, the reprogramming control level was made the line item but the trigger level for changes to be approved was $3 million or 10 percent. The change was the result of an intentional effort to give these agencies more budgetary discretion.

While reprogramming requirements were loosened, the Interior Subcommittee added new strictures on other sources of flexible money. For example, the committee required that when secretaries assessed programs to pay for departmental overhead, the amounts and purposes of the assessments had to be spelled out clearly. Departments were forbidden to use such funds to pay for programs that Congress had cut or for new permanent staff positions or for any spending that could have been foreseen. In other words, overhead assessments were treated as a potential source of reprogramming funds. Also, extra rules were promulgated for the Forest Service, which was forbidden to change the boundaries of a region or to move or close any regional office for research or any state or private forestry or National Forest System administrative office without the consent of the House and Senate Committees on Appropriation, the Senate Committee on Agriculture, Nutrition and Forestry, and the House Committee on Agriculture.

As this example suggests, it is not clear whether the level of agency discretion over reprogramming was going up or down. Several factors, including the National Performance Review (NPR), pressed for less congressional control over agency budgets. The NPR was staffed by officials on loan from agencies across the federal government who identified the features they liked least about their jobs, one of which was the overregulated environment in which they worked. The NPR reports demonstrated a clear belief that managers needed to be freed from regulations controlling inputs in favor of accountability for outputs. At the same time, both in Congress and in OMB, there was emphasis on increasing competition and incentives to operate more effectively. Internal markets (called *internal service accounts* at other levels of government) were supposed to provide such incentives. Agencies could purchase services they needed internally, but because it cost them money, presumably they would economize and use the minimum they could get away with. In order to receive motivation for saving in this manner, the agencies had to be able to keep the savings and use them where they were most needed. Incentives were to take the place of regulations, and the result was to be better, more cost-effective management. These pressures for decontrol were offset by congressional concerns that agencies might cut congressional priorities or restore congressional cuts. Also working toward tighter regulation was the history of prior abuse of discretion that made some members of Congress suspicious about potential new sources of discretion and unofficial reprogramming.

Not only were there pressures and counterpressures, but even in agencies where the clear direction was to reduce legislative controls over the budget, the results did not confirm expectations for improved management and therefore did not provide an impetus for more decontrol. Two initiatives launched in the 1990s to give agencies more discretion over their budgets brought into question the assumption that more agency discretion leads to better financial management. One initiative was the creation of the Defense Business Operating Fund (DBOF); the other was a reform of the Forest Service's budget structure.

DBOF combined a series of existing operating capital funds in the Defense Department to form a huge internal service account. The military branches each purchased supplies and repairs from this huge, departmentwide fund. Because it was so large and crossed services, DBOF created massive amounts of discretion. Moreover, military accounting procedures were so poor that overseers in Congress could not figure out what was going on inside the DBOF, further adding to the level of discretion in the Department of Defense. Formed in 1991, DBOF was terminated in 1995, decentralized back to the services from which it came. The DoD never got the financing or accounting under control, and the advantages the fund was supposed to achieve were not realized.

The second initiative was a 1995 budget reform of the Forest Service, which had been cited by the National Performance Review as having a budget structure so complicated and controlling that it hampered management and efficient uses of public money. The House and Senate Appropriations Committees agreed to increase the agency's budgetary flexibility, consolidating line items and increasing the agency's ability to move money between line items without approval. The appropriations committees expected improved performance and performance reporting in return; they wanted more focus on programs and performance reporting in exchange for weaker line-item controls.

The GAO reported in December of 1998 that the changes seemed to have made little difference to agency management. One reason seems to have been that the agency seldom requested changes between line items, either before the reforms or afterward. Part of the reform restructured the budget so that all the funding for a project was consolidated in the program that would benefit most from that project. Such an approximation to program budgeting would have improved accountability. GAO reported, however, that for a variety of reasons, including underestimating of project costs, some programs did not have the funds needed to implement a project, so other programs that were providing support services were required to absorb some of the costs.[22] Under the newer, more program-oriented system, flexibility between line items within a program was not the major concern; paying for a project with inadequate budget was the main issue, and for this, a different kind of flexibility was needed.

While there were many reasons for lack of results from the Forest Service experiment, one of them had to do with the politics of full costing, which sometimes makes programs or projects look too expensive. Simply removing or loosening some of the line-item controls did not address the perceived need to underestimate costs. When costs are underestimated, they have to be made up somehow, because of federal antideficiency regulations. In this case, costs were made up not by formal reprogramming but by informally putting more of the costs on supporting units.

The problem of setting and sticking to realistic cost estimates when those costs seemed too high plagued DoD as well. One of the goals of the Defense Business Operating Fund was to encourage the military services to sell back excess inventory to the DBOF for credits, turning inventory into budget dollars. When that happened, Congress claimed a savings, but the effect on DBOF was to reduce its operating capital below what it needed for cash flow on a week-to-week basis. Consequently, the DoD began to bill the services in advance, before services were rendered, to create enough cash to pay short-term bills. In order to eliminate the advance billing and build up a sufficient cash reserve, DBOF, and after 1995 the individual revolving funds had to increase prices, which in turn played havoc with army, navy, and air force budgets. Pressure to increase prices met up with counterpressures to hold budget outlays down. Proposed price increases were sometimes rolled back. Cash flow remained a problem and advance billings continued.

Some members of Congress were concerned that advance billings in these capital revolving funds might be used for reprogramming without formal notification. The following dialogue between committee members and witnesses from the General Accounting Office illustrates this concern:

Mr. Pickett: Well, is any of the cash that is collected from the depot advance billing used for any other purpose [besides depot repair]?

Mr. Pugnetti: It will then go into the overall—in the case of the Navy, into the Navy working capital fund overall pot; and then that cash will be used for paying any bills that come in, which could be for those Navy business areas, or other Navy business areas.

Mr. Pickett: So this is a nice way to have a reprogramming internally without having to go through Congress and getting it approved, isn't it?

Mr. Pugnetti: Except that they have to—the service, the working capital fund still has to perform that work. . . . they still have to either overhaul that ship or repair the aircraft. So I mean there is an obligation and a contractual agreement between the customer and the working capital [fund] for them to do that work.

Mr. Pickett: But the cash itself can be used for purposes other than paying the shipyard workers, and, for example, it's an advance billing for ship repair work, that cash could be used for repairing aircraft, or—

Mr. Brock: That is correct, although there is an obligation, you know, to pay your—the current expenses that would be incurred with doing the shipyard work, or whatever.[23]

According to this testimony, in the short term the cash from advance billings could be spent on other things, but sooner or later the work that was contracted for would have to be performed and the costs paid. What the GAO witnesses did not address, however, was whether the services, when finally delivered, were worth the amount paid. If some costs were overestimated or services underprovided, some slack could be created that could indeed be reprogrammed without any reporting. During hearings, spokespersons from DoD assured committee members that services were provided for advance billings just as they were for regular billings, just later on, and that the advance billings were a response to cash shortfalls, not a way of getting around budget controls.[24]

Congress's concern with advance billings in the Department of Defense reflected less a concern that DoD was not complying with reprogramming guidelines than that DoD was finding ways to shift money around that did not come under formal reprogramming guidelines. This was the same concern that the Interior Subcommittee on Appropriations had expressed about the use of overhead billings. To find other possible unregulated sources of reprogramming, the Military Readiness Subcommittee of the House Committee on National Security requested that GAO look into underspending and overspending in the DoD Operations and Maintenance (O&M) budget. Over- and underestimates of spending should be more or less random; if GAO could discover a pattern of underspending in some areas of the budget, the subcommittee might have evidence of intentional creation of funds for reprogramming in contravention of congressional policy.

MINICASE: DEPARTMENT OF DEFENSE AND THE O&M BUDGET

The Department of Defense spends a substantial portion of its budget on the Operations and Maintenance program. The department has considerable flexibility in the use of these funds. According to Representative Herbert Bateman, "the O&M accounts are the only ones in the department that have little if any restrictions on the movement of funds within or out of their original appropriation." The General Accounting Office, at the request of the Military Readiness Subcommittee, examined the differences between the amounts budgeted and the amounts obligated in different accounts and subaccounts within the O&M section of the budget. They found substantial differences between the budget and the obligations. Sometimes the changes were in random directions, too high one year and too low another year, but for some accounts, there seemed to be a systematic trend toward overestimating budgetary needs and then using the money elsewhere in the O&M budget, not always for the highest priority items.

Particular members of the Readiness Subcommittee of the House Committee on National Security were concerned lest this pattern represent an effort to get Congress to appropriate more money than was needed for approved expenses. DoD could claim it was behind in depot repairs, for instance, get an increased appropriation for depot repairs, use the increase for other purposes, and then come back to claim more budget for delayed depot repairs. The chair of the subcommittee was direct in his questioning:

> *Mr. Bateman*: The first question I have is whether or not there is any indication that somewhere in the DoD structure someone is gaming the system to overestimate on accounts where the accounts can't be—or underestimating on accounts where you can't do the transfers without reprogramming from activity to activity.[25]

To get the attention of the Defense Department, the House included in its version of the Defense Appropriations Bill for 1998 considerably more stringent constraints over the total allowable reprogramming in the O&M budget. The proposed language would require reprogramming notification from the secretary of defense for cumulative amounts of redirected dollars over $10 million. The Defense Department fought back vigorously, arguing that such constraints would prevent it from responding to emergencies because congressional approval would be required for even small amounts of money if they exceeded a modest total. The DoD prevailed, and the new constraint was not included in the final legislation, but members of Congress had done what they intended, which was to get the attention of DoD officials, who indicated that the committee members indeed had their attention and that they would work on the problems.

Reprogramming can be a more or less important problem, depending on whether the reprogramming guidelines are too strict to allow the agency to adapt to contingencies during the year, whether the agency is likely to try to evade reprogramming guidelines, and whether the legislative body has detailed priorities that it is trying to ensure are observed. In addition, if the accounts or funds are small, there is not much discretion to move items around inside them, but if the accounts or funds are very large, the possibilities for evading policy directives are more substantial. Budgetary cutbacks increase the pressure on executive agencies to reprogram as a way of adapting to reduced funding and, at the same time, intensify legislators' fears that some of their priorities may be cut as a way to pressure them to restore funding. Agencies that often deal with emergencies arising during the year are more likely to have to worry about reprogramming, especially when supplemental appropriations are hard or impossible to get. Flexibility that is provided to deal with uncertainty can be abused.

Congress has generally been reluctant to put stringent reprogramming restrictions into law. Most often, reprogramming requirements appear instead in committee reports, which do not have the force of law but often get the point across that Congress is concerned about the level of reprogramming or possible intent to evade controls. An agency history of prior evasions makes legislators who have followed the agency for years highly skeptical of present intentions, but agency insistence on the need for flexibility often dominates the outcome.

Contingency Funds

Contingency funds are sums of money budgeted for unknown or unstated purposes. There are some contingency funds, or discretionary funds, at the federal level, but they are less important at the federal level than at state and local levels. At the national level, contingencies are generally funded by supplementals, which usually increase the size of the deficit; at state and local levels, it is illegal to run deficits, so a variety of special funds are set aside for different contingencies. In addition, at the local level, departmental budget justifications are normally included in the budget, so a detailed plan of how the money is to be spent is part of the budget legislation. Most city agencies thus do not have much flexibility regarding how budgeted money will be spent. To create discretion during the year, administrators have to build it into the budget in terms of pools of uncommitted revenues to be allocated during the year.

Cities normally aim for year-end balances between 5 and 10 percent of their budgets. In any given year, the amount may be lower. The more money there is in contingency funds, the less is needed in the year-end balance, and vice versa. The money for salary increases is normally placed in one or more contingency accounts and transferred from the contingency funds to the departmental accounts after labor negotiations. Often a city with a very large year-end balance is planning some capital project and saving up for it.

Most of the uses of formal contingency funds are technical, but the informal creation of funds may be a way of rebudgeting during the year. In a study of Cincinnati during a period of fiscal stress, the city cut back expenditures in line with a worst-case revenue scenario. The process of worst-case planning created moderate amounts of slack in the retrenchment budget. The council used the slack to add police and fire personnel after the 1976 cuts. In 1980, the manager elicited supplemental requests from departments to use revenues that exceeded the somewhat pessimistic predictions in the budget. The manager then selected from these supplemental requests those that dealt with the managerial problem he saw as high priority, deferred maintenance.[26] How such "savings" will be used and who will control their expenditure are policy-laden issues.

The use of funds built up through conscious overestimation of expenditures and/or underestimation of revenues occurs in cities not experiencing cutbacks. The following excerpt from an interview with a city manager indicates that he believes some other cities use their balances to make minor but policy-related changes during the year:

Q. What about year-end balances, how are they used?

A. They are strictly an accounting device. We don't play any games at all with the statements. I could, because most people don't read accounting statements. Some managers do use it. They purposely underestimate revenues and overestimate expenditures, so that will happen. The council may ask the manager to find money to fund a project during the year. The manager then can do it. The council thinks it's magic.

The project for which the council is asking midyear support may be one for which the need developed during the year, or it may be a pet project with political payoff that could not be funded as part of the regular budget but could be funded midyear without much budget scrutiny or comparison to other projects.

While the need for contingency funds at the local level is substantial, year-end balances combined with contingency funds seldom exceed 8 to 10 percent of the budget. One of their major purposes is to fund labor agreements, which represent no policy change. The level of the contingency funds will normally remain constant from year to year, unless it is drawn down to fund a particular capital project or tide the city over in a recession. In some cities, at some times, a portion of the contingency funds may be spent for special council projects, with explicit council approval. The budget may thus change somewhat during the year, with negative impact on public accountability, but the amounts involved are normally quite small, maybe 2 percent of the total budget.

Interfund Transfers

Interfund transfers are shifts of money between appropriation accounts or funds. At the federal level, because the amounts of the individual appropriation accounts can be very large, most of the need for transfers can be accommodated within accounts, and without fanfare. Why go between accounts, which requires legislative approval, when there is sufficient discretion within accounts, which requires no approval? In cities, however, individual funds (the local analog to federal appropriation accounts) are sometimes narrow, covering only one function and having only a limited number of dollars. Some of these funds may be related in function, so interfund transfers may be planned and budgeted in advance. Formal transfers occurring during the year are treated as budget amendments and need to be approved by the council. Hence they are neither secret nor do they bypass the regular budget process, although they occur during the budget year.

There should be little reason for unanticipated transfers, and normally there are few of them. Sometimes, however, there is some informal borrowing, especially from cash-rich to cash-poor funds. If the borrowing is not approved by the council or becomes a long-term loan, or if a loan is not fully repaid, the implications are policy laden rather than technical.

For example, if a general fund borrows from a water fund and does not repay the loan, the water fund may develop deficits.[27] The fund showing the deficit will have to cut services or increase user fees or taxes to eliminate the deficit. The result may be to raise water fees to pay for police services, a result that is not only inequitable but secret. If the deficits are not eliminated, bond costs may go up, costing the city unnecessary interest charges on future water projects. This practice is probably not common, but it does sometimes occur, and when it does, there are policy implications.

Summary and Conclusions

For the purposes of accountability to the public and for managerial predictability, most of the budget is implemented as passed. Nevertheless, some flexibility has to be built into budget implementation because budgets are open to the environment. Rivers flood, countries invade each other, hurricanes knock down trees and houses. The economy waxes and wanes, reducing or increasing revenues beyond expectations and reducing or increasing the number of those eligible for entitlements. If more people commit crimes and are caught and sentenced to prison, there has to be some way to pay for their imprisonment, even if the numbers were not correctly predicted when the budget was put together. Budgets also adapt to the priorities of newly elected officials, who must initially work within the framework of budgets put together by their predecessors.

Budgets adapt through a variety of techniques, including supplemental appropriations, rescissions, deferrals, reprogramming, contingency funds, and interfund transfers. Some techniques are more common at one level of government than another. The federal government can run deficits, so it can respond to an emergency with a supplemental appropriation; state and local governments cannot generally run legal deficits and so have to build up various reserve and contingency funds to draw down in case of emergency, and often hold back on spending during the year in case revenues do not materialize. Contingency funds and deferrals of this sort are common at state and local levels, but supplementals are relatively rare. Interfund transfers are fairly common at the local level; reprogramming within accounts is more important at the national level because accounts are so large that moving money around inside them usually provides sufficient flexibility.

Most of the changes in the budget during implementation are the result of technical changes and adaptation to the environment, but the flexibility that is absolutely necessary to budgeting also allows for some changes due to policy considerations. If Congress adds on to the president's budget, the president may try to rescind or defer that unwanted spending; if Congress disapproves of some spending program the president favors, it may try to rescind that spending by packaging it with supplementals that the president wants. Revenues may be intentionally underestimated and then put into a pool for allocation to council members' favorite programs or projects. Agencies may reprogram money approved by the legislature and the executive to spend on priorities they prefer. In general, the amount of money spent on policy-motivated changes during the year is quite limited and in some cases, as in the policy-related deferrals at the national level, has been reduced to near zero. Supplemental appropriations at the national level for policy reasons have been controlled, and reprogramming is under legislative control. Once in a while, though, issues of budget implementation take center stage.

CHAPTER EIGHT

Budget Implementation and Control

THE BUDGET IS generally implemented almost exactly as passed. Most of the changes that occur are made for widely accepted reasons, and very little rebudgeting takes place out of public view or outside regular budget processes. Nevertheless, the discretion granted to the executive to carry out the budget is sometimes used for political and policy purposes during the year. Not all of this policy-related activity is unacceptable or threatening to democratic values. But sometimes changes in the budget during the year have the effect of rendering the publicly circulated budget document obsolete. Sometimes the discretion to adapt the budget to changing circumstances is abused or is perceived as a perversion of legislative intent. If there is some indication of overspending or underspending, or of corruption, fraud, or purposeful thwarting of the policies and priorities in the budget, the elected officials are likely to increase the level of their control over budget execution.

The Discretion, Abuse, Control Cycle

Senator Edmund Muskie described the impulse to increase control over implementation when agencies defy congressional will. In 1973, when he learned that the Environmental Protection Agency (EPA) had abused its discretion to implement the budget, Muskie said, "The clear language and debate was what we were giving you, in what we understood to be legitimate administrative discretion to spend the money, not defeat the purposes. Then to have you twist it as you have, is a temptation to this Senator to really handcuff you the next time."[1] "Handcuffing" involves writing detailed constraints into legislation and thereby reducing the agency's discretion over budget implementation.

The dynamics of control tends to follow a pattern over time: (1) an initial grant of broad discretion to the agencies; (2) a perception of abuse; (3) increased budgetary control, in the form of increased supervision and oversight, increased reporting responsibilities, and additional constraints written into committee reports and statutes; and (4) agency reaction to reduced flexibility. If reduced flexibility sufficiently hampers management, or if politicians become overburdened with politically irrelevant decisions about budget execution, there may be (5) a gradual reduction in the level of implementation of budgetary controls.

The National Level

At the federal level, for the most part, Congress's control of agencies' budget execution is informal. There is an initial broad grant of discretion to the agencies and to the executive branch over budget execution. There are conversations between legislators and agency heads during budget hearings or suggestions for restrictions on spending in committee reports, neither of which has the status of law. Congressional committees request and agencies prepare detailed budget justifications, but these justifications are not part of the appropriations; they are just part of the informal understanding between agency officials and members of Congress. But if the agency does not adhere to informal advice, congressional committees may increase their controls and put restrictions or advice into the appropriations act, giving them the force of law. "Usually when restrictive provisions are written into appropriations acts, it is because the agency has failed to comply with these less formal types of guidance or the Congress is not satisfied with how a particular agency is progressing toward some congressionally desired goal."[2]

One example of a broad grant of discretion followed by a perception of abuse and a threatened and actual increase in controls over budget implementation has occurred in response to reprogrammings. Departments have sometimes taken money intended for one approved program and spent it on another program expressly disapproved by Congress. The problem of controlling reprogrammings accelerated after 1949, when Congress began to consolidate a number of appropriation accounts.[3] Reprogramming can occur only within a single appropriation account, so the move toward more lump-sum appropriations with many programs in a single appropriation increased the amount of discretion and the amount of reprogramming that could be done.

One department that has used reprogramming in ways that have sometimes provoked congressional ire is the Department of Defense. The ability to reprogram was abused during the Vietnam war. For example, the Pentagon used other appropriated funds to pay for projects Congress had disapproved. Congress took control of this particular reprogramming in 1974, with legislation prohibiting the Defense Department from reprogramming funds to any items previously denied by Congress. As a further discouragement of reprogramming, Congress took a more active stance in recommending rescissions of unspent money so there would be less temptation to reprogram.[4]

Although Congress tried to increase controls over Defense Department spending in most areas, some problems remained in the late 1970s and early 1980s, provoking congressional threats of still more detailed control over spending. Congressman Joseph Addabbo complained in 1981 hearings that the Department of Defense had avoided specific congressional instructions and threatened detailed, line-item control in the operations and maintenance section of the Defense Department budget. Addabbo asked whether Congress had come to the point "when we should get the Congressional Budget Office to prepare a computer printout and we line item. When we cut, say, 'this is it' and the money will be spent in all of the other items."[5]

Addabbo charged that the Defense Department was funding a number of items during the year that were not even in the budget request and for which funds had not been appropriated.[6] Addabbo also complained that Defense Department officials were reprogramming in such a way as to try to force Congress to pass supplementals to restore the lines from which the reprogramming funds were taken. Addabbo described this ploy in the following terms:

> Well, take the Indian Ocean operation, moving the task force in there, you proceed to do that and within that category, the same category, you have a ship overhaul. You take the money from ship overhaul, which is a high priority item, and use it for this. I am willing to venture a guess that within that same category there are many items which we discussed and which there should have been a more careful look at. . . . You don't grab where it's easiest to grab and say we are going to get that back anyway. That is what we have seen.[7]

Defense Department officials, according to this description, transferred money (reprogramming) out of top-priority rather than low-priority programs, because they knew that Congress would have to pass a supplemental appropriation to replenish the funds for the high-priority programs. Congressman Addabbo, in particular, was not pleased by this maneuver and threatened to reduce Defense Department autonomy over spending even further. Departmental representatives vigorously resisted the imposition of further controls.

Congressman Addabbo also argued that the Defense Department used appropriations for ammunition (which Congress thought very important) as a source of reprogramming funds. Congress would appropriate the money for ammunition, and the Defense Department would reprogram the funds into other areas and then come back to Congress with an emergency request for additional funds for ammunition.[8]

The Defense Department did indeed come back later with requests for supplemental appropriations. During the hearings on the supplemental request, Congressman Addabbo pointedly argued that the Defense Department had tried to avoid cuts specifically recommended by Congress through reprogramming.

> Last year in R.D. and T.E. [the research and development programs] the Congress said you had too much budgeted for inflation. We cut, and all we got back was a lot of nonsense, a lot of wording that we cut so dramatically that many things are going to go wrong. You decided to teach Congress a lesson. You took the reductions out of add-ons by the Congress and we had to hold action on reprogrammings. Because action was required on the supplemental, you started taking it out of where you should be taking it out.[9]

The reprogramming Congressman Addabbo was describing represented not only an agency attempt to avoid specific congressional cuts but also an attempt to implement the president's budget over congressional preferences. That is, the Defense Department chose to take the cuts in those areas where Congress had added to the president's request. The usurpation of congressional prerogatives by the executive branch was not lost on the appropriations subcommittees, which held up the supplementals until the cuts were taken as specified.

MINICASE: ABUSE AND CONTROLS AT THE DEPARTMENT OF DEFENSE

At the end of September 1985, the House Armed Services Committee took the deputy secretary of defense to task for what many committee members perceived as a violation of the reprogramming procedures.[10] Apparently, the Defense Department had proceeded with a contract bid even though the committee had denied the reprogramming approval necessary for funding the contract. There was some discussion on the committee as to whether the congressional interest stemmed from narrow concerns about who the low bidder was or broader concerns about cost effectiveness of the bid itself, but in any case the result of Defense's bypassing the committee's controls was considerable anger.

The first step was to bring the deputy secretary before the committee to explain what had happened and to reaffirm his understanding of the informal agreements between the committee and the department about the rules of reprogramming. The deputy secretary shifted the blame to a number of other locations and promised to try to do better in the future. He did reiterate a clear understanding of what the rules were.

Some committee members were not content with what they called "wrist slapping." The second step was to call in the General Accounting Office to review the Department of Defense's procedures on reprogramming and to have that office review all the Defense requests for reprogramming to see if they complied with the committee's rules. If not, the committee was determined to reject the request.[11] Then GAO was instructed by the Senate Armed Services Committee to evaluate reprogramming in the Defense Department and suggest improvements. The GAO found that the Defense Department was doing a reasonable job complying with the committee's rules but that the reporting procedure was such that the department did not sort out by fiscal years the reprogramming requests and did not highlight the items of interest to congressional committees. Nor did the department tell the committees of other pending requests that might give congressional committees a clue about what policies were being pursued. The GAO also found that there was considerable reprogramming that went on below the limits required for reporting.

Part of Congress's concern was where the money for reprogramming was coming from, not just where it was going to and whether the object was one Congress had forbidden. As a GAO report described, the Defense Department had proposed a $60.8 million reprogramming from a single program, the Small Intercontinental Ballistic Missile program, without indicating that this request was part of a $330 million sum that it had or was in the process of reprogramming out of that program. When Congress understood the full impact of the proposed reprogramming, it denied use of the Small Intercontinental Ballistic Missile program as a source of most of the requested reprogramming funds. Then it rescinded $266 million of the program's funds, eliminating it as a source of reprogramming.[12] In 1989 the Defense appropriations conference report included language requiring Congress to review decreases in spending resulting from reprogrammings, not just increases.

The ongoing battle between the Armed Services Committees and the Department of Defense continued when a new controversy broke out over a request to reprogram "M" account funds. "M" accounts are a merged pool of lapsed appropriations.

According to a Senate Armed Services Committee report in 1989, the committee was "disturbed to discover that the air force was planning to use the so-called 'M account' to fund approximately $944 million in major corrections to the B-1 bomber."[13] The committee reported that the air force was using the funds in a manner totally inconsistent with usage over the past fifteen years. The issue highlighted for committee members a broader problem of controlling lapsed appropriations.

The House Armed Services report on the authorizing legislation claimed there was even more money involved; the committee was faced with a $1.5 billion recovery plan for the B-1B's electronic countermeasure system. The committee recommended a measure to restrict the way the air force could fund the work.[14] The plan they set up limited the amounts and controlled the manner in which unobligated balances could be restored after they had been withdrawn from availability for obligation. Any amounts over $4 million had to be approved by the secretary of defense or his designee. If the amounts were greater than $25 million, the secretary of defense had to notify, thirty days in advance, both the Armed Services Committees and the Appropriation Committees and provide a description of the proposed action, the legal basis, and the policy implications.[15]

The story did not end there.[16] The conference report on 1990 appropriations for the Defense Department specified that use of the M funds for funding changes in the B-1B should be handled by the secretary as a normal reprogramming requiring advance notice. In January 1990, the secretary informed the Appropriations Committee of its intent to use the M funds but did not use normal reprogramming procedures, as he had been directed to do.

House Appropriations Subcommittee chair John Murtha was only partly mollified by the explanation that the money was coming from accounts approved for the same purposes as the money was now being spent for, and so did not require formal reprogramming, and that the department had not in fact committed the funds yet. Murtha began to pressure the department, saying that the committee had been working on reducing the constraints that appear in the Defense Department appropriation,[17] implying that this effort could be suspended if the Defense Department did not cooperate.[18] Even more bluntly, Murtha told the Defense Department representative, "I hope you will take my message back. We can go one step further to putting it into the law and then you will have no leeway."[19]

The authorizing committee (Armed Services) did indeed go one step further and changed the law.[20] These changes eliminated merged M accounts five years after the ending date of an appropriation account. If further obligations resulted from an expenditure more than five years earlier, they were to be paid from some other account set up for similar purposes.

The House Armed Services Committee explained its action in its report on the 1991 National Defense Authorization Act. It described the origin of M accounts in 1956 and the intent to provide a way of paying obligations for which no current unexpired appropriation exists. They argued that generally the M accounts had been well used, but that they had occasionally been abused by the Department of Defense. There was currently nearly $50 billion in the Defense Department M accounts, some of which was truly for paying bills incurred but not yet paid out, and some of which consisted of excess funds that were no longer needed. The M funds had not been audited in recent memory, and no one knew if all the claims on the fund were valid. The committee called for an audit that would determine the legitimate claims on the funds and would terminate the unobligated balance. They estimated that about $38 billion of old spending authority would be eliminated.

The authorizing legislation amended the statutes to eliminate all M funding and require extensive reporting of all obligated and unobligated balances, regardless of agency. Though the M funds were technically eliminated at that point, the Department of Defense seems to have used them one more time, but in this case not to reprogram funds but to cover up overspending that violated the antideficiency act. The episode illustrates the continuing battles between Congress and the Department of Defense over legitimate financial management issues and the need, from Congress's point of view, to reduce the discretion of the Department of Defense.

MINICASE: THE LAST USE OF THE M FUNDS?

Senator Charles Grassley of Iowa, a self-designated Defense Department watchdog, flagged an inspector general's report noting that the air force was asking for $649 million in supplemental appropriations to cover expenditures already made. Grassley threatened to cut out the $649 million from the supplemental appropriation bill; the threat got the attention of the Defense Department and the chair of the Senate Appropriations Subcommittee on Defense. The story came out in pieces. It seems that the air force had no way of reconciling bills coming in with orders it had made and often paid for bills it did not owe or overpaid, and sometimes overspent its budget for lack of basic accounting. More peculiarly, in 1993 the air force took money from the moribund M accounts that had theoretically been closed ten months before to make up for a $649 million gap. The negotiated solution between Senator Grassley, the gadfly, and Senator Inoue, who was defending the air force, was to ask the inspector general to examine the apparent inappropriate use of the M funds and the lack of adequate documentation on what the money was spent on.[21] Grassley wanted the specificity of illegal acts and culprits, not only to show the public that the problem was being taken care of, but to remind the Defense Department not to try this again and to keep working on getting an accounting system that worked.

The tension between the Defense Department and the congressional committees over reprogramming was not resolved with the dissolution of the M funds. Eventually the committees did resort to what Muskie had called handcuffing the agencies. Specific constraints were written into the appropriations forbidding the agency from reprogramming money for specific purposes. For example, the 1994 Defense Department appropriation suggests a prior conflict without satisfactory resolution. The 1994 appropriation states that during the current fiscal year and thereafter, there shall be no reprogramming or transfer or shift of money by other means between the CIA and the Defense Department for any intelligence or specific activity different from that previously justified to the Congress unless the director of the CIA or the secretary of defense has notified the House and Senate Appropriations Committees of their intent to do so and described the project. The legislation also included a series of rescissions, which would prevent the accumulation of funds that could be used for reprogramming. Moreover, the appropriation legislation specified where money could be transferred from and where it could go for particular purposes.

Reading the 1994 Department of Defense appropriation would initially make one sympathetic to the complaint of the Department of Defense that Congress is micromanaging the Defense Department, especially because so many of the prohibitions seem narrowly political—don't move the 116th Fighter Wing of the National Guard from Dobbins Air Reserve Base to Robins Air Force Base—but in the light of prior history of Congress trying to get compliance in gentler ways and persistent Defense Department defiance, the degree of detail and control seems more understandable, if not ideal. Moreover, some of the controls do seem to have clear policy implications, such as forbidding transfers between the CIA and the Department of Defense for unapproved projects.

Part of the congressional effort to respond to apparent abuses of accountability was to eliminate or reduce the discretionary funds that misbehaving agencies controlled. In addition to the M funds, Congress also went after carry-forward funds, intended to tide an agency over the beginning of the fiscal year in case appropriations did not come through on time. The effort to control this type of fund only occurred after an agency had flouted congressional controls. For example, the formerly secret National Reconnaissance Office, after defying congressional oversight, was discovered to have accumulated a carryover fund of $1.5 billion (on a budget of about $6 billion). Congress trimmed back the fund to one month of the agency's budget (about $500 million), forbidding the agency to allow the fund to grow any larger and inviting the inspector generals of the CIA and Defense to examine the agency's spending controls and recent financial history.[22]

Earmarking is another common congressional response to agencies that evade congressional priorities through extensive reprogrammings, and it is also a constraint that may be written into the law and last for many years. Congress may specify in legislation that so much money or such a percentage of the appropriation be spent on a particular program. The earmarking may be less formal if it appears in committee reports instead of laws. For example, the judiciary committees of both houses initially granted wide discretion over spending to the Department of Justice, but some committee members were concerned that some programs in the Justice Department were not being funded because the Justice Department's priorities were different from those of the committee. One program the committee supported that they felt was being obliterated was the program to catch and deport Nazi war criminals. The committee proceeded to earmark money for that specific purpose.

Another example of the broad grant of discretion followed by abuse and tightened congressional control occurred over the use of *impoundments*—the president's unilateral withholding of funds authorized by Congress for expenditures. Historically, Congress allowed the president to withhold some authorized spending for technical reasons. But under President Nixon, such withholding was used to increase the president's power over the budget and defy congressional intent.

> Executive officials seized on discretionary language in statutes to suspend or cancel programs. Through strained legal analyses, administrative officials contended that permissive language in authorization and appropriation bills allowed the president to terminate programs. Also the Nixon administration treated the president's budget as a ceiling on Congress. Any funds that Congress added to the president's budget could be set aside and left unobligated.[23]

The Nixon administration was also fairly free about reprogramming funds to get around congressional opposition to the administration's policy in Vietnam.

President Nixon's abuse of his discretion over budget implementation led to increased congressional control of budget execution, especially on the issue of whether the president could withhold spending that Congress had authorized. In 1974 Congress passed the Congressional Budget and Impoundment Control Act, part of the intent of which was to control presidential impoundments. The act divided withholding of funds into two categories, rescissions and deferrals. The law required Congress to approve presidentially proposed rescissions. For deferrals, if Congress took no specific action to deny, the deferral proposed by the president would take place. Either house could block a deferral. The law also set up the GAO as watchdog, to make sure that the administration was not withholding funds from agencies without reporting the withholding to Congress.

After 1974, rescissions were still often used for programmatic and policy purposes. "President Ford tried to cancel billions of dollars added by Congress for social programs; President Carter persuaded Congress to rescind funds it had appropriated for military weapons."[24] More than 90 percent of the rescissions during the Carter years were in defense.[25] And under President Reagan, the rescissions were again in social programs. These policy-related rescissions had to be approved by Congress before they could take effect.

President Reagan was still submitting policy deferrals in 1986 and 1987, but Congress was no longer able to overturn such deferrals with one-house vetoes because the Supreme Court, in *Immigration and Naturalization Service* v. *Chadha*, had ruled such one-house vetoes unconstitutional. Congress then took the offensive to prevent the president from submitting such policy deferrals at all, and was successful in getting the courts to rule such deferrals illegal. Thus by 1988, Congress had good control over policy-related rescissions and had virtually eliminated policy-related deferrals.

As the determination of Congress to control impoundments (now called rescissions and deferrals) shows, Congress can be brought to the boiling point when the executive branch simply cuts out any additions to the budget that Congress makes. Such action implies that Congress is just a rubber stamp and whatever the executive wants is what the budget should be. Treatment of pay raises further illustrates what Congress perceives as an abuse of discretion and its determination to respond by tightening controls.

Salary increases have for years been determined government wide, without giving agencies enough money to cover the mandated salary increases. The logic was to force agencies to take money that had been unspent in other accounts to contribute to the salary increase. The intent is to reduce the need for, and the size of, supplemental appropriations to cover mandated salary increases. The process sounds like a technical and routine matter, but it has a definite political implication. First, Congress often sets targets for how much of the salary increase the agencies should aim to absorb. This amount has been in the range of 30 percent. Agencies do not necessarily have that much unspent money in personnel lines. OMB has encouraged agencies to transfer surplus funds from other accounts to salary. This practice raises the questions as to what is surplus, and whether program funds are being used to absorb salary increases, and if so, which programs are being cut to fund the salary increases.

The agencies sometimes have to guess at how large or small a supplemental appropriation OMB will approve, and create the surplus to make up the balance. That may mean leaving positions purposely unfilled or even increasing the size of a reduction in force, or using a furlough (mandatory, unpaid leave of absence) to save money in the salary lines. In short, OMB can force an agency to cut its personnel budget to absorb some portion—not necessarily the congressional target—of the salary increase costs. The issue becomes less one of efficiency improvements and using unspent money and more one of forcing unpublicized cuts on an agency midyear, without explicit congressional approval.

In the late 1970s OMB used salary absorption to discriminate against congressional add-ons.[26] OMB placed an inordinate burden on those agencies with salary and expense lines increased by Congress above the level of the president's request. "Administration officials were using their powers of implementation to frustrate congressional priorities."[27]

Congress responded to this arrogation of power with the threat of increased legislative controls and in some cases with a requirement that the agency seek supplementals for salary increases rather than try to absorb the costs from existing lines. Senator Lawton Chiles warned in 1979 that "continuation of this practice might prompt Congress to write into the appropriation bill the instruction that absorption cuts be made on a pro rata basis."[28] That restraint would eliminate discretion to cut some programs and leave others alone to fund the salary increase. The Senate Committee on the Judiciary added a section to the annual authorization bill stipulating that the Department of Justice would not be required to absorb any salary increases.[29]

The State Level

The cycle of broad discretion, abuse, and tighter control also applies at the state level. Traditional line-item controls (restrictions on spending according to the object of the expenditures, such as personal service, travel, or contractual services) became less effective as the level of state expenditures grew from $27.6 billion in 1964 to over $100 billion in 1976. Not only is there a lot of money in each line, which creates a lot of discretion, but funds appropriated for a line item can be disbursed legally for a wide variety of purposes. "Moreover, expanded federal grants in aid—from $1.6 billion in 1948 to $16 billion in 1969 to over $40 billion in 1976—vitiate legislative oversight by creating opportunities for state administrators to initiate new programs or to transfer funds among activities during budget execution."[30]

The list of techniques widely used at the state level to change the budget during the year is suggestive of the possibility of abuse of discretion, at least as perceived by the state legislatures. Techniques included padded requests, artificial accounting balances, and improper interfund transfers. Transfer authority also allowed funds to be shifted between line items and appropriation accounts.

In a survey in 1976, 62 percent of 324 state agency directors in eight states responded that they transferred money between line items; 66 percent of the directors reported that they engaged in reprogramming within appropriation accounts. These reprogrammings were used to compensate for cuts in priority items, to engineer expansions in programs, and to initiate programs that lacked legislative support. The more different federal programs the agencies received funding from, the more likely the agencies were to report that they were reprogramming funds.[31]

State legislatures gradually reacted to what they perceived as an abuse of discretion. One report noted in 1975 that "legislatures are paying increased attention to expressing their intent more clearly as a means of exercising policy control." The report continued, ". . . executive agencies' fun and games with the enacted budget are the cause of much of this concern."[32]

By 1984 major changes had been made in legislative control over state budget execution.[33] In the 1960s legislatures began to assume the postauditing function that had been independent of the legislatures. By 1980, four out of five state legislatures selected a postauditor responsible to the legislature. The activities of these auditors expanded to include program and performance auditing. In addition, "Legislatures began to appropriate federal grant in aid monies in an effort to assure legislative rather than executive priorities in the spending of state funds, to guard against commitment of future state dollars for matching programs without legislative approval, to avoid pursuit of programs the legislature had disallowed through use of substitute money, and to guarantee effective delivery of services."[34] As of 1988, thirty-six state legislatures made specific appropriations of federal funds, and seventeen controlled appropriations of federally funded staffing levels. Another six states controlled the federally funded staffing in some cases.[35] By 1998 forty-three states appropriated federal funds for specific agencies, and twenty-six appropriated federal grants.[36]

The Local Level

At the local level, the discretion, abuse, control cycle is even clearer than at state and federal levels, although it is primarily state control over local governments, rather than the legislature controlling the executive. Local governments are creatures of the states, and when their finances get out of hand, the state governments step in to increase control levels. Two historical examples illustrate, in addition to the abuse and control cycle, managerial problems resulting from too-tight control and gradual relaxation of control under changing conditions.

MINICASE: MASSACHUSETTS OVERCONTROLS THE CITIES, 1875–1933

After the Civil War, local debt grew enormously in Massachusetts.[37] The growth was in response to rapid urbanization and the need for infrastructure, but it also reflected the desire to keep property taxes low. Some of the borrowing was for current expenses and for railroads. The growth in borrowing was accompanied by increased assessed valuations until the fiscal crisis of 1873, but during the following recession the burden of debt was keenly felt, and taxes had to go up to cover debt payments when people could least afford the increased taxes.

By 1875 the state had stepped in to curtail and regulate local debt, and in 1876 the state limited cities' investments in railroads. The debt limit was lowered in 1885, from 3 percent of assessed valuation to 2.5 percent and then 2 percent. Also, in 1885 municipal tax levies were curtailed in an effort to control municipal expenditures, which were increasing rapidly. Debt declined from 1875 to 1882, then climbed slowly until 1890. But from 1890 to 1905 net debt more than doubled, and the annual tax levy increased 80 percent. The increases continued after 1905.

Increase in population and changes in social and economic conditions created new administrative problems for local governments, and a rising standard of public consumption pressed on the tax and debt limits. Cities had begun to petition the legislature for exemptions almost immediately after the 1875 legislation. More than 1500 special exemption acts were passed between 1875 and 1911. These exemptions allowed about $73 million in debt outside the limits.

In addition, cities got around the limits on long-term indebtedness by borrowing more short term, in excess of anticipated revenues, and through demand notes. They refunded these notes without appeal to the legislature, rolling over short-term debt for ten, twenty, or even fifty years. Cities also borrowed for operating purposes for periods of less than ten years, another loophole in the law. Taxes that remained uncollected for long periods contributed to the buildup of debt.

Part of the cause of the buildup of debt was the limitation on property taxes. Because cities could not tax legitimately to cover their expenses, they resorted more frequently to borrowing. State mandates for spending also added pressure to local governments to bypass restrictions. The tax limit, like the debt limit, was loosened in application by legislative exemptions.

By 1913 the state had passed a new law attempting to fix some of the problems with the previous legislation. Tax limits were taken off all cities except Boston; debt limits were raised somewhat; and the state tried to improve record keeping and data presentation so that the legislature would have some independent basis on which to evaluate requests for borrowing outside the limits. Short-term debt was controlled.

Borrowing for current purposes was reduced by this legislation until the depression of the 1930s increased welfare expenditures and reduced revenues. From 1913 to 1920, debt increased only moderately, partly because of World War I and the suspension of improvement projects. From 1920 to 1926 aggregate debt grew by 41 percent, then the rate of growth tapered off until 1930. In the early depression years, debt grew rapidly. The state responded to the depression-caused financial problems of the cities by loosening debt limits and loaning cities money.

To summarize, the state stepped in when debt got out of hand and popular pressure against increased taxes provided a base of support for state intervention and control. For a time, the controls had their intended effect, but they also had unintended effects; the tax and borrowing limits increased short-term borrowing beyond expected revenues. When controls are too tight, there is enormous pressure to evade them, and some of the evasions cause additional abuses that invite a new round of controls. Over time, the circumstances that brought about the original control may disappear, and changing circumstances, such as the depression of the 1930s, may require a loosening of controls.

MINICASE: OHIO'S 1 PERCENT LAW

Ohio imposed tax limitations from 1859 to 1911, but they were not restrictive, and there was no machinery for enforcement.[38] But in 1910 and 1911 the Smith 1 percent law was enacted, and it was stringent and enforceable. The context of the increased control was the Progressive era expansion of expenditures and the growth in the functions of government, combined with a very poor system of assessment for real estate and personal property taxes. Assessment reform could not take place without some kind of guarantee that taxes would not increase as assessments went up to 100 percent. Also, a lowering of rates was thought to encourage the reporting of personal property. The 1 percent limit was the total for all local governments, including cities, school districts, counties, and townships.

Before long, most cities were taxing at or near their limits. When a state law reducing liquor revenues was factored in, many cities received less revenues in 1914 than they had in 1910. By the end of 1914, there had developed an epidemic of floating debt. Cities were reportedly not being profligate but were not receiving enough revenues to handle state-mandated expenditures, inflation, and the growing demands of increased population. The legislature exempted the principal levies of counties and townships from the Smith 1 percent law but kept the limits on cities.

As inflation continued to rise, floating debt increased to the point that in places it could no longer be carried. Bonds had to be authorized for their retirement. Efforts to educate the public to pass these bonds helped build pressure to revise the tax system. As inflation continued, cities had to raise salaries of employees, and the floating debt levels continued to rise.

By 1919 the legislature began to make serious adjustments. First, they authorized new and expanded nonproperty taxes that would help pay local bills. Then the legislature loosened the limits somewhat for school districts. Then all levies for existing indebtedness were excluded from the limit, if public support could be garnered. Since the cities had such a heavy debt load, this was a major relief. During the next session of the legislature, citizens were empowered to overrule the Smith law for up to three years by a 60 percent vote. The Smith law was repealed in 1923.

The 1 percent law was too strict. It did not allow for rapid population growth or make provision for very rapid inflation. The result was an accumulation of short-term debt to balance the budget, some of which was funded by deficiency bonds. The legislature made adjustments gradually, but not before considerable damage had been done.

The control cycle does not necessarily end with ever tighter effective controls. At the federal level, for example, the consolidation of appropriation accounts represented a lessening of legislative controls on expenditures. The result was increased agency discretion over reprogramming. The cycle of control began with a lessening of control from the previous cycle. At the state level, it was clear that line-item controls were weakened by both increases in total dollars and increased complexity resulting from federal grants. At the local level, overly harsh state controls have generally loosened over time.

When controls are tight, they make routine management problematic and adaptation difficult. Managers under these circumstances will often try to re-create flexibility within the existing constraints. For example, managers dealing with tight line-item controls have generated a system of invisible swaps between line items. Legislative controls on impoundment spawned ways of getting around the controls, such as executive reduction in staff. It can be difficult to devise a system of controls that will not be evaded and simultaneously will not be so rigid as to make good management impossible.

Sometimes legislatures may, in moments of pique, set up rigid oversight of implementation, and then gradually lose interest in maintaining the oversight. The initial issues that seemed such an affront to legislative power may have receded, or the amount of detailed work involved may not be paying much in the way of political dividends, and other issues press to the fore. Under these circumstances, the laws are likely to remain on the books, but the level of surveillance is likely to ease. An understanding may emerge that the agencies need no longer conform to the letter of the law.

Implementation and Control: The Politics of Finding Waste, Fraud, and Abuse

Efforts to control waste, fraud, and abuse illustrate a second strategy for maintaining budgetary accountability. Here it is not policy divergence from the budget that threatens accountability, but accounting systems that do not work, programs that are poorly designed, and excessive claims for funding. Intentional fraud and just plain waste both interfere with carrying out the intent of the budget. These campaigns may seem technical, managed by accountants who work out improved techniques for financial control, but as elsewhere in this book, what is technical may also be highly political. First, whoever is chosen to be the auditor must have enough independence to be credible, but enough cooperation to get reliable information and to carry out recommendations for improvements. Gaining that independence and negotiating for cooperation are themselves political efforts. Second, the effort to reduce waste, fraud, and abuse may become a highly visible political campaign, one with a large number of pitfalls.

The Inspector General system at the national level is a good example of efforts to control waste, fraud, and abuse, and to increase the overall accountability of the budget. Inspectors General are auditors who work with a team within specific departments or agencies. The first Inspector General was appointed in the Agriculture Department in 1961, but the idea gradually spread to other departments and agencies. The Inspector General Act (P.L. 95-452) was passed in 1978, establishing Inspectors General in twelve federal departments and agencies. The system has gradually expanded; in 1993 there were sixty Inspectors General with a staff of 15,000.[39]

Like other forms of financial control described in this chapter, the Inspector General system was created in response to perceived abuses. "It was a series of scandals and abuses within government as well as a renewed emphasis on prevention and detection that led to congressional realization of the need for an I.G. concept within the federal government and subsequent passage of the act."[40] Congressional intent was to create a powerful instrument to root out fraud, waste, and abuse in government by creating a semi-independent, centralized auditing and investigatory team for each major department. The intent of Congress was to create a dual structure of reporting, to see that the Inspectors General reported to Congress as well as to the executive branch.

Almost every increase in the coverage of the Inspector General system occurred as a response to a perceived abuse and widely publicized scandal. The first one, in the Department of Agriculture, was established as a response to the Billy Sol Estes scandal. "Estes had been revealed to have parlayed fraudulent warehouse receipts, mortgages, and financial statements into a fortune from the Department of Agriculture despite the fact that his activities were suspected by three different audit units within the Department."[41]

After 1969 Congress began to lose interest in the Inspectors General.[42] But in 1974 reports of widespread cheating in Medicare and student loans in the Department of Health, Education, and Welfare reinvigorated congressional interest. Reports of doctors overbilling and overtesting Medicaid patients further stimulated Congress; the HEW Inspector General Act was passed in 1976.[43] By the time the Inspector General model was extended to many other departments in 1978, Congress had come to accept that "government programs were rotten with massive fraud, waste, and abuse and that neither the political executives nor the career civil servants who managed the programs could be relied on to root it out."[44]

The Inspector General system was designed by Congress to increase and improve controls over implementation of the budget when signs of waste, fraud, or abuse were observed. But the ability of the system to work as planned was questionable because of its odd structure and its need for independence in order to function.

Legislators felt that other kinds of investigations lacked independence, and put into the 1978 law features they felt would enhance the independence of the Inspectors General.[45] To ensure independence, the Inspectors General would be appointed by the president and report both to the department head and to Congress. This dual reporting system is supposed to make them more independent, but it also inevitably makes them somewhat more political.

The independence of the Inspectors General is necessary to carry out an investigative role, but the independence is compromised by political appointment, and by responsibility to both Congress and the departmental secretaries. The early Inspectors General in the Department of Agriculture were especially politicized because the two top positions were presidential appointees subject to Senate confirmation; and in addition, two assistant Inspectors General were presidential appointees not subject to Senate confirmation, in an office that never exceeded forty-seven employees.[46] That is a very high proportion of political appointees in one office.

The Inspectors General can get caught between departments and Congress and can be rendered useless. The GAO evaluated the first Inspector General in the Department of Agriculture negatively. There was "limited use of the office as a management tool, partly because of concern over external disclosure of inspection findings through routine distribution of reports to congressional committees and others."[47] Reported one observer of the Inspector General system, "In my opinion, the IG's independence will not be any better defined than it has been and will always be a subject of dispute. IGs are 'straddling a barbed wire fence.' "[48]

Because the Inspectors General are located in departments and do not always have their own appropriation accounts, they come under departmental personnel ceilings. Thus if a secretary is threatened by the activities of an Inspector General, he or she may reduce the staffing levels of the Inspector General's office. Presumably, the knowledge that secretaries can do this curtails the Inspector General's independence.

The issue of independence of the Inspectors General became even more salient when President Reagan fired all sitting Inspectors General in 1981 and began to replace them with his own appointees.[49] Presumably the president wanted to make sure the Inspectors General were not going to embarrass the administration, but in doing so he harmed the appearance of neutrality necessary for any kind of waste/fraud investigator. Some congressmen were very upset by this action.

> The Reagan massacre established for all time in the minds of many on the hill . . . when a position is created as a presidential appointment, a president is going to appoint the kind of people he wants . . . Congress can add all the provisos it wants about being notified for reasons for removal—the fact remains that appointed incumbents serve at the president's pleasure. The unnecessary rubbing of people's faces in this fact was the costly aspect of the massacre.[50]

Once skepticism had been raised about the objectivity of the Inspectors General, future pronouncements by them were treated as campaign stances rather than statements of fact. The Inspectors General reported at the end of 1981 a savings of $2.1 billion, a figure that Congressman John Dingell and the GAO took apart as grossly exaggerated. In a subsequent report, the Inspectors General restated the $2.1 billion figure as $5.4 billion, by adding in savings from the Defense Contract Audit Agency—not a part of the Inspector General system. The DCAA's role is in preaward audits, preventing misclaims later. These were not dollars of money misspent and recovered, but the operation of routine controls. How much money one saves by preventing false claims through good contract management is no more than a wild guess.

The political will of department secretaries has clashed with the autonomy of the Inspectors General. Congress expanded the Inspector General system in 1988 to include several more cabinet departments, one of which was the Department of Justice. Like many other departments that had been subject to Inspector General programs, the Department of Justice firmly opposed having an Inspector General. The major reason given was that the attorney general (the political appointee of the president who heads the Department of Justice) would be unable to direct or stop investigations. That was indeed part of the intent of establishing the program—that Inspectors General could carry out investigations without departmental obstruction. Nevertheless, Congress, in recognition of the sensitive matters dealt with by the Department of Justice, gave the attorney general permission to halt some cases if he gave Congress warning that he was about to do so.

MINICASE: TENSION AT THE CIA

Congress created an Office of the Inspector General at the Central Intelligence Agency in 1989; the first Inspector General took office in 1990. As might be expected, the CIA did not want an Inspector General looking over its shoulder, and the agency's displeasure was frequently expressed in terms of criticism of Fred Hitz, the IG. As Senator Bob Kerrey put it, "The CIA has a proud but insular culture which tends to resist the scrutiny of an independent examiner."[51] But precisely because of the agency's secret missions, Congress felt the need for an independent Inspector General.

The IG was not only thrust between an agency that did not want it and Congress, which wanted good audit information in a secret environment; he also had to wrestle with the possible consequences of overcontrol. This possibility, that IGs would intimidate public officials into not taking risks, was mentioned for all agencies in the National Performance Review organized by Vice-President Gore in 1993 and 1994. Kerrey described the dilemma for the IG at the CIA:

> ... an independent IG must not contribute to a climate in which the CIA is afraid to take risks when vital U.S. interests are at stake. An independent IG must not create an internal empire of inspectors which has the same chilling effect on creative action in Government that excessive regulation has on business. Like the congressional oversight committees, a good IG must ensure that the Agency acts in accordance with U.S. law and U.S. values without inhibiting the Agency's ability to act boldly.[52]

Successfully negotiating this kind of environment with these kinds of constraints requires more than good accounting and auditing skills. The difficulty of getting information and the sensitivity of each possible report make political skills essential.

When the solicitor at the Department of Labor tried to stop an investigation by the Inspectors General at that department, the matter came to the Department of Justice for resolution. Did the Inspectors General have authority to make the kind of investigation they were making? The Department of Justice not only said no, they did not, but made a general statement applying to all Inspectors General, limiting the scope of their investigations.

The crux of the matter seemed to lie in the kind of investigation, which the Office of Legal Counsel of the Department of Justice called "regulatory." What they specifically opposed was when the Inspectors General, finding that a department had not deployed resources to investigate some regulatory compliance issue, took it upon themselves to do it. The Inspectors General claimed they had the authority to investigate fraud in federal programs; the Office of Legal Counsel said they had the authority to investigate only if the matter involved fraud or corruption of public officials and the expenditure of federal funds.[53]

The Legal Counsel opinion was based on a selective reading of the history of the Inspectors General law and ignored other specific delegation of authority in laws after 1978.[54] Still more disturbing, individual Inspectors General stated that the Department of Justice was threatening them and that it would not defend them in case of lawsuit if they pursued cases beyond Department of Justice's judgment of appropriate scope. Said Senator John Glenn, chairman of the Committee on Governmental Affairs: "As I understand it, your people have been told that if they don't get prior approval in particular areas, you were told by the head of the DOJ Office of Consumer Litigation that continued investigation of FDA cases by Inspector General employees would place your special agents in jeopardy of personal tort liability. In other words, if there is a suit filed against you, they would not defend you, as would be the normal case; is that correct?" Richard P. Kusserow, Inspector General, Department of Health and Human Services, answered: "That's correct, sir."[55] The implication was that the Inspectors General had better clear every dubious case with the Department of Justice. Such action would have given the Department of Justice enormous power to cut off any investigation of regulatory matters.

The intent of the Department of Justice in this matter became clear when the name and policy position of Elliott Levitas was taken as evidence of the intent of Congress in passing the Inspectors General legislation. Levitas in a brief congressional career made a name for himself as a defender of the regulated against the regulators.[56] He argued on the floor of Congress that the Inspectors General should be engaged in watching government officials, not in finding non-compliance and fraud in business people subject to government regulations.[57]

After the Department of Justice memo limiting the scope of their investigations, Inspectors General from different departments found that subjects of some of their investigations were claiming the inspectors had no authority in the matter. The inspectors were forced in a number of instances to drop investigations in progress. They reported difficulty in interpreting what they were obliged to do under the law and what they were forbidden from doing. Collectively, they tried to negotiate the matter with the Department of Justice but reported no progress. They then came to the Senate Governmental Affairs Committee to suggest that Congress strengthen and clarify the law to make their jurisdiction clearer. The committee called a hearing, with both sides present.

During the hearings, Chairman Glenn managed to get Department of Justice spokesmen to back down verbally from the threat to force inspectors to hire their own attorneys if sued on a case where the Department of Justice disapproved of the appropriateness of the investigation. The Department of Justice spokesmen took a somewhat conciliatory view. They would meet with the Inspectors General at any time; many of the investigations questioned by inspectors after the DOJ policy statement were judged to be legitimate. But the Department of Justice spokesmen did not budge on the issue of preventing Inspectors General from investigating regulatory matters that the agencies were supposed to investigate themselves, even when the agencies lacked the resources or skills or determination to do the investigations. The Governmental Affairs Committee recommended additional time to work out a negotiated settlement.

The problem of proper scope of Inspectors General investigations was ultimately determined in favor of the IGs and a broad scope of investigations. Symbolic of this resolution was the public call of President Clinton for a crackdown on Medicaid and Medicare fraud in May 1995. The major sources of fraud in these programs are unscrupulous doctors and nursing homes who prescribe unnecessary tests or overbill. The campaign was spearheaded by the Inspector General of Health and Human Services and clearly established the idea that Inspectors General could and should investigate fraud perpetrated on the government.

The tension between policy control over investigations by appointed officials and the independence of the Inspectors General is endemic to the structure of the Inspector General system and adds a political dimension to budget implementation. A second source of political infusion in a technical process occurs when the effort to reduce waste, fraud, and abuse becomes a political campaign. During his first term, President Reagan, like his immediate predecessors, launched a national campaign to reduce the amount of waste, fraud, and abuse in the federal government. Not only did his campaign make headlines, but examples of fraud and waste kept hitting the newspapers, making the issue particularly salient. Military purchases of $2,000 toilet seats, $600 hammers, and $7,600 coffeepots became public knowledge; military procurement became the subject of congressional hearings. During Reagan's second term, military procurement became a widely publicized scandal.

A public effort to reduce waste, fraud, and abuse seems like an ideal political campaign issue, because it fits the public conception of waste in government, promises to clean it up, and offers to reduce tax burdens by cutting fat and leaving services alone. If done properly, it also helps cover over currently occurring scandals or abuses. On closer examination, however, such a campaign is fraught with difficulties both political and technical.

Campaigns against waste, fraud, and abuse often make the naive assumptions that there is fat in the public budget and that the fat is easily recognizable and surgically removable. In fact, the amount of fat is not easily determined, and it is almost always attached to something of value. For example, trying to get able-bodied people off the handicapped rolls requires tightening eligibility requirements. Inevitably, some people who are both eligible and needy will also be taken off the rolls. Should their plight become public knowledge, the result is likely to be worse publicity than if some undeserving person got public aid. There is a very real tradeoff between denying some people aid who need it and preventing the undeserving from getting it.

Second, waste, fraud, and abuse keep recurring, no matter how much is reported eliminated, because a small number of mistakes is inevitable in any large and complex operation.[58] Thus a campaign to eliminate waste, fraud, and abuse can be embarrassing, because the more you "save" the more you demonstrate how much more waste, fraud, and abuse exist. "No matter which administration is blamed, constant harping on fraud and abuse goes beyond its necessity as a deterrent to the point of further weakening an already dangerously tottering image of the governmental process."[59]

Moreover, much of the source of waste is systemic, which means that really getting to the basis of the problem may mean major revelations of structural problems and major reorganizations. To eliminate wasteful purchasing in the military would require a drastic overhaul of the military. Such a change is a long-term proposition, not a short-term political campaign with highly publicized results and then silence.

Campaigns against waste, fraud, and abuse are useful political tools to bring down an opponent or discredit a predecessor, but they can boomerang and be used against one's own administration. Hence such campaigns are inherently political, regardless of their technical components.

To summarize, some waste, fraud, and abuse is inevitable in complex programs, so continual efforts to remove them only reinforce their existence in the public mind and can undermine governmental legitimacy. Second, political campaigns to reduce waste, fraud, and abuse can boomerang, making the current administration look riddled with scandal. That possibility creates the desire to control the auditors politically, and underscores the need for independence of the auditors. To be effective, Inspectors General have to work with department administrators, but still be independent; and to serve the purposes of control, they must also be responsible to Congress. The Inspectors General have to struggle continuously to maintain independence and effectiveness in this environment.

Summary and Conclusions

Periodically the flexibility in the budget is abused, and legislative will is thwarted. Legislators may become angry and increase controls over an agency or program. Such controls may accumulate over time and remain in place long after they are needed. A morass of controls invites efforts to evade them, and even the legislature may gradually lose interest in enforcing outdated overcontrols.

Legislative bodies tend to get excited when they think their will has been thwarted. They do not tend to get as excited about poor financial management, but the General Accounting Office and the Inspectors General at the national level and Inspectors General and auditors at the state level get upset about poor financial management, especially when it leads to major losses of money. Unlike the legislatures, auditors do not have line authority to make improvements. At the national level, the Inspectors General have to persuade the management of their agencies to make improvements. They have to develop a working relationship with the managers whom they are observing, while maintaining their independence and reporting to Congress.

Improving financial management is not a neutral and technical topic even when it is handled quietly, but when mismanagement involves millions or billions of dollars and makes government look bad, those who report it become unwelcome presences. Efforts to control the auditors or put a particular spin on their findings have sometimes marred the independence of the Inspectors General.

The National Performance Review put some of the blame on auditors for creating an atmosphere of fear and overcontrol, but generally all they do is call attention to violations of rules and in some cases suggest new ones. The source of overcontrol is occasional intentional abuses of discretion that generate increasing controls. Not enough attention is paid to moderating and eliminating the controls when they are no longer needed. This is not to argue that legislators are always on morally high ground in terms of what they want the agencies to do—they may insist that a contract go to a specific company, for example. Rather, the argument is that agencies should be extremely careful to avoid abusing grants of discretion, and legislatures should use the minimum amount of control necessary to regain compliance should they detect such abuse.

CHAPTER NINE

Budgetary Decision Making and Politics

BUDGETARY DECISION MAKING includes five distinct but linked clusters: revenues, process, expenditures, balance, and implementation. Describing each decision stream separately tends to emphasize their independence. This chapter is more about how they fit together into one decision-making process. Looking at the decision strands together also permits an examination of their common themes and differences.

Real-time Budgeting

I call the pattern of decision making that results from the integration of the five streams of decision making *real-time budgeting*. "Real time" refers to the continual adjustment of decisions in each stream to decisions and information coming from other streams and from the environment. Budgeting, like the complex computer programs aboard spaceships, continually readjusts, in real time, for changing information.

Budgeting is characterized by semi-independent, overlapping streams of decision making that depend on one another for key pieces of information. What makes this process complex and interesting is that the clusters are not timed sequentially to feed into one another. The clusters occur at different intervals and last for different lengths of time. In order to make the key decisions in any one stream, actors may have to look backward, to the last time the decision was made in another stream, or forward, to anticipated decisions, or even sideways, to decisions being made at the same time. Much of this information is tentative; it can and does change as the budget moves toward implementation.

Budgetary decision making takes the shape it does because of the characteristics of public budgeting described in chapter 1. First and foremost, budgets are open to the environment—to the economy, to the weather, to a variety of emergencies, and to changes in public preferences and political leadership. Openness to the economy means that estimates of revenues, and to some extent estimates of expenditures, may have to be revised several times during the budget process as better information becomes known. Budgeters cannot make one estimate at the beginning of the budget process and stick to it. Openness to change in political leadership and public opinion means that budgets that were generally agreed to may need to be redone.

A second characteristic of public budgets is that a variety of actors with different goals compete for limited resources. Policy decisions that feed into the budget may cause controversy and delay. Budgets have to be able to deal with policy conflict among these actors and with competition between them. Some budget actors may want to limit revenues, which has implications for the expenditure stream; some actors may want to increase particular expenditures, which has implications for the revenue stream; the goals of these actors may clash. The result may be long-delayed decisions. Budgetary decision making has to accommodate this kind of conflict and this kind of delay. Budgets have deadlines. The later they are, the less use they are, so the problem of late decisions has to be handled in some way.

The solution to the problems of changing information and late decisions is a budget process that features fragmentation, with semi-independent decision streams, and interruptibility. Parts of the decision making may proceed without the rest in order to complete the budget in a timely manner. The different strands of decision making proceed as if they were independent, referring to one another, bargaining when necessary to reach accommodation. If one decision-making strand gets stuck, such as when a tax increase is being considered but no decision is yet made, other decision streams can proceed with their work, by making assumptions about what will occur in the revenue stream and adjusting their own work when the final outcome is known in the revenue stream.

The decision clusters are mostly independent, but they need information from one another to complete their work. The revenue cluster cannot proceed without some knowledge of spending requirements and balance constraints. Decisions about how to reduce a deficit are dependent on revenue estimates and spending estimates. Spending estimates depend on revenue, balance, and implementation streams. Implementation depends on decisions throughout the process to that point, especially on the degree of underestimates of revenues or overestimates of expenditures, and the constraints of balance and handling of deficits. Revenues, expenditures, balance, and implementation all depend on the process stream to organize them and allocate power to them.

Information coming from other decision streams may appear as a constraint, but one that is flexible rather than rigid. Thus a figure for estimated revenues already fed into the expenditure stream may change if the prediction of the economy changes. Or it may change if a decision is made in the expenditure stream that requires more revenue.

Constraints from other decision streams are flexible not only because the environment changes but also because actors in one stream can sometimes force a change in another stream. Actors who want to spend more money may be able to force a change in the tax structure or even in revenue estimates; they may also be able to force a change in the definition of balance. Actors who want to reduce revenues may act to cut expenditures and define balance to suit their purposes.

Budgetary decision making is not linear and sequential, in the sense that some decisions are made first and form the frame for the other decisions. A simple model of decision making would argue that the definition of balance, the budget process, and the revenue estimates should be in place before the beginning of the decision making and that the decision making should begin with targets for spending that keep within revenue estimates. Then spending decisions should be made. Real budgeting does not look like this model for three by now familiar reasons. First, the budget is open to the environment, so new information becomes available at intervals. Second, decisions in the budget take different amounts of time to make and are remade at intervals that may be impossible to predict or schedule. Third, actors in one decision stream can jump over into other decision streams and force a change there in the middle of the decision making.

Consider, for example, recent revenue decisions at the local level. In Illinois, two recent changes in state laws have affected local revenues. In one case, the legislature passed a change in the law for tax increment districts, which is a form of project funding that uses the increased tax yield from property as a result of public development efforts to pay off the initial project costs. The state had agreed to help share the costs of redevelopment by offering increments from the state sales tax to the cities that had sales tax increment districts, but then found that some cities drew up their districts not to maximize development but to maximize the state funding offer. The size of the local demand on state funds was larger than anticipated. The state balked; it was no longer clear what proportion of the promised funds the state would provide. In the middle of a budget year, the state announced its revised guidelines and reduced funding levels. Spending decisions that had already been made had to be remade, and projects had to be reprioritized in the light of the changed law.

A second example occurred when the state changed the sales tax law to merge locally raised sales tax with the state-collected sales tax, requiring a uniform set of exemptions, but giving cities a little over two years to prepare for the change. The result for some cities would be a loss of revenues, because they would have to conform to the state exemptions. They would have two years to decide what to do and how to adapt and design alternatives and implement them. They might or might not get the decision making in the revenue stream accomplished in time. In any case, the decision began two years ahead of the event, and was thrust on the cities by the state at an unpredictable moment.

An example of a decision that may be remade in the middle of budgeting occurs when actors try to define or redefine balance during the budget process. If it appears that there is a conflict between the amount of revenues available and the amount of spending desired, and the conflict cannot be easily reconciled, one option is to attack the definition of balance and loosen it. For example, a requirement that budgets balance each year may be stretched out to balance over the life of the program. In the Highway Trust Fund, proponents of additional spending argued that if they spent more money now than was in the trust fund, they would just continue to collect user fees after the end of the building program and pay off the debt later. The intent was to redefine balance from an annual reckoning to a period of fifteen or twenty years.

Efforts to redefine balance were continuous at the national level for most of the 1980s. Gramm-Rudman-Hollings made this effort explicit by defining balance as a moving target of deficits of smaller and smaller sizes. Each year, then, the target for balance was to change. Unfortunately for the linear model of decision making, it was not clear that Gramm-Rudman-Hollings was constitutional, which made its targets somewhat dubious; and the response to its limits was to make the deficits look of appropriate size rather than be of appropriate size. The result was a shifting goal of balance that got defined each year as part of the budget process.

Budgetary decision making is not and cannot be made sequential. The solution is to make the key decisions in five parallel sequences and link them to one another for necessary information. The system of decision making by linking clusters in real time is wonderfully adaptive. Real-time decision making allows the streams to be disrupted, or interrupted, and repeated. Decisions can be adjusted or remade.

Budgeters have to have many contingency plans to deal with missing information or late decisions. To respond to missing information, they may rely instead on the last, most recent decision. If individual policy decisions are too slow, they may simplify and speed up the decision making by grouping many decisions together. They may push up the urgency of decisions that are causing roadblocks by linking them to other urgent matters. The overlapping nature of decision clusters allows solutions in one stream to resolve roadblocks in another stream. A solution in the revenue stream may unlock a problem in the expenditure stream; a change in process may solve problems of linkage between the streams.

A Comparison of the Decision-making Streams

The focus of this book is to make clearer the nature of politics in public budgeting. After examining each of the five decision streams, one would have to say that what politics looks like depends on where you look. In some areas of budgetary decision making, narrowly conceived interest groups compete with one another for tax breaks or spending increases; in others, coalitions of interest groups that approach class interests compete for control of the scope of government services; in still others, interest groups play little if any role. Some areas of the budget are policy laden, while others appear policy neutral and technical. From one perspective, changes in the budget process itself define the political maneuvering and coalition formation; from other vantage points, the politics of process seems to have little to do with the outcomes. To get anything like a realistic view of politics in the budget requires a look at each strand of budgetary decision making.

Revenue politics is characterized by both a policy orientation and active interest-group participation. The policy issues include who will be taxed and what the level of taxation will be. Narrowly defined interest groups get involved in trying to deflect taxes from their constituents; broader coalitions of interest groups get involved in efforts to determine the distribution of taxation between income groups and the overall level of taxation.

The politics of process revolves around two policy issues and bargaining among the actors. The first cluster of policy issues includes, ironically, how much of a policy focus the budget should have, how clearly policy issues should be articulated and, concomitantly, how much conflict should be expressed and resolved during budget decision making. The second and related policy issue is how much articulation of citizen and interest-group preferences the budget process should engage in. How much access should individuals, interest groups, agency heads, and the press have to budgetary decision making, and how much secrecy should there be? The result of these policy choices influences not only the level of accountability in the budget process but also, presumably, the level and nature of public expenditures and the amount of discipline in the budget process. The politics of process also revolves around the bargaining between budget actors for more power over budgetary choices. The bargaining over the distribution of power and the choices on key policy issues are often intertwined.

The politics of expenditures reflects several different aspects of politics. There is active interest-group involvement, as well as extensive bargaining and competition. The competition between interest groups generally prevents interest-group determinism. When budget actors manage to insulate their programs from competition, however, the result looks more interest-group dominated. At times, there is a compensating emphasis on policy, in the considered choice between programs and emphasis on formulating and achieving public goals. Legislators can resist even powerful interest groups when they choose; they use the budget process to insulate themselves.

The politics of budget balance is primarily a politics of policy. Three key issues are the role of the budget in managing the economy, the scope of government programs, and which level of government will balance its budget at the expense of which other level of government. These issues are often defined in terms of the target level of unemployment, the level of social services provided by the public sector and the number of programs or services provided by the public sector that could be provided by the private sector, and the degree of progressivity of the taxes that pay for governmental services. The outcome of each of these policy decisions is far reaching. As a result, coalitions of interest groups representing wide segments of society take different stands on the politics of balance; liberals and conservatives, Democrats and Republicans, take opposing stances. The politics of balance is often a partisan issue.

The politics of implementation is a contest between the technical goals of maintaining accountability and implementing the budget almost exactly as passed and the insertion of policy changes in the budget during the budget year. Generally, the technical model is triumphant, but at the cost of considerable effort in monitoring potentially policy-laden budget adaptations.

In short, no one view of politics in the budget stands alone. There is bargaining among actors in budget decision making, but it is framed by policy concerns expressed through the budget process; there are interest groups active in budgetary decision making, but they are controlled, or can be controlled, both by competition among themselves and by the budget process that gives or denies them access to decision making. There is a contest between more technical and more policy-oriented approaches to budgeting, but in most areas of budgeting there is a balance between them. There are policy issues in the budget, but they may be played up or toned down by the budget process and format.

The description to this point has been of a lively decision process that may occur over a period of years, but it says nothing of the patterns of change over time. Some of these patterns are cyclical, while others alternate, like a pendulum, between extremes.

Dynamics of Budgeting over Time

A number of long-term patterns have been identified in this book. In the revenue stream, tax breaks gradually eroded the tax base of broad taxes such as income and sales taxes, and encouraged honest taxpayers to cheat on their taxes because the system seemed so inequitable. When the savings from eliminating tax breaks was sufficient to distribute in the form of tax reductions to a broad base of citizens and interest groups, tax reform passed, cleaning the slate, and readying it for new demands for tax breaks.

Another pattern in the revenue stream was the attempt to put beyond consideration taxes that would hurt some particular class of people. While some interest group or class was in power, it would try to find the longest-term protection for itself, often a constitutional prohibition of some tax that threatened its membership. Such restrictions have kept some forms of taxation off the agenda for many years, but many such restrictions have gradually been eroded or eliminated.

In the expenditure cluster, there was a long-term tendency toward trust funds, locking in revenue sources for particular expenditures to reduce competition with the rest of the budget. Other devices for reducing competition were also noted, including the establishment of public enterprises and the design and implementation of entitlement programs. Even right-based entitlements can be reduced over time if their legitimacy is eroded. Competition does not cease once programs or expenditures have achieved some privileged status; others find a way to latch on to the successful program's success. Thus mass transit managed to horn in on the Highway Trust Fund for a number of years.

The politics of process was also marked by long-term patterns. When debts or expenditures got out of hand, there was a tendency to blame the legislatures for lack of discipline and give increased budget power to the chief executives. If and when that power was used to thwart the policy intentions of legislators, the legislators often took back some of that delegated budget authority. Although the shifts have sometimes been extreme, the overall tendency in recent years has been toward balance, with the executive and the legislature each having staff capacity and overlapping budgetary powers.

When Congress is trying to reassert its budgetary power, it has to create both a policy capacity and a mechanism to coordinate revenues and expenditures; it has to exert some central discipline over legislators. When the president is trying to assert budgetary power, he is likely to exert more central power over the executive branch agencies. There is alternation between more top-down and more bottom-up approaches to budgeting in both branches, with a moving balance between individual or agency interest and a number of broader policy concerns.

The politics of balance has been marked by reaction after the fact to growing deficits. There has been a tendency to react through apparently rigid budgetary requirements, often written into constitutions or statutes. Such restrictions may ban or severely limit borrowing, or require budgets to be balanced when submitted. Over time, these restrictions are often bypassed.

The patterns in budget implementation have been clearly marked, beginning with a broad grant of spending discretion to the executive, followed by some scandal or attempt to bypass the policies established by the legislature. The conflict results in increasingly detailed legislative controls over spending. The agencies may gradually try to evade the controls, or the legislature may gradually relent in the enforcement of the detailed controls.

Common Themes: The Roles of Competition and Secrecy

Much of what goes on over time in budgetary decision making has to do with the channeling, control, and even elimination of competition. Competition in budgeting is strong and always present, but handled in different ways. The allocation of proportional shares of new money to existing departments or programs is one way to limit competition, but it is not the only way. Competition is limited also by the tendency to compare seriously only items in the same part of the budget. Paper supplies typically are not compared with garbage trucks; soldiers are not traded off for buildings and grounds maintenance staff. Within each capital budget, or within each department, even dissimilar items may be compared. Thus the capital budget is intensely competitive, and competition within departments is keen, with some program requests cut back and others expanded. Competition sometimes occurs between portions of the budget, but this kind of competition occurs only occasionally.

The level of competition is so high within portions of the budget that those seeking to protect programs try to reduce the level of competition by getting out of those areas of the budget. Thus program supporters try to set up trust funds, entitlement programs, or public enterprises, which buffer a program or project from competition.

The level and kind of competition vary correspondingly with the kind of interest-group involvement. The budget implementation period is not generally seen as highly competitive; the spending stream of decisions is seen as highly competitive. There is a difference in kind between many small interest groups each pleading for some benefit and groups that represent broad political and social cleavages competing for control over policy. Thus competition between classes and regions of the country over the form of taxation is of a more enduring and important sort than competition between clusters of small interest groups. Competition between business and labor over the definition of balance and the scope and role of government services is also deep and enduring.

Controlling the demands of multiple small interest groups can be achieved either through directing their competition against one another or structuring the budget process to buffer their direct demands. This restructuring has often involved some level of secrecy. The competition between social classes over the form and level of taxation and the competition between business and labor over the scope of government and the definition of balance are not curtailable in the same sense; they are part of the broader political process. Over time, the domination of one set of interests or the other brings one solution or another to the fore, creating some of the typical patterns of change over time.

Competition is one general theme of this book that cuts across several streams of decision making. A second general theme is the level of secrecy in the budget and the role of the budget as a tool of public accountability. There is inevitably some selectivity in all public budgets; it simply is not possible to tell all in a public budget. In addition to this minimum level of selectivity, however, there are three other sources of secrecy. The first is the effort to buffer the budget process from interest-group pressure; the second is the effort to spend taxpayers' money differently from the way taxpayers would choose to spend it; the third is the effort to cover up attempts to avoid hard choices between cutting spending and increasing taxes by running deficits.

The budget process can be insulated from interest-group pressure by closing the proceedings, or by concentrating decision-making power in a small group of powerful decision makers who may choose to exclude interest groups. Meetings can be held at inconvenient times and places. The budget document can describe expenditures in such a way that it is difficult for interest groups to see if they have won or lost; agencies can be organized in such a way that interest groups have to lobby for their programs in half a dozen or more places. It can be made difficult for them to know who has decision-making power, or who exercises discretion.

Budget decisions may be insulated from the public at large and its preferences by too high a level of secrecy. Expenditures that take from all taxpayers and benefit a narrow group of citizens or companies or a specific geographical area are likely to be controversial unless positive spillovers to others can be demonstrated. Under these circumstances, potential competitors for funds may be bought off or included, or the source and amount of funding may be obscured.

Most governments, most of the time, balance their budgets; when they do not achieve balance, it may be for both good and temporary reasons. Nevertheless, when governments run deficits because they lack internal discipline, or ignore or redefine the constraints of balance, they may be embarrassed by the consequences, and in the face of what would be widespread public disapproval, and in view of the politically unpleasant tasks of cutting expenditures and raising revenues, they sometimes choose to hide the deficits.

Although there are continuing sources of secrecy in budgeting, there are also continuing pressures for maintaining openness and accountability. Expenditures that seem to benefit broad groups of people and programs that citizens can easily imagine themselves using or needing tend to generate little controversy and can use resources that are highly visible. And budget implementation is generally very close to the budget that passes in full public view; there is very little behind-the-scenes redoing of the policy choices in the budget. Actors who need to come to agreement on the next budget do not wish to see the last set of agreements come undone or be remade by someone else during the budget year. To keep the whole decision-making process going, the budget actors need to believe that their previous agreements will be implemented without change. The end of the Cold War has helped to reduce the level of secrecy in the Defense Department; pressure from the deficit to find and reduce waste and shrink the scope of programs has also contributed to congressional pressure to take programs out of the black budget.

Reconceptualizing Reform

This description of real-time budgeting and the patterns of change over time is intended to contribute to a descriptive theory of public budgeting. The theory is suggestive of how the politics of budgeting works and what kinds of reforms are likely to be desirable or effective.

The description of budgeting offered here suggests that there are multiple actors, with differential power over time, and that the actors' motivations are multiple and variable. Legislators are interested not only in constituency benefits but also in maintaining their own power and the power of the legislature. Equally important, at times they are interested in providing for the public good. When their individual interests clearly clash with the public good, they are often able to opt for the public good. Sometimes they do not see a problem coming or they underestimate the severity of the public consequences of their individual actions, but they learn from disasters and are often able to restructure their processes to increase discipline or delegate decision making to a location that is more buffered from interest groups. This pattern suggests that more of reformers' attention might be profitably directed to making clear the consequences of similar actions taken in the past or documenting the likely outcomes for the future. Restructuring can be successful when there is a consensus that it is necessary to avoid a disaster.

The swings in budgetary decision making suggest there are some internal mechanisms for balance, but they are not well regulated. They depend on knowledge of outcomes that is often not there. When constraints are devised, they usually address the last huge swing, not the next potential one. For example, when cities and states ran extraordinary amounts of debt, the response was to limit the amount of borrowing and to make state and local governments incapable of an activist role. States live with outmoded restrictions in their constitutions for decades or even centuries. The initial problem is extreme, the response in turn is extreme, and the quality of government is reduced. In recent years, at the national level, huge deficits have prompted calls for a constitutional amendment; again, a problem was allowed to get out of control, and the proposed solution is extreme in its constraints and duration.

The historical pattern suggests that research and reform should concentrate on identifying the places and times, the mechanisms, that allow balances to swing wildly or too widely, and the turning points or mechanisms that have historically brought the extremes back from danger or uncontrolled spiraling outcomes. It may be that the size of the swings can be narrowed.

For example, a more careful monitoring of deficits and intense publicity about early warning signs may be helpful in averting the huge accumulation of deficits that sometimes occur when small deficits are hidden or overlooked. A belief that all budgets should balance and that most do balance has left the public sector without a series of fallback positions and triggers for corrections. Building a consensus about what kinds of deficits will be acceptable and for how long may be helpful; devising a series of measures of deficits and counting how many of them are in the "red zone" may also be helpful. This may help avert the argument that deficits are not harmful, so we can allow them or ignore them. It may be that we are willing to accept deficits from some sources but not others, for some periods of time but not longer than a certain number of years. If the conceptual murk can be cleared by a series of definitions, each acceptable to some major groups, then the level and degree of deficits may be plainer, and the efforts to eliminate them more effective.

A second theme for reform that emerges from this book has to do with the interchangeability of budget roles. Reforms that simply gave the executive more power were not long-term solutions to budget discipline or balance. Governors sometimes played restrictive roles and sometimes expansionary ones; similarly, legislatures were sometimes restrictive and sometimes expansionary. History does not support the position that increased power to the executive will solve deficits or other budgetary problems.

Reform, in the sense of changing budget processes that shift the location of budget power, changes the outcomes in the short run by shifting power to actors who have a particular point of view. If there is a reform governor and an unreformed legislature riddled with corruption and eager for pork, then shifting power to the governor may bring about short-term improvement. But endless reinforcement of the governor's powers does not bring evermore budget improvement. Illinois may have the strongest governorship in terms of budget powers, but Governor Thompson shifted from more to less fiscally conservative accounting, he routinely hid deficits, and he was oriented to patronage spending for capital projects. Under his leadership the state ran deficits despite the strong executive budget.

A balance of power between the executive and the legislature, so one actor can catch the other at bad practice, is probably more sound over the long run than the weakening of one and the continual strengthening of the other. The arrangements of the mid-1800s, when distrust of government drastically curtailed the powers of both the governor and the legislature, were not particularly successful; it is not weak government that is required, but fairly balanced powers. This conclusion has echoes of the debate over the founding of the nation. Over the past decade, supporters of increased presidential power have argued that the president needs more budgetary power to control the deficits. The argument is that Congress is profligate, and only the president can exercise discipline. The experience of the states suggests that shifting more power to the president is no long-term improvement.

Overall, this book suggests that there is a relationship between budget process and outcomes, but that there is no one ideal process that will guarantee balance and limit taxation over time. The budget process allocates power to different budget actors, each of whom has ideologies, values, and goals. When the budget process shifts power more to one actor than to another, it influences the likely outcomes. The process also tends to reinforce or weaken top-down control. That control may be narrowly political, in the sense of maintaining the power of a small elite of legislative and executive branch officials, or it may be broadly policy oriented, in the sense of trying to control spending or shift spending priorities. It may be intended to buffer budget actors from certain kinds of demands, or it may emphasize budget balance over the achievement of constituency services or the delivery of capital projects. But budgetary reform that emphasizes discipline has to have the serious support of key actors in order to work; if the recognition of the need for discipline erodes, or if the case is never well made, the process will not create the desired outcome. Process does not sit out there by itself exerting discipline on unruly and unwilling actors. The actors create the process and try to abide by it once it exists, but if it is not working, they change the process, formally or informally.

This book offers no clear guidance on reforms that would alter the degree of secrecy in the budget. Secrecy performs several functions, some of which are more legitimate than others. Secrecy may simultaneously reduce the role of interest groups and help maintain the integrity of budget processes, while it blocks out the role of the public and minimizes accountability. What is done behind the cover of secrecy is, of course, not always known. Openness in budget processes may reduce the level of hidden subsidies or politically unacceptable subsidies, or it may force more reliance on user fees to break the linkage between public disapproval and spending for narrow interests.

A third suggestion about reform concerns budget formats and the amount of information for decision making. Traditional efforts to reform budgeting by including broader consideration of the options and making sure that there is enough time and enough easily accessible information to make intelligent decisions are still reasonable in the framework of this book, but perhaps less urgent, since the book does not portray much or all of budgetary decision making as routine, mindless, and opaque. If there is a demonstrated need for clearer formats or consideration of additional options, then those formats and options should be advocated. There is nothing impossible or necessarily undesirable about this kind of reform. It may increase the burden of work, however, and hence should address only clear needs and not be done excessively. It may increase the level of competition, but competition can be handled in many ways. It may be better public policy to allow a controversy to be stated than to use the power of budgeting to prevent an issue from reaching the public, where it can be dealt with and resolved. Budgeting handles controversy all the time; it is designed to cope with the interruptions resulting from unresolved and controversial policy matters.

Avenues for Research

This book suggests many avenues for productive research, for students as well as scholars. It also suggests some lines of inquiry that probably will not be productive. Studies that compare last year's total appropriations to this year's total appropriations are unlikely to contribute much understanding of budget processes; they examine too small a portion of the budget, and over too short a period of time. Studies of budgetary tradeoffs may well produce major insights, if they adopt a realistic view of the way budgeting works. That is, they must assume that revenue constraints are variable, not fixed; that most routine tradeoffs occur within departments and within the capital budget, rather than across sections of the budget; that major changes in spending priorities occur only over fairly long periods of time; and that budgets are structured so that some expenditures are much more flexible than others. The kind of expenditure makes a difference, since much of the politics of budgeting revolves specifically around the degree of flexibility and the attempt to lock in some expenditures.

The descriptive outline of budgeting presented here needs to be documented, elaborated on, and filled in. Much more research is needed on state and local budgeting, and on the linkage between the decision clusters. One issue glossed over in this book for lack of information is the relationship between microbudgeting and macrobudgeting. Given a particular set of budget processes, what strategies do budget actors use, under what circumstances? How effective are these strategies? Once it becomes clear that strategies are highly variable, not fixed, the way is opened for exploring those variations and the success of those strategies. How do budget actors anticipate or measure the environment, and how do those estimates affect their strategies? To what extent does the allocation of power implicit in the budget process determine the outcomes independent of strategies?

Another issue barely touched on is the tension between discretion and control. This book describes a discretion-and-control cycle for budget implementation, but does not deal in any detail with the ways in which administrators re-create discretion within a control budget. More needs to be described about these internal dynamics and the different political value of different resources depending on the degree of discretion they entail. New money, unencumbered money, money without strings, has a special value in a tightly controlled budget, so that there may in fact be two budgets, one with less and one with more discretion. Administrators may strive to get more money into the budget with greater discretion. When circumstances reduce the discretionary money, the impact on the politics of budgeting may be very different from a reduction in the more tightly controlled portion of the budget. The elimination of revenue sharing (unencumbered money with virtually no strings) from state and local governments' budgets thus provides a test case for observing how officials adapt to sharp reductions in the more discretionary portion of the budget.

A third theme that warrants future investigation is the process of locking and unlocking decisions. Budgeting involves a number of decisions that budget actors at the peak of their power try to make permanent. There are often attempts to unlock decisions, to reverse them, once they are made. Under what circumstances do locking or unlocking strategies work? More study needs to be made of these processes, such as the efforts to put bans in state and national constitutions on certain forms of taxation, or the establishment of trust funds or public enterprises. Efforts to create right-based entitlements need more explicit study. In each of these cases, more attention should be focused on the processes and circumstances for undoing them or reversing them.

A fourth theme of the book that needs further exploration is the relationship between the technical and political aspects of budgeting. The technical concerns of the budget include accurate estimates of expenditures and revenues, realistic evaluations of the economy, compliance with balance requirements (no matter how formulated), timely completion of decisions, prevention of overspending by agencies, and the creation of a plan that puts enough resources in the right places to get mandated work accomplished. The political concerns of budgeters include establishing and enforcing priorities, getting sufficient support for taxation to allow expenditures to occur and balance to be achieved without being thrown out of office, the creation of a workable budget process, the design and implementation of rules of balance, and the satisfaction of perceived needs for constituency benefits. These functions are not neatly divided into those performed by elected officials and those performed by career bureaucrats. Who performs which functions? How do they balance? When does political distortion of projections of the economy become so severe as to force the creation of an alternative, more neutral projection system; when do technical efforts to achieve balance cause major policy changes? Whose responsibility is it to maintain the informational integrity of the budget and its usefulness as a tool of accountability to the public? How far can that integrity be eroded before counterpressures are exerted?

More broadly, this book has characterized budgeting changes over time as the pendulum swings. Changes in one direction begin to garner support for the opposite, or flaws in the current system make it obvious that a new system is needed. But more research is needed on turning points, on the dynamics and timing of shifting from one policy extreme back toward the center or toward the other extreme.

These suggested topics are only a preliminary list; there are many more possibilities. Such research could meaningfully be quantitative or qualitative, as long as it had a sufficiently long time span, viewed budget constraints as flexible, and was sensitive to the different kinds of resources in a budget and the different streams of budget decision making.

Summary and Conclusions

Public budgeting is highly political, but it is not the same thing as politics in general. It represents a special corner of politics, with many of its own characteristics. The peculiar politics of extraction called taxation may illustrate broader political desires to avoid unpopular decisions, but the process of turning taxation into distributive politics through the award of tax breaks and the eventual need for reform, the tension between spending and taxing, and the occasional passage of new or increased taxes are unique to the politics of budgeting. Real-time decision making is peculiar to budget decision making with its intense sensitivity to the environment, its interruptibility, its nested options, and its time constraints. Budgeting has a bottom line and a due date, which distinguish it from many other political decisions. Budgeting carries in itself a way of measuring failure that creates pressures for action and reaction over time.

Budgeting is a particularly important arena of politics because many policy decisions are meaningless unless they can be implemented through the budget process. When political actors want to enhance their power, they often focus on power over budgeting as a way to do it. Consequently, battles over budgeting processes, which might otherwise seem dry, technical, internal matters, turn out to be lively contests. Individuals try to get into positions of budgetary power and then try to enhance the power of the positions they hold. Budgeting is the setting for major contests over the separation of powers and the balance between the legislature and the executive. Legislative committees battle with one another for jurisdiction, budget power gets highly fragmented, and coordination becomes a major issue.

The budget document itself plays a unique role in the political system. It is a management document designed to help plan expenditures and maintain financial control; it may reflect major policy decisions made during the budget process and thus represent a summary of major government actions; and it presents to taxpayers an explanation of how their money is being spent. The role of the budget in providing public accountability is a crucial one in a democracy. Yet budgets do not always play this role well. Budgets sometimes change during implementation; the figures in the budget are not always accurate; and the information may be displayed in such a way as to obscure rather than elucidate key decisions. Budgets have to remain somewhat flexible, which may reduce their usefulness as tools of public accountability; secrecy in making decisions may be necessary in order to buffer decision makers from the pleadings of special interests; and secrecy may be used to do something desired but formally prohibited.

The level of secrecy in budgeting needs to be carefully monitored, but at present, it remains relatively low. Most public budgets are fairly accurate representations of the activities and spending decisions of their governments. They thus provide an excellent vantage point from which to observe government and a way of holding government accountable. Citizens may be forced by the coercive power of government to pay taxes for programs they do not want, but this is a democracy, and citizens may and do rebel. Citizens are important budget actors.

Notes

CHAPTER 1

1. Faculty Senate minutes, Northern Illinois University, 4 November 1998, 6.
2. Patricia Ingraham and Charles Barrilleaux, "Motivating Government Managers for Retrenchment: Some Possible Lessons from the Senior Executive Service," *Public Administration Review* 43, no. 3 (1983): 393–402. They cite the Office of Personnel Management Federal Employee Attitude Surveys of 1979 and 1980, extracting responses from those in the Senior Executive Service, the upper ranks of the civil service and appointed administrators. In 1979, 99 percent of the senior executives said that they considered accomplishing something worthwhile very important; 97 percent said the same in 1980. By contrast, in response to the question, "How much would you be motivated by a cash award?" only 45 percent said either to a great extent or to a very great extent.
3. Twelve percent of LeLoup and Moreland's Department of Agriculture requests between 1946 and 1971 were for decreases. See Lance LeLoup, *Budgetary Politics*, 3d ed. (Brunswick, Ohio: King's Court, 1986), 83. For a more recent case study of an agency requesting decreases, see the case study of the Office of Personnel Management, in Irene Rubin, *Shrinking the Federal Government* (New York: Longman, 1985). See Irene Rubin, *Running in the Red: The Political Dynamics of Urban Fiscal Stress* (Albany: State University of New York Press, 1982), for an example of a department refusing additional employees.
4. For a good discussion of this phenomenon, see Frank Thompson, *The Politics of Personnel in the City* (Berkeley: University of California Press, 1975).
5. See Rubin, *Shrinking the Federal Government*, for examples during the Reagan administration.
6. U.S. Senate, Committee on Governmental Affairs, *Office of Management and Budget: Evolving Roles and Future Issues*, Committee Print 99-134, 99th Cong., 2d sess., prepared by the Congressional Research Service of the Library of Congress, February 1986. OMB's role has changed some in the 1990s, as it has engaged in helping implement GPRA, the Government Performance and Results Act, and various efforts at downsizing to help balance the budget. But it still remains a more top-down agency, implementing presidential policy, doing analysis, and making recommendations to the president. See Shelley Lynn Tomkin, *Inside OMB: Politics and Process in the President's Budget Office* (Armonk, N.Y.: M.E. Sharpe, 1998), for both the history of OMB and its recent roles.
7. See, for example, Kenneth Shepsle and Barry Weingast, "Legislative Politics and Budget Outcomes," in *Federal Budget Policy in the 1980s*, ed. Gregory Mills and John Palmer (Washington, D.C.: Urban Institute Press, 1984), 343–67.
8. Rubin, *Running in the Red*, 56.
9. For a vivid account of the relationship between pork-barrel spending and building political coalitions, see Martin Shefter, "New York City's Fiscal Crisis: The Politics of Inflation and Retrenchment," *Public Interest* 48 (Summer 1977): 99–127.

10. See John Ellwood, "Comments," in Mills and Palmer, *Federal Budget Policy in the 1980s,* 368–78.
11. Douglas Arnold, "The Local Roots of Domestic Policy," in *The New Congress,* ed. Thomas Mann and Norman Ornstein (Washington, D.C.: American Enterprise Institute, 1980), 252, quoted in Ellwood, "Comments."
12. Arnold, "Local Roots," 282.
13. Ellwood, "Comments," 370.
14. Linda Harriman and Jeffrey Straussman, "Do Judges Determine Budget Decisions? Federal Court Decisions in Prison Reform and State Spending for Corrections," *Public Administration Review* 43, no. 4 (1983): 343–51.
15. Irene Rubin, *Class Tax and Power: Municipal Budgeting in the United States* (Chatham, N.J.: Chatham House, 1998).
16. See H.L. Platt, *City Building in the New South: The Growth of Public Services in Houston, Texas* (Philadelphia: Temple University Press, 1983).
17. On the symbolic aspects of mandates, see Paul Posner, *The Politics of Unfunded Mandates: Whither Federalism?* (Washington, D.C.: Georgetown University Press, 1998).
18. Stephen Barr, "Congress Seeks a Seat at the Table," *Washington Post,* 7 March 1997.
19. Prepared Statement of Honorable Janice R. Lachance, Director, Office of Personnel Management, Before The House Committee on Appropriations Subcommittee on Treasury, Postal Service, and General Government, 13 March 1998, Friday.
20. Some of the GPRA material was prepared by Wouter Van Reeth, a visiting scholar from Belgium, in spring 1999.
21. For more on contemporary budget strategies, see Irene Rubin, "Strategies for the New Budgeting," in *Handbook of Public Administration,* 2d ed., ed. James Perry (San Francisco: Jossey-Bass, 1996), 279–96.

CHAPTER 2

1. This case study draws extensively on Joan Parker, *The Illinois Tax Increase of 1983, Summit and Resolution* (Springfield: Sangamon State University, Illinois Issues, 1984).
2. Ibid., 20.
3. This case study is taken from Timothy Riordan, "The Dayton Income Tax Increase: A Summary of Success," *Urban Fiscal Ledger* 1, no. 3 (August–September 1984): 1–3.
4. Ibid., 3.
5. Susan Hansen, "Extraction: The Politics of State Taxation," in *Politics in the American States: A Comparative Analysis,* 4th ed., ed. Virginia Gray, Herbert Jacobs, and Kenneth Vines (Boston: Little Brown, 1983), 434–36.
6. John F. Witte, *The Politics and Development of the Federal Income Tax* (Madison: University of Wisconsin Press, 1985), 77.
7. Ibid., 97.
8. Catherine Rudder, "Tax Policy. Structure and Choice," in *Making Economic Policy in Congress,* ed. Allen Schick (Washington, D.C.: American Enterprise Institute, 1983), 196–220.
9. Rudder argues that committee members tended to be party regulars, "with relatively high scores on party unity." Ibid., 197.
10. Ibid., 212. The reader should note that any attempt to add up the value of tax breaks is approximate. Nevertheless, this description of trends is probably fairly accurate.
11. Ibid., 211.
12. Randall Strahan, "Committee Politics and Tax Reform" (paper prepared for the 1987 meetings of the American Political Science Association, 3–6 September 1987). See also Randall Strahan and R. Kent Weaver, "Subcommittee Government and the House Ways and Means Committee" (paper presented at the Southern Political Science Association meetings, Memphis, Tennessee, 2–4 November 1989). Randall Strahan's book, *The New*

Ways and Means: Reform and Change in a Congressional Committee (Chapel Hill: University of North Carolina Press, 1990), deals with these themes at length.

13. Robert Pastor, "The Cry and Sigh Syndrome: Congress and Trade Policy," in Schick, *Making Economic Policy in Congress*, 158–95.
14. General Accounting Office, *Budget Issues: Earmarking in the Federal Government* (Washington, D.C.: Government Printing Office, 1995).
15. Martha A. Fabricius and Ronald K. Snell, *Earmarking State Taxes*, 2d ed. (Denver: National Council of State Legislatures, September 1990), 26; Arturo Pérez and Ronald Snell, *Earmarking State Taxes*, 3d ed. (Denver: National Council of State Legislatures, 1995), 3, 5, 22.
16. Advisory Commission on Intergovernmental Relations, *Significant Features of Fiscal Federalism, 1988* (Washington, D.C.: Government Printing Office, 1989), 1:96–97.
17. Ibid., 1 and tables 7 and 8.
18. Pérez and Snell, *Earmarking State Taxes*, 3.
19. Charles Spindler, "The Lottery and Education: Robbing Peter to Pay Paul?" *Public Budgeting and Finance* 15(3) (Fall 1995): 54–62.
20. Susan MacManus, "Florida: Reinvention Derailed," in *The Fiscal Crisis of the States: Lessons for the Future*, ed. Steven Gold (Washington, D.C.: Georgetown University Press, 1995), 250.
21. Fabricius and Snell, *Earmarking State Taxes*, tables 4, 5, and 7.
22. Timothy Clark, "Taking a Regional Stand," *National Journal*, 22 March 1986, 700.
23. Witte, *Politics and Development of the Federal Income Tax*, 68.
24. C.K. Yearley, *The Money Machines: The Breakdown and Reform of Governmental and Party Finance in the North, 1860–1920* (Albany: State University of New York Press, 1970), 39.
25. Terrence J. McDonald, "San Francisco: Socioeconomic Change, Political Culture and Fiscal Politics," in *The Politics of Urban Fiscal Policy*, ed. Terrence J. McDonald and Sally K. Ward (Beverly Hills, Calif.: Sage, 1984), 51.
26. Arnold Meltsner, *Politics of City Revenue* (Berkeley: University of California Press, 1971). See also Charles Levine, Irene Rubin, and George Wolohojian, *The Politics of Retrenchment: How Local Governments Manage Fiscal Stress* (Beverly Hills, Calif.: Sage, 1981). The authors state that although Oakland's property tax base was rising very slowly during the 1960s and 1970s, the city reduced property tax rates whenever possible. The property tax rates declined in 1968, 1969, 1970, and 1971, and then again in 1976, 1977, and 1978. (After 1978, the city was affected by Proposition 13, which eliminated the city's discretion and forced further cuts in property tax rates.) These declines occurred despite increasing costs.
27. Hansen, "Extraction," 429.
28. Ibid., 434, and Susan Hansen, *The Politics of Taxation: Revenue without Representation* (New York: Praeger, 1983).
29. Hansen, "Extraction," 428.
30. Allen Schick, *Capacity to Budget* (Washington, D.C.: Urban Institute, 1990), 144.
31. David Osborne, *Laboratories of Democracy* (Boston: Harvard Business School Press, 1988), 27.
32. See Bryan Jones and Lynn Bachelor, with Carter Wilson, *The Sustaining Hand: Community Leadership and Corporate Power* (Lawrence: University Press of Kansas, 1986), for the relationship between economic decline and tax breaks for General Motors in Detroit; see Daniel Mandelker, Gary Feder, and Margaret R. Collins, *Reviving Cities with Tax Abatements* (New Brunswick, N.J.: Rutgers University, Center for Urban Policy Research, 1980), for the connection between economic decline and property tax abatements in St. Louis. For the relationship between declining economy and tax breaks in Cook County, where Chicago is located, see Arthur Lyons, Spenser Staton, Greg Wass, and Mari Zurek, "Reducing Property Taxes to Promote Economic Development: Does It Work?" Report prepared for the Comptroller of the City of Chicago, January 1988.

33. Stanley Surrey and Paul McDaniel, *Tax Expenditures* (Cambridge: Harvard University Press, 1985), 3, make this distinction. Tax exceptions are sometimes called tax expenditures because they reduce the revenues that would normally have been raised by the tax, and because the stated goal of such tax reductions is to achieve some programmatic goal using tax incentives instead of spending programs.

34. Louis Eisenstein, *The Ideologies of Taxation* (New York: Ronald Press, 1961).

35. *U.S. Budget, Fiscal Year 2000, Analytical Perspectives*, table 5-3.

36. Witte, *Politics and Development of the Federal Income Tax*, 214.

37. Howard E. Shuman, *Politics and the Budget: The Struggle Between the President and the Congress* (Englewood Cliffs, N.J.: Prentice Hall, 1984), 105.

38. Schick, *Capacity to Budget*, 144.

39. Thomas Neubig and David Joulfaian, "The Tax Expenditure Budget Before and After the Tax Reform Act of 1986," OTA Paper 60, Office of Tax Analysis, Department of the Treasury, October 1988, 1–2.

40. Congressional Budget Office, *The Effects of Tax Reform on Tax Expenditures* (Washington, D.C.: CBO, 1988), cited in Schick, *Capacity to Budget*, 148.

41. Allen Manville, *Tax Notes*, 10 April 1995, 293.

42. Ben Wildavsky, "Where Social Programs Go to Hide," *National Journal*, 7 February 1998, 294.

43. Iris Lav, "The Final Tax Bill: Assessing the Long-term Costs and the Distribution of Tax Benefits," Center on Budget and Policy Priorities, 1 August 1997. The bill that passed both houses and was sent to the president was HR 2015 Enr.

44. Paul R. McDaniel, "Overview of Tax Expenditures in the Budget," *Hearing Before the Committee on the Budget, Concurrent Resolution on the Budget for Fiscal Year 1994*, U.S. Senate, 1st sess., 3 February 1993, 362.

45. Based on an analysis of information presented in "A Layman's Guide to Illinois Taxes, Illinois Department of Revenue, September 1989, 23–25.

46. Frederick W. Derrick and Charles E. Scott, *Maryland's Sales and Use Tax: Past, Present and Future* (prepared for the Maryland Commission on State Taxes and Tax Structure, 31 October 1989), 1.

47. Ibid., 9.

48. Jay Ladin, *The Maryland Personal Income Tax* (prepared for the Maryland Commission on State Taxes and Tax Structure, January 1990), 21.

49. Ibid., 19.

50. Nebraska's 1998 Tax Expenditure Report.

51. Texas Comptroller of Public Accounts, "Tax Exemptions and Tax Incidence, School Property Tax," table 1, http://www.window.state.tx.us/taxinfo/incidence/ptoptax.html.

52. Department of Revenue, Washington State, "Property Tax Statistics 1998, Senior Citizens Property Tax Relief," http://dor.wa.gov/reports/te98/taxstats98/sencitizen.htm.

53. Lee Walker, *The Changing Arena: State Strategic Economic Development* (Lexington, Ky.: Council of State Governments, 1989); and Paul Peretz, "The Market for Industry: Where Angels Fear to Tread?" *Policy Studies Review* 5, no. 3 (February 1996): 624–33.

54. Charles Spindler, "Winners and Losers in Industrial Recruitment: Mercedes Benz and Alabama," *State and Local Government Review* 26, no. 3 (Fall 1994): 192–204.

55. Ibid., 202.

56. Ibid., 198.

57. Peter Eisenger, *The Rise of the Entrepreneurial State: State and Local Development in the United States* (Madison: University of Wisconsin Press, 1988).

58. Don Sherman Grant II, Michael Wallace, and William Pitney, "Measuring State-Level Economic Development Programs, 1970–92," *Economic Development Quarterly* 9, no. 2 (May 1995): 134–45; and Peter Eisenger, "State Economic Development Policies in the 1990s: Politics and Policy Learning," *Economic Development Quarterly* 9, no. 2 (May 1995): 146–58.

59. David Postman, "Tax Breaks for New Industry? Some Lawmakers Say No," *Seattle Times*, http://www.seattletimes.com/news/local/html98/alttax_021198.html. See also "Company Rules Out Steel Plant for Washington," *Seattle Times*, 17 February 1998.

60. Samuel Nunn, "Regulating Local Tax Abatement Policies: Arguments and Alternative Policies for Urban Planners and Administrators," *Policy Studies Journal* 22, no. 4 (Winter 1994): 574–88.

61. J.E. Harris and S.A. Hicks, "Tax Expenditure Reporting: The Utilization of an Innovation," *Public Budgeting and Finance* 12, no. 3 (Fall 1992): 32–49; the figure of twenty-one states is cited on p. 33.

62. Karen Benker, "Tax Expenditure Reporting: Closing the Loophole in State Budget Oversight," *National Tax Journal* 39, no. 4 (December 1986): 403–17.

63. Douglas Snow, "The Strength of Tax Expenditure Claims on State Financial Resources," unpublished dissertation, Political Science Department, Northern Illinois University, 1996.

64. Benker, "Tax Expenditure Reporting," 412.

65. "California Tax Expenditure Report, 1998–99," http://www.dof.ca.gov/html/fs_data/taxexpend.pdf, accessed 27 March 1999.

66. Commonwealth of Massachusetts, "The Governor's Budget Recommendation, Tax Expenditure Budget, FY 1997," http://www.magnet.state.ma.us/bb/fy97h1/appendb.htm.

67. Texas Comptroller of Public Accounts, "Texas Taxes, Tax Exemptions and Tax Incidence," April 1999, http://www.window.state.tx.us/taxinfo/incidence/overview.html.

68. John Sharp, Texas comptroller of accounts, sales and franchise tax exemptions, *A Report to the Governor and Texas Legislature*, January 1991; and letter from John Sharp, 16 December 1992. Texas Comptroller of Public Accounts, "Texas Taxes, Tax Exemptions and Tax Incidence," April 1999.

69. "Executive Budget Proposal, State of Ohio, Fiscal Years 2000 and 2001," and companion "Tax Expenditure Report, 1998, 1999, 2000, and 2001."

70. Paul Carrier, "Business Tax Break 'Eating Budget,'" *Portland Press Herald*, 3 February 1999, http://www.centralmaine.com/copy.html.

71. Jesse Hughes and Janne Moteket, "Tax Expenditures for Local Government," *Public Budgeting and Finance* 8, no. 4 (Winter 1988): 68–73.

72. Ann H. Elder and Nancy S. Lind, "The Implications of Uncertainty in Economic Development: The Case of Diamond Star Motors," *Economic Development Quarterly* 1, no. 1 (February 1987): 30–40.

73. Nunn, "Regulating Local Tax Abatement Policies," 582.

74. Michael Barker, ed., *State Taxation Policy* (Durham, N.C.: Duke University Press, 1983), 94.

75. Lyons et al., "Reducing Property Taxes," 50.

76. "Local Tax Exemptions Drying Up," *Business News of Dayton*, 2 December 1996, http://www.amcity.com/dayton/stories/1996/12/02/story1.html.

77. For an account of the federal government's efforts to control this tax break, see Dennis Zimmerman, *The Private Use of Tax Exempt Bonds: Controlling Public Subsidy of Private Activity* (Washington, D.C.: Urban Institute Press, 1991).

78. Texas Comptroller of Public Accounts, "Texas Taxes, Tax Exemptions and Tax Incidence," April 1999.

79. Robert Lehnen and Carlyn E. Johnson, "The Impact of Tax Increment Financing on School Districts: An Indiana Case Study," draft manuscript, 1999.

80. William Celis III, "Schools Lose Money in Business Tax Breaks," *New York Times*, 22 May 1991, 1.

81. Lyons et al., "Reducing Property Taxes," 57.

82. One example of the relative inefficiency of tax expenditures as a means of achieving program goals occurred in housing. In 1975 Congress passed a tax credit for the purchase of new homes, reportedly to encourage building and sales of new homes, at a cost of $600 million. Housing was increased by fewer than 105,000 units, which amounted to a sub-

sidy of $5,700 per unit. More efficient subsidies could have been used, according to Thomas Reese, *The Politics of Taxation* (Westport, Conn.: Quorum Books, 1980), xvi.

83. Ibid., xix.

84. Timothy Clark, "How to Succeed against Business," *National Journal*, 3 May 1986, 1059.

85. Ibid.

86. For an account of the lobbying to protect tax breaks, see Jeffrey Birnbaum and Alan Murray, *Showdown at Gucci Gulch: Lawmakers, Lobbyists, and the Unlikely Triumph of Tax Reform* (New York: Random House, 1987).

87. Eileen Shanahan, "Congress Expected to OK Tax Overhaul Bill," *National Journal*, 23 April 1986, 1951.

88. Benker, "Tax Expenditure Reporting," 412.

89. John F. Witte, "Wisconsin Income Tax Reform," in *State Policy Choices: The Wisconsin Experience*, ed. Sheldon Danzinger and John F. Witte (Madison: University of Wisconsin Press, 1988), 108–29.

CHAPTER 3

1. Prepared Testimony of Christopher Cox Before the House Budget Committee, Subcommittee on Budget Process Reform, 18 June 1998; see also John F. Cogan, Timothy Muris, and Allen Schick, *The Budget Puzzle: Understanding Federal Spending* (Palo Alto, Calif.: Stanford University Press, 1994), esp. chap. 3, "The Uses and Abuses of Budget Baselines," by Tim Muris; and Center on Budget and Policy Priorities, "Concerns Regarding the Nussle-Cardin-Goss Budget Process Bill," 14 May 1999, at http://www.cbpp.org and the related sign-on letter urging opposition to the bill.

2. "Stupid Budget Laws: Remarks Before the American Association of Law Schools," by Bill Dauster, 5 January 1996, and *Congressional Record*, 27 October 1995.

3. *Congressional Record*, 27 October 1995.

4. Jennifer Grooters and Corina Eckl, *Legislative Budget Procedures: A Guide to Appropriation and Budget Processes in the States, Commonwealths and Territories* (Denver, Colo.: National Conference of State Legislatures, 1998), table 6-3.

5. Irene S. Rubin, *Class, Tax, and Power: Municipal Budgeting in the United States* (Chatham, N.J.: Chatham House, 1998).

6. Zander Navarro, "Affirmative Democracy" and "Redistributive Development: The Case of 'Participatory Budgeting' in Porto Allegre, Brazil, 1989–1997," Universidade Federal do Rio Grande do Sul, Brazil, December 1997.

7. Allen Schick, "The Road to PPB: The Stages of Budget Reform," *Public Administration Review* 26 (December 1966): 245–56.

8. Thomas Anton, *The Politics of State Expenditure in Illinois* (Urbana: University of Illinois Press, 1966), 73.

9. See Gloria Grizzle, "Does Budget Format Really Govern the Actions of Budget Makers?" *Public Budgeting and Finance* 6, no. 1 (Spring 1986): 64.

10. Grooters and Eckl, *Legislative Budget Procedures*.

11. Glenn Abney and Thomas B. Lauth, *The Politics of State and City Administration* (Albany: State University of New York Press, 1986), esp. chap. 9.

12. Allen Schick, *The Capacity to Budget* (Washington, D.C.: Urban Institute Press, 1990), chap. 6. See also Shelley Tomkin, *Inside OMB* (New York: M.E. Sharpe, 1998).

13. Grooters and Eckl, *Legislative Budget Procedures*, table 6-4.

14. Grooters and Eckl, *Legislative Budget Procedures*.

15. Beryl Pettus and Randall Bland, *Texas Government Today: Structures, Functions, Political Process* (Homewood, Ill.: Dorsey Press, 1979).

16. Ibid., 341.

17. Ibid., 343.

18. Ibid., 344.
19. Ibid.
20. Ibid.
21. James Gosling, "The State Budget Office and Policy Making," *Public Budgeting and Finance* 7, no. 1 (Spring 1987): 51–65.
22. Ibid., 57.
23. Barbara Yondorf and B.J. Summers, *Legislative Budget Procedures in the 50 States*, Legislative Finance Paper 21 (Denver, Colo.: National Conference of State Legislatures, 1983), 198.
24. Grooters and Eckl, *Legislative Budget Procedures.*

CHAPTER 4
 1. Charles Stewart III, "Budget Reform and Its Consequences: Agencies, the Committees, and the House, 1865–1921," paper presented at the 1987 American Political Science Association meeting, Chicago, 3–7 September. Also see Charles Stewart III, *Budget Reform Politics* (New York: Cambridge University Press, 1989).
 2. For the state level, see ACIR, *The Question of State Government Capability* (Washington, D.C.: Government Printing Office, 1985), 146ff.
 3. Howard Shuman, *Politics and the Budget: The Struggle Between the President and the Congress* (Englewood Cliffs. N.J.: Prentice Hall, 1984), 27.
 4. Ibid., 28.
 5. Frederick Mosher, *A Tale of Two Agencies: A Comparative Analysis of the GAO and OMB* (Baton Rouge: Louisiana State University Press, 1984), 27.
 6. Allen Schick, *Congress and Money* (Washington, D.C.: Urban Institute Press, 1980), chap. 2.
 7. Congressional Budget Office, *The Economic and Fiscal Outlook: Fiscal Years, 1992–1996* (Washington, D.C.: Government Printing Office, January, 1991), chap. 2.
 8. Ibid., 57.
 9. Allen Schick, *The Federal Budget: Politics, Policy and Process* (Washington, D.C.: Brookings Institution, 1995), 41.
10. For a description of some of these summit negotiations, see Allen Schick, *The Capacity to Budget* (Washington, D.C.: Urban Institute Press, 1990), chap. 6; and Joseph White and Aaron Wildavsky, *The Deficit and the Public Interest: The Search for Responsible Government in the 1980s* (Berkeley: University of California Press, 1989), 235–41, 298, 319–22.
11. Janet Cornelius, *Constitution Making in Illinois, 1918–1970* (Urbana: University of Illinois Press, 1972), 13.
12. Ibid., 14.
13. Ibid., 68.
14. William T. Hutchinson, *Lowden of Illinois,* vol. 1 (Chicago: University of Chicago Press, 1957).
15. Ibid., 295.
16. Jennifer Grooters and Corina Eckl, *Legislative Budget Procedures: A Guide to Appropriation and Budget Processes in the States, Commonwealths and Territories* (Denver, Colo.: National Council of State Legislatures, 1998), 6.7–6.9.
17. James Gosling, *Budgetary Politics in American Governments*, 2d ed. (New York: Garland, 1997), 158.
18. Hutchison and James, *Legislative Budget Procedures*, 1988, p. 12.
19. Data come from the NCSL, *Legislative Budget Procedures in the 50 States*, 1983; *Legislative Budget Procedures in the 50 States*, 1988; and Grooters and Eckl, *Legislative Budget Procedures*, 1998.
20. National Association of State Budget Officers, "Budget Process in the States," 1997, table N, posted on NASBO's website: http://www.nasbo.org/pubs/budpro/frame.htm.

21. James Gosling, "Patterns of Influence and Choice in the Wisconsin Budgetary Process," *Legislative Studies Quarterly* 10, November 1985, 457–82, cited in Gosling, *Budgetary Politics*.

22. Glenn Abney and Thomas Lauth, "The End of Executive Dominance in State Appropriations," *Public Administration Review* 58, no. 5 (1998): 388–94.

23. Thomas Lauth, "The Executive Budget in Georgia," *State and Local Government Review* 18 (Spring 1986): 56–64; and Thomas Lauth, "Exploring the Budgetary Base in Georgia," *Public Budgeting and Finance* 7 (Winter 1987): 72–82.

24. The material through the 1950s is from Thomas Anton, *The Politics of State Expenditure in Illinois* (Urbana: University of Illinois Press, 1966).

25. Edgar Crane, "The Office of the Governor," in *Illinois: Political Process and Governmental Performance,* ed. Edgar Crane (Dubuque, Iowa: Kendall/Hunt, 1980), 74.

26. Ibid., 78.

27. Ibid., 77.

28. Irene Rubin, Jack King, Steven Wagner, and Ellen Dran, "Illinois: Executive Reform and Fiscal Conditions," in *Governors, Legislatures, and Budgets: Diversity across the American States,* ed. Edward Clynch and Thomas Lauth (Westport, Conn.: Greenwood, 1991).

29. Joseph Kyle, "Florida Legislative Budget Review Process," in *The Political Pursestrings: The Role of the Legislature in the Budgetary Process,* ed. Alan P. Balutis and Daron K. Butler (New York: Wiley, 1975), 78.

30. Karen Stanford, personal communication, 18 March 1999.

31. Gloria Grizzle, "Florida: Miles to Go and Promises to Keep," in Clynch and Lauth, *Governors, Legislatures and Budgets*, 98–99.

32. Karen Stanford, personal communication, 18 March 1999.

33. Grizzle, "Florida," 98.

34. Karen Stanford, personal communication, 18 March 1999.

35. This case is taken from Charles C. Williamson, *The Finances of Cleveland* in the series *Studies in History, Economics and Public Law* 25, no. 3, ed. Faculty of Political Science, Columbia University (New York: Columbia University Press, 1906–7).

36. Ibid., 22.

37. Ibid., 44.

38. Martin Schiesl, *The Politics of Efficiency: Municipal Administration and Reform in America, 1800–1920* (Berkeley: University of California Press, 1977), 90.

39. Ibid., 91.

40. Ibid., 92.

41. Charles Phillips Huse, *The Financial History of Boston, From May 1, 1822 to January 31, 1909* (Cambridge: Harvard University Press, 1916), 62.

42. Ibid.

43. Ibid., 177.

44. Ibid., 233–34.

45. Charles Glaab and A. Theodore Brown, *A History of Urban America,* 3d ed. (New York: Macmillan, 1983), 200.

46. Stanley Botner, "Trends and Developments in Budgeting and Financial Management in Large Cities in the United States." *Public Budgeting and Finance* 9, no. 3 (Autumn 1989): 41.

47. See Carolyn Adams, *The Politics of Capital Investment: The Case of Philadelphia* (Albany: State University of New York Press, 1988), chap. 5, for an illustration of the interaction between neighborhood loyalties, fiscal stress, and council participation in the capital budget process.

48. See George Terhune, *An Administrative Case Study of Performance Budgeting in the City of Los Angeles, California* (Chicago: Municipal Finance Officers Association, 1954); and Ali Eghetedari and Frank Sherwood, "Performance Budgeting in Los Angeles," in *Perspectives*

on Budgeting, 2d ed., ed. Allen Schick (Washington, D.C.: American Society for Public Administration, 1987).

49. Selma Mushkin et al., in cooperation with the Council of State Governments, the International City Managers Association, the National Governors Conference, the National League of Cities, and the U.S. Conference of Mayors, *Implementing PPB in State, City, and County: A Report on the 5-5-5 Project* (Washington, D.C.: State and Local Finances Project of George Washington University, June 1969).

50. Ibid., 13.

51. See Charles Levine, Irene Rubin, and George Wolohojian, *The Politics of Retrenchment: How Local Governments Manage Fiscal Stress* (Beverly Hills, Calif.: Sage, 1981), 76–77.

CHAPTER 5

1. Representative Rogers, House of Representatives, *Congressional Record,* 11 March 1997.

2. House of Representatives, Supplemental Appropriations Bill, *Congressional Record,* 31 March 1998, H1780.

3. See Richard Stubbing, "The Defense Budget," in *Federal Budget Policy in the 1980s,* ed. G. Mills and J. Palmer (Washington, D.C.: Urban Institute Press, 1984), 81–110.

4. Office of Management and Budget, "Major Policy Initiatives," FY 1987 budget, 12, quoted in Roy T. Meyer, "Microbudgetary Strategies and Competition," Ph.D. diss., University of Michigan, 1988, 305.

5. This occurred while I was doing participant observation on the Finance Advisory Board of DeKalb, Illinois. I was the citizen involved, and the event left me chagrined.

6. James Savage, *Funding Science in America: Congress, Universities, and the Politics of the Academic Pork Barrel* (Cambridge, England: Cambridge University Press, 1999).

7. These arguments were all used in the 1986 and 1987 hearings before the Finance Advisory Board in DeKalb.

8. Meyer, "Microbudgetary Strategies," 284.

9. Meyer discusses a wide variety of strategies to make federal programs look less expensive than they are.

10. Roy Meyers, *Strategic Budgeting* (Ann Arbor: University of Michigan Press, 1994), 85ff.

11. On the Export-Import Bank, see Jordan Jay Hillman, *The Export-Import Bank at Work: Promotional Financing in the Public Sector* (Westport, Conn.: Quorum Books, 1982), xiv–xv. See also *Congressional Record,* House of Representatives, H6361, 30 July 1997.

12. Genie Stowers, "Earmarking as a Strategy against Budgetary Constraints: San Francisco's Children Amendment," *Public Budgeting and Finance* 15, no. 4 (Winter 1995): 68–85.

13. This minicase is summarized from Savage, *Funding Science in America.*

14. From the now defunct *PoliticsNow* website, run by the *Washington Post,* 11 January 1997.

15. Jeffrey Straussman, "Rights-Based Budgeting," in *New Directions in Budget Theory,* ed. Irene Rubin (Albany: State University of New York Press, 1988).

16. Kathryn Foster, *The Political Economy of Special Purpose Government* (Washington D.C.: Georgetown University Press, 1997).

17. U.S. Congress, Senate, *Social Security Tax Cut: Hearings Before the Committee on Finance on S. 2016,* 101st Cong., 2d sess., 5, 8, and 27 February 1990, 14.

18. Ibid., 8.

19. Ibid., 5.

20. U.S. Congress, Senate, *Social Security Preservation Act, Report 101-426 of the Committee on the Budget, to Accompany S. 2999, to Exclude the Social Security Trust Funds from the Deficit Calculation,* 4 August 1990, 29.

21. Meyers, *Strategic Budgeting,* 70, 71.

22. Statement made in House Of Representatives by Representative Charles W. Stenholm, 17 April 1996, Concerning H.R. 842, "Truth in Budgeting Act."

23. "Aid to Elderly Divides Young, Old and Politicians," *New York Times,* 23 June 1988.
24. Ibid.
25. U.S. House of Representatives, Committee on the Budget, *Hearing Before the Task Force on Urgent Fiscal Issues, U.S. Farm Policy: Proposals for Budget Savings,* 101st Cong., 2d sess., 28 June 1990, 11.
26. Ibid., 16.
27. Nancy Blanpied, ed., *Farm Policy: The Politics of Soil, Surpluses, and Subsidies* (Washington, D.C.: CQ Press, 1984), 80.
28. Congressional Budget Office, *The Economic and Fiscal Outlook: Fiscal Years 1992–96* (Washington, D.C.: Government Printing Office, January 1991), 100.
29. U.S. Congress, House, *Federal Credit Reform: Hearings Before the Task Force on Urgent Fiscal Issues of the Committee on the Budget,* 101st Cong., 2d sess., 11 April 1990, 1.
30. Ibid., 3.
31. General Accounting Office, *Federal Credit Programs: Agencies Had Serious Problems Meeting Credit Reform Accounting Requirements,* no. AFMD-93-17 (Washington, D.C.: GAO, January 1993).
32. Marvin Phaup, "Conceptual Dissonance and Utility of the New Credit Accounts in the Budget: FHA under Credit Reform," *Public Budgeting and Finance* 16, no. 1 (Spring 1996): 23–36.
33. General Accounting Office, *Credit Reform: Speculative Savings Used to Offset Current Spending Increase Budget Uncertainty,* no. AIMD-94-46 (Washington, D.C.: GAO, March 1994).
34. For a summary of the arguments about how to treat administrative costs, see Phil Joyce, *Budgeting for Administrative Costs under Credit Reform* (Washington, D.C.: Congressional Budget Office, January 1992).
35. Senator Bumpers, *Congressional Record,* 11 August 1995, S. 12516.
36. Senator Bond, *Congressional Record,* 11 August 1995, S. 12515.
37. Congressional Budget Office, *Curtailing Indirect Federal Subsidies to the U.S. Postal Service* (Washington, D.C.: Government Printing Office, August 1984, ix.
38. See Congressional Budget Office, *Federal Subsidies for Rail Passenger Service: An Assessment of Amtrak* (Washington, D.C.: Government Printing Office, July 1982).
39. Material from Gloria Simo, University of Arkansas, Little Rock, 1999.
40. See Blanpied, *Farm Policy,* for a good summary of various kinds of agricultural subsidies through 1984.
41. Tim Weiner, *Blank Check* (New York: Warner Books, 1990), 5.
42. Ibid., 10.
43. Ibid.
44. Ibid., summarized from chapter 4.
45. "Spy Satellite Unit Facing a New Life in Daylight," *New York Times,* 3 November 1992.
46. "House Approves Intelligence Funds," *Chicago Tribune,* 22 December 1995.
47. "Spy Satellite Unit."
48. "Disclosure of Spy Agency's $1.5 Billion Fund Leads to Shake-up," *New York Times,* 25 September 1995.

CHAPTER 6

1. Alan Blinder and Douglas Holtz-Eakin, "Public Opinion and the Balanced Budget," *American Economic Review* 74 (May 1984): 144–49.
2. Advisory Commission on Intergovernmental Relations, *Significant Features of Fiscal Federalism,* vol. 1, *Budget Processes and Tax Systems, 1992* (Washington, D.C.: ACIR, 1992), table 3.
3. Congressional Research Service Report for Congress, "Transportation Trust Funds: Budgetary Treatment," by John W. Fischer, Economics Division, updated 6 April 1998, 98–63 E.

4. *Historical Tables of the United States Budget* (Washington, D.C.: Government Printing Office, January 1996), table 1.1.
5. David Stockman, "The Crisis in Federal Budgeting," in *Crisis in the Budget Process: Exercising Political Choice*, ed. Allen Schick (Washington, D.C.: AEI Press, 1986).
6. Ibid., 65.
7. Allen Schick, "The Evolution of Congressional Budgeting," in Schick, *Crisis in the Budget Process*, 53.
8. Norman Ornstein, "The Politics of the Deficit," in *Essays in Contemporary Economic Problems*, ed. Phillip Cagan (Washington, D.C.: AEI Press, 1985), 311.
9. "Stockman Book Offers An Inside View," *New York Times*, 13 April 1986, sect. 1.
10. David Stockman, *Triumph of Politics* (New York: Harper & Row 1986), 124.
11. U.S. Congress, House, *Hearings before the Ways and Means Committee, Administration's Views on the Deficit and Possible Revenue Increases for the Next Three Fiscal Years*, 14 June 1983, 15.
12. U.S. Congress, House, Subcommittee on Monopolies and Commercial Law of the Judiciary Committee, *Hearings, Constitutional Amendments Seeking to Balance the Budget and Limit Federal Spending*, 97th Cong., August 1982, 351–64.
13. U.S. Senate, *Balanced Budget—Tax Limitation Constitutional Amendment*, Senate Report 98-628, 1984, 13.
14. From speech given to the Association for Budgeting and Financial Management, Washington D.C., 15 October 1993.
15. Jeffrey Birnbaum, "House Rejects Bid to Require Balanced Budget," *Wall Street Journal*, 12 June 1992, A2.
16. Statement submitted to the Task Force on Spending Limitations, Committee on Rules, U.S. House of Representatives, 20 March 1980.
17. U.S. Congress, House, *Hearings of the Task Force on Federal Spending Limitation Proposals of the Committee on Rules, on Legislative Measures to Amend the Congressional Budget and Impoundment Control Act of 1974*, 96th Cong., 2d sess., 1980, 133.
18. Ibid., 127.
19. Ibid., 123.
20. Ibid., 193.
21. U.S. Congress, Senate, *Budget Reform Proposals, Joint Hearings before the Committee on Governmental Affairs and the Committee on the Budget*, 101st Cong., 1st sess., 18 and 26 October 1989, 167. Roy Meyers, *Strategic Budgeting* (Ann Arbor: University of Michigan Press, 1994), 75, lists the government sponsored enterprises that were proposed in 1986–1987: the Corporation for Small Business Investments, the Airways Corporation, the National Public Works Corporation, the National Long-Term Care Corporation, and several GSE-style corporations to carry out uranium enrichment.
22. *Budget Reform Proposals*, 147.
23. Tony Hutchison and Kathy James, *Legislative Budget Procedures in the Fifty States: A Guide to Appropriations and Budget Processes* (Denver, Colo.: National Conference of State Legislatures, 1988), 92–93. Jennifer Grooters and Corrina Eckl, *Legislative Budget Procedures: A Guide to Appropriations and Budget Processes in the States, Commonwealths, and Territories* (Denver, Colo.: NCSL, 1998), table 7-2.
24. John G. Cross, "Michigan State Expenditures and the Provision of Public Services," in *Michigan's Fiscal and Economic Structure*, ed. Harvey Brazer and Deborah Laren (Ann Arbor: University of Michigan Press, 1982), 379.
25. Statement of Lowell Weicker, 13 May 1992, U.S. Congress, House, *Hearings before the Committee on the Budget*, 102d Cong., 2d sess., 12, 13, 19 May and 3 June 1992, 216.
26. State of Connecticut, *Governor's Budget Summary, 1992–1993*.
27. U.S. Congress, House, *Hearings before the Committee on the Budget*, 12 May 1992, 8.
28. Example modified from ibid., 14.

29. Robert Albritton and Ellen Dran, "Balanced Budgets and State Surpluses: The Politics of Budgeting in Illinois," *Public Administration Review* 47, no. 2 (March–April 1987): 135–42.
30. Illinois Economic and Fiscal Commission, *Revenue Estimate and Economic Outlook for FY 1978,* Springfield, Ill., June 1977, 17; cited in Albritton and Dran, "Balanced Budgets," 144.
31. Naomi Caiden and Jeffrey Chapman, "Constraint and Uncertainty: Budgeting in California," *Public Budgeting and Finance* 2, no. 4 (Winter 1982): 114–15.
32. Albritton and Dran, "Balanced Budgets," 145.
33. Harvey Brazer, "The Anatomy of a Fiscal Crisis: The Michigan Case," *Public Budgeting and Finance* 2, no. 4 (Winter 1982): 140.
34. Ibid.
35. Mandy Rafool, "Fiscal Perspective, State and Local Tax and Expenditure Limits," *The Fiscal Letter,* National Conference of State Legislatures, Denver, Colo., September/October 1996.
36. Steven Gold, "Preparing for the Next Recession: Rainy Day Funds and Other Tools for States," Legislative Finance Paper no. 41, National Conference of State Legislatures, Denver, Colo., 30 December 1983, 2; ACIR, *Significant Features of Fiscal Federalism, 1989,* table 74.
37. ACIR, *Significant Features of Fiscal Federalism, 1994,* vol. 1, table 4.
38. Iris Lav and Alan Berube, "When It Rains, It Pours," Center on Budget and Policy Priorities, 1999.
39. Gold, "Preparing for the Next Recession," 7–8.
40. "Learning to Live in an Age of Strict Limits," *New York Times,* 13 April 1986, Week in Review, 5.
41. ACIR, *Significant Features of Fiscal Federalism, 1985–1986,* 163. See also Janet Kelly, *State Mandated Local Government Expenditures and Revenue Limitations in South Carolina* (Columbia: South Carolina ACIR, June 1988).
42. ACIR, *Significant Features of Fiscal Federalism, 1988,* 48–59. Later years calculated by the author directly from the Census of Governments, U.S. Census.
43. Steven Gold, "State Fiscal Problems and Policies," in *The Fiscal Crisis of the States,* ed. Steven Gold (Washington, D.C.: Georgetown University Press, 1995), 14.
44. Ibid., 33.
45. Ibid.
46. Jeffrey Chapman, "California: The Enduring Crisis," in Gold, *Fiscal Crisis of the States,* 125–26.
47. Thomas Luce Jr., "Innovation in an Era of Constraint," in Gold, *Fiscal Crisis of the States,* 338.
48. Charles Levine, Irene Rubin, and George Wolohojian, *The Politics of Retrenchment* (Beverly Hills, Calif.: Sage, 1981).
49. Irene Rubin, *Running in the Red: The Political Dynamics of Urban Fiscal Stress* (Albany: State University of New York Press, 1982).

CHAPTER 7

1. Congressional Budget Office, *Supplemental Appropriations in the 1970s* (Washington, D.C.: Government Printing Office, July 1981).
2. P.L. 98-8, 96 stat. 13.
3. "Hard Times Lead to Budget Cuts in Seventeen States," *New York Times,* 16 March 1986.
4. Peter Applebome, "Officials Report Texas Is Falling Short on Budget," *New York Times,* 15 February 1986.
5. Robert Suro, "Texas Governor Is Elusive on Taxes," *New York Times,* April 1991, 13.

6. Kenneth Kirkland, " 'Creative Accounting' and Short Term Debt: State Responses to the Deficit Threat," *National Tax Journal* 36, no. 3 (September 1983).

7. Thomas Lauth, "Midyear Appropriations in Georgia: Allocating the 'Surplus,' " *International Journal of Public Administration* 11, no. 5 (1988): 531–50.

8. Ibid., 538.

9. Ibid., 542.

10. Ibid.

11. Alan Saltzstein, "Changing City Policies in Times of Fiscal Uncertainty" (paper presented at the meetings of the American Political Science Association, Washington, D.C., 1986).

12. Congressional Budget Office, *Emergency Spending Under the Budget Enforcement Act* (Washington, D.C.: Government Printing Office, December 1998), 9.

13. Ibid., 14.

14. *Analytical Perspectives, Budget of the U.S. Government, FY 1999*, Section 8, "Underwriting Federal Credit and Insurance," at http://www.gpo.gov/usbudget.

15. Testimony of James Lee Witt, director of FEMA, at *Hearing on Budgeting Treatment of Emergencies, before House Task Force on Budget Process, Committee on Budgeting*, 23 June 1998.

16. *Analytical Perspectives, Budget of the U.S. Government, FY 1999*, pp. 183ff.

17. Figures are taken from Allen Schick, *Capacity to Budget* (Washington, D.C.: Urban Institute Press, 1990), table 4.4, p. 112, based on OMB data.

18. For a fascinating discussion of this case, see Barbara Hinkson Craig, *Chadha: The Story of An Epic Constitutional Struggle* (Berkeley: University of California Press, 1990).

19. Schick, *Capacity to Budget*, 113.

20. Senate Report 100-48 on the 1987 Supplementals, to accompany H.R. 1827, 4–5.

21. *City of New Haven, Connecticut* v. *United States of America*, slip opinion 86-5319, DC Circuit (1987). See also Walter Oleszek, *Congressional Procedures and the Policy Process*, 3d ed. (Washington, D.C.: CQ Press, 1989), 65.

22. General Accounting Office, *Forest Service Management: Little Has Changed as a Result of the Fiscal Year 1995 Budget Reforms*, A Report to the Subcommittee on Interior and Related Agencies, Committee on Appropriations, House of Representatives, GAO/RCED-99-2 (Washington, D.C.: Government Printing Office, December 1998).

23. "Operation and Maintenance Financial Management Practices," *Hearing before the House Committee on National Security, Military Readiness Subcommittee*, 105th Cong., 1st sess., 22 July 1997. Available at http://commdocs.house.gov/committees/security/has203030.000/has203030_1.htm.

24. Ibid.

25. Ibid.

26. Charles Levine, Irene Rubin, and George Wolohojian, "Resource Scarcity and the Reform Model: The Management of Reform in Cincinnati and Oakland," *Public Administration Review* 41, no. 6 (November/December 1981): 619–28.

27. See Irene Rubin, *Running in the Red* (Albany: State University of New York Press, 1982), for an example of a general fund borrowing from the water fund and causing deficits in the water fund.

CHAPTER 8

1. U.S. Congress, Senate, *Joint Hearings before Committees on Government Operations and on the Judiciary, Impoundment of Appropriated Funds by the President*, 93d Cong., 1st sess., 1973, 411; quoted in Louis Fisher, "The Effect of the Budget Act on Agency Operations," in *The Congressional Budget Process After Five Years*, ed. Rudolph Penner (Washington, D.C.: American Enterprise Institute, 1981), 173.

2. Frank Draper and Bernard Pitsvada, "Limitations in Federal Budget Execution," *Government Accountants Journal* 30, no. 3, (Fall 1981): 23.

3. Fisher, "Effect of the Budget Act," 156.
4. Ibid., 157.
5. U.S. Congress, House, *Hearings before a Subcommittee of the Committee on Appropriations, DOD Appropriations 1981,* 96th Cong., 2d sess., 1980, pt. 4, p. 308.
6. Ibid., 246.
7. Ibid., 309.
8. U.S. Congress, House, *Hearings before Subcommittees of the House Appropriations Committee, Supplemental Appropriation and Rescission Bill,* 1981, 97th Cong., 1st sess., 1981, pt. 4, p. 31.
9. Ibid., 119.
10. U.S. Congress, House Committee on Armed Services, *Full Committee Consideration of Reconciliation Recommendations and Hearings on Reprogramming Process and Procedures,* 99th Cong., 1st sess., 30 September 1995.
11. U.S. Congress, House Committee on Armed Services, *Full Committee Organizational Meeting and Consideration of Defense Department Reprogramming,* 100th Cong., 5 February 1987, 10–11.
12. General Accounting Office, *Budget Reprogramming: Opportunities to Improve DoD's Reprogramming Process* (Washington, D.C.: Government Printing Office, July 1989), 14–15.
13. U.S. Senate Committee on Armed Services, *National Defense Authorization Act for Fiscal Years 1990 and 1991,* Report to accompany S. 1352, 19 July 1989.
14. U.S. House, *Defense Authorization Act for Fiscal Years 1990 and 1991,* Report 101-21, 841, in *U.S. Congressional and Administrative News,* 101st Cong., 1st sess., vol. 3.
15. See P.L. 101-89.
16. U.S. Congress, House Appropriations Committee. *Hearings on Defense Appropriations for 1991,* pt. 6.
17. Of which there were many.
18. U.S. Congress, House Appropriations Committee, *Hearings on Defense Appropriations for 1991,* 124.
19. Ibid., 125.
20. P.L. 101-510.
21. *Congressional Record,* 22 June 1993, 7551ff.
22. See The Defense Appropriation for 1996, P.L. 104-61, sec. 8070, and the Intelligence Authorization Act, H.R. 1655, the authorization of the secret portion of the budget. Amendments 2881, 2882, 2883, and 2884 were discussed en bloc in the Senate, as reported in *Congressional Record,* 29 Sepember 1995.
23. Fisher, "Effect of the Budget Act," 150.
24. Allen Schick, *Congress and Money* (Washington, D.C.: Urban Institute Press, 1980), 403.
25. Ibid., 406.
26. Fisher, "Effect of the Budget Act of 1974," 170.
27. Ibid.
28. Cited in ibid., from U.S. Congress, House, *Hearings before the Committee on Appropriations, Departments of labor and Health, Education, and Welfare and Related Agencies Appropriations for Fiscal Year 1980,* 96th Cong., 1st sess., 1979, 175–76.
29. Fisher, "Effect of the Budget Act," 171.
30. Hale, "State Budget Execution," 284.
31. Ibid., 285.
32. *The State Legislative Appropriations Process* (Lexington, Ky.: Council of State Governments, 1975), 36.
33. ACIR, *The Question of State Government Capability,* 116.
34. Ibid., 117.
35. Tony Hutchison and Kathy James, *Legislative Budget Procedures in the Fifty States: A Guide to Appropriations and Budget Processes* (Denver: National Conference of State Legislatures, 1988), 108.

36. Jennifer Grooters and Corrina Eckl, *Legislative Budget Procedures: A Guide to Appropriations and Budget Processes in the States, Commonwealths, and Territories* (Denver: National Conference of State Legislatures, 1998).

37. This case is taken from Royal S. Van De Woestyne, *State Control of Local Finance in Massachusetts* (Cambridge, Mass.: Harvard University Press, 1935).

38. This case is taken primarily from Raymond Atkinson, "The Effects of Tax Limitation upon Local Finance in Ohio, 1911 to 1922" (Ph.D. dissertation, Columbia University. Printed in Cleveland, Ohio, 1923, n.p.).

39. National Performance Review, *From Red Tape to Results: Creating a Government That Works Better and Costs Less* (Washington, D.C.: Government Printing Office, 1993), chap. 1.

40. Charles Dempsey, "The Inspector General Concept: Where It's Been, Where It's Going," *Public Budgeting and Finance* 5, no. 2 (Summer 1985): 39.

41. Mark H. Moore and Margaret Jane Gates, *Inspectors-General: Junkyard Dogs or Man's Best Friend?* (New York: Russell Sage Foundation, 1986), 11.

42. Ibid., 11.

43. Ibid., 12.

44. Ibid.

45. Dempsey, "Inspector General Concept," 40.

46. Thomas Novotny, "The IG's—A Random Walk," *Bureaucrat* 12, no. 3 (Fall 1983): 35.

47. Ibid., 39.

48. Ibid.

49. For accounts of these events, see Chester Newland, "A Midterm Appraisal—The Reagan Presidency: Limited Government and Political Administration," *Public Administration Review* 43, no. 1 (January/February 1983): 1–21; and Novotny, "The IG's."

50. Novotny, "The IG's," 38.

51. *Congressional Record*, 21 December 1995, S.19138.

52. Ibid.

53. See William Barr, Assistant Attorney General, Office of Legal Counsel, "Testimony," *Oversight Hearings of the Operations of the Inspector General Offices*, 267–85; and Office of Legal Counsel, "Authority of the Inspector General to Conduct Regulatory Investigations," policy memo, 9 March 1989.

54. James Naughton, "Authority of Inspectors General to Conduct Criminal Investigations Relating to Regulatory Programs," *Oversight Hearings*, April 1990, 147–200.

55. *Oversight Hearings*, 10.

56. See Barbara Hinkson Craig, *Chadha: The Story of an Epic Constitutional Struggle* (Berkeley: University of California Press, 1990), 40–46.

57. *Oversight Hearings*, 103.

58. The complexity of federal programs and the inevitability of some waste, fraud, and abuse are the central points made by John Young, "Reflections on the Root Causes of Fraud, Abuse, and Waste in Federal Social Programs," *Public Administration Review* 43, no. 4 (July/August 1983): 362–69.

59. Novotny, "The IG's," 37.

Name Index

Subject Index